WINDOWS
NT
Professional
Library

WINDOWS NT

Windows NT Troubleshooting

D1304799

About the Author...

Kathy Ivens has authored and contributed to more than 30 books on computer subjects. She is a frequent contributor to national magazines, writing articles and reviews.

Before becoming an expert in computing, Ms. Ivens spent many years as a television producer, where she had fun producing sports and was mildly amused producing news and entertainment programs. Preceding that career was some time spent as a community organizer for social agencies, and she also spent a few years as a political consultant. She still doesn't know what she wants to be when she grows up.

WINDOWS
NT
Professional
Library

WINDOWS NT

Windows NT
Troubleshooting

Kathy Ivens

Osborne **McGraw-Hill**

Berkeley   New York   St. Louis   San Francisco
Auckland   Bogotá   Hamburg   London   Madrid
Mexico City   Milan   Montreal   New Delhi   Panama City
Paris   São Paulo   Singapore   Sydney
Tokyo   Toronto

Osborne/**McGraw-Hill**
2600 Tenth Street
Berkeley, California 94710
U.S.A.

For information on translations or book distributors outside the U.S.A., or to arrange bulk purchase discounts for sales promotions, premiums, or fund-raisers, please contact Osborne/**McGraw-Hill** at the above address.

Windows NT Troubleshooting

1234567890 AGM AGM 901987654321098

ISBN 0-07-882471-0

Publisher
  Brandon A. Nordin

Editor-in-Chief
  Scott Rogers

Acquisitions Editor
  Wendy Rinaldi

Project Editor
  Cynthia Douglas

Editorial Assistant
  Ann Sellers

Technical Editor
  Bob Chronister

Copy Editor
  Rebecca Pepper

Proofreader
  Carroll Proffitt

Indexer
  David Heiret

Computer Designers
  Jani Beckwith
  Roberta Steele

Illustrator
  Arlette Crosland

Series Design
  Peter Hancik

This book is dedicated to Carl Callini of Mantis Computers,
with thanks for his expertise, help, patience, humor,
and all-round general niceness.
Everybody who makes a living with a computer
needs a hardware supplier as perfect as Carl.

WINDOWS NT
Professional Library

CONTENTS

Part II

Troubleshooting Startup Problems

Part IV

Troubleshooting Peripherals

Part VI
Using Troubleshooting Tools

Part VII

Appendixes

ACKNOWLEDGMENTS

One of the best reasons to write this book was the chance to meet and work with Wendy Rinaldi, who is a wonderful Acquisitions Editor and a splendid person. Cynthia Douglas is a terrific Project Editor who works well even under the strange and harried circumstances I managed to foist on her. Ann Sellers, the Editorial Assistant for this book, kept her cool, her competence, and her humor under some of the most stressful conditions I could manage to create. Rebecca Pepper is the best. She's one of the most professional copy editors in the world—you cannot get an extra comma or an inconsistency past her. Bob Chronister checked the technical accuracy of every word in this book with his usual level of expertise.

I owe very special thanks to Bruce Hallberg, one of the world's great authors of computer books, who contributed some of his knowledge to this book.

INTRODUCTION

This book is written for network administrators and power users who spend a substantial amount of time trouble-shooting Windows NT servers and workstations. I collected the problems I address in this book from a variety of sources: clients; adminstrators and users who called me with conversations that started with "did you ever see..."; and by trolling some of the newsgroups on the Net. I found an astounding rate of repetition as questions were posed and strange computer behavior patterns were defined; it seems we're all facing a consistent pool of problems.

You've probably had some Windows NT 4 problems I haven't covered, and you may see problems in this book that you've never encountered. There is, of course, no way to do the ultimate and perfect book on troubleshooting a complicated and powerful operating system.

I've divided this book into parts, based on logic that is solely my own.

Part I is all about installation, but it's really about installation and configuration. These are both processes that can be fraught with problems. Within the Installation section you'll find chapters on hardware, installation procedures including network share point installations, domains, and re-installations (including updates).

Part II is all about startup problems. There's a chapter on operating system startup failures and another chapter on startup as it affects users; logging on and getting the rights and access they need.

Part III concerns itself with users and access of network resources. This is the stuff an administrator's day is made of. The chapters cover shares, user profiles, registry controls, and the controls you can impose with the System Policy Editor.

Part IV is dedicated to peripherals, the ones that drive you nuts with their strange behaviors: printers and modems (RAS).

Part V is about safety and security, the nagging concern we all carry around with us like a little black cloud over our heads. There are chapters on securing servers and backing up.

Part VI is a guide to tools. I cover the standard NT 4 tools, the wonderful nifty stuff that you can find in the Resource Kit, and then, for real fun and power, the Microsoft PowerToys.

Part VII contains four appendices, which are chock full of details that you might find interesting or helpful.

Once in a while, when there's some feature or function that I know will change dramatically with Windows NT 5, I'll point that out. I've been playing with NT 5 for several months and these little pointers throughout the book should serve as a warning that NT 5 is not simply an update, it's a whole new ballgame.

PART I

Troubleshooting
Installation

WINDOWS
NT
Professional
Library

CHAPTER 1

Hardware Problems in Setup

One of the most frustrating experiences for Windows NT administrators is dealing with hardware issues during the installation of the operating system. Most of the time the problems aren't fatal, and you only have to make some adjustments to your system. Sometimes there are outright compatibility problems that you have to work around (most companies have neither the financial resources nor the inclination to discard all the legacy computer equipment they've accumulated over the years when they want to change operating systems), but sometimes you'll just have to tell the purchasing department there isn't any workaround and new equipment needs to be installed.

This chapter covers some of the hardware problems that are encountered most often and offers some solutions and workarounds you can try.

INSTALLATION FLOPPY DISKS DON'T WORK

Believe it or not, this problem occurs more often than you'd expect. I've experienced it several times and found several different causes. The symptoms vary:

▼ The Windows NT boot floppy disk is ignored and your operating system boots as if no boot disk were in drive A.

■ The light goes on to indicate that drive A is being accessed, but nothing else happens (and the light stays lit).

▲ An error message appears, such as "Operating system not found" or "Cannot read from Drive A."

Of course, the first thing you're going to think of is that the floppy disk is bad. While this could be the reason for failure, don't assume it—investigate further before tossing the floppy disk into a trash can.

Check the BIOS

Restart your computer and go into the BIOS setup. Check the boot sequence to make sure that drive A is included in the bootable drives sequence. If it is, try making drive A the first drive checked for booting.

TIP: For reasons of security, it's not uncommon to change the BIOS default so that drive A is not included in the boot sequence. If you've used this security technique, after you finish installing Windows NT go back and reestablish the setting because I've found it really does help with security issues. If drive A is bootable, users who can't break into your computer because they don't know your logon password might still get to your files if you're using the FAT file system. It's also a good technique for safeguarding your computer against certain viruses.

The Windows NT 4 CD is bootable, and this can really confuse the installation program. Turn off the option to boot from the CD in your BIOS (if you have a CD-ROM drive that is boot-capable). Or take the Windows NT CD out of the drive until after the floppy disk has booted the system.

Turn off BIOS virus checking, which frequently interferes with the installation process, sometimes at this point and sometimes later in the setup process.

NOTE: If your floppy drive is connected to a SCSI controller, you may have a hardware setup problem (such as termination mistakes) or a controller compatibility problem (check the HCL).

Create Your Own Floppy Disks

Sometimes one or more Windows NT floppy disks are bad, and sometimes your floppy drive is out of calibration (which means it can read only disks it writes). In fact, sometimes the boot floppy disk works fine and then you receive an error message indicating that the system cannot read the disk when you move on to disk 2 or disk 3.

The solution is to make your own set of floppy disks for installing NT. You'll need three blank, formatted floppy disks to accomplish this task (you can't create just one of the floppy disks; if you have one bad one, you have to create the whole set).

If you have a fresh box of preformatted floppy disks, use those. If you have a fresh box of unformatted floppy disks, you must format them. Don't start yet, though—there are potential problems with some formatting methods. Don't format the floppy disk by using the Format command on a Windows 95 machine; there are sometimes problems with such floppy disks. That caveat also includes using the command line on a Windows 95 machine to format. Instead, boot from a real, bootable DOS floppy disk and perform the format from there.

Put a label on each of the floppy disks (I mean a paper label, of course; don't use the Label command during the format). In the order in which they are created, the labels read Disk 3, Disk 2, and Boot Disk (you can label it Disk 1).

To create the disks, you have to get to the Windows NT CD-ROM. You can do this on any computer that can access the CD-ROM (either by loading the drivers in a DOS boot sequence or by accessing the drive in a computer running any version of Windows). Then use the Run command on the Start menu to execute the command *d:*\i386\winnt /ox, where *d:* is the drive letter for your CD-ROM and \i386 assumes you are installing to an Intel computer (use the appropriate directory on the CD-ROM for other platforms). The /ox parameter indicates that you are creating the installation floppy disks only, so no files will be transferred to your hard drive and Windows NT Setup will not run.

TIP: If you enter *d:*\i386\winnt without any parameters, the Setup process will start after you are walked through the creation of the floppy disks.

By the way, if you think the problem is that the floppy disk drive for the computer to which you're installing is out of calibration, you must create the set of floppy disks on that computer. Then, go buy a new floppy drive.

Bypass the Floppy Disks

You can install Windows NT 4 without the floppy disks. Although it isn't recommended by Microsoft for an installation from DOS or Windows 3.x, and in fact is called an unsupported installation technique, I've used it on several occasions when there were problems with the floppy drive.

Use the command *d:*\i386\winnt /b, where *d:* is the drive letter for your CD-ROM and \i386 assumes you are installing to an Intel computer (use the appropriate directory on the CD-ROM for other platforms).

The /b parameter instructs the installation program to move the files that are contained on the floppy disks to a directory on your hard drive (\Win_nt.~ls)and run the operating system setup from there.

If you're performing the installation on a computer that has Windows NT installed, use Winnt32 instead of Winnt.

SETUP CANNOT ACCESS THE HARD DRIVE

While it's not a common problem, sometimes the installation program can't find or can't communicate with your hard drive. Of course, you might just have a bad drive or a bad controller; you'll have to run diagnostic software under your current operating system to find out. If either is bad, it's time to call your hardware vendor. If both the drive and the controller are healthy, however, there are a couple of investigative processes to pursue in order to install Windows NT.

Virus Problems

A boot sector virus on the hard drive will frequently prevent Windows NT from accessing (or even finding) the drive. Use a virus program to check for (and eliminate) such a virus, or try **fdisk/mbr**.

In addition, sometimes a BIOS virus-checking procedure interferes with Windows NT as it tries to access the drive, so if you have such a feature turn it off.

More than 1,024 Cylinders

Years ago, if you had a hard drive with more than 1,024 cylinders you had to boot with a software program that translated the configuration into one that your computer could handle. Today, however, the system BIOS can handle disks that exceed 1,024 cylinders because a system of Logical Block Addressing (LBA) is built into the BIOS. LBA is used by the BIOS only when a drive with more than 1,024 cylinders is installed (there is native BIOS support for hard drives that don't exceed this number).

You may see LBA choices in your BIOS setup program, and if you do there is probably a choice of enabling or disabling the function. Disabling it (perhaps because you didn't realize your hard disk exceeds 1,024 cylinders) doesn't necessarily disable your hard drive—you just don't get to use all the available megabytes. In some cases, however, you will lose the hard drive if you inappropriately disable LBA.

When you install Windows NT, which is extremely sensitive to hardware, you may find that the LBA scheme being used to run your hard disk is incompatible with Windows NT. If that's the case, Windows NT won't be able to access the drive. Contact the BIOS vendor; sometimes an updated BIOS will solve the problem. If not, try disabling LBA and performing the installation again. If that doesn't work, you have an incompatibility problem that cannot be overcome.

NOTE: These problems are generally found only on Intel-based computers. RISC-based computers don't have Master Boot Records that can become infected with viruses, nor do they have differences between disk configurations of the hard drive, controller, and system hardware. Even on Intel-based computers, SCSI controllers and drives don't have configuration differences. Therefore, you should be concerned about these issues only if you are using IDE or ESDI hard drives.

ESDI Drive Problems

Sometimes when you install Windows NT on an ESDI drive with more than 1,024 cylinders, the installation seems successful, and then the first time you boot the operating system you see an error message followed by a total freeze. Most of the time the error is "0x0000006B: Phase 1 Process Initialization failed" (followed by a lot of hex). This almost always indicates that the controller for your ESDI drive is not supported in Windows NT, and you'll have to contact the manufacturer. I have no explanation for the fact that the operating system happily installs under these circumstances; it doesn't seem fair.

Cannot Find Hard Drive After Restart

During setup, after the Setup program restarts your computer, you may see an error telling you that Setup cannot locate the hard drive partition prepared by the MS-DOS portion of Setup. This is frustrating because obviously the hard drive is there; Setup has already accessed it, and there's no logical reason why it has suddenly become lost.

Winnt.exe puts the temporary files needed to continue the installation on the first drive it finds that has sufficient free space. Winnt.exe can see drives that Windows NT may not be able to see or support, and as a result the temporary files aren't accessible to the Setup program after the first Setup reboot. Most of the time this means that the drive in question is compressed or is on a secondary controller (IDE or ESDI). It might also be the result of the drive being an unsupported SCSI drive.

The solution is to fix the problem (uncompress the drive or install a supported SCSI device). If the problem is that the temporary files are on a secondary controller, you can specify that drive by entering **winnt /t:***driveletter* to start Setup. The switch /t, along with the drive letter, specifies the target drive for temporary files, and Setup will know where to look for the temporary files when it needs them.

SETUP CANNOT FIND A CD-ROM

Incompatibility problems with CD-ROM drives are usually easy to learn about; you just have to check the Hardware Compatibility List (HCL) that is in the documentation for Windows NT.

SCSI CD-ROM drives are generally not a problem (assuming they're connected to a compatible SCSI adapter). You cannot take it for granted that an IDE CD-ROM drive is supported, although the list of supported drives grows longer as manufacturers join the Windows NT ranks. Make sure the IDE CD-ROM is ATAPI 1.2 compatible. Check with Microsoft on the Internet (www.microsoft.com) to download the latest list.

Use DOS Drivers to Access the CD-ROM

Boot your computer with a floppy disk that has the CD-ROM drivers and the appropriate lines in Config.sys and Autoexec.bat to put the drive into service. For example, your Config.sys file might contain a line (or lines) similar to this:

```
DEVICE=ASPI4DOS.SYS /D
DEVICE=ASPICD.SYS /D:ASPICD0
```

And Autoexec.bat will have a command to load Mscdex, along with parameters, such as this:

```
MSCDEX.EXE /D:ASPICD0 /M:12 /V
```

All of the files specified in these lines must be on the boot floppy disk you're using.

Then insert the Windows NT CD-ROM in the drive and make the CD-ROM drive your current drive. From the subdirectory for your platform (probably \i386), enter **winnt/b**.

Help Setup Find an IDE CD-ROM on Sound Cards

If your IDE CD-ROM drive is hooked into the IDE interface on a Sound Blaster card and the IDE interface on the sound card is not ATAPI 1.2 compliant, Setup probably won't find it. Here are the steps you can follow to try to resolve this:

1. Connect the CD-ROM drive to an available port on your computer's main IDE controller. This controller must be ATAPI 1.2 compliant also.

2. Disable the IDE interface on the sound card, so you don't confuse Setup with an extra IDE controller. (Check the documentation for the sound card.)

Use a Different Driver

You may have a CD-ROM drive that is supported because it emulates another manufacturer's drive that is supported. In that case, Windows NT won't have a driver for your device, but it will have one for the emulated device. You might be able to install your CD-ROM by telling Windows NT Setup that it's a different brand (this is one of those times when it's perfectly okay to lie).

During installation, Windows NT finds any supported CD-ROM device and tells you about it with an on-screen message. You also have an opportunity to tell Windows NT about additional devices ("additional" means devices beyond those automatically found by the Setup program). Follow the steps to do this and tell your lie to Windows NT. This frequently works.

COMMON INSTALLATION ERROR MESSAGES

One of the most vexing experiences is staring at an error message that is nothing but numbers and hex dumps, although sometimes there's a word or two of plain English that seems to point you in the right direction as you try to figure out what's going on. This section covers a few of the common error messages that can appear during installation of Windows NT.

Stop: 0x00000050

This error message is usually accompanied by the message "PAGE_FAULT_ IN_NONPAGED_AREA." The translation for the message is that you received a "Stop 50," and you can pretty much bet that you have a problem with memory (RAM). Unfortunately, the message isn't terribly specific, because it could be any RAM in the system: motherboard memory, video memory, or secondary RAM for caching. You'll have to determine the source of the faulty RAM. My own philosophy in these circumstances is to follow two rules:

1. Change only one thing at a time.
2. Start with the easiest task.

In fact, I follow those rules whenever I'm faced with what seems to be a hardware problem and it's not apparent what the specific problem is.

Disable Caching

The first thing to do is go into your BIOS setup and disable all caching. Look carefully through the options to make sure you've caught all the caching that's enabled, such as CPU caching and the L2 cache. Then try the installation again.

If that seems to cure the problem, stop the installation and enable one of the caching schemes, then start the installation again. Stop and enable another cache and try again. Continue to do this until you've discovered the bad caching process. Check the documentation for your computer to learn where to find the RAM you have to replace.

If you can't install the operating system after you disable all caching, reenable the caching and move on to test the next potential problem.

Change the Video Controller

Pop in a video controller from another machine (or from the supply closet if you keep extra video boards around), and try the installation again. If this works, the RAM on your video card is bad and you'll have to replace the controller.

Change the Main Memory

This can get complicated. I've found it best to open a computer that is working properly that has SIMMs the same size as those on the faulty computer and begin a system of trading. Your trading scheme will depend upon the size and number of SIMMs in the system. Before you begin, however, take one step to ensure your sanity—build yourself a little diagram and give yourself tools to represent different SIMMs. Here's what I do:

1. On a piece of paper, I draw a large rectangle for each SIMM, each larger than the SIMM module. I also note the positions by writing "power supply" at the appropriate place.

2. I fish around the bottom of my pocketbook and find coins to represent the different SIMMs; for instance, if I have four SIMMs to investigate I'll find four pennies and four nickels.

3. At the top of my paper I write the key—for example, pennies represent the SIMMs from the faulty computer, nickels are for the good computer.

4. I pull a SIMM from the bad computer and place it on the rectangle and put a penny in that rectangle. Then I put a good SIMM into the computer and try the installation.

5. If the installation doesn't work, I put the original SIMM back, place the borrowed SIMM on the rectangle, and replace the penny with a nickel.

Just keep swapping SIMMs in this fashion, and if the installation works at any point, you've found your problem. Of course, if the computer from which you are borrowing SIMMs is within reach, you won't need the coins; you just put the SIMMs back as you go.

The only flaw in this scheme is that it doesn't work if you have more than one bad SIMM module, but that's rare, so the odds are with you.

You could also reverse the process, replacing all of the SIMMs and then withdrawing them one at a time to insert an original SIMM module in order to find the point at which the installation fails.

The big decision you face when you've discovered that SIMMs are your problem is which computer gets to keep the good SIMMs. I have no advice on that one.

NOTE: Once in a while this error message appears during an installation from a network share (instead of the CD-ROM). This is due to a virus protection program that's running on the server. Check that first, and then if you can't install, start working on a RAM problem.

Stop: 0x0000001E

This error appears with annoying frequency during installation, and unfortunately it's pretty much generic, meaning that Windows NT is telling you, "I found something I don't like." It indicates an exception code that the Setup program was unable to handle.

The error message conveys additional information but it's all in hex, so you'll have to call Microsoft Support for a translation. Here's the syntax you'll see:

```
Stop 0x0000001E [A] [B] [C] [D]
```

where:

A is the specific exception code that was not handled.B is the address where the exception occurred.C is the first parameter (called parameter 0) of the exception code.D is the second parameter (parameter 1) of the exception code.

Actually, in many cases this error message translates to one of three specific problems, so you might want to try a quick fix if you think any of them is pertinent:

▼ An incompatible third-party video driver is loaded. Remove it and try again.

■ You do not have enough disk space to perform the installation. Do some housekeeping and start again.

▲ Your BIOS is not compatible. Contact the manufacturer and get an upgrade.

SETUP HANGS DURING HARDWARE INSPECTION

At one point during installation, Setup sends a text message saying that it's inspecting your hardware. The actual message is "Setup is inspecting your computer's hardware configuration." A minute passes, perhaps two minutes. You begin to think that nothing is ever going to happen. Go into another room, make a phone call, make a pot of coffee, run to the nearest deli and get a sandwich to go. When you return, if Setup is still inspecting your hardware, you have a problem. Your computer is hung, frozen, dead. The reason I say that you should find something to do before deciding this is that sometimes the hardware inspection really does take a couple of minutes (perhaps even more), and I don't want you to declare a hung computer too early.

You have to shut off your machine and start it again, but you'll experience the same thing unless you take some steps to determine and correct the problem. I'll go over the possibilities here, starting with the most common problem and working my way down to the less common ones.

Take the Windows NT CD-ROM out of the CD-ROM Drive

If your BIOS supports bootable CD-ROMs, that's probably the problem. Take the Windows NT disk out of your CD-ROM drive. In fact, as the computer restarts, enter the Setup program and disable CD-ROM booting, and also take the CD-ROM out of the boot sequence list of drives.

NOTE: The cause of this is that the BIOS recognizes the NT CD-ROM as bootable and grabs it during the POST.

Check CMOS Settings for Memory Use

Go into CMOS setup and disable caching (external caching seems to be a real problem with hardware detection) and shadowing. While the logic of this escapes me, it frequently works to cure the hardware inspection hang. I have no idea why this would interfere with Setup's ability to read the hardware.

Check IRQs

Make sure you don't have devices in your system that are causing IRQ conflicts. I keep a little "table" for every computer, in which I list every device and its IRQ and I/O address. As I add devices to computers and have to set their configuration, I have an easy reference for ascertaining what's available. It's quite possible that you have an IRQ conflict that didn't bother your previous operating system—Windows NT 4 is hardware sensitive (which means it gets hysterical about things like this).

Change the Video Card

If you have a powerful video card, even if it's supported, replace it with a plain vanilla video controller (make sure it's also supported). This is my own personal advice; I've only heard of this suggestion being made by Microsoft technical support people a couple of times. I've had powerful video cards that were on the HCL (right down to the model number and installed RAM). The Setup program would hang, or other weird things would occur. Putting the plain vanilla card in worked like a charm. After the operating system is installed and things seem to be running just dandy, change back to the original video card. Boot to VGA mode, install the drivers for the card, and everything will work fine.

Pull the NIC

I've had the same problem with NICs as with video cards. And the solution is almost the same. Pull the NIC out of the machine, install Windows NT 4, and then install the NIC into your running operating system.

Use the Debug Version of Ntdetect.com

Ntdetect.com is the application that finds and builds the hardware component list (for Intel-based computers). You can use the debug version of this program to learn why Setup is hanging during hardware inspection.

From another computer, perform the following steps:

1. Use **diskcopy** to copy the contents of the Windows NT Setup floppy disk (Disk 1) to a formatted, blank floppy disk.

2. Delete Ntdetect.com from the copy of Disk 1.

3. Copy Support\Debug\i386\Ntdetect.chk from the Windows NT 4 CD-ROM to the copy of Disk 1.

4. Rename Ntdetect.chk Ntdetect.com.

Now you can use this Setup floppy disk on the target computer (the one you're trying to make a Windows NT 4 computer).

The debug version of Ntdetect.com doesn't work privately or secretly; it tells you what it's doing. It displays information about what it is looking for and each piece of hardware it finds. It does not move on to the next step until you press a key (any key). Keep pressing keys until Setup hangs. The contents of the screen continue to display during the lockup, so you should have a pretty good clue about where your problem lies. Replace the hardware or change its configuration.

BOOT LOADER SCREEN CYCLES ENDLESSLY

All of the stories you've heard (and perhaps your own prior experiences installing Windows NT 4) indicate that almost all of the serious problems occur during the text-mode portion of Setup. Finally you get to the GUI-mode phase of Setup. The boot loader screen counts down 5 seconds to 0, the screen goes black, and you think the worst is over—you're finally off and running. Then the boot loader screen appears, counts down from 5 seconds to 0, the screen goes black, then the boot loader screen appears, counts down . . .

You almost certainly have a boot sector virus. Shut down and run a DOS-based virus program (do not use **Fdisk/mbr**; in this situation it will probably do more harm than good).

TROUBLESHOOTING HARDWARE WITH NTHQ

The Windows NT 4 CD-ROM has a terrific diagnostic utility named NTHQ. It's in \support\hqtool. You can use this program utility to detect your system components before you install Windows NT 4. NTHQ does not run in Windows NT or Windows 95.

It works by creating a bootable disk that will run a hardware detection program under DOS and output what it finds to a log file.

To create an NTHQ bootable disk, follow these steps:

1. Put a formatted 3.5-inch 1.44MB floppy disk into drive A.

2. Insert your Windows NT 4 CD-ROM into your CD-ROM drive and go to \support\hqtool.

3. Double-click Makedisk.bat.

4. Restart your computer, leaving the floppy in drive A.

The system boots to the floppy in drive A, and the NTHQ utility performs the following steps (displaying an on-screen message to announce each step):

1. Creates a 4MB RAM drive

2. Copies Zipfile.exe from the CD-ROM to the RAM drive

3. Extracts Zipfile.exe

4. Starts Nthq.exe

A dialog box appears, with "Hardware Query Tool 4.0 for Windows" in the title bar. The dialog box message enumerates the tasks the program will perform, as follows:

This program will:

Identify PCI devices and resources

Identify ISA Plug and Play devices and resources used

Identify EISA and MCA devices

Identify Legacy devices and system components and resources used

Create a log file of the results of the detection

The log file this program creates is called NTHQ.TXT.

The help file included called README.TXT explains how to interpret the log file and use it for troubleshooting.

The NTHQ.TXT log file and README.TXT will be saved automatically to your A: drive when you exit the program.

The detection could take 3-5 minutes to complete.

Would you like to continue with the device detection?

Choose Yes to move on. Another dialog box appears with a title bar that reads "Detection Method—Comprehensive or Safe." The dialog box contains the following information and choices:

Is it OK to perform comprehensive detection? The
default Yes will start comprehensive detection,
choosing No will start safe detection. If comprehensive
detection fails, restart the system and choose No for
safe detection.

It's best to choose No because there's no reason to risk a problem unless the safe detection process fails to give you the information you need.

System detection starts with a progress bar displaying the percentage of detection accomplished. A display of the device types that are being sought is updated continuously, and the last detected device is presented.

When the detection process ends, a dialog box displays information about your system. There are buttons across the bottom of the dialog box you can use to see details about your motherboard, network card, video controller, and so on. All of the information is in the log file that will be written to the floppy disk, but you can peek at the results if you wish. The choices for user action in this dialog box are Save, Help, and Exit. Choose Exit.

You are at a C:\ prompt, and you can power down or use the Reset button to start your computer again (don't forget to remove the floppy disk during restart). Use any Windows NT machine to view the log file (Nthq.txt). Here is a typical log file:

```
Hardware Detection Tool For Windows NT 4.0
Master Boot Sector Virus Protection Check
Hard Disk Boot Sector Protection: Off.
No problem to write to MBR
ISA Plug and Play Add-in cards detection Summary Report
No ISA Plug and Play cards found in the system
ISA PnP Detection:  Complete
EISA Add-in card detection Summary Report
Scan Range: Slot 0 - 16
Slot 0: EISA System Board
EISA Bus Detected: No
EISA Detection:  Complete
Legacy Detection Summary Report
System Information
Device: System board
Can't locate Computername
Machine Type: IBM PC/AT
Machine Model: fc
Machine Revision: 00
Microprocessor: 80486DX
```

```
Conventional memory: 655360
Available memory: 36 MB
BIOS Name: American Megatrends
BIOS Version:
BIOS Date: 07/25/94
Bus Type: ISA
Device: Programmable interrupt controller
Hardware ID (for Legacy Devices): *PNP0000
I/O: 20 - 21
I/O: a0 - a1
IRQ: 2
Device: Direct memory access controller
Hardware ID (for Legacy Devices): *PNP0200
I/O: 0 - f
I/O: 81 - 83
I/O: 87 - 87
I/O: 89 - 8b
I/O: 8f - 8f
I/O: c0 - df
DMA: 4
Device: System CMOS/real time clock
Hardware ID (for Legacy Devices): *PNP0B00
I/O: 70 - 71
IRQ: 8
Device: System timer
Hardware ID (for Legacy Devices): *PNP0100
I/O: 40 - 43
IRQ: 0
Device: System speaker
Hardware ID (for Legacy Devices): *PNP0800
I/O: 61 - 61
Device: Numeric data processor
Hardware ID (for Legacy Devices): *PNP0C04
I/O: f0 - ff
IRQ: 13
Device: Standard 101/102-Key or Microsoft Natural Keyboard
Hardware ID (for Legacy Devices): *PNP0303
I/O: 60 - 60
I/O: 64 - 64
IRQ: 1
Device: ISA Plug and Play bus
Hardware ID (for Legacy Devices): *PNP0A00
Didn't detect system resources being used.
Device: Tseng Labs ET4000/W32
```

```
Hardware ID (for Legacy Devices): *PNP0912
I/O: 3b0 - 3bb
I/O: 3c0 - 3df
Memory: a0000 - affff
Memory: b8000 - bffff
Memory: c0000 - c7fff
Device: NE2000 Compatible
Hardware ID (for Legacy Devices): *PNP80D6
I/O: 300 - 31f
Device: Standard Floppy Disk Controller
Hardware ID (for Legacy Devices): *PNP0700
I/O: 3f2 - 3f5
IRQ: 6
DMA: 2
Device: Communications Port
Hardware ID (for Legacy Devices): *PNP0500
Friendly Port Name: COM1
I/O: 3f8 - 3ff
IRQ: 4
Device: Logitech Serial Mouse
Hardware ID (for Legacy Devices): *PNP0F08
Didn't detect system resources being used.
Device: Adaptec AIC-6X60 ISA Single-Chip SCSI Controller
Hardware ID (for Legacy Devices): *ADP6360
I/O: 340 - 35f
Memory: dc000 - dffff
IRQ: 11
Device: Printer Port
Hardware ID (for Legacy Devices): *PNP0400
Friendly Port Name: LPT1
I/O: 378 - 37a
Parse Legacy Data: Complete
MicroChannel (MCA)card detection Summary Report
Scan Range: Slot 0 - 16
Only MCA IDs are detected
MCA Bus Detected: No
MCA Detection: Complete
Enumerate all IDE devices
IDE Devices Detection Summary Report
IDE/ATAPI: Complete
PCI Add-in card detection Summary Report
PCI Access Mechanism Support: 0
Number of Last PCI Bus: 0
```

```
PCI Detection: Complete
================End of Detection Report====================
Adapter Description: Tseng Labs W32/W32i/W32p
Listed in Hardware Compatibility List: Yes
Adapter Description: NE2000 compatible
Listed in Hardware Compatibility List: Yes
Adapter Description: Adaptec AHA-1522
Listed in Hardware Compatibility List: Yes
```

You've probably run into a slew of problems that I haven't covered here, but most of the time those problems are the result of compatibility issues. You really can't get away with cheating on the HCL, although occasionally you can take advantage of any emulation your devices are supposed to contain.

WINDOWS
NT
Professional
Library

CHAPTER 2

Troubleshooting Network Sharepoint Installations

You can install Windows NT 4 by copying the installation files to a *sharepoint* (a shared directory) on a network computer and using those files for installation on other computers. Of course, this works only if you have some existing form of networking, some way for the target workstations to connect to the source computer.

In this chapter we'll discuss the troubleshooting techniques for this method, assuming you're installing Windows NT 4 Workstation (because that's generally the operating system requiring multiple installations). However, everything is the same if you are installing Windows NT 4 Server onto additional computers.

The most obvious advantage of the sharepoint technique is that it enables you to install NT 4 on workstations that do not have CD-ROM drives.

In addition, there are tools available to administrators that help control the installation process. You can create files that enable installation to proceed without user intervention (the files have the answers to all the questions users are asked during installation), and you can customize the installation to control which optional features are installed. You can customize installation only if you are installing from a shared directory on a hard drive—you cannot customize installations that use the Windows NT CD-ROM.

An overview of some common customization techniques, along with some of the problems you might encounter, are the stuff of this chapter.

USING A NETWORK SHAREPOINT FOR INSTALLATION

To eliminate the need for the CD-ROM, you can copy the operating system files needed for installation to a computer and access that computer to perform the installation. Assuming you are installing Windows NT 4 on the Intel platform, copy the \I386 directory from the CD-ROM to a directory on the computer that will act as the host (I always name the directory \I386). Make sure the directory is shared and accessible to Everyone.

The way in which this directory is accessed by the workstations varies depending upon your current connectivity. It could be that workstations load DOS drivers for network access and map the sharepoint, or you might have existing Windows networking (Windows for Workgroups [WFW], Windows 95, or an earlier version of Windows NT) that can access the sharepoint.

Once the workstation is connected to the sharepoint, the executable file for installation is launched from the command line (or from the Run box if the workstation is running Windows).

The command is **winnt /b** unless the workstation is running an earlier version of Windows NT, in which case the command is **winnt32 /b**. The /b parameter tells Setup to copy the setup boot files to the workstation's hard drive instead of creating floppy disks for the installation.

Problem: Windows 95 Workstations Fail to Complete the Installation

For some reason (I use that phrase because I haven't seen a pattern to the problem), you can have a problem installing Windows NT client software to a Windows 95 computer when using **winnt /b** from the sharepoint. I've found that when this happens, using the three Windows NT Workstation floppy disks for the process produces a clean installation. You can use the sharepoint to create the disks (**winnt /ox**) and then direct the installation program to the NT Workstation files (on a connected CD-ROM, or on a local directory that you created and then copied the \I386 files to).

Problem: The Workstation Is Not Currently Running Networking Software

If you have workstations that are running MS-DOS (perhaps with Windows 3.x but not WFW), they won't be able to boot into the network and find the sharepoint. Once you've installed the NIC, you can let NT 4 put together a startup disk to get those workstations to the sharepoint.

The startup disk is used to boot the computer, get it to the sharepoint, and make it easy to install the operating system with the proper configuration. We'll cover all the steps here in some detail because I've found it almost impossible to get detailed information about this process in other books (including those from Microsoft).

You'll need to know these things in order to create a startup disk:

▼ The name you want to assign to the computer

■ The name of the domain or workgroup that the computer joins when logging on

■ The logon user name (usually Administrator)

■ The NIC installed in the computer

▲ The network protocol being used

Create a Startup Disk

Start by formatting a floppy disk and placing the system files on it. (Boot to DOS and use the command **format a:/s** for an unformatted floppy disk, or use the command **sys a:** for a floppy disk that is formatted but not bootable). Be sure to do this from MS-DOS, not from a Windows 95 or Windows NT computer.

Place the formatted bootable floppy disk in the floppy drive of a Windows NT server and follow these steps at the server:

1. Put the Windows NT Server CD-ROM in the server's CD-ROM drive, or copy the \Clients directory and all the subdirectories to the hard drive of the server.

2. From the Administrative Tools group of the Program menu, open Network Client Administrator. The program window looks like this:

3. Choose Make Network Installation Startup Disk.

4. Specify the path for the client files, as seen in Figure 2-1 (*d:***clients**, where *d:* is the drive letter for either your CD-ROM or your hard drive), and select Share Files. Then choose OK.

NOTE: Notice the other choices in the Share Network Client Installation Files dialog box shown in Figure 2-1. You can use the choices to place the copy of the \Clients directory on your server's hard drive, which includes the automatic creation of a share. If you copied the files manually and created a share for the directory, you can choose Use Existing Shared Directory. Hereafter, as you create additional client startup disks, the system will use the same share you're using this time if you specify Use Existing Path.

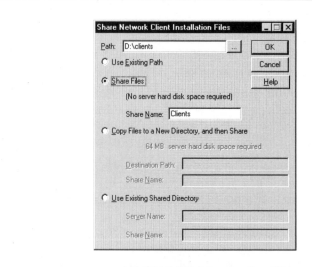

Figure 2-1.   The first step is to locate and share the necessary client files

5. Specify the appropriate information in the Target Workstation Configuration dialog box, as seen here, and choose OK.

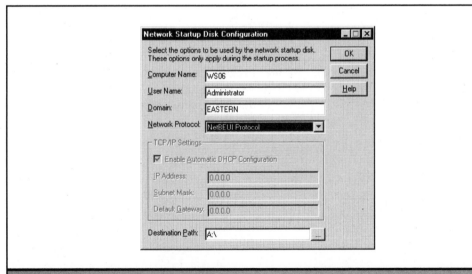

6. In the Network Startup Disk Configuration dialog box (shown in Figure 2-2), enter the specific information for this computer and choose OK.

Figure 2-2.   The options you specify are for the startup disk and can be changed after this computer is on the network

7. The Startup Disk Configuration program displays a summary of the specifications that will be used on the disk. Choose OK to continue, or choose Cancel to back up and make changes.

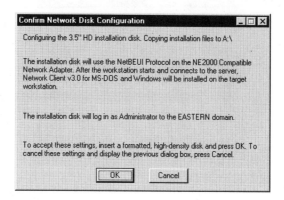

8. The appropriate files are copied to the floppy disk.

After the files are copied to the floppy disk, an information dialog box appears that is more or less a readme file. It explains how to check and use the startup disk.

Correct the Startup Disk Information

The startup disk is created with default information, some of which may not be accurate and therefore might interfere with installation.

The files on the disk consist of the standard files needed to boot a computer (Command.com, Config.sys, Autoexec.bat, and the hidden system files), but the contents of the files are specific to the installation of the client software from the sharepoint.

There is a subdirectory named \Net on the floppy disk that contains files specific to the network hardware and protocols you used. For example, these are the files created as a result of the process detailed in this section:

System.ini	Wcsetup.inf
Protocol.ini	Wfwsys.cfg
Ifshlp.sys	Shares.pwl
Ndishlp.sys	Himem.sys
Net.exe	Emm386.exe
Net.msg	Ne2000.dos
Neth.msg	Protman.dos
Setup.inf	Protman.exe

You must open and read the Protocol.ini file and make corrections if necessary. The startup disk procedure specifies default settings for the IRQ and I/O of the NIC, and you have to insert the correct information if you're not using default settings. (Since the default settings match those of COM2 for most computers, it's quite common to have changed those settings when you set up the network card, either by moving jumpers or by using a software configuration program.) Here is the section of Protocol.ini you're looking for:

```
[ms$ne2clone]
drivername=MS2000$
;  INTERRUPT=3
;  IOBASE=0x300
```

The first line of this section is the name of the NIC you specified during the creation process (in this case, it's an NE2000-compatible NIC). The INTERRUPT and IOBASE settings must match your NIC's configuration. Make the changes and save the file.

TIP: It's pretty obvious, but I'll point it out anyway—your rollout of Windows NT with this startup disk is a lot easier if you install the same brand NIC with the same settings in every computer.

Now boot the client computer with this setup disk in drive A, and you are taken through the process of joining the network and connecting to the host computer. If the system displays a message asking about a password-list file, respond with **N** and press ENTER.

When the startup disk has completed its task and logged the computer on to the network, you can use the network sharepoint on the host computer to install the operating system, or use the host CD-ROM drive.

You are at a command prompt when the boot process finishes, so you need only map the appropriate file directory (for instance, \I386 for Intel machines) with the Net Use command and enter **winnt /b**.

You can modify Autoexec.bat so it performs this task for you. The Autoexec.bat file on the setup disk has the following lines:

```
path=a:\net
a:\net\net start
net use z: \\EAST\Clients
echo Running Setup...
z:\msclient\netsetup\setup.exe /$
```

In this example, \\EAST is the name of the server that created the setup disk and to which the client files were moved.

If the \I386 directory has been moved to the host computer as a sharepoint, substitute the following lines in Autoexec.bat:

```
net use z: \\ServerName\Share_Name_for_Hard_Drive
z:
```

```
cd \I386
winnt /b
```

For instance, in the preceding example the name of the server is East, and the share name for drive C is EastDriveC. The Intel directory (\I386) from the CD-ROM has been placed on the server. Thus, the commands in Autoexec.bat would be

```
net use z: \\East\EastDriveC
z:
cd \I386
winnt /b
```

If the host computer has the Windows NT CD-ROM in its CD-ROM drive and you want to use it, place these lines in Autoexec.bat:

```
net use z: \\ServerName\Shared_CD_Name
z:
cd \I386
winnt /b
```

You would, of course, substitute the share name for the CD-ROM on your server for the entry *Shared_CD_Name*.

CAUTION: If the protocol you use is IPX, be sure you check the Protocol.ini file for the Frame information. The default is 802.2; if you're running 802.3 as the frame type, make the correction before using the disk.

Error: NetBEUI Protocol Failed

NetBEUI works only on a LAN, between computers directly connected by cable. If you are using routers to get to a server, you cannot use NetBEUI, because it doesn't support traffic across routers.

Error: Not Enough Memory

This error usually appears when you use a network setup disk that's configured for TCP/IP protocol. Change the Config.sys file on the setup disk to use extended memory (you can use Emm386.exe). If that doesn't work, you'll have to use NetBEUI or IPX protocol.

Error: The Specified Shared Directory Cannot Be Found

The most frequent cause for this error message during a sharepoint installation is that the directory isn't shared (not that it isn't there). Create a share for the directory. Or check your typing and make sure you have spelled the share name correctly.

Another cause for this error could be that you entered a command (either in the Autoexec.bat file on a setup disk or at the command line) that attempts to access a directory instead of a share. If you are installing from C:\I386, you cannot enter **net use z:** *ServerName***c:\i386**, nor can you enter **net use z:** *ServerName**Share_Name***i386**. You must first establish the mapping for the share, as it is named. Then move to the share, and finally, change directories.

> **TIP:** You could use the directory that has the files as the sharepoint. For instance, if you create a share on the host computer for C:\I386 named NTFILES, you can use the command **net use z: \\ServerName\NTFILES** followed by **z:**. Then issue the command to start the installation **(winnt /b)**.

Insufficient Space

The /b switch for Winnt.exe places the installation files on your local hard drive, which is a necessity if the computer does not have a CD-ROM drive. (Even if you have a CD-ROM attached, using this switch is faster than going through the installation with the three installation disks). However, you must have about 100MB of free space available for these files in order to perform the installation in this manner (there are a lot of temporary files in addition to the installation files). If the computer does not have enough space and also does not have a CD-ROM, just back up some of the existing files on the drive and delete them. After the installation is completed, much of the space occupied by the installation files is returned to you (because the temporary files are deleted), and you can restore your original files.

TROUBLESHOOTING CUSTOMIZED INSTALLATIONS

You have the ability to customize the Windows NT 4 installation on each workstation, either making each workstation identical or creating specific customized installation procedures for specific computers. This means you can make administrative decisions about which features you want to install and which you want to skip. While you can instruct users about company policy regarding the installation of games or certain accessories, you have no control over the final installed product unless you control the installation process. That is a daunting task if you are supporting a great many seats, but utilities are available to make the chore less onerous.

The easiest way to install Windows NT onto multiple computers is to push it (send it to the workstation from a server) or pull it (start an automatic or semiautomatic installation as a result of a batch file or login script that's been launched on the workstation).

To perform any sort of automatic installation, you must first install Windows NT 4 on one computer, and then use that computer's installation and configuration as the source of your companywide rollout. (In fact, you could create several source installations to speed the process.)

You can also create files that control the installation, at the same time customizing the operating system for your own needs, as you roll out Windows NT throughout your organization. There are several tools available to assist you in this effort:

▼ *Control files* on the Windows NT CD-ROM (both Server and Workstation) manage the installation process. These files can be altered to change the basic setup options.

■ *Answer files* are used to automate installation by providing some or all of the answers that are required via user response during the installation process. When the answer file contains all of the responses, it is usually referred to as an *unattended answer file*. See the section "Troubleshooting Unattended Installations" later in this chapter for more on this topic.

■ *Uniqueness database files* are used during unattended installation procedures to provide configuration data that is unique to a specific computer (for example, the computer name).

■ *Setup Manager* is a utility on the Windows NT 4 CD-ROM (\support\deptools\<platform>) that guides you through the process of creating answer files that help to automate the installation.

▲ *Systems Management Server* (SMS) is a Microsoft BackOffice application that provides a host of easy-to-use functions for deploying operating systems and software across a network. You can download a 120-day evaluation copy of SMS from the Microsoft web site (www.microsoft.com).

The fact is that none of these solutions are cakewalks, but the effort required to use these tools properly is certainly worthwhile when compared to installing the operating system one computer at a time (or leaving the installation to users).

Omitting Components

You can omit components of the operating system with Syssetup.inf. All you have to do is comment out the appropriate lines by placing a semicolon at the beginning of each line.

Syssetup.inf is in the platform directory (\I386) on the Windows NT 4.0 CD-ROM, so it should have been moved to your network distribution share. It's compressed, so the filename is Syssetup.in_. Working on the network share, use the Expand command to uncompress the file. The syntax is **expand syssetup.in_ syssetup.inf**.

CAUTION: You must be working in Windows NT to use the Expand *application.*

The NT Control Files

A number of files are used to control the installation process, and some of them pass controls on to other files:

▼ Txtsetup.sif controls the basic files that are transferred during the first phase of installation, which is a text-based process.

■ Dosnet.inf tells the installation program which files to copy to a temporary directory on a local drive if you launch the installation by entering **winnt /b** or **winnt32 /b** at a command line instead of using the floppy disks.

■ Layout.inf controls the geography of the installation. It directs the locations and directories for both the source and target disks.

■ Ipinfo.inf controls the installation of IP addresses.

▲ Syssetup.inf controls the structure of the installation. This file is compressed and is expanded during setup. It points to other .inf files to control the setup of particular components.

After the file is expanded, you have to change the name of the original expanded file, because if the Setup program sees both the .inf file and the .in_ file, it will use the compressed version. I usually change the extension from .in_ to .ori (for original).

Now you can open the expanded Syssetup.inf file and manipulate the contents. Since this file points to other .inf files for information about component setup, you'll be looking for lines that read *xxxxx*.inf, where *xxxxx* is the component you want to omit.

For example, examine the section of Syssetup.inf that looks like this:

```
[BaseWinOptionsInfs]
accessor.inf
communic.inf
games.inf
imagevue.inf
mmopt.inf
msmail.inf
multimed.inf
optional.inf
pinball.inf
wordpad.inf
```

Omit the Exchange Inbox

If you're planning to install e-mail with a client application such as Outlook, you won't need to install the Exchange client that comes with the Windows NT operating system.

Comment out the msmail.inf line in Syssetup.inf by placing a semicolon in front of it. This choice won't be available during setup.

Omit Games

Comment out the games.inf and pinball.inf lines if you don't want to put games onto the target computers. The choice won't be available during setup.

Omit Other Choices

Use your judgment, company policies, and common sense to eliminate other parts of the operating system from the installation choices.

Omitting Directories

You can also save time and disk space by preventing millions of bytes from being copied to the target computer's drive. Of course, you do this only if you know that you don't need the files in question. For instance, the expendable files for most installations are the third-party drivers for NICs, which take up about 20MB of disk space.

The file Dosnet.inf controls the directories that are copied during the text mode phase of setup. To prevent a directory from being copied, you have to comment out the appropriate line. In this case, the directory is \Drvlib.nic, and it is listed in the [OptionalSrcDirs] section of Dosnet.inf. To comment out the line, put a pound sign at the beginning of the line. That section would then look like this:

```
[OptionalSrcDirs]
inetsrv
#drvlib.nic
```

TIP: Microsoft's documentation, including its white paper on this subject that resides on its Internet site, tells you to use a semicolon to comment out these lines. That is not correct; the Dosnet.inf file requires pound sign commenting.

Don't comment out this directory unless you're sure the NICs you're installing are all in the \I386 (or other platform) directory and you have no need of this optional library.

TIP: The \Drvlib.nic directory contains many subdirectories. If you do need files from this directory, delete the subdirectories you don't need from your network sharepoint. This will save time and disk space.

Incidentally, the \Inetsrv directory listed in the [OptionalSrcDirs] section is for installing Peer Web Services, and it is about 5MB in size. This directory is copied by default during all installations of Windows NT 4. However, the option to install Peer Web Services is not available during installation of Windows NT 4 Workstation; it is a Server application (although it can be installed later on Workstation). For Workstation installation rollouts, comment out the line for that directory as well to save time and disk space.

TROUBLESHOOTING UNATTENDED INSTALLATIONS

You can eliminate the need for users to answer questions and make decisions by providing an answer file. As its name implies, this file provides the answers to all of the installation questions.

Answer files are enormously efficient but are also very unforgiving—leaving out an answer or making an error that causes the installation program to burp and stop (because there's no built-in dialog box that says "Huh? That makes no sense") defeats the purpose.

There are two ways to provide an answer file: use Setup Manager to fill out dialog boxes that provide the answers for the file, or create one from scratch (it's a text file).

To tell the Setup program that this is an unattended installation and that an answer file is available, start the installation with the command **winnt /u:<*answer file*> /s:<*install source*>**, where

> /u indicates that this is an unattended setup.
> <*answer file*> is the name of the answer file you created (the most common choice is Unattended.txt).
> /s:<*install source*> is the source location of the Windows NT installation files.

(If you are installing NT 4 onto computers that already have a version of NT, use the command **winnt32 /u:<*answer file*> /s:<*install source*>**).

TIP: The word "unattended" is defined in a variety of ways when you use the term to describe the installation of Windows NT 4. Sometimes, because of specific differences in computers or because you want different components on different computers, it might be wise to create a semiattended installation. This means that much of the user interaction is eliminated by predefined configuration options, but some responses are required from the user during specific parts of the installation procedure.

Problem: Target Computers Are Not Identical

If you look ahead to the data in the answer file that's created as a result of the information you're placing in the User Information tab, you can smell a problem coming. All the computers will have the same name because you must enter a computer name in the User Information tab. In addition, there may be some differences in hardware, or you may not want identical configuration options for every target computer.

There are three solutions to this problem:

▼ Create separate answer files.

- ■ Edit the generic answer file on the target computer during the installation process.

- ▲ Create a uniqueness database file (UDF), which is used along with a generic answer file. The UDF provides Setup with information that is unique to each computer.

More information about the latter two options is found later in this chapter in the section "Configuring the Differences."

Using Setup Manager to Create an Answer File

The easiest way to provide an answer file is to use Setup Manager for a "fill in the blanks" approach. Transfer the program from the CD-ROM to the computer that has had the Windows NT software installed (that installation is your source, and you'll want to put the answer file on the same drive). Open the program and begin providing data about the installation options.

You don't have to fill in all the blanks in Setup Manager, but there are some required entries. Unfortunately, Setup Manager doesn't have a Help button or a Help menu item, so it seems appropriate to provide a brief discussion here.

There are three sets of dialog boxes available in Setup Manager (see Figure 2-3). The first time you use this application, you start with the General Setup and then you move

Figure 2-3. There are three sections to configure in Setup Manager

on to the Networking Setup and the Advanced Setup. Afterward, clicking those buttons displays the information you entered so you can edit it, or you can choose New to create a new answer file.

General Setup for Setup Manager

The first section you fill in for Setup Manager is the General Setup Options dialog box, which has a number of tabs.

Required User Information

The information in the User Information tab, shown in Figure 2-4, is required. The product ID is the serial number on your Windows NT CD.

General Information About the Target Computer

The information you place in the General tab depends on whether or not this is a first-time installation, and it also is a measure of your confidence in how well you know the hardware installed in the target computers. As shown here, there are several options and suboptions available.

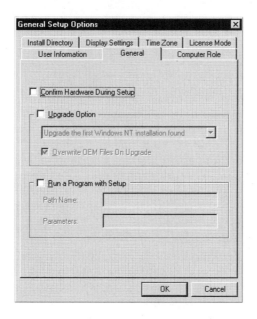

Here are some guidelines for supplying information in this tab:

Select Confirm Hardware During Setup if you are sure the hardware settings of the target computer are correct. Otherwise, Setup will perform diagnostics.

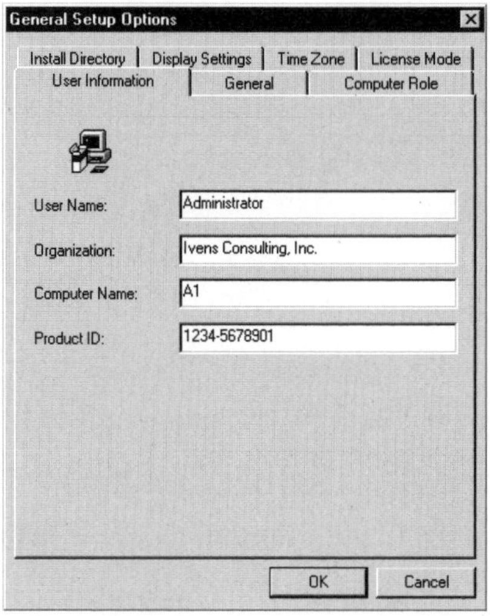

Figure 2-4. This basic information must be available to the Setup program

If you are upgrading to Windows NT 4, select Upgrade Option. Then choose the method for replacing the existing operating system. The choices are

▼ Prompt user for Windows NT installation to upgrade

■ Upgrade the current single Windows NT installation

■ Upgrade the first Windows NT installation found

▲ Upgrade Windows 3.1 or Windows for Workgroups

If you are doing an upgrade, selecting the Overwrite OEM Files on Upgrade option causes Setup to delete the files for existing Windows installations before installing the files for Windows NT 4.

If you want to run a program while you're installing Windows NT 4, select the Run a Program with Setup option and then enter the path/filename of the program and any parameters. You can even use this option to install software at the same time, getting a two-for-one unattended installation (but in view of the complexity of the task I'd recommend sticking to the operating system installation alone).

Choose a Role for This Computer

The Computer Role tab, shown in Figure 2-5, specifies the role of the target computer. Part of the decision is already made (whether or not you're preparing this answer file for installation of Windows NT 4 Server or Windows NT 4 Workstation).

The choices available for the role of the computer are

▼ Workstation in workgroup

■ Workstation in domain

■ Server in workgroup

■ Server in domain

■ Primary domain controller

▲ Backup domain controller

Enter the name of the domain or workgroup the computer will join.

The computer account field is optional (and appears only if you're assigning a role connected to a domain), and in fact you should not enter anything in this field for a companywide rollout.

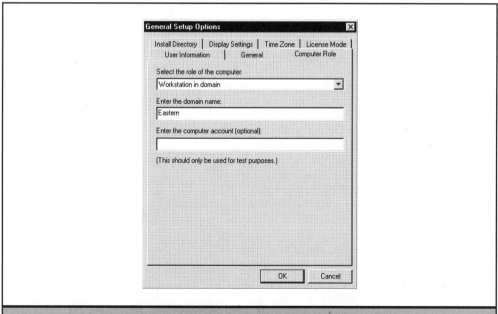

Figure 2-5.   You must choose a role for the target computer

Choose a Directory for Windows

Specify the directory where Windows NT 4 will be installed on the Install Directory tab:

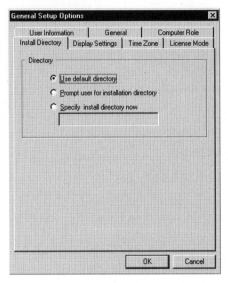

The default directory is \Winnt, or you can specify a user prompt during installation or indicate a target directory of your own choosing.

Specify Settings for the Display

The Display Settings tab holds the configurations for the video display:

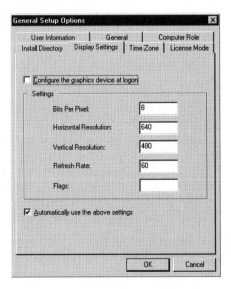

Most video cards will support the default settings already in place in this dialog box. (I'm tempted to say that all video cards will support these settings, but I couldn't prove it.) However, if you're sure of the hardware in the target computer(s), you can change the settings. The safest, most appropriate way to handle this tab is to leave it alone—you can always change the settings later.

Wrong Video Settings Can Be Fatal

Having the wrong video settings is often disastrous. Sometimes Setup dies a quiet death with no explanation after the first reboot (following the text portion of the installation), and sometimes the GUI portion of the installation procedure starts, but then you face the Blue Screen of Death. Video configuration problems account for a great many failed installations (and that's true as well for Windows 95 and Windows 98). On a companywide rollout, play it safe and opt for low resolution and low refresh rates.

Set the Time Zone

The Time Zone tab asks for your time zone information, which requires no assistance from me.

License Mode Required for Servers

If the target computer is a server, you must specify a license mode for your use of Windows NT 4. As shown here, there are two choices:

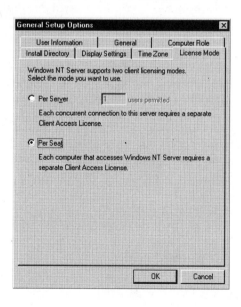

▼ Per server licensing means the server holds all the licenses for every simultaneous connection. For example, if you've bought 100 licenses, you can have up to 100 concurrent connections.

▲ Per seat licensing means each computer running Windows NT must have its own license. There is no server limit on this license type.

Network Setup for Setup Manager

When you have entered all the General Setup information, you're returned to the Setup Manager opening window. Now you can begin to configure your network by choosing the Networking Setup icon.

Establish Networking Installation Parameters

The General tab for the Networking Setup section is the place to configure the approach you want to use for installing network options. As seen in Figure 2-6, there are a variety of choices.

In effect, this tab governs whether or not the installation of networking information is handled automatically or manually.

If you choose a manual network installation, all the other choices on this tab are dimmed and all the other tabs disappear. During installation, user response is required to select the network settings for the computer.

If you choose an unattended network installation, you then have to specify the manner in which you want the installation to proceed:

▼ Choose Automatically Detect and Install First Adapter to have Setup search for a network adapter. As soon as it finds one, it will install it. The adapter in the computer must be one that is recognized correctly by Windows NT Setup.

TIP: If you have two adapters in the computer (usually this occurs only in a server), you will have to go back later and install the second one. If you want both adapters configured during the initial installation, you have to select manual network installation.

■ Choose Specify Adapter(s) to Be Detected to tell Setup that you know which adapters you want the installation routine to look for. The information about the adapter is specified on the Adapters tab of this dialog box.

▲ Choose Specify Adapter(s) to Be Installed to tell Setup which adapter to install.

The choice you make determines the fields that will be available to you on the Adapters tab.

Specify Information About Adapters

The Adapters tab is a chameleon—it changes itself in response to the input of the General tab.

If you chose Automatically Detect and Install First Adapter, you won't have access to the Adapters tab.

If you chose Specify Adapters to Be Selected, the Adapters tab looks like Figure 2-7. In effect, you're building the section of the answer file that Setup needs to automate the process.

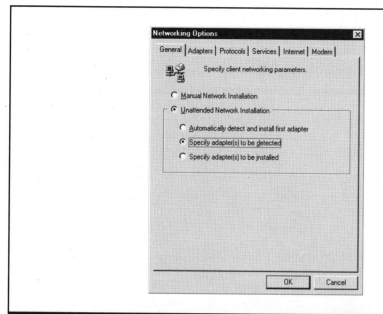

Figure 2-6.   The General tab is the place to specify how you want the installation program to handle networking information

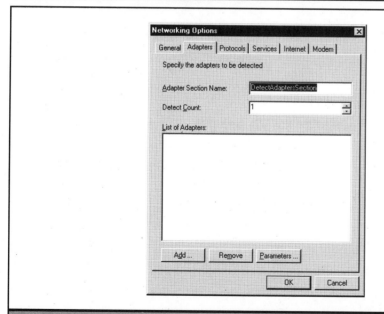

Figure 2-7.   Specify the adapters you want to put into the DetectAdaptersSection of your answer file

Even though this dialog box offers you a chance to change the name of the DetectAdaptersSection, there's no particular reason to do so.

The Detect Count box lets you specify the number of attempts you want Setup to make as it detects the adapter. Usually the default of 1 is sufficient.

You build the information needed for automatic setup by entering information in the List of Adapters section of this dialog box:

1. Choose Add, then click the down arrow to see the list of available adapters and select the appropriate ones, in order to build a list. Setup will use the list on each computer.

2. Choose OK; the adapter is entered into the List of Adapters box.

3. Select each adapter on your list and choose Parameters to enter information about the IRQ, I/O base address, and so on. There are some optional fields that apply only to specific types of networking setups. You'll know if you need to use them.

If you chose Specify Adapters to Be Installed, the Adapters tab looks the same as Figure 2-7, except there is no Detect Count field (since there's no detection and the system moves right on to install the adapter you list).

TIP: Use the Specify Adapters to Be Installed option when all of the computers that will use this unattended file have the same adapter with the same configuration.

Set the Protocols

You can establish the protocol settings for your installation with the Protocols tab, shown in Figure 2-8. As with the Adapters tab, use Add to choose a protocol (the choices are NetBEUI, IPX, and TCP/IP).

If you select TCP/IP, and you will not be using DHCP, choose Parameters to configure the TCP/IP information shown here:

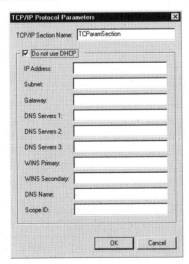

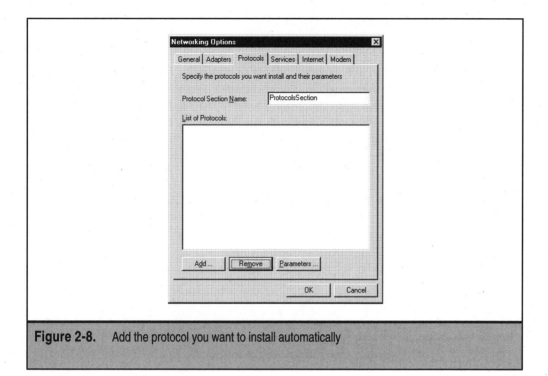

Figure 2-8. Add the protocol you want to install automatically

Configure Network Services

Use the Services tab to select the network services you want to install. You can use the Parameters button to configure any service you choose. The parameters you can set vary from service to service, of course.

Configure Internet Services

This is a euphemism for installing Internet Information Server (IIS), and you can install this application only if you are setting up unattended installation for Windows NT Server. If you do install IIS, you can configure the services (ftp, Web, Gopher) as well as other options.

Configure RAS Modems

The Modem tab is available only if you've chosen RAS in the Services tab (where you should have configured the port). Use the Modem tab to select the modem, connect it to the configured port, and add any other configuration details your modem needs.

Advanced Setup for Setup Manager

This section of Setup Manager (see Figure 2-9) has a number of tabs you can use to set discretionary advanced configuration options.

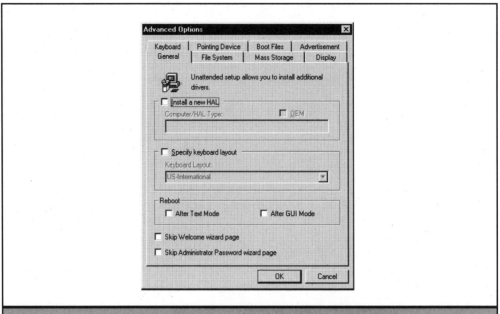

Figure 2-9. Set additional options for your unattended installation answer file

Check the Setup Manager Answer File

When you've completed your entries in Setup Manager, choose Save and name the file. I've found it better to give this file a name other than "Unattend.txt," because I end up creating a variety of answer files to fit the variety of target computers. Name the file something that reminds you of its configuration.

Here is a sample answer file created by Setup Manager:

```
[Unattended]
OemPreinstall = yes
NoWaitAfterTextMode = 0
NoWaitAfterGUIMode = 0
FileSystem = LeaveAlone
ExtendOEMPartition = 0
ConfirmHardware = no
NtUpgrade = no
Win31Upgrade = no
TargetPath = *
OverwriteOemFilesOnUpgrade = no
```

```
[OEM_Ads]
Banner = "Ivens Consulting, Inc. Workstation Setup"

[UserData]
FullName = "Administrator"
OrgName = "Ivens Consulting, Inc."
ComputerName = A1
ProductId = "1234-5678901"

[GuiUnattended]
OemSkipWelcome = 1
OEMBlankAdminPassword = 1
TimeZone = "(GMT-05:00) Eastern Time (US & Canada)"

[Display]
ConfigureAtLogon = 0
BitsPerPel = 8
XResolution = 640
YResolution = 480
VRefresh = 60
AutoConfirm = 1

[Modem]
InstallModem = ModemParameters

[ModemParameters]
COM1 = "sportster 33.6 fax modem", "u.s. robotics"

[Network]
DetectAdapters = DetectAdaptersSection
InstallAdapters = SelectedAdaptersSection
InstallProtocols = ProtocolsSection
InstallServices = ServicesSection

[DetectAdaptersSection]
DetectCount = 1
LimitTo = NE2000
NE2000 = NE2000ParamSection

[NE2000ParamSection]
InterruptNumber = 15
IOBaseAddress = 0x300

[SelectedAdaptersSection]
```

```
[ProtocolsSection]
NBF = NBFParamSection
TC = TCParamSection

[NBFParamSection]

[TCParamSection]
DHCP = yes

[ServicesSection]
RAS = RASParamSection

[RASParamSection]
PortSections = PortSection1
DialoutProtocols = TCP/IP

[PortSection1]
PortName = COM1
DeviceType = Modem
PortUsage = DialInOut
```

Create Your Own Answer File

You can create your own answer file from scratch, or use the file you create with Setup Manager as the basis for a more complete answer file.

As a troubleshooting technique, you should be aware of the conventions expected in an answer file:

▼ Section headings must be surrounded by square brackets, for example, [Display]. Mandatory section headings must appear, even if you're not providing answers for that section.

■ Key names may not be changed. The key names are those that define an option, such as InstallAdapters. They always appear as the first word on a line.

■ Equal signs must have a space before and after, such as InstallAdapters = AdaptersList.

▲ Empty values are indicated by double quotes with no space between them ("").

Problem: OEM NICs Must Be Installed in Unattended Mode

One of the problems with an unattended install is that you are basically relying on drivers and files from the Windows CD-ROM. A problem arises when you have OEM NICs and drivers, because they don't appear on the list in Setup Manager and they aren't in the drivers library on the CD-ROM. The solution is to create the necessary files and make them a part of your network sharepoint, as if they'd been copied from the CD-ROM.

TIP: This is only worth going through if you're installing the OEM NIC on a lot of computers. For one or two of them, just do a manual installation.

These NICs are not detectable, but they are installable. Here's how to make this happen:

1. In the OEM files you were sent, find the file named Oemsetup.inf.

2. Go to your third-party drivers and look for a file called Oemsetup.inf.

3. Use a text editor to open the file. The top of the file should look like this:

```
[Identification]
     OptionType = NetAdapter
[PlatformsSupported]
     ISA
     EISA
     PCMCIA
     "Jazz-Internal Bus"
[Options]
     ACCURA
```

4. Write down the name under the [Options] section (there may be additional names in this section, usually commented out with a semicolon); you'll need it later.

5. Search for the [OptionsTextENG] section, and write down the values in this section; you'll need them later (there may be additional names in this section, usually commented out with a semicolon). This section should look like the following:

```
[OptionsTextENG]
     ACCURA = "Accura MX32 Ethernet Adapter"
```

6. On the \I386 sharepoint, create a subdirectory under the \Drvlib.nic\netcard subdirectory with the name of the NIC. In this case, I'd name the directory \Accura.

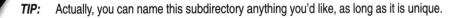

TIP: Actually, you can name this subdirectory anything you'd like, as long as it is unique.

7. Copy all the driver files for this NIC into the new subdirectory. (Most of the time, there is at least an .inf file, a .sys file, and a .hlp file).

8. Expand the file named Oemnadzz.in_ , which is in your \I386 share, and name it Oemnadzz.inf (see the information about expanding files in the section "Omitting Components," earlier in this chapter).

9. Use a text editor to open Oemnadzz.inf. The file has four sections named [Options], one each for PCI, MCA, EISA, and ISA. Beneath each [Options] sections are additional sections for the bus type named [Filename] and [OptionsTextENG]. Move to the section that matches the type of NIC you want to install.

10. Add the name of your NIC (the name you wrote down in step 4). For example, if this NIC is for an EISA machine, you look for [EISAOptions] and add the name to the first line under the section heading.

11. Go to the next section, which is [Filename] (in this case [EISAFilename]), and enter the path to the .inf file (which is in the subdirectory you created in step 6). Put this entry right below the section heading.

12. Go to the next section, [OptionsTextENG] (in this case [EISAOptionsTextENG]), and enter the value you wrote down in step 5.

Here is a look at some of the relevant parts of this file after the new information is added:

```
[EISAOptions]
ACCURA
NiwRAS
DigiSyncX25
DigiSyncFR
Diehl_DIVA
[EISAFilename]
drvlib\netcard\accura\oemsetup.inf
drvlib\netcard\x86\NiwRAS\oemsetup.inf
drvlib\netcard\x86\DIGIX25\oemsetup.inf
drvlib\netcard\x86\DIGIFR\oemsetup.inf
[EISAOptionsTextENG]
ACCURA = "Accura MX32 Ethernet Adapter"
NiwRAS       = "Niwot Networks NiwRAS Adapter"
DigiSyncX25 = "Digi SyncPort X.25 Adapter"
DigiSyncFR  = "Digi SyncPort Frame Relay Adapter"
```

Now you have to tell your answer file about all this work you just did. Check the [NetWork] section, which should resemble the following:

```
[NetWork]
JoinDomain = domain_name
CreatComputerAccount = user_name, password
```

```
InstallAdapters = InstallACCURANetcard
InstallProtocols = ProtocolsList
InstallServices = SelectedServicesList
[InstallACCURANetcard]
ACCURA = ACCURAParams
[ACCURAParams]
!AutoNetInterfaceType = "1"
!AutoNetBusNumber = "0"
IOBaseAddress = "768"
DMAChannel = "3"
InterruptNumber = "5"
```

Your answer file may have slightly different entries, but the important things are

▼ There is no reference to detecting adapters, just to installing adapters.

■ There is a specific data item calling for the installation of your OEM adapter.

▲ There is a specific section for your OEM adapter.

This process makes it possible to have your OEM NIC on the list of NICs, just as if your brand had been included in the Windows NT 4 files.

Problem: OEM NIC Install Is Prompting for Information

You may have to make some changes to the Oemsetup.inf file for your OEM NIC in order to prevent it from prompting for user input. The sections of the file that are important in this regard are

▼ STF_UNATTENDED

■ STF_GUI_UNATTENDED

▲ STF_UNATTENDED_SECTION)

In effect, you have to make sure that the .inf file has made provisions for an unattended install. It does this by answering "Yes" at all the appropriate places—except, of course, it isn't that simple; the language and structure are a bit more complicated than a simple "yes to unattended stuff."

You're looking for lines that resemble the following:

```
ifstr(I) $(!STF_GUI_UNATTENDED) == "YES"
        ifstr(I) $(!AutoNetInterfaceType) != ""
          set BusInterfaceType = $(!AutoNetInterfaceType)
        else
          set BusInterfaceType = 1
        endif
        ifstr(I) $(!AutoNetBusNumber) != ""
```

```
        set BusNumber = $(!AutoNetBusNumber)
    else
        set BusNumber = 0
    endif
    goto adapterverify
endif
```

If Setup is unattended, you must omit or comment out any commands that open a user interface (UI), such as a dialog box. These commands usually look like this:

```
read-syms FileDependentDlg$(!STF_LANGUAGE)
ui start "InputDlg"
```

TIP: If you're comfortable with programming standards, you can use GOTO to skip sections of the .inf file.

Then, when the network component .inf file verifies that Setup is running in unattended mode, it will use the STF_UNATTENDED symbol to fetch the unattended filename. This STF_UNATTENDED_SECTION symbol will be established by Setup so that the .inf file code can read it whenever it needs to.

Problem: Configuration Information for OEM NIC Can't Be Found

Sometimes you can't find the configuration information (IRQ, I/O base address) for your NIC in the OEM files. Here's how to get the data you need. Install one of these NICs manually on a single computer. Then use the information that's written to the registry. You can find these parameters in HKEY_LOCAL_MACHINE\System\CurrentControl Set\Services\<%OemNetcardKeyname%>X\parameters).

Notice the X in the next-to-last subkey. The registry has a subkey for the card name (called the product name) and another subkey for the card name with a number after it (called the service name). The first entry is really an option for the card, and the second entry is the actual instance of the card (usually the product name with "1" added on).

For example, look at Figure 2-10, which shows the registry entries for a computer that has an NE2000 NIC.

CAUTION: The values in the registry are in hex, but in your answer file they must be decimal. For instance, an I/O base address of 0x300 in the registry must appear as IoBaseAddress = 768 in the answer file. You have to obtain the information and translate it.

Other Common Answer File Problems

If a group of administrators who have rolled out NT 4 with answer files gets together to discuss the process, there's a good chance you'll find some agreement about the problems

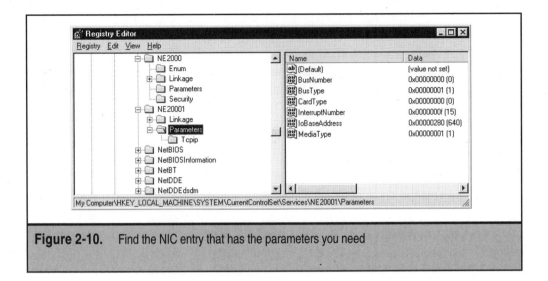

Figure 2-10.   Find the NIC entry that has the parameters you need

they faced as they prepared to rewrite the answer file. In this section I'll tell you what I've learned from participating in those conversations and also by eavesdropping.

The parameter for the answer file used in the installation command must match the name of the answer file. If it doesn't, it's a fatal typo. Check your spelling.

The first section heading must say [Unattended], and you may not use any other section heading in front of it. This is the only section heading that has a determined order (it must be first); the other section headings can be in any order you wish.

The decision about the response for the key name OemPreinstall (under the Unattended section heading) is extremely important:

A No value tells NT 4 that this is a standard unattended installation, where you've provided configuration parameters but you understand that there are a couple of things that have to be done by the user. For example, the user will have to reboot the machine after each successful section of installation (after the text-based portion of Setup is completed and also after final installation to go to the first logon). In addition, the user will have to agree to the licensing terms (unless you prevent it with this key name and value: **OemSkipEula = yes**).

A Yes value causes subdirectories to be transferred to the target machine, some of which may contain additional applications you're installing along with the operating system. However, the more significant side effect of a Yes value is that you can add keys in order to avoid any user action. Those keys are

▼ NoWaitAfterTextMode, where a value of 1 tells Setup to reboot automatically into the GUI mode when the text mode portion of the installation is complete, and a value of 0 prevents automatic rebooting.

▲ NoWaitAfterGuiMode, where a value of 1 tells Setup to reboot automatically when the installation is finished, and a value of 0 prevents automatic rebooting.

The key name FileSystem specifies the way the NT partition on the target computer is formatted. The choices are ConvertNTFS or LeaveAlone (Setup assumes a FAT volume). Be sure you understand the significance of your data for this key, and remember that you'll probably have a different answer depending on whether your answer file is being used for NT Server or NT Workstation.

CONFIGURING THE DIFFERENCES

No generic answer file works on all the target computers—at the very least the computer name must be unique. If you don't want to create individual answer files for each unattended installation, you have two methods for conforming the answer file for a specific computer:

▼ Edit the answer file after it is transferred to the target computer.

▲ Use a uniqueness database file (UDF) to provide the unique information.

We'll go over both methods in this section.

Modify the Answer File on Each Target Computer

During the first part of the installation process, the text mode phase, the files needed for installation are transferred to the local hard drive. You must have set up the answer file so that NoWaitAfterTextMode has a value of 0 (which prevents automatic rebooting).

Then, instead of restarting the operating system, turn off the machine and insert a bootable MS-DOS floppy disk into drive A. When the machine is up and running, go to drive C and look for C:\win_nt.~bt\winnt.sif. This is the name of the file that is copied to the target hard drive (in fact, it's not a full, identical copy of your answer file). However, you can use it to substitute unique settings for the generic settings contained in your answer file. Then remove the floppy disk and restart the computer to continue the installation process.

The best way to prepare an answer file for this type of after-the-fact editing is to enter information that makes it easy to find and replace data. For example, in the computer name section, use PutNameHere (or something similar); then a simple search and replace process in a text editor takes care of it. Or, for a network adapter, use NameNICHere.

CAUTION: This won't work if the hard drive is formatted with NTFS and you're using Winnt32.exe.

Use a UDF

You can attach the unique information for each computer with a uniqueness database file. To tell Setup that the file exists, you must add these parameters to your Winnt or Winnt32 command: /UDF:ID[filename.udb] where:

ID is a UniqueID for this computer
filename is the filename for the UDF, including the full path

TIP: Note that the filename for a UDF has the extension .udb.

The UDF is copied to the target computer during the text mode phase of Setup, and its contents are used during the GUI mode phase.

Using both an answer file and a UDF means that your command to install Windows NT reads like this:

winnt /s:*z*:\ /u:*answerfilename*.txt /udf:*UniqueID,UDFfilename*.udb /b

where:

s:z: is the source:network sharepoint drive letter
u:*answerfilename*.txt is the answer file to be used
udf:*UniqueID* is the uniqueness ID for this installation
UDFfilename.udb is the uniqueness database file to be used
/b specifies that you don't want to create install disks (the data is transferred to the hard drive of the target computer)

Remember that you must use the Net Use command to establish the source drive letter (see the discussion in the section "Correct the Startup Information," earlier in this chapter).

Letting the User Take Care of Giving Setup the UDF

You have another alternative for distributing a UDF. You can put it on a floppy disk, with the filename $Unique$.udb. Then start Setup at the target computer with only the UniqueID for the computer in the part of the parameters that calls for the UDF (/udf:id). After the text mode phase of Setup is complete, the installation program will ask the user to insert the floppy disk with the UDF.

This means you can sit at your workstation, create all the files you need on floppy disks, and distribute them.

Create a UDF

You can use any text editor to create the UDF, because it's a simple text file.

The first section must be [UniqueIDs]; it lists all of the UniqueIDs that are included in the UDF file. The listings in this section consist of two parts: the UniqueID and the name of the section(s) containing specific information for that UniqueID. The two parts are separated by an equal sign.

CAUTION: The UniqueID can have any characters except asterisk, space, comma, or equal sign.

The format for the UniqueIDs section is

```
[UniqueIds]
id1 = section,section
id2 = section,section
id3 = section,section,section
```

For instance, if you want to use computer names based on user names as the UniqueIDs, the UniqueIDs section could look like this:

```
[UniqueIds]
BeverlyT = UserData,Unattended
JudithB = UserData,GuiUnattended
DeborahL = UserData,GuiUnattended,Network
```

All of the other sections of the UDF are referred to in this [UniqueIds] section. The section names can be in one of two formats:

▼ The section names can match section names in the answer file (for example, [Unattended] is a section in the answer file).

▲ The section names can be specifically created for the UDF, in which case they are preceded by the UniqueID and a colon (such as JudithB:GuiUnattended).

TIP: If both a general section (such as [Unattended]) and an ID-specific section (such as [BeverlyT:Unattended]) have been entered in the UDF, the data in the ID-specific section wins.

The sections in the UDF can contain any keys and data for the same-named sections in the answer file. That way you can change, add, or delete data values in the answer file. During installation, each data item in a UDF-referenced section overrides the data for the same key in the answer file. If there is a data item in the answer file, and there is no data for that item in the section referenced by the UniqueID in the UDF, the data value in the answer file is used during installation.

The following sections can be referenced in the [UniqueIDs] section, but they cannot exist as sections of the UDF (they are found only in the answer file):

```
[UNATTENDED]
[MassStorageDrivers]
[KeyboardDrivers]
[PointingDeviceDrivers]
[OEMBootFiles]
```

```
[OEM_Ads]
[Display]
[Modem]
```

You can create one UDF that lists UniqueIDs for all of your target computers, or you can create individual UDFs for each computer. My own experience has been that where there are a number of differences, creating individual files for every computer is actually easier than having one enormous file that has to provide sections and data values for all those differences. If the only difference is the computer name and other basic data, it's not quite so difficult to keep track of data in a single UDF.

How the UDF Is Used During Unattended Setup

The UDF and the answer file are actually merged during Setup, and the merged information becomes the answer file for Setup questions. This merging takes place before all of the component installation procedures need the information. Here are the "merge" rules:

▼ If the answer file and the UDF sections have the same data value in a data item line, when the data items are merged the value in the UDF is used. In effect, the merge has caused a replacement of a data item in the answer file.

▲ If a UDF section has a data item that is referenced by the UniqueID, but the answer file does not contain that data item, the data value in the UDF is used. In effect, the merge has added a line to the answer file.

We can use the data from the example files in the preceding section to illustrate the effects of this merging process.

The top of the UDF reads as follows:

```
[UniqueIds]
BeverlyT = UserData,Unattended
JudithB = UserData,GuiUnattended
DeborahL = UserData,GuiUnattended,Network
```

For one of the user IDs, DeborahL, we've indicated there is a unique data item in three of the sections. For instance, in the Network section, the UDF has the following information:

```
[DeborahL:Network]
JoinDomain = "Eastern"
```

Now, back in the answer file we created, we have information that looks like this:

```
[Network]

DetectAdapters = DetectAdaptersSection
InstallAdapters = SelectedAdaptersSection
InstallProtocols = ProtocolsSection
InstallServices = ServicesSection
```

When Setup gets to the network installation, it will merge the items in the two sections (in this case, the domain information is added to the information in Network).

Error: Setup Asks for the UDF Disk Even Though a UDF Filename Is Specified

This error means that information is needed that is not supplied by the UDF. Missing values cause Setup to ask for the UDF floppy disk. There are two common causes of this error:

▼ A section is referenced in one of the lines in the [UniqueIDs] section, but the section doesn't exist in either the answer file or the UDF.

▲ A data item is specified in the UDF, but the data value is blank. Values in the answer file are not used when data items are specified in the UDF, so the value is assumed to be missing.

TIP: The correlation between missing data values and the request for a floppy disk containing the UDF is proven by the fact (stated earlier) that the disk is requested if you do not enter a filename on the command line. It is the missing data (the filename) that launches the request for the disk.

WINDOWS NT
Professional Library

CHAPTER 3

Troubleshooting Domains

A *domain* is a group of connected computers that share a security database and a specific list of users who belong to the domain. All of the security information for a domain is kept on computers called domain controllers. Only users who have been added to the domain's user list by a system administrator can join (log on to) a domain.

The connections that group computers together to make up a domain can be of any type—a domain does not have to be connected via a network leg. The computers can be scattered around the globe, communicating by any available method. (However, most of the time companies create domains that are connected through a LAN.)

Domains maintain an individual account for each user who logs on, and that user is logging on to the domain, not to the server that handles the logon for the domain. The server is merely the vehicle, not the ultimate destination of the logon process. (The user is also logging on to his or her local computer if that local computer is running Windows NT.) The domain enforces the security (rights and permissions for each user) through a directory database called SAM (Security Accounts Manager).

How a Workgroup Differs from a Domain

Unlike a domain, a *workgroup* is a group of computers identified by nothing more than a group name. Any user can be a member of any workgroup just by logging on to the workgroup. In practice, workgroups are consistent, meaning that there are users who routinely log on to that workgroup, usually sharing directories and peripherals with the other users in the same workgroup. However, there is no workgroup user list against which their logons are checked for rights and permissions, because there are no workgroup security features.

TROUBLESHOOTING DOMAIN CONTROLLERS

Within each domain there is a computer running Windows NT Server, which is the primary domain controller (PDC) for that domain. Changes made to the domain's directory database are tracked by the PDC. In addition, one or more backup domain controllers (BDCs) can exist on a domain (backup domain controllers are optional, but they're a good idea), and those computers must also be running Windows NT Server. BDCs receive copies of the directory database through regularly scheduled replications.

A BDC can share the workload in verifying user logons. However, changes to the database cannot be made at the BDC (even if the PDC has had a problem and is not running), because any changes to the database can be written only to the PDC.

Of course, there's plenty that can go wrong with this setup, whether it's a user problem during logon, a replication problem between domain controllers, or any of a host of other misadventures.

Stand-Alone Servers

There are frequently additional servers within a domain, usually employed as application servers or print servers. These are called stand-alone servers, and they have no influence on logons or security. The fact that they don't have to deal with the overhead of domain business makes them better candidates for hosting multiuser applications. You cannot change a stand-alone server into a PDC or a BDC unless you reinstall the operating system.

PDCs Disappear with NT 5

Just as a peek into the future, with Windows NT 5 there is no PDC or BDC. Instead there are DCs (domain controllers). You can have one or more domain controllers on a Windows NT 5 domain, and they all maintain the database as if they were PDCs. Changes made to one DC are replicated quickly to the others. If two changes are made to the same item, the last write wins.

Printing a List of Domain Users

For some inexplicable reason, the User Manager programs (User Manager and User Manager for Domains) don't provide a way to print a list of users. In fact, if you open the help file for User Manager and search the index or the database (with the Find tab) for the word "print," you won't find any entries. You also cannot print information about users from Microsoft Exchange Server or System Management Server, so this is obviously a Microsoft design. There are, of course, a gazillion reasons to have a hard copy of the user list. Here are two methods for getting a printout:

▼ Open a command window on a domain controller and enter **net user >** *filename***.txt** (invent your own filename for the redirected list).

▲ Open a command window on an NT workstation that is part of the domain and enter **net user /domain >** *filename***.txt**

TIP: There are two things to be aware of when you use this method to print a list of users. First, you don't have to use the .txt extension. (I use it because it's so easy to open the file later from Explorer when the extension is registered and associated.) Second, when you use the command at a workstation, you must enter the word **domain**; don't replace that word with the actual domain name.

Since you also cannot obtain a list of users for the local NT workstation from User Manager, use the command **net user** > *filename*.txt (without the word "domain") at an NT workstation command prompt to get a list of local users.

Of course, once you have the file you can print it from any editor or word processor (or the command line, for that matter).

Renaming the Primary Domain Controller

There was a time when I would have asked, "Why in the world would you need or want to rename a computer, especially a primary domain controller?" Over the years, however, I've learned that the decision to rename domain controllers sometimes makes sense. Companies grow, and additional sites are added to the infrastructure, and the sites become domains (or multiple domains). After a while, this growth develops into an illogical set of names, and users have a difficult time keeping track of departments and company services. Somebody with a logical mind arrives at a logical conclusion: the computer system naming scheme should reflect the company's structure. Thus, the domain for a division headquartered in New York should have a name that is a little more illustrative than DomainC, perhaps FifthFloorNY. And the name of the PDC for this domain should offer some information, perhaps NYAccntg, which makes more sense than naming it PDCNY4. Even if there aren't multiple sites around the country (or the world), as companies grow and occupy additional floors of a building, sites and domains are created. The domains and the primary domain controllers should be named to give information about their place in the corporate structure.

To change the name of a PDC, follow these steps:

1. At the PDC, open the Network applet in Control Panel, which presents the Identification tab in the foreground. The current computer name and domain name are displayed.

2. Choose Change to display the Identification Changes dialog box, as seen here.

Identification Changes   ? X

Windows uses the following information to identify this computer on the network. You may change the name for this computer or the name of the domain that it manages.

Computer Name: EAST

Domain Name: EASTERN

OK   Cancel

3. Enter a new name for the computer—the name must be unique to the network, and you can use up to 15 characters.

Reboot the computer to have the name change take effect.

TIP: While technically a computer name can be 15 characters long, you should try to keep the name to 13 or less characters if you haven't installed Service Pack 3 for Windows NT. This is because the Policy Editor has a problem with applying policies to groups if the server name is longer than 13 characters. Of course, if you think you'll never use the Policy Editor it doesn't matter (but you're missing out on a very useful tool). SP3 corrected the problem.

Problem: A Renamed PDC Isn't Listed in Server Manager

Sometimes the renaming goes awry (sorry, but "sometimes" is as specific as I can be, since I've never figured out a pattern for this problem), and the newly named computer isn't listed as a PDC. To see if there are ramifications to your renaming adventure, launch Server Manager (in the Administrative Tools program group).

If the new computer name isn't listed, you have to add it, using these steps:

1. Choose Computer, Add to Domain from the menu bar. The Add Computer To Domain dialog box appears, as seen in Figure 3-1.

2. Select Windows NT Backup Domain Controller as the computer type, and enter the name you gave the PDC. (Don't worry; it will become a PDC. There's just no choice for that on the dialog box.) Choose Add, then choose Close.

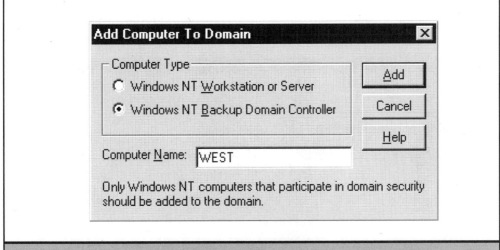

Figure 3-1.   I renamed my PDC WEST but it didn't appear in Server Manager, so I have to add it

3. When you return to the Server Manager window, select the old computer name and choose Computer, Remove From Domain (you could also press the DEL key). Answer Yes to the confirming dialog box.

Since the computer you just removed from the domain was the PDC, the newly added BDC is automatically promoted to a PDC. Now everything is the way it should be. Well, maybe not; I've also seen cases where the promotion to PDC leaves the newly added computer listed as a BDC also, meaning that it's listed twice. If that happens, select the BDC version of the name and remove it. Now, for sure, things are the way they should be.

Problem: A Renamed PDC Is Listed Under Both Names in Server Manager

Very often the new name makes it to Server Manager, but the old name still exists and the operating system thinks it's a BDC (see Figure 3-2). If the system thinks that a BDC by that name exists, it will try to include it in the replication process, which can really confuse things.

Select the old name and remove it. When the confirmation dialog box appears, choose Yes. After you confirm the removal of the computer, you may see a dialog box telling you that even though the computer name is listed it isn't part of the domain, and the system will remove it during the next update of the database. It's as if the operating system is saying, "I know, I know; I just didn't get around to removing the name yet. It doesn't mean anything." Just click OK (and check back in about half an hour to make sure).

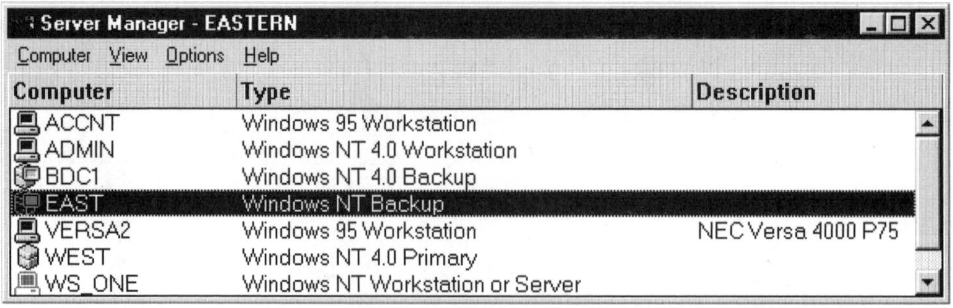

Figure 3-2. The old PDC, EAST, is still listed, even though I changed its name to WEST

Renaming a Backup Domain Controller

Renaming a BDC is a bit different from renaming a PDC. You have to give the PDC some advance warning, registering the new name before you can apply it.

Don't Rename a BackOffice Server BDC

You don't want to rename a BDC that is being used as a server for a BackOffice application such as Exchange Server. While technically it is probably possible to perform this task and fix all the ensuing errors, it takes almost forever to catch all the pointers and paths and then reconfigure your BackOffice program and the clients that access it. Don't bother; it isn't worth it.

Follow these steps to change the name of the BDC:

1. At the PDC, open Server Manager and add the new computer name to the domain, specifying that it will be a backup domain controller.

2. Move to the BDC that you want to rename and use the Network applet in Control Panel to change the name. You'll see a warning message saying that if you do this without having the administrator change the name first on the domain, you'll be unable to log on. (There is no menu item on Server Manager that would permit the administrator to change the name, so you couldn't do this if you wanted to.) Confirm the name change by choosing Yes.

3. Reboot the BDC. After you log on you'll see a Service Control Manager dialog box informing you that a service failed and telling you to check the Event Viewer (there may be several errors relating to the effects of the renaming process, but you'll fix everything by following the next steps).

4. Open a command window on the BDC and enter the command **net accounts /sync**. This synchronizes the domain database between the BDC and the PDC.

5. Open the Services applet in Control Panel and start the Net Logon services.

6. At the PDC, launch Server Manager, select the old BDC name from the list and choose Computer, Remove From Domain.

TIP: If you enter the command **net accounts /sync** from the PDC, it synchronizes all the backup domain controllers on the domain. Entering the command from the BDC synchronizes only that BDC.

Renaming a Domain

You can't. Well, you can, but only by reinstalling the operating system on the computer. What you can do is invent a new domain and move an existing PDC to it, which in effect amounts to renaming the domain if you don't put another PDC in place of the old one in the old domain.

Before I spell out the steps for doing this, I think it's prudent to point out the complications you'll face. You will have to be prepared to do the following:

▼ Redo the logon configuration of every workstation that currently joins the domain you're planning to eliminate.

■ Reconfigure all persistent network connections to the PDC throughout the organization for the new UNC. Remember that specific shares on the PDC may be involved in these connections (and multiple shares may be involved).

■ Reconfigure all trust relationships that involve this domain in both directions.

▲ Install new BDCs for the new domain, since you cannot move a BDC the way you can move a PDC.

If you still have a need to move the existing PDC to a new domain, follow these steps to achieve your goal:

1. At the PDC, open the Network applet in Control Panel.

2. Choose Change on the Identification tab to open the Identification Changes dialog box.

3. Type the new domain name in the Domain Name text box.

4. If you wish, you can also change the name of the PDC by entering a new name in the Computer Name text box.

5. Choose OK.

There's a short delay as Windows checks around the network to see if there's already a domain using this new name (if there is, you're told the name exists and the process ends). When the name is determined to be unique, a message dialog box appears warning you of some of the consequences of this action. If you want to continue with this procedure, choose Yes; otherwise choose No.

Promoting a BDC

A BDC can be promoted to a PDC, which is why having a BDC is a good idea. The database is there, having been replicated regularly, so you don't have to rebuild a PDC from scratch and restore a tape (one of the slowest processes in computing). There are two reasons to promote a BDC to a PDC:

▼ The PDC is unavailable, having crashed, burped, been stolen, or otherwise been rendered not usable.

▲ You are planning to shut down the PDC to perform maintenance such as adding more memory or larger storage capacity.

TIP: There is a slight difference in this procedure, depending on whether or not the PDC is up and running at the time you promote the BDC. If it is, when the BDC is promoted, the PDC is automatically demoted. If it isn't, you will have to demote the old PDC manually when it comes back online.

To promote a BDC, follow these steps:

1. At the BDC, open Server Manager (it's in the Administrative Tools submenu).
2. Select the BDC you want to promote.
3. Choose Computer, Promote to Primary Domain Controller from the menu bar.
4. Read the warnings (all connections to both the BDC and the PDC will be closed), then answer Yes to continue or No to cancel.

If the PDC is running, it is automatically demoted to a BDC.

Demoting a PDC

If the PDC was not running when you promoted the BDC, you may eventually get the computer fixed and boot it. Once the operating system is running, you'll see a message that at least one service failed, along with a suggestion to check the Event Viewer. If you do check the Event Viewer, you'll learn that an event was logged because a PDC was already running for this domain during logon of this PDC. Now you must demote this PDC to a BDC, by using these steps:

1. Open Server Manager (in the Administrative Tools menu).
2. Select the PDC you want to demote.
3. From the menu bar, choose Computer, Demote to Backup Domain Controller.

When you want to restore the original PDC to its role, just reverse the two preceding processes, promoting the newly created BDC and demoting the newly created PDC. If both are running (this is usually the case when the promotion/demotion was planned in order to upgrade hardware or otherwise mess around with the original PDC), promoting the original PDC back automatically demotes the new PDC to its former role as a BDC.

Warning Users Before Closing Connections

It's a good idea to warn all the users connected to the PDC or BDC before you perform tasks that shut the connections. There are two ways to do this: by contacting users who are currently connected to a server, or by broadcasting a message to a group of users. (Of course, these instructions work for message handling under any circumstances, not just for sending warnings before shutting down domain controllers.)

To send a message to all the users connected to a server, take these steps:

1. Open Server Manager.

2. Select the server whose users you want to contact.

3. Choose Computer, Send Message to see this Send Message dialog box:

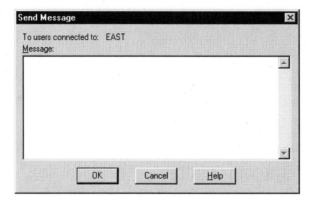

4. Enter the message, then choose OK.

The message is sent to all computers that have active connections to the selected server:

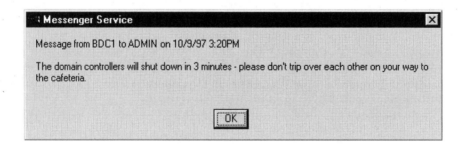

The problem with this method is that it sends messages only to computers with active connections, which means the server is mapped or a user is currently logged on and accessing a share. Remember that logging on to a domain controller doesn't necessarily establish an active connection. As a result, your message may reach only a few members of your domain.

It's usually more expedient to broadcast a message, which reaches all computers that are physically connected. You can broadcast a message from any Windows NT computer, whether a server or a workstation. To do so, open a command window and use this command: **net send /xxx message**, where *xxx* can be

/domain (the word "domain," not the name of the domain), which sends the message to all computers on the domain.

/domain:*name*, which sends the message to all the names in the named domain (used for connected domains other than your own).

/*name*, which can be a user name or computer name (enclose computer names that have spaces in quotation marks).

/users, which sends messages to all users with current connections to this computer (the same as using the Server Manager feature).

Problem: Some Computers Don't Receive Messages

If computers that are physically connected to the sending machine don't receive the message, the solution depends on the operating system platform.

Troubleshooting Windows NT Message Problems

Windows NT computers must be running the Messenger service (this is the default, so it would be unusual to have this problem, but it does happen). You can check for the problem (and resolve it) either from the server or from the computer that's having the problem.

To solve the problem from the server:

1. Open Server Manager.

2. Select the computer that did not receive the message.

3. Choose Computer, Services from the menu bar to open the Services applet from that computer's Control Panel. (If you are working at the affected computer, just open the Services applet in Control Panel.)

4. Scroll to the Messenger service (the services are in alphabetic order), and make sure it is enabled. The information should look like this:

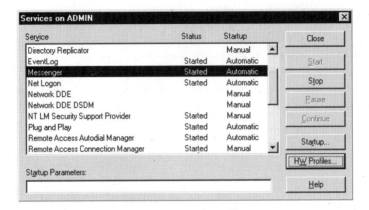

5. If the Messenger service does not have a status of Started, you must reconfigure it. Make sure the Messenger service is selected, then choose Startup from the Services dialog box to see the Service dialog box shown in Figure 3-3.

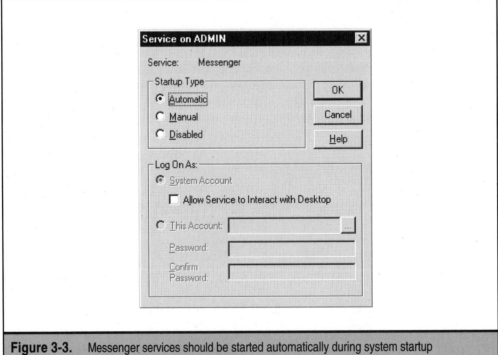

Figure 3-3.   Messenger services should be started automatically during system startup

6. Choose a Startup Type of Automatic. Be sure to select System Account in the bottom section of the dialog box. Then click OK to return to the Services dialog box.

7. Although you have specified automatic startup, this does not start the Messenger service for the current computer session. You could reboot to force the automatic startup, but it's faster and easier to start the service manually from the dialog box. Choose Start to activate the service immediately. Then close the dialog box.

TIP: You can also go to a command line and enter **net start messenger**. (If the service is already running when you use this command, Windows NT returns a message telling you of that fact.)

If the Messenger service is running when you check the Services dialog box, you probably have a problem with cable connections.

Troubleshooting Windows 95 Message Problems

When you have Windows 95 clients on your network, the problem is a bit more complicated because there aren't any Messenger services running. Instead, you must configure your Windows 95 clients to run Winpopup.exe. This application is part of Windows 95 (and, for that matter, of Windows 3.x if you have those clients on your network too).

Since it's asking too much of a Windows 95 user to guess when a message is about to be sent and launch Winpopup.exe in time to receive it (and calling or yelling to a Win95 user seems silly since if you wanted to yell you could yell the message you're trying to send), put the application in the Startup folder so that it's always ready.

The odds are you already know how to add an application to the Startup folder, but just in case you're out of practice, let's review the three methods for doing this:

▼ Use the Taskbar Properties dialog box.

■ Use the Start menu folder.

▲ Use Explorer.

To use the Taskbar Properties dialog box to add the program to the Startup folder, follow these steps:

1. Right-click on any blank spot on the taskbar and choose Properties.

2. When the Taskbar Properties dialog box opens, move to the Start Menu Programs tab.

3. Choose Add to open the Create Shortcut Wizard, and enter the path to Winpopup.exe (\%SystemRoot%\Winpopup.exe). Then choose Next.

4. In the Select Folder window, find the Startup folder and select it. Then choose Next.

5. In the Select a Title for the Program window, enter the name you want to use for this program (Winpopup.exe seems rather appropriate). Then click Finish.

To use the Start menu folder to add the program to the Startup folder, follow these steps:

1. Right-click the Start button and choose Open.

2. Open the Programs folder, and then find and open the Startup folder.

3. Choose File, New, Shortcut from the menu bar.

4. Enter the path to Winpopup.exe (\%SystemRoot%\Winpopup.exe). Then choose Next.

5. In the Select Folder window, find the Startup folder and select it. Then choose Next.

6. In the Select a Title for the Program window, enter the name you want to use for this program. Then click Finish.

To use Explorer to add the program to the Startup folder, follow these steps:

1. Open the folder that contains the Windows 95 software and find Winpopup.exe.

2. Scroll up in the left pane to find the Profiles subfolder under the Windows 95 folder.

3. Expand the Profiles folder to find the user name (or default user), and expand that subfolder until you can see the Startup folder (under the Programs folder).

4. Right-drag the Winpopup.exe file object to the Startup folder. Choose Create Shortcut(s) Here from the menu that appears when you release the right mouse button.

Okay, there are actually four ways to do this—if you use the Taskbar Properties dialog box and choose Advanced (instead of Add), you're taken into Explorer at just the right spot (the Profile subfolders for the current logged-on user). Expand the Programs folder to reach the Startup folder. Select it, then right-click in the right pane of Explorer and choose New, Shortcut from the shortcut menu. Then follow the steps above to fill in the information about the path of the application for which you need a shortcut.

Problem: Windows 95 Clients Are Not Listed in Server Manager

Sometimes the Windows 95 computers on your network are not displayed in the computer list in Server Manager. It's disconcerting because it makes you unsure of the connection, and it's annoying if you want to send that computer a message.

This happens when the selected View for Server Manager is Show Domain Members Only. Windows 95 machines are not really considered members of the domain in the same way Windows NT clients are. Remember, the Identification tab of the Network applet in

Control Panel for a Windows 95 machine has no field for a domain name. Instead, Windows 95 clients enter the name of a known domain in the Workgroup field and then can access the domain shares and resources because an administrator has added the logged-on user name to the domain's user list. Windows 95 computers log on to a domain, Windows NT computers join a domain. Technically, the difference between logging on and joining involves the presence or absence of a SAM on the client computer. Since there is one on the NT client, that user logs on to the local computer and then joins the domain.

What causes the problem is the fact that when you activate the Show Domain Members Only view, browser enumeration is turned off. The Windows 95 computers are listed only when the browser is displaying the list. To see the Windows 95 computers in Server Manager, be sure to deselect View, Show Domain Members Only.

NOTE: Incidentally, a similar problem occurs if your domain has stand-alone servers that run Windows NT 3.51—they're seen as workstations if the selected view is Show Domain Members Only. That's because it's the browser that discerns the difference between workstation and server for NT 3.51 computers that aren't domain controllers.

Problems with Roaming Profiles for Windows 95 Users

Sometimes roaming Windows 95 users report that they're not getting their configured desktops (instead they get the configuration for the default user).

If you have load balancing in effect and the Windows 95 user was validated by a BDC (or the PDC was down, so the BDC validated the logon), this is probably the cause of the problem. Windows 95 clients can receive roaming profiles only from a PDC. This is a bug in Windows 95, and you'll have to apply a workaround. The easiest way to fix this is to create a default user profile that is acceptable to roaming users—even if it's not exactly the configuration they prefer.

Problem: Windows 95 Logon Script Is Ignored

If you have configured Windows 95 workstations to log on to a PDC with a centralized logon script (usually a Winlogon batch file), you may find that sometimes the script file isn't processed. This problem occurs only if the Windows 95 client attempts to access the logon script file while another Windows 95 client is doing the same thing. The first access of this file is read in exclusive mode, and therefore any other user attempting to read the file while it's being used is denied access. This is a known bug; at the moment the only solution is to wait a bit and log on again.

Fixing Corrupt Built-In Accounts

Sometimes the built-in accounts and groups become corrupt. If this problem occurs, the odds are that the corrupt portion of the database has been replicated to any existing BDCs, so you have to start with a clean BDC. Install a new BDC on the domain, using a computer that has never been a BDC before.

TIP: If you don't have a spare machine hanging around, you can make an existing workstation a BDC if it has the necessary memory and disk space. Then, if you add another machine to the domain later and make it a BDC, you can boot the workstation into Windows NT Workstation and give the machine back to the user you borrowed it from.

Immediately promote this new BDC to a PDC. Immediately means at once, without any hesitation, as the last step of the installation process. If you don't promote the computer as soon as the installation is complete, it will quickly perform its primary BDC task—requesting a copy of the database from the existing PDC. This defeats the purpose.

Then synchronize the entire domain to this new PDC by opening a command session and entering **net accounts /sync**.

Because the built-in accounts are part of the installation you performed when you created this BDC, you have a clean set. When this replication runs, it cannot overwrite and therefore damage the SAM on the original PDC or any other BDCs. Only the built-in accounts are overwritten (which is the whole idea, since by overwriting them you're correcting them).

You can now promote the original PDC back to its primary role and remove the new BDC.

If this doesn't work, you will have to restore a backup that was made before the built-in accounts became corrupted.

Built-In Groups

Built-in groups are the default groups provided with Windows NT. They are usually comprehensive enough to provide all the security management needed by an organization. They cannot be deleted.

The built-in groups for Windows NT Server 4.0 are the following:

- ▼ Administrators
- ■ Domain Administrators
- ■ Users
- ■ Domain Users
- ■ Account Operators
- ■ Backup Operators
- ■ Print Operators
- ■ Server Operators
- ■ Replicators
- ■ Domain Guests
- ▲ Guests

Problem: Unable to Connect to a Remote Domain to Administer It

You can administer any domain (with the proper permissions, of course) by opening Server Manager and selecting the domain you want to work with. There's something terribly frustrating about seeing a domain listed in Server Manager and then getting error messages that indicate it can't be found. Actually, it's most common to receive an error message that the domain controller (not the domain) can't be found.

In effect, you're having a domain name problem when this happens. It's not that the name of the domain that appears on the list is wrong; it's that Windows NT 4 can't translate the name properly. The name that's listed is a NetBIOS name, and the connection requires the NetBEUI protocol (which translates NetBIOS names). If you're dialing in using a RAS connection, the RAS configuration may have disallowed NetBEUI. Or if you're using RAS for all your connections, you may have disabled NetBEUI (or not installed it).

The solution is to enter the name of the domain's PDC in the domain text box instead of selecting the domain name from the list.

TIP: If you're using TCP/IP, you can put the remote domain controller's name and IP address in the Lmhosts file. The IP address can then be resolved from the name.

TROUBLESHOOTING TRUST RELATIONSHIPS

One of the concepts that cause confusion for some administrators is the trust relationship, and this is probably because it's really not a simple concept. Adding to the perplexity is the fact that there are multiple types of trusts. If you're running an organization that has established trust relationships between domains, it's likely you've encountered problems, confusion, and some annoyed users. Before we discuss the problems and how to troubleshoot something this intricate, let's take a quick look at trusts and how they work.

To oversimplify a bit, a trust relationship is a connection that links two domains into an administrative unit that users can move between. This is because the resulting effect of the trust relationship is that the logon security for one domain is recognized and approved (and therefore matches) the other domain. For instance, my office in Philadelphia is a domain, and it has a trust relationship with my office in New York City. That trust is set up so that the New York City domain trusts the users in the Philadelphia domain. As a result, when Philadelphia users log on to the New York City domain, their accounts are validated without any problems, and the logon is as smooth as if they were logging on to the Philadelphia PDC. In this scenario, New York is the trusting domain and Philadelphia is the trusted domain. If a user in the Philadelphia office needs a file from the hard disk of a user in the New York office, she logs on to the New York domain to get it. As she goes through the logon process, her user account information does not have to be moved to the New York user database, because the New York domain has access to all of the user information in the Philadelphia user database.

Of course, I made sure that Philadelphia trusts new New York, so the New York users can log on to the Philadelphia domain with the same ease.

Trusts are one-way relationships, but it's common for two domains to create the same type of trust in each direction, giving the illusion of a two-way trust. That is just an illusion, however; there are no two way trusts, only one way trusts. Domains that trust each other in both directions do not have a two-way trust; they have two one-way trusts. (Having said that, I'll admit that everyone calls such a combination of trusts a two-way trust, even though they know it's technically inaccurate).

NOTE: One-way trusts are very common when the users of the trusted domain need to access the trusting domain for resources, such as software applications. In that case, there's no reason for a trust relationship in the other direction.

Each trust relationship has a communications process, which you can think of as a pipe, or a tunnel, or any other metaphor you want to envision. It's usually referred to as a communications channel, and there is a discrete communications channel whenever there is a trusting domain and a trusted domain partnership. For the scenario I just described, there are two communications channels, one for New York as the trusted domain in its relationship to Philadelphia (the trusting domain) and another for New York as the trusting domain in the relationship with Philadelphia as the trusted domain. Two trusts, two channels, but feel free to call it a two-way trust—as long as you understand that there isn't one fat channel handling the trusts in both directions at once.

NOTE: It's beyond the scope of this book to enter into a full discussion of the various types of trusts and their hierarchies.

How Trusts Are Loaded for Users

While an NT computer is loading the operating system, it begins looking for a domain controller before the CTRL-ALT-DEL logon dialog box appears. Actually, what occurs is that the machine is searching for a secure channel to a domain controller in the local domain in order to have that controller validate the machine account. Then the user logon completes the user connection to the domain.

TIP: The machine's search for a channel to a domain before user logon, and its ability to fetch information when it finds that channel, is the reason that workstations must have unique names in an NT network and must have a computer account registered with the domain.

If the local domain has a trust relationship with another domain, the machine account fetches the list of trusting domains from the local domain controller, and the user then has the opportunity to log on to another domain. If that happens, the user's credentials are sent from the client machine to a domain controller in the local domain, using the secure channel that was established by the machine during the startup of the operating system. The local domain controller passes authentication of the user to the target domain through the communications channel that exists between the domains. The passing of credentials is transparent to the user.

NOTE: In fact, the relationship between the booting machine and the domain is also a trust. After all, it has a secure channel that provides information from the trusting domain to the trusted computer. This trust relationship is an implicit trust, and it exists between a domain controller and every computer that logs on to the domain.

Trust relationships aren't shared, which means that if my Philadelphia office has a trust relationship with my New York office and has the same trust relationship with my San Francisco office, there is no inherent trust between New York and San Francisco.

Setting Up a Trust Relationship

Here's how to create a relationship in which your local domain is trusted by another domain (the trusting domain).

First you have to tell each domain about the relationship and identify their roles (trusted or trusting). To do so, start by telling the local domain (the trusted domain) about the trusting domain, using these steps:

1. On your local domain, open User Manager for Domains.

2. Select Policies, Trust Relationships from the menu bar.

3. Choose Add.

4. Enter the name of the trusting domain in the Trusting Domain box.

5. Supply a password to establish the trust relationship and confirm it. Then choose OK.

Now the trusting domain must identify the trusted domain, which you accomplish with these steps:

1. Log on to the trusting domain by choosing User, Select Domain from the menu bar.

2. Select the trusting domain from the Select Domain list box. Then choose OK.

3. Choose Policies, Trust Relationships.

4. Choose Add.

5. Enter the name of the trusted domain (your local domain).

6. Enter the password you used to set up this trust relationship, and choose OK.

7. A message tells you that the relationship has been established. Choose OK.

You have successfully implemented a one-way trust relationship. If you want to establish trust in the other direction, repeat this procedure with the trusted and trusting roles reversed.

Error: Trust Creation Isn't Verified

After you've created a trust relationship as described in the previous section, you may see the following error message:

```
The trust relationship cannot be verified because this machine has a
session open to North, the Primary Domain Controller of domain
Northern. Do you wish to continue setting up the trust relationship?
```

(Of course, the PDC in your error message probably won't be named North, and the domain you're establishing trust with is probably named something other than Northern.)

Don't panic, you probably have a totally secure, beautifully working trust relationship. It just couldn't be verified because a user from one domain was connected to the other domain (getting some work done). If there is an existing connection between the two domains at the time a trust relationship is created between the same two domains, verification isn't possible. This is because Windows NT can handle only one user account for each server for a remote session, and the returned message of verification is considered a user action.

Ending a Trust Relationship

Ending a trust relationship also requires action on both sides of the arrangement—you have to end the trusting relationship from the trusted domain and also end the trusted relationship from the trusting domain.

Start on the trusting domain with these steps:

1. Open User Manager for Domains.
2. Choose Policies, Trust Relationships from the menu bar.
3. From the list box, select the trusted domain you want to end the relationship with and choose Remove. (You'll have to confirm the removal.)

Now log on to the other domain and remove the other side of this trust relationship by following these steps:

1. Choose User, Select Domain from the menu bar.
2. Select the name of the trusted domain from the list box and choose OK to log on to that domain.
3. Choose Policies, Trust Relationships from the menu bar.
4. Select the trusting domain from the list box and choose Remove. (You must then confirm the removal.)

Local Permissions Aren't Automatic for Users in Trusted Domains

The trusted domain's groups aren't added to the trusting domain's local group automatically, so you'll have to perform that task. For example, you may want a user or multiple users from the trusted domain to have permissions to administer the server. You must add those users to the local Administrator group.

It may be clearer to illustrate this with names instead of the terms "trusted" and "trusting." Picture me in Philadelphia, where the domain is named Eastern and the PDC is named East. I trust the New York office, which has a domain named Northern and a PDC named North. Eastern is the trusting domain and Northern is the trusted domain. I'm sitting in front of the computer named East, and I want a user named BillT from Northern to be able to administer this computer. Using the User Manager for Domains application, I add Northern\BillT to the Administrator's group for East. This means BillT has local rights to this particular server (the trust established his domain rights).

TIP: You aren't restricted to individual users in this procedure; you can choose to add one of the other domain's groups. The group entry follows the same format, which in this case might be Northern\Domain Admins.

More Than You May Have Wanted to Know About Trust Communications

The way trusted/trusting domains communicate is really quite interesting. Here's a description of the processes, which are based on keeping the secure channel secure.

Again, to make it easier to picture things, I'll use real-world examples to describe what goes on between trusted domains. I'm still in Philadelphia, where the domain is named Eastern. I trust my New York office, where the domain is named Northern. So the trusted domain is Northern and the trusting domain is Eastern. Northern has information about its user accounts, and Eastern trusts Northern to validate those user accounts when they want to access Eastern. Both domains need to trust the security of their communications channel.

On all of the domain controllers in Eastern, the presence of this trust is represented by an object that represents a Local Security Authority (LSA). This object contains the name of the trusted domain (Northern) and the domain security ID (SID). The PDC on Eastern replicates the LSA object to all of the BDCs in Eastern.

Every DC in Eastern keeps a password in an LSA secret object G$$<*TrustedDomainName*> (in this example, G$$Northern). This object is in the registry key HKEY_LOCAL_MACHINE\Security\Policy\Secrets.

On every domain controller in Northern, a password is stored in a SAM user account marked as Interdomain_Trust_Account (in this example, Eastern$). This can be found in the registry key HKEY_LOCAL_MACHINE\ SAM\SAM\Domains\ Account\Users\Names. This account is replicated from the PDC to the BDCs.

These accounts are created when the trust relationship is created. User Manager on Northern is launched to configure Eastern to trust Northern's accounts. When the domain is added in the Permit to Trust dialog box, a password is furnished by the administrator and a hidden user account is created in Northern's SAM for the trusting domain (Eastern). This account has that password (for this example, Eastern$).

At the trusting domain, Eastern, an administrator creates the trust and enters the password created earlier, and then User Manager creates the LSA secret object. The server in Eastern then tries to establish a session with Northern, using the account Eastern$. The domain controller in Northern sends back an error "0xc0000198, Status_Nologon_Interdomain_Trust_Account."

In effect, the request for a session has failed. Don't worry, though; it's supposed to, because this Interdomain_Trust_Account can't participate in a regular session logon. In fact, Eastern wants this error message, because it proves that the trust account exists, and if the trust account exists, you can have a trust relationship.

Eastern happily sets up a null session and uses RPC transactions and remote API calls to create the trust relationship. Later, the netlogon service establishes the secure channel necessary for a trust relationship, using all of the information mentioned above.

After the trust is created, the Eastern PDC changes the password of the trusted domain object and tells Northern to change the password up there too. All of the domain controllers in both domains receive the trust account objects (with the new passwords) through the normal synchronization of the SAM (Northern) and the LSA databases (Eastern). Now that these objects are in place, a domain controller in Eastern can establish a secure channel to a domain controller in Northern.

It doesn't end with that password change, however, because the password for the trusted domain object is changed every seven days by Eastern's PDC (and is replicated to all of the BDCs in Eastern). Eastern then sends a message to Northern, instructing the PDC to change the password for the SAM user account on Northern (which is, of course, replicated throughout Northern's BDCs). These automatic password changes are always initiated at the trusting domain's end (using an I_NetServerPasswordSet RPC call). The passwords must always match.

This seems just fine, except all administrators know that the time will come when Eastern changes the password of the LSA and sends the new password to Northern, along with an order to change the password in the SAM, but Northern goes down during this process. Eastern has the new password, but Northern didn't receive it and still has last week's password.

For just such contingencies, both the old and new passwords are always stored in the LSA secret object on the trusting domain. To make everything even safer, the weekly password change isn't considered correct until there has been a successful connection through the secure channel with the new password. If authentication for the connection fails with the new password, the trusting PDC uses the old password. When that works, it passes the new password along immediately.

Letting Users Access Domains Without a Trust Relationship

If there are only a couple of users who need to access files in another domain, you may not want to go to the trouble of creating trust relationships. You can configure other domains to accept these users without any trust involved (and without the overhead of trust communication and replication). In fact, some companies deliberately avoid trust relationships for certain domains. For example, if the accounting department is a specific domain, it's probably not a good idea to have a trust relationship with any of the other domains in the company. However, some of the executives may need or want to see certain accounting reports (like today's bank balance or the amount of total accounts receivable outstanding for more than 90 days). These users can be set up as users in that domain in order to be able to access those files.

The steps required to do this are pretty obvious—you just add each user to the other domain. However, there are some guidelines you might want to think about when establishing this other domain identity for the user.

Let's use names to help paint this picture. President Billy Bigshot has a desktop computer on his desk (a beautiful desk on the top floor), and the computer and he are both part of the domain named Admin. The President's logon name is Prez. Down on the third floor (or 500 miles away in another city) is the accounting department, where 60 people sit at computers that are part of the domain named Accntg. There are a couple of ways to get President Billy onto the Accntg domain.

Use the Same Name and Password for Both Domains

You can add user Prez to the domain Accntg with the same password he uses to log on to domain Admin. This is the simplest way and actually makes it possible for him to switch back and forth between domains at will. However, there are some security risks here. If President Billy is logged onto the Admin domain and leaves his desk, anyone who uses his computer has his access rights (which may be perfectly okay with him insofar as the information on the Admin domain is concerned but can be worrisome if the visiting user decides to sneak a peek at the payroll records). In addition, if both domains have enforced password changes at specific (but not matching) intervals, there's going to be some extra administrative work. His password will have to change on both domains every time one domain demands a password change in order for his logon to work. Of course, if the company doesn't require new passwords at certain intervals and President Billy can log on forever with the same name and password, this is a great solution.

Use Different Names and Passwords for Each Domain

Another option is to create a new logon name and password for President Billy for those times he wants to access the domain Accntg. Then, when he logs on to his machine, he enters the name and password connected to the domain in which he wants to work. Of course, this means that when he finishes looking at the bank balance and wants to look at his word processing documents (which are on a computer in the Admin domain), he has to log on again as the new user. That's time consuming, even possibly annoying, but not as confusing as changing passwords on both domains when one domain insists on it.

When to Give Up and Create a Trust

If it were just President Billy who needed to cross into other domains, the fact that you have to go through the steps to set him up in a second domain isn't bothersome. In fact, even if he decides he needs access to a third domain, or a fourth, you have some extra work to do, but that's why they pay you those big bucks.

The day that First Executive Vice President Wally Wannabe calls you with all his reasons for needing access to the domain Accntg and perhaps another domain, you begin to see the handwriting on the wall. Second executive vice presidents, department heads, and division directors will be dialing your extension demanding accounts on other domains. This is the time to think about creating a trust relationship.

TROUBLESHOOTING REPLICATION

The most common replication on a network is the process of replicating the domain's database from the PDC to all of the BDCs of a domain. This replication is called *synchronization,* and it's performed automatically. You can, however, synchronize manually if you need to. In fact, during a manual synchronization you can choose to synchronize all of the BDCs in the domain or only one (if a particular BDC has gotten out of sync).

The most prevalent problem with synchronization among domain controllers is that sometimes one or more controllers are down. When that occurs, you'll want to catch up and synchronize the controllers manually. To do this, use the command **net accounts /sync** in a command prompt window:

▼ To synchronize all of the BDCs with the PDC, open a command session on the PDC.

▲ To synchronize one BDC with the PDC, open a command session on that BDC.

Don't Use Server Manager for Manual Synchronizing

The menu items (and the help files) in Server Manager suggest that you can be at the PDC and select the BDC computer to synchronize it manually (using Computer, Synchronize With Domain Controller from the menu bar). Don't believe it—if you perform this procedure it seems to work (a dialog box even opens to tell you it may take some time to do this and asks you to choose Yes to agree and proceed). In previous versions of Windows NT, this worked just fine.

Starting with Windows NT 4.0, however, it doesn't work properly, because the manual synchronization process employed by the operating system has changed. If you use the Server Manager menu commands at the PDC instead of the command line option, you get only a partial synchronization (but the system doesn't report that back as an error).

Check the Replication User Configuration

The replication user you created for each of the export and import computers must have sufficient permissions to get the work done. Make sure the replicator's user account is a member of the Backup Operators group (or has equivalent permissions), has no limits on the hours allowed for logon, and has a password that never expires.

Check the Replication Service

Synchronization (or replication) is a Windows NT service and is found in the Services applet in the Control Panel. The service is named Directory Replicator. By default, the service startup type is Manual. For every computer involved in replication, do the following:

1. Select the Directory Replicator service and choose Startup.

2. Select Automatic as the Startup type.

3. Set the replication user as the logon user.

4. Enter the password for the replication user.

5. Choose OK.

The Services applet shows the new, correct startup type, but that won't take effect until the next time you start the operating system (notice that the Status column does not say "Started"). So select the Directory Replicator service and choose Start. You'll see a message telling you that the system is trying to start the service, and eventually the Status column will indicate that the Directory Replicator service is running.

TIP: You can always check the status of the Directory Replicator service by entering **net start** at the command line and seeing if the Directory Replicator service appears on the services list.

Replication Across a Router

If the replication is being processed across a router, replication will not occur without forcing name resolution for the computer on the other side of the router. The export computer broadcasts to the subnet on which it resides, using the name of the domain for which it is broadcasting. Import computers listen for the broadcast and answer, replicating if their domain name is the same as the domain name on the export packet. Computers that are across routers (or bridges) from the source of the broadcasts don't get the notification from the export server unless the export server has been specifically configured to broadcast to those computers.

To ensure (actually, to force) name resolution:

1. Open the Server applet in Control Panel and click the Replication button.

2. When the Directory Replication dialog box opens, choose Add for the Export or Import directories.

3. Enter the machine name in the format *domain**machine*.

For machines on the LAN leg, this step isn't necessary, because the export computer and import computer find each other via broadcasts without the need to add the computer names to this dialog box manually.

Replicating Logon Scripts

If you look at the directory structure of the import/export directories tree, you'll see that there is a subdirectory named \Scripts at the bottom of the tree. Windows NT is designed to adapt to the organizations that still use logon scripts. If you do use logon scripts, of course, you must make sure they're part of the synchronization process. Just set up your system so that logon scripts are placed in \%SystemRoot%\System32\Repl\Export\Scripts, and they'll travel throughout the domain via synchronization.

Logon script paths are set in the domain controller's Properties dialog box in Server Manager. Choose Replication and use the Logon Script Path field at the bottom of the dialog box, as seen here:

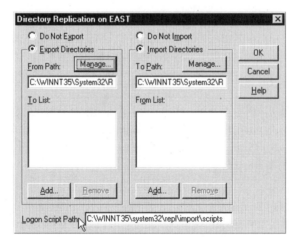

Replicating Additional Directories

By default, Windows NT computers have built-in directories that are used for importing and exporting: \%SystemRoot%\System32\Repl\Import and \%SystemRoot%\System32\Repl\Export. (These directories exist in all Windows NT machines, both servers and workstations, as part of the installation of the operating system.)

If you want to export and import additional directories during synchronization, you can add subdirectories to this default location, and they'll be included in the export/import scheme when synchronization takes place.

CAUTION: Note that I said directories, not files. The process is actually called Directory Replication. Files that sit in the path \%SystemRoot%\System32\Repl\Export are not replicated. You must create a directory below that level and place any files you want to replicate within that directory

---

To add directories to the export process, open Explorer and move to \%SystemRoot%\System32\Repl\Export. Add a subdirectory at this point in the tree. You can call it whatever you want (except \Scripts, because that subdirectory already exists).

What's important about this instruction is that many administrators don't realize that the work is performed in Explorer. Instead, they open Server Manager and use the feature that lets them manage exporting (there's a Manage button on the Directory Replication dialog box). The Manage Exported Directories dialog box has an Add button, and if you click it you see this dialog box:

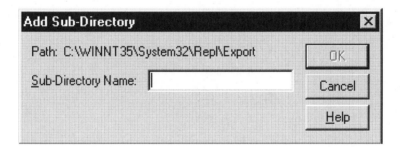

It seems logical and productive to add the name of a new directory here. It may be logical, but it isn't productive, because it's meaningless. Entering the name of a new subdirectory does not create the new subdirectory; it just adds an entry to the list. The only way to add the subdirectory is through Explorer or the command line. In fact, it's really unnecessary to add the new subdirectory to the list, because once the new subdirectory is in place and has files in it, it's exported. The import side works with the same logic.

NOTE: The Entire Subtree option at the bottom of the Manage Exported Directories dialog box must be selected to ensure that all subdirectories are exported.

Adding Target Computers to the Export

You can replicate directories throughout your organization, to computers other than the domain controllers involved in synchronization. In fact, many organizations use replication to make sure that data files are available throughout a domain, a site, or a company.

There are some important guidelines you must be aware of before you begin:

▼ Any Windows NT computer can be involved in replication, but only computers running Windows NT Server can export. Both servers and workstations can import.

▲ The default synchronization export/import that is established for your domain controllers becomes invalid as soon as you add an additional computer to your list of target computers. You must reenter the synchronization export/import as a discrete export/import. (Don't ask me what the logic is behind this; write to Microsoft.)

To set up additional replication targets, you can use either the Server applet in Control Panel or Server Manager in the Administrative Tools section of your Programs menu. If you use Control Panel, you have to go to each computer you want involved in the scheme to set it up, while Server Manager offers the ability to configure computers remotely. Choose your weapon depending on how much exercise you need. I'm lazy, so I'll use Server Manager to demonstrate. Here's how to add computers to the To list (for adding targets to an exporting computer) or the From list (for adding source computers to an importing computer):

1. Open Server Manager, select the computer you want to configure, and choose Computer, Properties (or double-click the computer listing).

2. Click the Replication button to display the Directory Replication dialog box.

3. If you are adding target computers to the To list for an export, click the Add button on the Export pane. If you are adding source computers to the From list for an import, use the Add button on the Import pane. Either action displays the Select Domain dialog box.

4. Double-click the domain that has the computer you want to add—the double-click action expands the listing so it displays all the computers in the domain.

5. Choose the computer(s) you need (remember that only servers can be exporters).

6. If you are involving any domain controllers that are part of your synchronization process in this procedure, you must add another listing in the To list (or From list) and reproduce the default replication. Once you add anything to the To and From lists, the default synchronization data is lost and must be added back.

Troubleshooting Replication Among Domains

The process of replicating within a domain isn't terribly complicated, although you do have to go through a number of steps to configure the computers, create the directories that are replicated, and so on.

However, if you are going to be replicating to and from computers in other domains, you must make sure that your replication user has the same user name and password on both domains.

Other Replication Issues to Consider

You may or may not come across some other potential problems in replication (depending on your network setup), but just in case, here are a few of the common problems I've seen:

▼ If you are exporting from an NTFS partition, be sure that permissions for the export directory and all of the files inside it are adequate. The replicator user (or group) must have Change privileges at a minimum.

■ If you are using an NTFS partition and replication updates existing files on the target (import) computer, be aware of filename and directory case. If filenames are the same except for case, sometimes the export computer picks one file and the import computer expects a different file. This means you don't have a real sync.

■ Check the clocks between the two computers. If they're more than a couple of minutes apart, it could interfere with replication.

▲ Keep an eye on the Application log in Event Viewer to track replication problems.

WINDOWS
NT
Professional
Library

CHAPTER 4

Troubleshooting Reinstallations and Updates

There will be times when you have to make some sort of substantial change to the operating system. I see that task as involving either of two objectives. To make sure we're all talking about the same things, here are my definitions:

Reinstall: To run the installation program again in order to fix problems or add components you didn't select when you originally installed the operating system.

Update: To take advantage of updated files for your current version as they become available from Microsoft. This includes Service Packs and bug fixes. (Updating can also mean installing updated drivers for installed devices, but I won't cover that here, since there's not much troubleshooting involved.)

TROUBLESHOOTING REINSTALLATION

If your Windows NT operating system has become corrupted to the point that your computer is no longer usable, it's time to consider reinstalling it. This doesn't necessarily mean the computer fails to boot the operating system; there are a host of other symptoms that indicate a serious problem. For example, my BDC once went through a petulant phase and balked at performing any task. With no software open, the simplest request (opening Explorer) produced an error message telling me there was not enough memory to complete the operation. Since I happened to believe that 64MB of RAM was sufficient to open Explorer, I figured something was very wrong. I've had clients report similar problems: messages like "Not enough system resources to complete this task" or "Cannot find <insert name of any important .dll here>" every time a user tried to do something.

I can't give you any specific reasons for why this happens, and it may or may not be user induced. Personally, I think it usually is, even if the human error is peripheral to the operating system. In my own case, I frequently install beta software, including operating system utilities, that throw my computers for a loop (it's a necessary part of training and writing books).

Reinstalling to Repair the Operating System

Here are the basic steps needed to reinstall the operating system in order to repair it. The actual process varies, depending upon the configuration of your Windows NT computer and the problem you're having. Treat these procedures as guidelines, and be aware of the responses you receive from Setup as you go through these steps.

1. With the Emergency Repair Disk (ERD) for the computer firmly in your grasp, turn off the computer and put the Windows NT Setup Disk 1 into the floppy drive. Then turn on the computer.

TIP: If you can't find your Setup floppy disks, run **winnt32 /ox** from the Windows NT 4 CD-ROM or a network sharepoint that holds the Windows NT 4 files. Of course, you may have to use another computer to do this if your computer won't boot.

2. Put the Windows NT Setup Disk 2 into the drive when you're instructed to, and press ENTER, which displays the "Welcome to Setup" message.

3. Choose **R** for Repair. Then press ENTER to see the repair options that use the ERD:

   ■ **Inspect Registry Files** displays another screen on which you can select the registry files you want the repair process to check. Setup tries to load each of those files to see if it is corrupted. A recommendation to restore any corrupted files is displayed, and you can accept or reject the recommendation.

   ■ **Inspect Startup Environment** checks the boot files (Ntldr, Ntdetect.com, and so on). If necessary, you will be asked to replace them.

   ■ **Verify Windows NT System Files** uses a checksum to verify every file in the installation by matching it against the file that was installed originally. Any files that are corrupted or missing can be restored from the installation media.

   ■ **Inspect Boot Sector** repairs the boot sector on the boot drive.

   Select the repair options you want to use.

CAUTION: Avoid the option for registry files unless you know that's where the problem is and you know what specific object you want to fix (and you have a backup of the registry). You could lose even more of your operating system with an inappropriate attack on the registry.

4. When you've made your choices, Setup presents more options (that depend on your original choices). Use the arrow keys to move to the choice that lets you continue with your selected options, and press ENTER.

5. Setup wants to identify your mass storage devices, so press ENTER (press **S** if you have other mass storage devices that should be identified). Or you can press ESC to skip disk verification.

6. When told to, put the Windows NT Setup Disk 3 in the floppy drive and press ENTER. A message appears listing the mass storage devices detected. Accept the list, or press **S** to identify any other storage devices.

7. If files need to be transferred from the original media, you'll be asked to put the Windows NT 4 CD-ROM in the CD-ROM drive.

8. If repairs can be made from an ERD, you'll be asked if you have one. Press ENTER to tell Setup that the Emergency Repair Disk is available. Then put the ERD into the floppy drive and press ENTER.

9. When the repair process is finished, Setup displays a message informing you of that fact. You can now restart the computer.

If you chose the Inspect Registry Files option, use the arrow keys to move to the specific task you want to perform and press ENTER to select it. The choices are

▼ SYSTEM (System Configuration)

■ SOFTWARE (Software Information)

■ DEFAULT (Default User Profile)

■ NTUSER.DAT (New User Profile)

▲ SECURITY (Security Policy) and SAM (User Accounts Database)

CAUTION: Don't select SECURITY (Security Policy) or SAM (User Accounts Databases) unless you are sure your problem is connected to those registry items, because this is a dangerous part of the registry to play with.

Forcing the Creation of Up-to-Date ERDs

Unless your network is made up of the most phenomenally responsible users in the world, the computers on your network probably don't have a current ERD. You can force the creation of up-to-date ERD information for computers on your network with the Windows NT scheduler (the AT command).

The process involves several steps, and you can write a batch file (and schedule it with the AT command) that performs them all.

You'll need a share on the server (it should be a hidden share for safety) to hold the repair information for each computer, and you'll need a subdirectory in that share for each target computer for which you're keeping repair information.

For this example, the server share is named ERDShare$, and subdirectories under the share are created for each target workstation.

The AT command is **AT \\<*target computer*> 01:00 /interactive /every:M,T,W,Th,F,S,Su *ServerName*\ERDShare$\MakeERD.bat.**

The contents of MakeERD.bat should be similar to this:

```
%windir%\system32\rdisk.exe /s-
net use x: /delete
net use x: \\ServerName\ERDShare$/persistent:no
if not exist x:\%targetname% md x:\%targetname%
Copy \%SystemRoot%\repair\*.* X:\%targetname%\*.*
net use x: /delete
exit
```

where %targetname% is the subdirectory for the target computer under the ERD share on the server.

NOTE: The /s switch for rdisk tells the program to copy the SAM.

To create the actual ERD for a computer, just format a diskette on your server and copy the files from the %targetname% subdirectory.

There are a couple of things to be aware of before you rush to create this handy function:

▼ Use full path names for all processes and steps.

■ Create a user (with administrative privileges) for this process and give that user a password that never expires.

■ Be sure the scheduler runs under the context of an administrative user.

▲ Do not use the system account—it has no network access for copying files, and therefore the last step of the batch file will fail (the copy across the network to your server).

Don't Reinstall NT 4 over NT 4

If the operating system is so corrupted that you decide you have to do a total reinstall of the operating system, don't use the same directory for installation. Instead, create an entire new installation.

In fact, if you do that, after you mount the new operating system you can use a backup tape to restore your original system. This restores all of the additional files (such as .dll files) that you'd added over the course of time. It also restores your users and all the other important information you'd rather not configure from scratch. However, before trying this technique, create an ERD for the new installation and back up the registry.

After the restore, modify Boot.ini to point back to the original directory. If the old system still doesn't work (it usually will if you also restored the registry), modify Boot.ini again and use the new installation (restore the registry from the new installation).

NOTE: If you purchased the Update version of Windows NT 4 (instead of the full version) and you try to use it on a machine that is already running Windows NT 4, you'll see an error message, and the Setup program will not run. The Update version is designed to install over (and replace) earlier versions of Windows NT. The sniffer will not look for or recognize version 4, and it will not install on a computer that doesn't have an earlier version. It thinks there is no version of NT on the computer. Your solution is either to install Windows NT 3.x and then install Windows NT 4 to replace it, or buy the full version of NT 4.

Reinstalling to Upgrade a Workstation to a Server

You can upgrade a workstation to a server, but that server cannot become a PDC or BDC; it can only become a standalone server. By "upgrade" I mean reinstalling the operating system into the same directory as the one that the NT Workstation installation used. If you do that, the user information and other settings will be there when the machine boots Windows NT Server.

If you install the Server version of the operating system into a separate directory and dual-boot, you can make the workstation a domain controller, but it would be very unusual to want a dual-booting domain controller.

Follow the standard installation procedures to upgrade from Workstation to Server.

> **NOTE:** I've found one extremely annoying side effect of this procedure, and it's something that isn't supposed to happen. Sometimes the server carries over one undesirable configuration from the workstation—the 10 user limit. It's especially frustrating if the reason for upgrading to Server is that the computer has a popular printer attached and you wanted to use this new server as a print server to replace the limitations of the workstation's print server services. As of this writing, I haven't gotten a reason or a fix from Microsoft.

TROUBLESHOOTING UPDATES

Whether it's a Service Pack or a hotfix, updating your Windows NT system is a procedure that many administrators approach warily. While it's true that sometimes things don't go as expected during the update, and it's even more true that there can be some strange and troubling side effects afterwards, most of the time an update is a smooth procedure. For those vexatious experiences, however, I'll steer you through my world of fixes, collected as a result of some of the most frustrating hours I've spent.

Preparing for a Service Pack Update

To twist a previously coined phrase, prevention is the better part of valor. It's fine to be brave as you enter the world of updating an operating system, but you need to perform all the important preliminary steps to prevent a total disaster. After you've made a full backup of your system, including the registry, take the following precautions before you begin installing the Service Pack.

Service Packs Are Not Really Updates

Regardless of the terminology I'm using here ("update"), a Service Pack isn't an update. It's a repair. And you should install a Service Pack only under one or more of the following conditions:

▼ You have a problem that is solved by a Service Pack.

■ You need to install software that requires the presence of a Service Pack (for example, some of the Microsoft BackOffice applications require a specific Service Pack update to the operating system).

▲ You need to use or add an operating system service or utility that doesn't exist, or doesn't work properly, without the Service Pack.

In other words, if it ain't broke, don't fix it.

Disk Space Requirements for a Service Pack

Make sure you have enough disk space for the update and the work it has to do. You'll need approximately 60MB of free space on the drive in addition to whatever space you reserve for swapping. While you aren't required to install the update with the uninstall directory option, it's foolish not to. You'll need about 60MB of hard drive space to create the uninstall directory, but after the temporary files are removed, the directory itself will use about 30MB. Incidentally, the uninstall directory is located below the \%SystemRoot% directory, and it is hidden.

Update the ERD

Before installing a Service Pack, be sure to update the ERD for the current installation. During the Service Pack update, you'll have an opportunity to create an ERD, so when you finish you'll have one for each configuration.

Disable Certain Services

Disable any third-party services you find in the Services applet in Control Panel. Don't change them to manual startup; totally disable them. This is especially important if any of these services access your file system, such as virus software or scheduling applications.

While you're in the Services applet, change nonessential, high-impact Windows NT services to manual startup. This includes BackOffice services (such as Exchange and SQL Server) and, if the computer is a print server, the Spooler service.

If you are running any form of remote control software that controls the screen display, uninstall it. That's right: You need to uninstall it; merely not launching it is not enough.

Run a Pristine Startup

Reboot your system and watch the startup process carefully. Make sure you have an error-free startup. If there is a message about an occurrence that was reported to the Event Viewer, check the event and correct the source. Keep doing this until you have a perfect startup. Do not attempt to install a Service Pack update on a machine that does not boot cleanly.

Save Previous Service Pack Uninstall Files

If this isn't the first Service Pack you've installed, you should save the last Service Pack's uninstall folder. That way you'll be able to get your system back to the configuration that existed before you began installing Service Packs. The easiest way to do this is to create a new directory for the old uninstall files and copy those files to it. Name the directory SP*X*uninstall, where *X* indicates the SP level. When you install the new Service Pack, the uninstall files will be placed in the original uninstall directory.

If you don't save the uninstall files from the previous Service Pack, uninstalling the new Service Pack puts your system back to the configuration it had after the installation of the last Service Pack. You will have no way to remove that Service Pack to get back to your original configuration. You'd be surprised how often that need arises, by the way. You may install software later that doesn't want to run with, or is somehow negatively affected by, the Service Pack.

If you do use the uninstall feature, and later want to reinstall the Service Pack, another uninstall directory will be formed.

Installing a Downloaded Service Pack

If you download the Service Pack, the executable file (Nt4sp3_i.exe for SP3) is a self-extracting file. It extracts into the TMP environment location (set in your environment variables). After the files are extracted, Update.exe is launched and the \%SystemRoot% directory is updated.

Changing the Working Drive for a Service Pack Installation

If the drive on which your temporary directory resides is near its capacity, as the files begin expanding you'll see an error message indicating that there is not enough space on the drive. Service Packs do not have a Setup program that checks for drive space before installation begins.

If you have a second drive in your computer that has 60MB available, you can use it for the Service Pack installation. To do that, you have to change the environment variable that sets the TMP location. Open the System applet in Control Panel and move to the Environment tab (Figure 4-1).

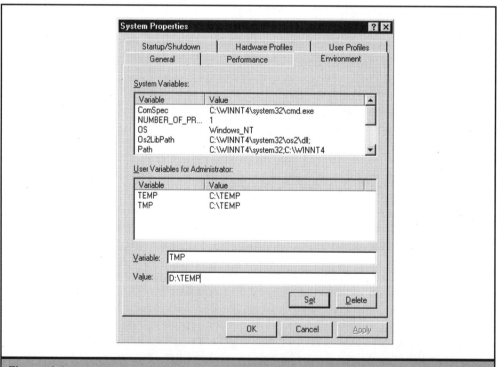

Figure 4-1.   Change the environment variable for TMP to extract the Service Pack to a drive that has more free space

Select TMP from the User Variables list. The current location of the variable appears in the Value box at the bottom of the dialog box. Enter $D:\backslash$**temp** in the Value box (substitute the appropriate drive letter for $D:$). Click OK and restart the computer.

Using a Downloaded Service Pack on a Network Sharepoint

If you want to use the Service Pack to update other computers from a sharepoint on a network server, you have to get the Service Pack files into the sharepoint. The trick is to extract the downloaded file without launching it. The file is preset to launch the update as soon as the extraction is completed.

You can prevent the launch by entering your extraction command as **nt4sp3_i.exe /x.** The /x switch means "extract only." You'll be asked for the name of the target directory, which becomes your sharepoint.

Using a Service Pack CD-ROM

A CD-ROM of SP 3 is about $15 plus shipping. Compared to the time spent downloading a Service Pack (these are really big files), it seems a pittance. Call (800) 370-8758 to order it.

A CD-ROM install of a Service Pack is very much like an installation. You can run the update from the CD-ROM, move appropriate directories to a sharepoint, or run an unattended update. The steps and the cautions are the same as described in this chapter for a downloaded Service Pack.

Troubleshooting Problems After Service Pack Installation

Unfortunately, there are sometimes problems after the installation of a Service Pack. In fact, Microsoft usually publishes a list of known problems and then fixes them in the next Service Pack (seems like a perpetual job security scheme). In truth, the problem isn't usually that the Service Pack is buggy, it's that the process of updating sometimes overwrites configuration information.

Most of the time there's a simple fix, and a call to Microsoft Support will gain you the information you need to reconfigure. Sometimes you have to reinstall a service after the installation of the Service Pack; other solutions include tweaking configuration options in the Control Panel or hacking the registry.

Reinstalling a System Service

If you find you have to reinstall a system service or protocol after you've installed a Service Pack, you will have to install the Service Pack again. And you must complete the Service Pack installation before you reboot your computer. (If the installation of the service or protocol requires a reboot, do not perform the reboot until you have reinstalled the Service Pack.)

Create a new uninstall directory during the reinstallation of the Service Pack. In fact, every time you reinstall a Service Pack you must create a new uninstall directory.

Clients Cannot Log On with IPX

After the installation of SP3 on a server, clients who attempt to try to log on to the server using the IPX protocol may have difficulty. This problem is usually limited to non–NT 4 clients. The error messages vary, but the essence of the error is that logon access is being denied. (Users frequently assume they've missed a required password change or have had an administrative change made to their passwords.)

The fix is a registry change that fixes the changes made by the Service Pack. Open a registry editor and follow these steps:

1. Go to HKEY_LOCAL_MACHINE\System\CurrentControlSet\ Services\LanManServer\Parameters.

2. Create a new DWORD item named MinClientBufferSize.

3. Enter the data value **500**. Be sure to choose Decimal instead of Hex data.

Poledit.exe Not Updated Correctly with SP3

Service Pack 3 included a fix for known problems with Poledit.exe, but there's a small problem in the way the Service Pack handles the replacement file—it totally fails to replace it (I guess that's not a small problem)—so you'll have to do it yourself.

Service Packs replace files that exist with updated/fixed versions. If the file doesn't exist (which means you aren't using it), it's not replaced. Unfortunately, SP3 looks in the wrong directory for Poledit.exe and, of course, doesn't find it, so it doesn't update it. Poledit belongs in \%SystemRoot%, and, if you use it, it's there. SP3 checks \%SystemRoot\System32.

You have two choices for addressing this problem:

▼ Before you run the update, change the Update .inf file so it looks in the right directory. Go to the section [MustReplace.System32.files] and remove Poledit.exe. Then go to the [SystemRoot.files] section and add Poledit.exe.

▲ Copy Poledit.exe to the \%SystemRoot% directory manually after you run the update.

If you are using a downloaded version of SP3 instead of the CD-ROM version, you'll have to expand the downloaded file without running the update. Use **nt4sp3_i.exe /x** to expand the files into a directory you've created for that purpose. As was mentioned previously, the /x switch only expands the files and does not automatically begin the update.

Reinstall Third-Party Drivers After SP3

The CD-ROM on one of my NT computers stopped playing audio after I installed SP3. The first time I'd installed the CD-ROM was after installation of the operating system, and I'd used the drivers provided by NEC. After SP3 was installed, the audio stopped working (everything else worked). Of course, what I had to do was reinstall the NEC drivers. This is a global consideration, not just a NEC CD-ROM problem. If you installed devices with manufacturer's drivers, a Service Pack installation could replace those drivers with Microsoft drivers. If your device wasn't 100 percent compatible (that is, if it was not on the HCL) during the initial installation of Windows NT 4, there's a good chance it still isn't compatible. Reinstall the manufacturer's drivers.

It seems inevitable to have problems after updates. If you know what's in your system—which devices have third-party drivers and which directory contains the uninstall files for each service pack—and you generally keep a written record of all of the things you do to your computer, troubleshooting the problems is much easier.

PART II

Troubleshooting Startup Problems

WINDOWS
NT
Professional
Library

CHAPTER 5

Troubleshooting Startup

This chapter covers some of the operating system startup problems that are experienced frequently enough by administrators to warrant discussion. You have, no doubt, encountered some strange and eerie problems that aren't covered here, but I had to make some choices. Here is how I decided what to include:

▼ I checked the notes I kept when I ran into problems and had to yell to Microsoft for help.

■ I talked to a number of network administrators.

▲ I browsed message boards throughout cyberspace.

I found an amazing similarity in problems, the same ones occurring over and over. Those are the problems I'm covering in this chapter (seems logical, doesn't it?).

PREVENTIVE TACTICS

Before you have a serious startup problem, do whatever you can to prepare for it. That means creating the items you need to get a computer up and running again. There are three items of particular importance:

▼ The ERD (Emergency Repair Disk)

■ A bootable floppy disk

▲ A backup of the important data on a computer

We'll discuss the first two items in this chapter. Check Chapter 14 for information about backing up the computers on your network.

First, let's straighten out the difference between an ERD and a bootable floppy disk. An ERD is not bootable; it merely holds information about your configuration. You can use that data to reconstruct your configuration if it becomes corrupt. If the system won't boot from the hard drive, you have to find another way to get the computer up and running so the information on the ERD can be used. You can either use the first Windows NT installation disk (then use R for repair instead of installing the operating system again) or use a bootable floppy disk you created for just such an occasion. This floppy disk is designed to boot the operating system so you can access your computer in order to repair the problems.

In fact, if you do try to boot with the ERD in the floppy drive, you'll see the following message:

```
The Emergency Repair Disk is not startable.
Repairing a damaged Windows NT installation is an option
available at the beginning of Windows NT Setup.
To start Setup, insert the Windows NT Setup Disk into Drive A:
Press control+alt+delete to restart your computer.
```

Updating Repair Information and the ERD

You should have created an ERD during the installation of the operating system. However, since that time the configuration of your computer has probably changed. It's a good idea to update the repair information and to create a new ERD at the same time.

The process of updating repair information has two steps: first, the new repair information is written to your hard drive; second, you are given the opportunity to save that information to a floppy disk (the ERD).

The Repair Disk utility in Windows NT 4 places a number of files in \%SystemRoot%\Repair, shown in Figure 5-1. The first two files in Figure 5-1 should be familiar to you. The other files are registry hives.

To run the Repair Disk utility, open a command prompt and enter **rdisk**. The Repair Disk Utility dialog box appears.

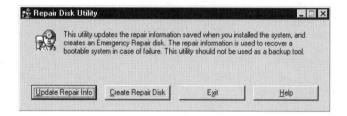

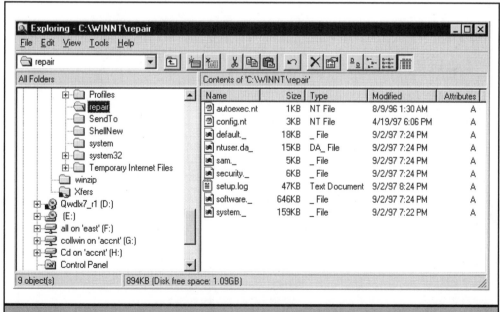

Figure 5-1. The files in this subdirectory can be used to repair the computer if the operating system becomes corrupted

If you cannot find your current ERD, choose Create Repair Disk and place a floppy disk in drive A. The information currently stored in \%SystemRoot%\Repair is copied to the floppy disk.

If you want to update the information in the subdirectory, choose Update Repair Info. When that process is completed, you're asked if you want to create an ERD. Answer Yes and put a floppy disk into the floppy drive. The floppy disk is formatted, and the information from the subdirectory is written to it.

There is a problem with the Rdisk command—without the parameter /s, the SAM and Security hives aren't updated. If you enter **rdisk /s** at the command prompt (instead of **rdisk**), two things change: the first dialog box asking you to make a choice is skipped and the updating process begins immediately; and the SAM and Security hives are updated. Then you are asked if you want to create an ERD.

TIP: If the SAM for your computer is enormous (the computer is a PDC), the information won't fit on an ERD. In that case, use Rdisk without the /s parameter and back up the \%SystemRoot%\Repair directory with your regular backup routine. In fact, think about running a special session of your backup software and just backing up that subdirectory and the registry. Mark and store that tape separately.

Creating a Bootable Floppy

It's a good idea to create a Windows NT 4 boot disk that can access the hard drive of your computer in case there's a problem booting. The following procedure will boot your computer regardless of whether you're running FAT or NTFS.

1. Format a floppy disk with the Windows NT Format utility (I usually open My Computer and right-click the floppy drive icon to choose Format).

2. Copy the following files from your computer to the floppy disk:

▼ Ntldr

■ Ntdetect.com

■ Boot.ini

▲ Ntbootdd.sys (if you have a SCSI controller for your hard drive)

NOTE: Ntbootdd.sys is a copy of the appropriate driver for a non-INT13 SCSI device. During installation the file is transferred to the target hard drive with this new name. If your SCSI controllers are installed as multi devices, not SCSI devices, you probably don't need the file. On the other hand, it couldn't hurt.

UNDERSTANDING THE STARTUP PROCESS

It's a good idea to understand what's happening during system startup, so the problems you encounter will fall into their proper place as you envision the process. Many of the steps described here involve system files and processes. You'll find troubleshooting solutions for their failures in the next section of this chapter.

It Starts with Hardware

The boot process starts with POST, RAM check, and any SCSI BIOS checking. See the section on hardware problems later in this chapter for a discussion of things to look for in the event of a problem.

Ntldr Loads

The Ntldr program starts the bootup of the operating system. This is when you see "OS Loader V4.00" on your screen. If you don't see that message, something is wrong with Ntldr.

Ntldr checks for the presence of certain files:

▼ Boot.ini, a text file that holds information about the operating systems installed on the computer and where to find them on the drive

■ Ntdetect.com, an application that performs the hardware detection process

■ Bootsect.dos, which exists if you dual-boot with DOS (or a Windows operating system that can run from DOS)

▲ Ntbootdd.sys, which exists if you boot from a SCSI drive

Then the following events are launched by Ntldr:

1. It starts a basic file system based on your boot drive. If you have a SCSI drive, Ntbootdd.sys is opened. Otherwise, the system known as INT13 is used.

2. It reads Boot.ini and displays the information it finds on your screen (the bootup menu).

3. It waits for user input about the choice of operating system, and starts the default operating system if the time for making a choice elapses. It uses the information in Boot.ini to do this.

Ntdetect Runs

Once the NT operating system starts, Ntdetect.com launches to check the hardware in your computer. It announces itself with an on-screen message, "NTDETECT V4.0 Checking Hardware."

Here's what Ntdetect looks at:

▼ The machine ID

■ The bus type

■ The video controller

■ The keyboard type

■ The serial ports

■ The parallel ports

■ The floppy drive(s)

▲ The mouse

Ntldr Loads the Startup Files

After Ntdetect has finished its work, Ntldr opens three files:

▼ Ntoskrnl.exe, which is the Windows NT kernel

■ Hal.dll, which is the Hardware Abstraction Layer

▲ \%SystemRoot%\System32\Config\System, which is the System hive in the computer's registry

If there's a problem, you'll get an error message. If everything is honky-dory you'll see the familiar "Press Spacebar to use Last Known Good" message.

Ntldr Loads the Drivers

The system hive tells Ntldr which drivers to load. You can see this information for yourself in the registry—go to HKEY_LOCAL_MACHINE\SYSTEM\CurrentControlSet\Services. (If you pressed the spacebar and indicated a different LastKnownGood, it will head for that configuration.)

As Ntldr loads the drivers into memory, it writes a period to the screen for each driver.

This is the end of the boot sequence. Now the load sequence begins. Ntldr passes control of the operating system startup to Ntoskrnl.

The Load Sequence Begins

When the NT kernel begins, the screen changes to blue and you'll see a display message about the operating system version, the number of processors, and the amount of memory. Then dots start appearing, indicating progress as the kernel does its work.

First the kernel copies the Current Control Set to a registry key named HKEY_LOCAL_MACHINE\SYSTEM\Clone (you cannot open this key; it's active and therefore protected).

Then it performs the following tasks:

1. It initializes the low-level drivers that were loaded by Ntldr.

2. It searches all of the drivers (using the System hive) and initializes any that have a Start value of 1. Each time a driver is initialized, another dot appears on the blue screen.

3. It loads Smss.exe (the Services Manager application), which checks the registry subkey HKEY_LOCAL_MACHINE\SYSTEM\CurrentControlSet\Control\ Session Manager. That subkey has a value item named BootExecute, and Smss runs whatever application is named in the data for that item. By default the value of that data item is AUTOCHK (Chkdsk), and there's no reason to add anything else.

4. Smss.exe loads the page file.

5. Smss.exe then checks the registry subkey HKEY_LOCAL_MACHINE\ SYSTEM\CurrentControlSet\Control\Session Manager\SubSystems. It uses the information it finds in the value item named Windows to start the Windows NT operating system.

The Subsystem Starts

Once the previous steps have completed, the Win32 subsystem takes over and begins the last processes:

6. Winlogon.exe launches, sending the first logon dialog box to the screen (the logo, then the "Press Ctrl-Alt-Del . . ." dialog box.

7. Lsass.exe (the Local Security Authority program) is launched.

8. Screg.exe (a Scan Registry program) is launched. It searches the registry for autoload drivers. One of the drivers it should always find (perhaps the only one) is Services.exe. This is the application that loads the workstation and server services.

The User Logs On

Now the user logs on, and the registry key Clone is copied to LastKnownGood. The operating system is up and running. Go get your work done.

SOLVING STARTUP PROBLEMS

Let's go over some of the startup problems you're likely to run into. This is by no means a comprehensive list of everything that can go wrong. It's mainly a list of things that frequently do go wrong, along with some suggestions for repairing the problems.

Hardware Problems

I have no plans to describe here everything that could go wrong with hardware—I'd grow old writing it, and you'd grow old reading it. However, there are some hardware issues that occur over and over again. If the computer just doesn't boot, check the following items first:

▼ The BIOS must be accurate, especially as regards the hard drive.

■ BIOS virus checking should be turned off; it can interfere with NT booting (and always interferes with NT installation).

■ Check the hard drive controller for incorrect settings. In fact, check the hard drive controller itself; they die, and not always from old age. If the controller is SCSI and provides setup during boot (usually CTRL-A, at least for Adaptec), go into the setup program and check everything.

■ IRQ conflicts can sometimes prevent bootup, when the conflict involves the boot drive. The most common problems are conflicts with IRQ 14 and IRQ 15 for IDE controllers and IRQ 10 or IRQ 11 for SCSI.

▲ Check the temperature of the air coming out of the back of the computer—you're looking to see if the power supply fan has stopped functioning or the baby fan that cools your processor has stopped spinning. Either failure can roast motherboard chips (or motherboards).

Depending on the hardware and peripherals in your computer, there may be other things to check; you probably know what they are. Of course, the most obvious place to start is the device you just installed.

EISA Devices Can Cause Unique Problems

If you have an EISA computer, you probably celebrated the fact that you didn't have to play around with dip switches or mess around with jumpers. (Don't you just hate it when a jumper falls onto the floor and you can't find it? I've learned to open every old machine I'm discarding and pull every jumper from the motherboard and bus devices and save them in a baby food jar.) However, as wonderful as software setup is, there is a problem with EISA when the setup is incorrect. If anything is wrong, everything is wrong. One little misconfiguration causes an error message during bootup that says "EISA CMOS FAILURE." This has to be one of the least helpful messages in the world of computers. If you just installed a new EISA NIC, and the bootup process doesn't like the configuration, it also doesn't like the hard drive controller or anything else it finds. It's not that the other devices are configured incorrectly; it's just that when it sees a problem, it refuses to look at any other device. The only solution is to rerun the entire software setup. As EISA matures, we can hope for better communication.

Using the Last Known Good

I hate to be trite and go for the obvious, but even if you haven't had to use it, you've seen the message about pressing the SPACEBAR to access the Last Known Good configuration. Sometimes, when the operating system has a problem booting, instead of an informative message, you are told to use the SPACEBAR. During the startup process the operating system displays this message: "System configuration invalid; Press the SPACEBAR during Setup." This almost always happens on the first reboot following some change you've made in the registry. Registry hacking can be dangerous to your computer's health.

If you see this message, restart the computer, and when you're prompted to press the SPACEBAR, do so. In fact, as soon as you see the word "SPACEBAR" on the screen, press the SPACEBAR (you can miss this opportunity easily; the window of time available to use the SPACEBAR option is quite narrow).

Use the arrow key to move to the Last Known Good configuration. If there are multiple choices (if you're using hardware profiles you could see several configuration choices), don't mess around with the arrow key; just press the letter **L**. Press ENTER and the last good configuration for your system will load—and all the changes you made to the registry that caused this problem will be discarded.

Nothing on the Monitor Is Readable

This usually occurs after you've made changes to the display configuration, either by changing settings or by installing a new video controller. Most of the time the problem is apparent when the Windows Logo window displays, and it gets worse when you see the "Press Ctrl-Alt-Delete" dialog box. In fact, if you do press the three-fingered salute to get to the Logon dialog box (to use the Shut Down command if you're running Windows NT Workstation), you can't make out the buttons on the dialog box and have to rely on your memory.

Shut down the computer and restart it. When the boot menu displays, choose "Windows NT Server Version 4.00 (VGA Mode)."

Error: Missing NTDETECT.COM

This error message usually results from an inadvertent deletion of Ntdetect.com or from a corruption of the file. You will have to copy the file to the root directory of the boot drive.

If the computer is running FAT, follow these steps:

1. Boot the computer from a DOS boot diskette.

2. From the root directory, enter **dir ntdetect.com /a** to see if the file exists.

3. If it is not in the root directory, copy it from the \I386 folder of the installation CD to the root directory.

4. If it is in the root directory (it's probably corrupt), change the attributes (-s-h-r) and copy the file from the installation CD.

If the computer is running NTFS, use a bootable floppy to start the operating system, then follow the steps just given.

The Bootup Menu Doesn't Appear

Even if you're not dual-booting between operating systems, Windows NT 4 presents a bootup menu so you can choose between regular mode and VGA mode. If you don't see the bootup menu, don't panic; the system will boot into the default choice. It means that someone has configured this computer to boot without the menu. This isn't a good idea, because you sometimes need that VGA mode choice to solve problems. To put the bootup menu back, follow these steps:

1. Open the System applet in Control Panel.

2. Choose the Startup/Shutdown tab.

3. Select the startup operating system choice you want from the Startup drop-down list box.

4. Specify a number larger than zero in the Show List For box.

5. Choose OK.

Error: I/O Error Accessing Boot Sector File . . . BOOTSS

Okay, the actual error message during startup is "Error: I/O error accessing boot sector file Multi(0)disk(0)rdisk(0)partition(1)\\BOOTSS." The important part is that the operating system couldn't access a necessary boot sector file.

This error occurs only in computers that dual-boot between Windows NT 4 and another operating system. When there is a dual-boot configuration, the operating system uses a hidden file named Bootsect.dos to boot into the non–Windows NT operating system. If the file disappears or becomes corrupted, the error message is displayed.

NOTE: For some reason the operating system (it's actually Ntldr that is sending the error message) misreads the name of Bootsect.dos and calls it Bootss. I have no explanation for this (and neither did anyone I asked at Microsoft).

Usually the computer continues to boot (you just won't be able to access the other operating system). If the computer doesn't continue to boot, use the steps described earlier in this chapter to boot the computer from a bootable floppy.

Look for Bootsect.dos in the root directory of your boot drive by entering **dir bootsect.dos /a** at a command prompt. If it is there, it's probably corrupted. Change the attributes (-s-h) and delete it, then restore it from a backup. If it's missing, restore it from a backup.

If you don't have a backup, why don't you? This is where you'll get religion about backing up, because re-creating this file is not a two-minute job. You cannot copy it from the original CD; it's created during setup.

With luck (if you've been good in your previous lives), you'll be able to find another computer with the same configuration as yours and copy Bootsect.dos to a floppy and use "sneaker net" to bring it to your computer.

Bootsect.dos is created by the Windows NT Setup program when an operating system exists on the computer at the time of NT installation. The existing boot sector found in sector 0 of drive C is copied to Bootsect.dos first, and then the Setup program writes the Windows NT boot sector to sector 0. Because the contents of Bootsect.dos are actually created by the previous operating system, it's not very simple to re-create it. In fact, you have to put the original operating system back onto sector 0, and then you have to write that information to Bootsect.dos.

To do this, use the appropriate procedure to install the original operating system. If it was DOS, boot the computer with a bootable MS-DOS floppy disk and enter **sys c:** from the command prompt. If it was Windows 95, you'll have to regenerate that operating system (don't let the installation program look for devices, deselect every option, and don't install anything except the bare minimum files needed to get the system installed). Now the original operating system occupies sector 0.

Follow these steps to create Bootsect.dos:

1. Insert the first floppy disk from your Windows NT software (usually called the Boot Disk) and reboot. When you see the first Setup screen, choose **R** to start repairing your system.

2. Follow all of the instructions Setup displays.

3. When the list of optional repair tasks appears, be sure to select "Verify boot files on your C: drive:."

4. Continue to follow instructions until you see the message "Setup Repair is complete."

5. Go to the nearest blackboard and write "I will back up regularly to avoid this torture" a thousand times.

NOTE: Setup will not overwrite an existing Bootsect.dos file, which is why you must delete the file if you found it and assume that it is corrupted.

Error: Missing NTLDR

If Ntldr is missing from the root directory, the computer is not going to boot. The file might not be missing; it might just be corrupted. Either way, you have to get a good copy of Ntldr onto your boot drive.

Use a bootable floppy to start the computer.

If you have a FAT system and are using a DOS bootable floppy, you can find Ntldr on Disk 2 of the diskettes that came with your operating system. It's also on the CD-ROM.

If you are using NTFS, use the NTFS bootable disk, then copy Ntldr from the floppy to drive C.

> **TIP:** If Ntldr already exists on drive C and you cannot write the good copy, change the attributes of the corrupted file (-s-h-r). In fact, after you do that, delete it.

Error: NTOSKRNL.EXE Is Missing, or Corrupt

If you see the error message "NTOSKRNL.EXE is missing, or corrupt" during system startup, don't rush to replace the file (although you may have to do that in the end). A more common cause for this error message is a problem in the Boot.ini file, usually because somebody has messed around with it. If Boot.ini does not have errors, you will need to replace Ntoskrnl.exe from the original Windows NT media.

Understanding Boot.ini

To determine whether Boot.ini has errors, boot with a bootable floppy disk and take a peek at the Boot.ini file. First of all, make sure it's there. If it is there, open it and make sure the lines in the file are pointing to the right place. It is common for the name of the subdirectory for the operating system to somehow have been changed.

Just in case it is a problem with Boot.ini, let's take a brief look at the way that file works.

During system startup, Ntldr looks for Boot.ini, which contains information about which operating systems are available and where their files are kept on the hard drive. Here's a typical Boot.ini file:

```
[boot loader]
timeout=30
default=multi(0)disk(0)rdisk(0)partition(1)\WINNT
[operating systems]
multi(0)disk(0)rdisk(0)partition(1)\WINNT="Windows NT Workstation
Version 4.00"
multi(0)disk(0)rdisk(0)partition(1)\WINNT="Windows NT Workstation
Version 4.00 [VGA mode]" /basevideo /sos
C:\="Microsoft Windows"
```

The first section, [boot loader], tells Ntldr which operating system should be loaded as the default and how long to wait for user intervention before loading the default operating system.

The second section, [operating systems], contains information about where to find the existing operating systems. The format of the information is independent of the architecture of the computer, and would be the same for RISC machines (which don't have drives named C or D).

The first part of the location information identifies the disk controller; then the drive is identified, then the partition. Finally, there's the subdirectory. Remember that for controllers and drives, computers start counting with 0, not 1.

For the disk controller, your Boot.ini file may contain the word "SCSI" instead of "multi." In fact, the computer from which I took the Boot.ini file shown here has a SCSI controller, but it lists "multi" for the controller because the BIOS knows how to boot from it. Not all SCSI controllers are BIOS booted; if you have one that isn't you'll see "SCSI" instead of "multi." Also, if you have two SCSI controllers, you'll probably see "SCSI" even if they are BIOS bootable. This allows the operating system to keep track of them. In such cases you might see a line that refers to "SCSI (1)."

Incidentally, if you have two EIDE controllers, you will not see "multi (1)" in Boot.ini, because the multi parameter will not accept it. That parameter is always pointed at the controller that holds the boot drive. Any other controllers are ignored.

The disk parameter is always 0 for "multi." For "SCSI," it is the device ID for the drive. Although the device ID can be any number between 0 and 6, most people set up SCSI controllers with the drive as the first device, so a value of 0 is most common here.

The rdisk parameter indicates which drive holds the NT files if your configuration has "multi." For SCSI, it is the LUN (Logical Unit Number) for the device. This should always be 0, because I don't know why any individual SCSI device should have two LUNs.

The partition parameter identifies the partition on the drive where the operating system is installed. Partitions are counted starting with 1 (instead of 0), so if you installed NT on drive C you should see a 1. If you partitioned your drive and installed NT on logical drive E, the value of the parameter is 3.

The next entry in the line is the name of the subdirectory where the system files were installed.

The last entry in the line (the stuff surrounded by quotation marks) is the text that is displayed when the boot menu is on the screen.

HELPFUL MISCELLANEOUS TROUBLESHOOTING INFORMATION

There are a few odds and ends of information affecting startup that you might want to make note of.

Problems with More than 4GB of RAM

You probably don't have a lot of computers around that have 4GB of RAM, but just in case you're planning to install that much memory, be aware that the computer won't boot if it's running FAT unless you install Service Pack 2 (or later).

Problems with Bootable CD-ROMs

On many computers, you can have a problem booting if the Windows NT CD-ROM is in the CD-ROM drive. The Windows NT CD-ROM is a bootable disk, but you don't want it to boot, and in most cases it wouldn't boot properly if you did want it to. The whole question of bootable CD-ROMs is a problem, and some computer BIOSes are more troublesome than others.

Follow two general rules to avoid boot problems caused by CD-ROMs:

1. Remove the CD-ROM from the drive during bootup.

2. In the System BIOS, change the boot sequence so that the CD-ROM is last.

If your BIOS uses software emulation to boot CD-ROMs, you'll see an error message on your screen during bootup: "There is no disk in the drive. Please insert a disk into drive A:." Windows NT does not support software emulation mode for booting CD-ROMs. Go into the BIOS setup and disable it. This software emulation mode is usually found in AWARD BIOSes with a date code earlier than 8/25/96. Restart the computer and press DEL to enter the BIOS setup, then disable software emulation and also put the CD-ROM last in the list of bootable drives.

Don't Enable ROM BIOS Shadowing

ROM BIOS shadowing means that the BIOS is copied from ROM into RAM. In MS-DOS, because the operating system uses the BIOS for performing some tasks (like writing to the screen), using RAM is faster than reading the BIOS. However, Windows NT does not use the BIOS (except during startup) so all this configuration option does is use up RAM that the operating system and applications could be using.

Go into BIOS setup and disable all ROM BIOS shadowing. There may be more than one choice, so look for:

▼ System BIOS

■ Video BIOS

▲ Any ROM BIOS for an adapter

The trick to troubleshooting startup successfully is to be prepared. Keep ERD disks current, and always know where your original media are (especially the Startup floppy disk). In fact, it's a good idea to use Diskcopy to make yourself safety backups of the Startup floppy disk.

CHAPTER 6

Troubleshooting Logons

An administrator's day is unpredictable, and a great deal of time is spent putting out fires. But there is one constant—you can be sure that every day will bring a call from a user who is having trouble logging on. Whether it's an error message that refuses to permit the user to join the domain, a forgotten password, or a successful logon with the wrong desktop presented, logon problems in one form or another are something you can plan on. In this chapter we'll look at some of the common problems and their solutions.

PREPARE FOR SOLUTIONS AHEAD OF TIME

I've frequently found that the easiest solution to some logon problems (especially password-related problems) is to log on to the troubled computer with administrative rights and straighten things out. However, the only way to accomplish this is to make sure the computer has an account and password it will accept in addition to the user account that is having a problem. If your users never log on as Administrator, just make sure the Administrator account password is not required to change. Rather than trying to track a gazillion Administrator passwords, use the same password on every computer on your network. Never tell a user this password. It's tempting, during phone support, to walk a user through a fix by letting him or her log on as Administrator. If you do that, however, you'll live to regret it.

If any (or all) of your users are logged on to their computers with the Administrator account (which is not a great idea because of the damage they can do), make sure you create a second account with full administrative rights on every computer. Employ the same logic so that you can keep things straight: use the same user name and password for each machine; make sure the password does not have to be changed; and never tell anyone the name or password.

You can also copy the Administrator permissions on a computer to another user (to save yourself the trouble of creating all those rights and permissions from scratch when you create the user). To do this, follow these steps:

1. Open the System applet in Control Panel and move to the User Profiles tab (see Figure 6-1).

2. Select the Administrator profile and choose Copy To.

3. In the Copy To dialog box, click Browse and then move to the \%SystemRoot%\Profiles subdirectory.

4. Select the folder for the target user.

5. Click OK until you've closed all the dialog boxes.

Now you have a second user with administrative rights on this computer.

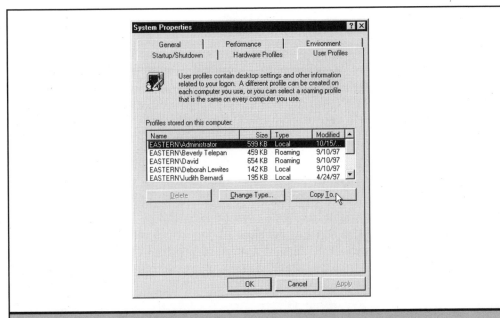

Figure 6-1.   Copy all of the Administrator's permissions and rights by copying the profile

TROUBLESHOOTING PASSWORD PROBLEMS

When you think of password problems, you remember all the times you've received calls for help from users who forgot their passwords or who went into a panic when they couldn't log on because they mistyped their passwords. The fact is, however, that many password problems stem from the password policies you set as an administrator. Some policies conflict, and others get so complicated that users are almost doomed to have problems. The way to avoid continuous password problems is to plan and implement password policies that provide the security you need without creating problems.

Setting Password Policies

Password polices for your network are set in the Account Policy dialog box (shown in Figure 6-2), which you reach by choosing Policies, Account from the menu bar in User Manager for Domains.

The following password policies are available:

▼ Maximum Password Age, which can be set for 1 to 999 days, or set as Password Never Expires.

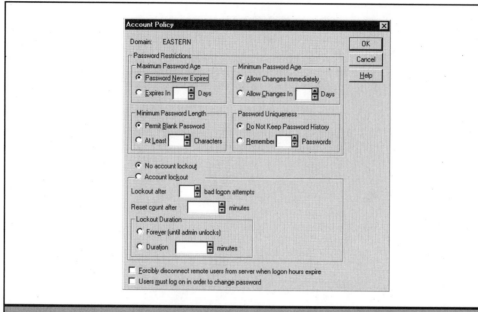

Figure 6-2.   User password policies are defined with the Account Policy dialog box

- Minimum Password Age, which can be set for 1 to 999 days, or set as Allow Changes Immediately.

- Minimum Password Length, which can be set for 1 to 14 characters, or you can release the requirement for a minimum length by setting Permit Blank Password.

- Password Uniqueness, which permits you to set a number of times that a new password must be created and used (the choices are 1 to 24 new passwords) before an old password can be reused.

▲ Account Lockout, which permits you to set the number of times a password fails (between 1 and 999) before the account is locked and no further attempt can be made to log on with that user name. There are other options you must specify if you choose this policy: you can use Reset Count After to specify the maximum number of minutes that can elapse between any two failed attempts in order to lock the computer (the range is from 1 to 99999); you can use Lockout Duration to specify that accounts are locked forever (an administrator must unlock the account) or for a specific duration (enter the number of minutes, from 1 to 99999, that must elapse before the account is unlocked).

NOTE: The Account Lockout policy counts only standard logons when it is tracking the number of times a user attempts to log on with the wrong password. Attempts made by a user to gain access from a workstation lockout that was initiated with CTRL-ALT-DEL, Lock Workstation don't count as tries under the Account Lockout policy. Neither do failed attempts to get past a password-protected screen saver.

▼ User Must Log On in Order to Change Password, which means that a user cannot change the password without being logged on to the network. If you set this policy, any user who has an expired password must ask the administrator to make the change. If the policy is not selected, the user will be able to change the expired password without involving an administrator.

Some of these policies are mutually exclusive, and there are also combinations of policies that have the potential to cause logon problems.

▼ If you establish the policy Allow Changes Immediately (in the Minimum Password Age section), do not establish a Password Uniqueness policy. Instead, be sure the Do Not Keep Password History radio button is selected. These policies, if used simultaneously, can cause problems.

■ If you establish Password Uniqueness, you must also enter a minimum number of days in the Minimum Password Age policy. This will avoid some potential clashes.

▲ If you want a policy that permits blank passwords, don't set a minimum password length.

Solving Password Problems

Several problems with user passwords occur so frequently that they seem almost endemic. Unfortunately, not all of them have simple, one-click solutions. Some are caused by user error, some by policy clashes, and some by what can only be explained as the caprice of the operating system.

The User Cannot Remember the Password

This, of course, will seem familiar to you. It's an administrator's most common troubleshooting task. To solve it, you have to set a new password for the user in User Manager. If that password is your choice instead of the user's, you can force the user to enter a new password at the next logon (which is one of the options in the User Properties dialog box).

The User Cancels the Action During a Password Change

Windows NT 4 apparently has no patience with people who can't make up their minds. If you've established a policy of requiring password changes, users are notified that a deadline is approaching when they log on. If a user receives a message indicating his or her password is about to expire, the operating system also offers an option to change the password during the current logon. Choosing Yes brings up the Password Change dialog box. If the user has a change of heart and chooses Cancel in that dialog box, the operating system permits the logon to proceed normally (the user will be reminded again at the next logon).

However, if the user locks the workstation with the CTRL-ALT-DEL sequence, or if a password-secured screen saver launches, the password doesn't work. The operating system displays the message "The password is incorrect. Please retype your password. Letters in passwords must be typed using the correct case. Make sure that Caps Lock is not accidentally on." The user is totally locked out of the workstation.

If you have installed Service Pack 3, this bug won't show up, but if you haven't installed SP3 you need a solution. The only solution is to unlock the workstation by logging on with a different administrative account (and I suggest you follow this with an Internet session in which you download SP3).

Unlocking a Locked-Out User

When a user is locked out, there are a couple of remedies, depending on the manner in which you configured lockout. However, one remedy that always works is to have the administrator unlock the workstation. Even if your lockout configuration doesn't specifically call for administrative unlocking, this solution works. To unlock a workstation, open User Manager for Domains and double-click the user entry. The Account Locked Out field (which is usually grayed out and inaccessible) is active and is selected with a check mark, as seen in Figure 6-3.

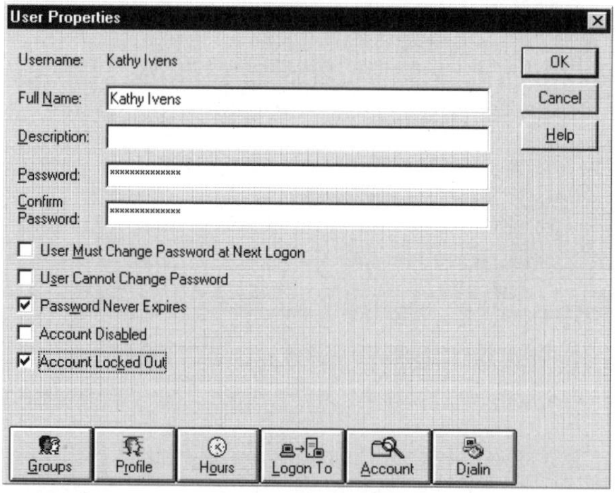

Figure 6-3. Regardless of your configuration for unlocking a workstation, you can always unlock it from User Manager

NOTE: Deselecting the Lockout doesn't change the configuration for this option; you're merely unlocking the workstation after this particular lockout incident. More bad passwords will result in another lockout.

If you've configured a lockout to end after a specific duration of time, the user who was locked out has two options (depending on the cause of the lockout):

▼ The user can wait for the specified duration and log on again, making sure to avoid typographical errors.

▲ The user can own up to forgetting the password, ask for a new one, and use it after an administrator has entered it in User Manager (and then unlocked the workstation).

The Lockout Duration Solution Doesn't Work

When you are configuring a lockout with a lockout duration solution, the figure specified for Lockout Duration must be equal to or larger than the figure specified for Reset Count After. If you don't set it this way, your configuration won't "take" in Windows NT 4.

Specifying the Advance Warning for Mandatory Password Changes

By default, Windows NT begins notifying users 14 days before they must change their password (assuming you've configured the system for mandatory password changes). You can change that advance warning interval by taking these steps:

1. Open a registry editor and go to HKEY_LOCAL_MACHINE\SOFTWARE\ Microsoft\WindowsNT\CurrentVersion\Winlogon.

2. Create a REG_DWORD data item named PasswordExpiryWarning.

3. Enter data that specifies the number of days before the password expiration date that you want the user to begin seeing the reminder.

Enabling Strong Password Functions

If you've installed Service Pack 2 or higher, you have the ability to institute even stronger password requirements than are permitted through the standard User Manager functions. Included in the Service Pack is a file named Passfilt.dll, and it should have been installed into the \%SystemRoot%\System32 directory (if it isn't there, search for it and move it there).

The strong password functions operate only on Windows NT 4 Servers. The functionality is available only to Windows NT and Windows 95 clients (16-bit Windows clients use password functions that don't work with this feature). These password requirements are as follows:

▼ Passwords may not contain the user logon name.

■ Passwords may not contain any string that is part of the user's full name.

■ Passwords must contain at least six characters.

▲ Passwords must contain characters from at least three of these four categories:

> Uppercase letters
> Lowercase letters
> Numbers
> Nonalphanumeric characters, such as punctuation characters

Unfortunately, these stringent rules make it more difficult for users to remember their passwords, so either they'll continually lock themselves out or they'll write the password down on a piece of paper and keep it where it's handy—which almost always means taping it to the monitor (along with a notation that says "password"). Therefore, if security isn't a major concern for your network, this may be more trouble than you want to let yourself in for. If security is a concern, however, this system makes it much more difficult to break into a computer with the normal password hacks (guessing a password connected to the user name or using the "password dictionary" approach).

NOTE: These password rules are in addition to any password requirements you've established, such as not repeating old passwords, requiring password changes at given intervals, and so on. This is not a replacement function; it's an add-on.

If you want to install strong password functionality (that's actually what it's called), you must make changes to the registry of every domain controller (PDC and BDCs). You must also make these changes to the registry of any stand-alone server that requires password validation. Take these steps to install this added functionality to passwords:

1. Open a registry editor and go to HKEY_LOCAL_MACHINE\SYSTEM\ CurrentControlSet\Control\Lsa.

2. Add a data key named Notification Packages, with a data type of REG_MULTI_SZ. If the key already exists, go to the next step.

3. Open the data item Notification Packages and add the value PASSFILT. If there is an entry in this value already (usually FPNWCLNT), add PASSFILT beneath it, as seen here:

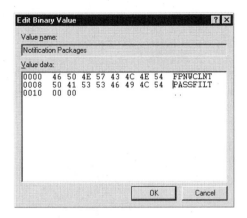

4. Choose OK and exit the registry editor.

You must reboot the computer to have these functions take effect. The new password functions take effect for users at the next change of password. For the creation of new user accounts, the strong functions are enabled immediately.

Strong Password Functions Can Be Ignored

This isn't really a problem that requires troubleshooting, but I mention it so you aren't surprised when it occurs. The strong password functions are enabled when a password change request is made by a client over the network (weak passwords will be rejected because the Passfilt.dll is implemented under these circumstances). If an administrator changes the password (or creates a password for a new user) via User Manager, however, the filtering for the strong password rules is not enforced (the administrator is writing directly to the SAM and the .dll is not active). This gives administrators the ability to make case-by-case decisions about password strength.

Create Your Own Password Rules

Passfilt.dll is Microsoft's implementation of the new Windows NT 4 capacity to permit programmers to write password rules that enhance security. You can have your own implementation if you program (or have programmers available). Information about this feature, along with sample code, is available in the Microsoft Win32 SDK, version 4.0. If you write your own scheme, you can decide on your own minimum length and type of characters required. The Microsoft implementation is not configurable—if you install it, it's "as is". The rules are hard-coded in the .dll file, and there are no registry entries or dialog box fields relating to Microsoft's implementation of the feature.

Reported Bug in Strong Passwords

It has been reported that occasionally the strong password feature produces an error message indicating that a new password doesn't meet the requirements, even when it does meet the requirements. I haven't seen this occur, but I do know that it has been reported to Microsoft often. A fix is in the works as of this writing; call Microsoft Support for more information.

Troubleshooting Password Problems with NetWare Servers

If you're running a mixed network environment, with both NetWare and NT on the net (which means you have clients running IPX), there are some logon/password problems you may run into.

Clients Running IPX Cannot Log On After Service Pack 3

It's been reported that after installing SP3 on NT servers, clients who are running the IPX protocol may have difficulty logging on to the domain. The error messages frequently indicate some form of password problem. The clients involved are MS-DOS, Windows for Workgroups (WFW), and Windows 95. There is no password problem; it's a side effect of SP3. You can fix it on the server by making this registry entry:

1. Open a registry editor and go to HKEY_LOCAL_MACHINE\SYSTEM\ CurrentControlSet\Services\LanManServer\Parameters.

2. Add a new REG_DWORD value named MinClientBufferSize.

3. Specify a value of 500.

Notice that this is a new value in the referenced subkey, not a new subkey.

Clients Cannot Log On to NetWare Server with Net Use

As convenient as it is, the Net Use command sometimes causes problems for Windows NT clients (both 3.51 and 4.0). An error message appears, indicating that the specified network password is not correct. The problem is not with the password; it's with the NetWare configuration, specifically Startup.ncf, if you are using the command SET ENABLE IPX CHECKSUMS=2. Windows NT does not support IPX checksums, and a value of 2 in this line enables them. The values this command can take include

▼ 0 = checksums disabled

■ 1 = checksums used if enabled by the client (this is the default value)

▲ 2 = checksums required

The reason the error message appears is that the Windows NT client has not enabled the checksum (which means that the checksum field in the IPX header is not filled in with any data that NetWare will recognize or accept). There are really no plans at Microsoft to change this, so you either need to disable the function or use it only if the client is sending checksum information (which means a non–Windows NT client).

NetWare Logons Fail with Unmatched Passwords

If a user has one password for logging on to the NT domain and a different password for logging on to the NetWare server, NT automatically tries to connect to the NetWare server using the password it knows. When that fails, the user is asked to select a NetWare server and is also asked for a password. As long as the user completes both logons, things are just hunky-dory.

However, if the user cancels the NetWare logon process (perhaps she doesn't feel like using the Accounts Payable software on the NetWare server at the moment), NT still tries to complete the connection. Of course, the only credentials NT knows about are the user name and password offered for the successful logon to the domain. In fact, NT doesn't know when to give up and keeps trying to connect. Not a lot of work is going to be accomplished on the user's workstation while this goes on.

Make the passwords identical to avoid problems. There's no particular reason to require a separate password for a NetWare server if you have good security in place for domain logons. Even if the user always, without fail, joins the NetWare server, why make her enter another password? Just let NT pass the credentials along.

TIP: Another reason to avoid separate NetWare passwords for users who log on to NetWare through a domain is that if you get fancy (okay, convoluted) about expiration dates for passwords, forced password changes, and so on, on both network operating systems, you can create an incredibly complicated system that no user could keep track of. In fact, even if you use the NetWare Compatible Password Expired option, you're likely to have a problem (there's a bug there that Microsoft has not yet fixed).

Securing Passwords for RAS and DUN

There are some methods for securing dial-in clients and dial-out clients, including password security, that you can use to assure yourself of the safety of your system.

Force CHAP Authentication

The host server for PPP dial-in traffic can be configured for more security during dial-in authentication. On the server side, make sure the client is forced to use Crypto-Handshake Authentication Protocol (CHAP) to be authenticated. This avoids acceptance of cleartest passwords, which can threaten the security level of your system. Doing this involves making a change to the registry in the subkey HKEY_LOCAL_MACHINE\SYSTEM\CurrentControlSet\Services\RasMan\PPP, which is shown in Figure 6-4. Look for the data item ForceEncryptedPassword (it's a REG_DWORD data type with a Boolean value), and change the data to 1.

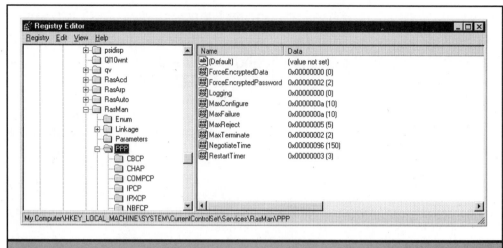

Figure 6-4. Settings for RAS/PPP communications can be checked or changed in the registry

TIP: It's probably a good idea to check the subkey CHAP (the next level under this subkey) to make sure the path to Raschap.dll is correct. It should be in the \%SystemRoot%\System32 directory. If the entry is there, it means the .dll file has been installed (the installation procedure wrote to the registry).

Disabling Stored Passwords in Dial-Up Networking

When users implement Dial-Up Networking to dial out to remote servers (or anywhere else), there's an option to save the password so that additional dialed connections won't require password entry. This is convenient, but it can be dangerous (unless those users never leave their computers). If your security protocols are such that this capability makes you nervous, disable the ability to save the password (technically it's cached, by the way). This is accomplished with the registry, as follows:

1. In any registry editor, go to HKEY_LOCAL_MACHINE\SYSTEM\ CurrentControlSet\Services\ RasMan\Parameters.

2. Add a new value with the name DisableSavePassword, making it a REG_DWORD type.

3. Enter a value of 1 to disable this feature (to enable it again, change the value to 0).

4. The option to save a password will no longer be available for Dial-Up Networking, even if the windows and dialog boxes are already established for doing so. Each time the user dials out, a password entry will be necessary.

CUSTOMIZE THE LOGON PROCESS

There are lots of ways to alter the logon process for users. You may want to use some of these methods either for convenience or for security.

Add a Custom Message

You can display a message during logon that is either specific to a workstation or global. There are plenty of reasons to do this, not the least of which is that it's just fun and interesting (I use funny messages on my system because a sense of humor is an employment requirement in my office.)

There are, however, more practical reasons to consider a message banner during logon. For individual workstations you might want to let users know of any special circumstances (perhaps the workstation's configuration is locked and desktop changes won't be saved). Globally, you might want to make company announcements, or just provide a warm, cozy note, such as "Welcome to Widget Wonderland, Inc., the Company That Cares."

Custom messages appear after the system message instructing the user to press CTRL-ALT-DEL to log on. The custom message remains on the screen until the user chooses OK, at which time the logon process continues as usual.

When you create a custom message, you can add both a heading (called a caption) and a message (called text). You can skip the caption if you wish (it appears in the title bar of the message box); the message text will still appear. Custom messages are added via the registry, so follow these steps to create one:

1. Open a registry editor and go to HKEY_LOCAL_MACHINE\SOFTWARE\Microsoft\WindowsNT\CurrentVersion\Winlogon.

2. Add a REG_SZ value item named LegalNoticeCaption.

3. Enter a data value for this item that is the text for the caption.

4. Add a REG_SZ value item named LegalNoticeText.

5. Enter a data value for this item that is the text for your message.

6. After entering your caption and message (as seen here), close the registry editor. The message is displayed at the next logon.

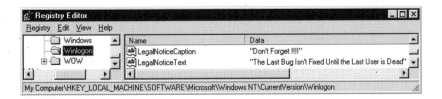

TIP: The quotation marks are added automatically by the system; do not enter them when you are typing.

Use Your Own Logon Graphic

If you want to replace the Microsoft logo that appears at logon with one of your own (usually the company logo), start by creating a bitmapped graphic. Place the graphic file in the \%SystemRoot% directory. Be sure the filename has eight or fewer characters and an extension of .bmp (yes, you need to follow the 8.3 convention for this file). Then follow these steps to use it:

1. Open a registry editor and go to HKEY_USERS \.DEFAULT\Control Panel\Desktop.

2. Find the value item Wallpaper. If it's not there, you can create it as a REG_SZ value item. Enter the data value, which is the complete path to your bitmapped file.

3. Find the value item TileWallpaper, or create it as a REG_SZ value item. Enter the data value, using 0 for Don't Tile, or 1 for Tile.

4. Find the value item WallpaperStyle, or create it as a REG_SZ value item. Enter the data value, using 0 for normal or 2 for stretch (stretch means it will fill the screen).

TIP: You cannot stretch the bitmapped graphic if you are tiling it.

You can also specify the position of your bitmapped logo on the screen by adding the necessary items to the same registry subkey, as follows:

1. Create a REG_SZ data item named WallpaperOriginX, and then enter data that represents the number of pixels from the left edge of the screen.

2. Create a REG_SZ data item named WallpaperOriginY, and then enter data specifying the number of pixels from the top of the screen.

Automate the Logon Process

There are some computers for which an automated, automatic logon makes sense. Print servers, RAS servers, and any other computer that exists to perform a specific function (and never has a user in front of it) are clearly candidates for this feature. So are workstations that are always occupied by the same user.

When a logon is automatic, the user just sits back and waits for the desktop to appear. There is no need to press the CTRL-ALT-DEL sequence, and there is no logon dialog box in which to enter a name and password.

TIP: If you are using the logon message feature, the message will display and the user will have to choose OK to clear it, which makes this a little less automated.

To automate logon, open a registry editor and go to HKEY_LOCAL_MACHINE\ SOFTWARE\Microsoft\WindowsNT\CurrentVersion\Winlogon. Notice that there's a data item named DefaultUserName. That's the user name for which you are creating this automatic logon.

TIP: You can do the same thing to your Windows 95 clients, using the registry key HKEY_LOCAL_MACHINE\SOFTWARE\Microsoft\Windows\CurrentVersion\Winlogon.

When you have determined that this is the user for whom you want to create an automatic logon, follow these steps:

1. Add a new REG_SZ type data item named AutoAdminLogon.
2. Enter a data value of 1 for the AutoAdminLogon item.
3. Add a new REG_SZ type data item named DefaultPassword.
4. Enter a data value for the DefaultPassword that is the password for the user named in the DefaultUserName data item.

The next logon for this computer will be automatic.

NOTE: Be sure to configure the user in an automated logon for "Password Never Expires."

Password Required for Automatic Logon

It seems logical to think that automated logons fit well with user names that require no passwords. After all, if you're merely mounting a print server and it's logging on automatically, what is the purpose of a password? Good question. However, regardless of the logic, a password is required for this feature. If there isn't a password, the first automatic logon will proceed with no problem, leading you to believe that everything is just fine. Then Windows NT will figure out that there isn't a password and change the Boolean data for AutoAdminLogon from 1 to 0. The next logon won't be automatic. You won't even be able to fake it by entering a DefaultPassword data item with blank data—which translates to two quotation marks. I've tried that and it doesn't work. You must have a real password (don't forget to perform the appropriate tasks for attaching a password to a user in the local and domain User Managers).

Bypass an Automatic Logon

Sometimes you need to log on to a computer with an automatic logon, and you need to use a different name. Perhaps you have to troubleshoot some problem and you need administrative rights (the automatically logged on user does not usually have full administrative rights).

To do this, when Windows NT starts booting (at the blue screen), hold down the SHIFT key. Keep holding it down until you see the Windows NT Welcome screen. (Incidentally, there's no "welcome" message on that screen, but that's what the screen with the Windows NT logo is called.) The Begin Logon dialog box with the instructions about CTRL-ALT-DEL appears, and you can log on as a different user.

When you have finished using this computer as the different (nonautomated) user, you must once again log on by holding down the SHIFT key. This time, manually log on to the computer with the name and password of the automated user (the one you entered in the DefaultUserName data item in the registry). Hereafter, automated logon will work. This is necessary because during the automated procedure the system uses the last logged-on user in the Logon dialog box (which it assumes will always be the DefaultUserName). You have to perform a manual logon in order to place that name back in the dialog box.

Hide the Last Logged-On User

It increases security if the name of the last user who logged on to the machine isn't showing when the Logon dialog box appears. This eliminates any password guessing based on the name. To display a blank logon screen so a user has to enter both a name and a password, follow these steps:

1. Open a registry editor and go to HKEY_LOCAL_MACHINE\SOFTWARE\ Microsoft\WindowsNT\CurrentVersion\Winlogon.

2. Add a new REG_SZ value entry item named DontDisplayLastUserName.

3. Make the value of this entry 1.

Shut Down from the Logon Window

For some reason, I keep running into administrators who want to debate whether there should be a shutdown option on the logon window. I have trouble coming up with good reasons for either side of the debate. I can't imagine why not, nor can I image why. I haven't heard any really good IS horror stories that ended with either, "What saved me was the fact that the user couldn't shut down from logon" or "What saved me was the fact that the user could shut down from logon."

Regardless of your position on this issue, here's how to configure a computer so that a user can shut down without logging on (or cannot shut down without logging on).

1. Open a registry editor and go to HKEY_LOCAL_MACHINE\SOFTWARE\ Microsoft\WindowsNT\CurrentVersion\Winlogon.

2. Find the value ShutdownWithoutLogon. If it's not there, you can create it as a REG_SZ value item.

3. Set the data value to 1 if you want to permit shutdown from the logon window; set the data value to 0 if you don't want a shutdown button on the logon window.

Now you can join the debate; you've taken sides.

TROUBLESHOOTING LOGON SCRIPTS

A logon script is a batch file that runs automatically when a user has logged on. You can create logon scripts to do any number of things for the user, such as creating a network connection to a drive or a shared folder. You can also use an executable program file as a logon script if you want an application to launch automatically at logon.

For MS-DOS, Windows 3.x, and WFW clients, the logon script is used to establish some of the environment variables that are in profiles. For Windows NT clients, logon scripts are a way to establish common or mandatory settings that may or may not have been established by the user in a profile. For instance, if you impose no controls over profiles and therefore have no way of making sure that every NT client has mapped a drive to a specific network connection, you can establish the connection in a logon script.

Just as a quick reminder, here's how you establish the logon script for a user:

1. Open User Manager for Domains.

2. Double-click on an existing user listing and choose Profile. If this is a new user, fill out the information in the New User dialog box, then choose Profile.

3. Enter the filename of the logon script in the Logon Script Name text box.

NOTE: If you want to put the logon script in a location other than the default subdirectory, enter the full path instead of just the script filename. See "Choosing a Logon Script Location" later in this section.

Use the Correct File Extension

The file extension for logon scripts is determined by the operating system of the user's computer. Here are the rules:

▼ Use .bat for MS-DOS, WFW, and Windows NT.

■ Use .cmd for OS/2.

▲ Don't use .exe for a script—a logon script that is named *filename*.exe launches the *filename* application. If there is no application, the logon script won't run.

Executable File Launches Without a Logon Script Command

You've done everything right—written a logon script and named it *something*.bat, and there's no command in the logon script to launch an application. And yet an application launches every time a particular user logs on. You check the Startup folder on your Start menu system and find that it's empty. You check Autoexec.bat, and it has nothing in it except a couple of environment commands.

Before you start believing in haunted computers and call somebody in to perform an exorcism, check the registry. Go to HKEY_CURRENT_USER\Software\Microsoft\WindowsNT\CurrentVersion\Windows (see Figure 6-5, which is a view from REGEDIT).

Look at the data in the entries named *load* and *run*. If there is any data (there should be a path statement that points to the application that seems to run itself), open the data item and delete the string.

Incidentally, the cause of this is usually rooted in a Win.ini file, perhaps left over from a migration from Windows 3.x. In fact, take a peek at your Win.ini file in Windows NT; you'll probably see a reference to this software application. With Windows 3.x, placing an application in a Run command caused that application to launch when Windows loaded. In Windows NT you can place an application name in Win.ini, but you also must enter it in the registry if you want it to run when you start Windows.

Choosing a Logon Script Location

Life will be a lot easier if you place user logon scripts in the default location, which is Server\%SystemRoot%\System32\Repl\Import\Scripts. The most important reason

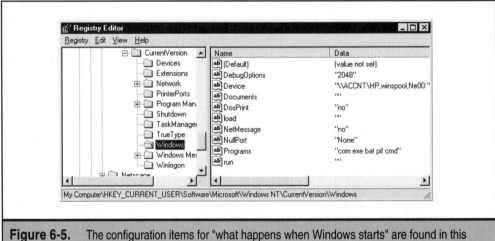

Figure 6-5. The configuration items for "what happens when Windows starts" are found in this registry key

for this is that you're guaranteed replication to all the domain controllers so that the script is always found, regardless of the authenticating controller at the time the user logs on..

However, you can create a subdirectory under the \Scripts subdirectory in the default path and then place logon scripts in that new subdirectory. In that case, you must enter the information about the relative path in the Logon Script text box of the User Environment Profile dialog box. This is accomplished by entering *newsubdirectory\filename.ext*, substituting the appropriate names. The system will append your relative path to the default path. This approach gives you the opportunity to group users and assign logon scripts specific to each group. See the next section on sharing logon scripts.

TIP: The reason the relative path works is that the replication process includes everything it finds below the \Repl subdirectory.

Sharing Logon Scripts

You can write one or several logon scripts and then point users to the appropriate script. In many companies, there's a single logon script, and it's entered in every user's account in User Manager.

I can think of many reasons for grouping users and assigning a logon script by group. You might want users who log on from a specific operating system to use a specific script. Or users who have to get to the same share on the network could use a script that maps that share.

For example, suppose you want everyone who uses the accounting software to have that connection explicitly established. If all of your users are connecting from Windows NT workstations and you've established control over profiles, you can set up the profiles to map the appropriate share and reconnect at logon. But if you're not dealing with a solid NT base, or you don't want to maintain administrative control over user profiles, a logon script accomplishes your goal.

First, create the logon script. For example, in my office the only command that's needed is **net use g: \\Accnt\MAS90**. This accomplishes the following:

▼ Establishes a drive letter for the share

■ Specifies the name of the computer that has the accounting software

▲ Specifies the name of the share that has the accounting software

Next, name the script, which in this case I call Accnt.bat.

Then indicate the path to the logon script in each affected user's account. In this case, I'd enter **accntg\accnt.bat**, because I created a new subdirectory named \Accntg under the default script path.

The users who need to access the accounting program can find their way to G: and go to work.

Other users who have to reach other software (shared documents for word processing for those people who spend their day writing training manuals, for example) are pointed to logon scripts that map the //computer and /share holding the word processing software.

Do You Need Separate Subdirectories?

In the example for my office, I indicated that I'd created a subdirectory under the default directory for logon scripts to hold the Accnt.bat script. That is really an unnecessary step; I could just as easily have entered **accnt.bat** in the Logon Script text box for each appropriate user. However, that logon script is for the people who use MAS90 accounting software. There are other users who use other accounting software to write training manuals. I prefer to keep all the logon scripts pertaining to accounting software in a discrete subdirectory just to make administration of all of this easier for myself (users change and/or the software changes frequently).

Your office probably doesn't have the same situation, but you might have the same reasons. If you're pointing a group of users to a logon script and later you find you want to separate that group in some way, you could add the new logon script to the default directory and point the users to the new script name. However, if your system gets a bit more complicated, it might be better to create subdirectories for similar groups. That makes it easier to change all of the logon scripts for a group after some global event (like moving software to a different server).

Use a Logon Script to Synchronize Time

One of the most popular uses for logon scripts is to synchronize the time of all your client machines with a server. This ensures the accuracy of file timestamping and date-sensitive software (such as accounting or scheduling software). The syntax for the command is **net time **server **/set /yes**, where:

net time is the command

\\server is the name of the server to which you want to synchronize the local computer's time and date

/set is the instruction to set the time to that server (without this parameter, the command returns the time on the server)

/yes confirms the fact that you want to set the local computer time and date to that of the server

---

TIP: If you fail to add the parameter /yes, the system asks for confirmation. Since a logon script file should carry out its commands in an unattended fashion, this parameter is important.

The only problem you have is finding a server that has an accurate clock. Remember that with computers, the word "accurate" is a relative term. (I know that's an oxymoron but that's as good as it gets with computer time.)

Don't Use Notepad to Create Logon Scripts

I have a habit of using Notepad to write myself all sorts of notes because it's quick and easy to load, enter text, and then print the note. In fact I keep a shortcut to Notepad on my desktop.

However, Notepad is not a clean, straight, absolute text editor. It inserts UNICODE characters, which may interfere with the execution of a logon script. What you need is a text editor that only uses ANSI characters. There are plenty of them around; the only guideline I can offer is that it's safest to use an editor that runs in MS-DOS. The one I use for this purpose is the built-in MS-DOS editor. I drop to a command line and enter **edit** *filename***.bat**, which invokes the DOS editor.

TIP: Frequently you'll find that you don't receive any error messages if a logon script doesn't run because of problems with UNICODE characters. You'll learn about the failure only when something you commanded in the script fails to happen—for instance, if you inserted a command to map a drive and the drive isn't mapped when the user tries to use the drive letter.

Don't Use Parameters for Windows 95 Clients

There's a bug that shows up when a Windows 95 client logs on to an NT 4 domain and the logon script has parameters for one or more of the commands. Actually, "shows up" is the wrong phrase because you don't see an error message, but the logon script doesn't work. It's known that many logon scripts with command line parameters on one or more lines of the script will fail, but as far as I know there has been no specific indication regarding which commands and parameters cause this problem. Therefore, the safest way to proceed is to avoid any command line parameters for logon scripts that belong to Windows 95 users. Stay in touch with Microsoft if you really need this feature, because a fix is being developed at the time of this writing.

Troubleshooting Logon Scripts with NetWare Services

If you have a gateway to a NetWare server, or your workstation is running NetWare Client Services, you probably will encounter a NetWare login script as you connect with the NetWare server. (For those of us who spent our professional lives solely in NetWare before adding Windows NT networking to our repertoire, scripts were a necessary fact of life—they are the only way to establish environment and user settings.)

This section describes some common errors you may encounter if you have NetWare services (along with solutions).

NetWare Mapping Fails When Drive Letter Is a Duplicate

During the execution of a NetWare login script, you may see this error at the point where the script tries to map a drive letter to a NetWare volume:

```
The following drive mapping operation was attempted on a non-NetWare
network drive. "Z:=Server/Volume:\Dir"
```

This happens because drive Z was already mapped at the point that the command was executed. If you have a persistent connection to drive Z on a non–NetWare server (through a profile or a logon file that executed when you first connected to your NT domain), that connection is made before the NetWare login script is run.

You must be aware of the drives you map in both NOS environments. Either change the drive letter for the NetWare mapping command, or don't create a connection with that drive letter during the logon to the domain.

NetWare Mapping Fails with IF MEMBER OF

When a computer running NetWare Client Services logs on to a NetWare 4.x server, the login script might fail to map drives if the command is preceded by IF MEMBER OF. However, this failure occurs only when there are a great many NDS groups and the group list exceeds 2048 bytes. The problem isn't with the number of NDS groups; it's that there is not a large enough buffer to handle the list, and so the IF statement isn't resolved. SP3 corrects this problem.

ENDIF Command Fails with CSNW and GSNW

If you write a login script that runs under Client Services for NetWare (CSNW) or Gateway Services for NetWare (GSNW), and the script has an ENDIF command, at the point that the ENDIF line executes you'll see an error message stating that the line could not be interpreted.

ENDIF can be used only in a login script that runs on a Novell NetWare client. For CSNW or GSNW clients, you must use END instead of ENDIF.

If NetWare Login.exe for FPNW Fails, It Maps Incorrectly

When you run Login.exe from the Microsoft File and Print Services for NetWare (FPNW), and there's any failure during execution, the server's login area (usually F:\Login) is automatically mapped to F:\. This is a problem, because you cannot move up the tree to get to another NetWare directory. In fact, of course, you can't get to an F:\Login prompt, which is where most NetWare login scripts expect you to land.

Most of the time this problem occurs because an invalid user name or password was supplied to NetWare before the program launched. Those are the two items to check if you're having this problem.

It's important to note that the problem isn't with the Login.exe program, which works perfectly well for NetWare clients. In fact, for NetWare clients, when there's an error in data being passed to NetWare, the user is sent to F:\Login after Login.exe executes. That's a good landing zone for correcting the problem and starting all over.

In this case, however, what causes the problem is the combination of bad information together with the use of FPNW. The fact that FPNW cannot handle bad information in the standard way makes this an FPNW bug. At the time of this writing, Microsoft had not fixed it.

Miscellaneous Troubleshooting Tips for Logon Scripts

This section describes common errors and problems that don't fit neatly into any category.

A New, Absolutely Perfect Logon Script Doesn't Work

The clue is in the word "new." If the client logged on to the domain and was authenticated by a BDC, the script probably hasn't arrived there yet. Rather than tell the user to wait until replication takes place, force the replication. Go to the command line at the PDC and enter **net accounts /sync**. See Chapter 3 for more information about synchronizing domain controllers.

Scripts Don't Work with WFW Clients

For Windows for Workgroups clients, you must specify the domain name in the Network applet in Control Panel in order to have the logon script aimed properly.

Scripts Generate Errors for Windows 3.x Clients

For Windows 3.x and WFW 3.x, the logon script runs in a virtual DOS session, which opens automatically to run the script. Unfortunately, this session also closes automatically in less than a minute. If the logon script hasn't finished running when the session ends, an error message appears announcing that the system's integrity has been compromised (which sounds like a terribly serious problem).

The solution is to use short logon scripts. This becomes extremely important if these clients are dialing in, because then everything happens more slowly.

Check Permissions on NTFS Servers

If the logon script is on a server using the NTFS file system, you must explicitly assign Read rights for the user(s) to whom the logon script is attached. If there are no rights for the user attached to the script's file, no error message appears when the logon script fails to run. This is the first place to look to solve the mystery.

TROUBLESHOOTING BINDINGS

Actually, there's not really too much troubleshooting you can do with bindings—they're either there or they're not. You can't rewrite them, use third-party bindings, or reconfigure the way a NIC–binding relationship interacts. However, there are a few things you can do to tweak the performance issues connected to bindings.

The most significant performance issue related to bindings is the order in which they are implemented. When Windows NT 4 uses the NIC to make a connection, the bindings for that NIC and the protocol are part of the set of rules the operating system uses to complete the connection. Bindings are used in the order in which they are registered, and if the binding you need is not first, there's a delay until the operating system gets to it (it tries the protocol bindings one at a time, starting from the top).

The bindings for protocols are displayed, in order, on the Bindings tab of the Network applet in Control Panel, as seen in Figure 6-6.

You can view the bindings by services, protocols, or NICs. If it seems to take too long to connect to the network and you're using NetBEUI, make sure that the NetBEUI binding to your adapter is first (there may be other bindings displayed for NetBEUI).

Select a binding and move it up or down with the selection buttons on the Bindings tab to arrive at the right order. You have to reboot when you make changes.

TIP: As with all things in tweaking or troubleshooting computers, make one change at a time.

If you begin to see error messages about failed connections, you may have corrupted bindings. Reinstall the protocol, then reorder the bindings list.

Incidentally, bindings affect other connections in addition to the connection to a server for logon or to a peer for share access. For example, if you're using Exchange Server on

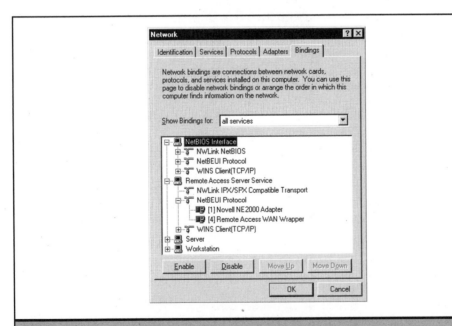

Figure 6-6.   The bindings for the installed protocols can be viewed and manipulated in the Network applet

your network, launching the client (for instance, Outlook) initiates a "try the bindings one at a time" process. The bindings are not read from the Network applet; instead, there is a discrete set of bindings for Exchange. If it seems to take forever for Outlook to display your Inbox, check the Exchange bindings. There isn't any dialog box for this; you have to hack the registry. As seen in Figure 6-7, the bindings are contained in HKEY_LOCAL_MACHINE\SOFTWARE\Microsoft\Exchange\Exchange Provider. You can open the data item and cut and paste to rearrange the order.

All the permutations and combinations of processes that run during network logons (or during the establishment of any network connections) can be daunting. Most of the troubleshooting you have to perform is repairing errors, many of them a result of the original configuration options during Setup. Take heart—once these problems are fixed, they usually stay fixed.

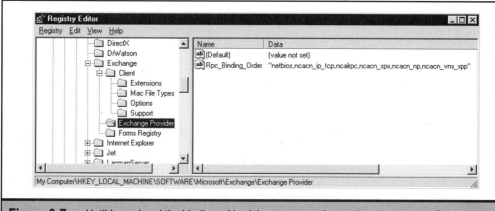

Figure 6-7. Until I reordered the bindings, I had time to empty the trash and sweep the floor while I waited for Outlook to load

WINDOWS
NT
Professional
Library

PART III

Troubleshooting User Rights and Access

WINDOWS
NT
Professional
Library

CHAPTER 7

Troubleshooting Shares

Unless a directory is configured as being shared, it cannot be accessed by users on other connected computers. Shared resources can be drives, directories, or peripherals. Both Windows NT 4 and Windows 95 users can create shares.

When NT (and Windows 95) users on a network open the Network Neighborhood folder or expand the Network Neighborhood object in Explorer, they can see every computer on the network. A computer's visibility is unrelated to whether or not there are any shared resources on that computer. (You can eliminate the display of computers from Network Neighborhood if you want to restrict their visibility; Chapters 9 and 10 have more information on this.)

In order to access a computer that's visible, one or more resources on that computer must be shared and the user must have permission to access a share.

In this chapter, we'll go over the different ways of creating and configuring shares, because most of the troubleshooting you have to worry about can be avoided if you perform these initial steps properly.

CREATING SHARES

The process of creating a share isn't terribly difficult. Any user with administrative rights can create a share on any computer. The easiest way to create a share is to open Explorer and find the drive and directory you want to share with network users. (A network user is defined as anyone who connects with the computer over a network connection.) There are two steps to creating a share:

▼ Naming it

▲ Giving users permission to access it

TIP: Actually, there are three steps. The third step involves specifying the number of users who can access the share simultaneously. However, I think of this as falling under the general category of giving permission.

Creating Shares for Directories

In Explorer or My Computer, start by right-clicking the directory you want to share, and then choose Sharing from the shortcut menu. This brings up a Properties dialog box for the share. The dialog box on a FAT system looks different from that on an NTFS system, because there are differences in the configuration options. Figure 7-1 is the dialog box for an NTFS system, and Figure 7-2 is the dialog box you'll see if you're running the FAT file system.

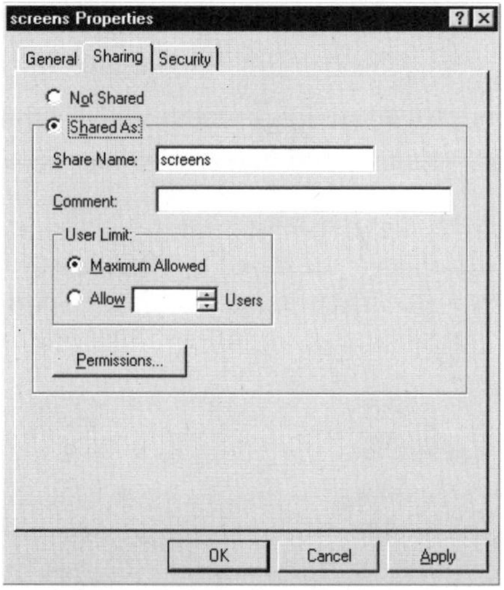

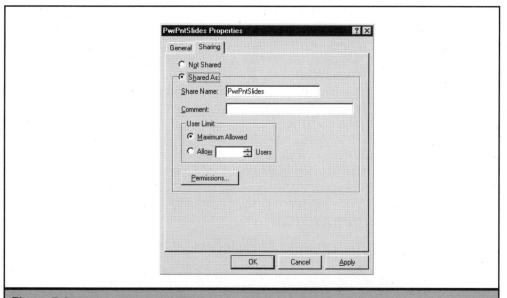

Figure 7-1. A Security tab on the Sharing Properties dialog box for NTFS lets you connect file and subdirectory permissions to share permissions

Figure 7-2. The permissions for a share are limited to the directory in FAT file systems

If you're running a gateway to a NetWare server, you have to create shares for any directory you want to make available to users. There are a few special things to remember while you are using Gateway Services for Netware to create and configure shares:

▼ The UNC for a NetWare share has the format *server**volume**directory*\ *subdirectory*.

■ You have to select a drive letter for the share.

▲ After you enter the share, the gateway service will validate it (which means it will try to find it and, if it does, will validate it) and then add it to the Share Name list in your gateway configuration dialog box.

Creating Shares for Drives

You can also give users access to an entire drive, which is very useful for servers that are used as application servers. The process is the same: Just right-click on the appropriate drive icon in Explorer and choose Sharing from the shortcut menu. Then name the share. The default name that appears is the drive letter, but you should enter a name that's descriptive. I usually use the computer name or something like *<Computername>*DriveX. For instance, for a computer named Admin, my share name for drive C is AdminDriveC. (See the "Allowed Length of Share Name Can Be Confusing" for more information on share name length restrictions if you have DOS computers on your network).

When you share a drive, it becomes just another share in the hierarchy that is displayed when connected users view a computer in Explorer or Network Neighborhood.

In addition to providing access to the entire computer by sharing the hard drive, you can share peripheral drives on any computer. That means a CD-ROM drive, a Zip drive, a Jaz drive, or even a floppy drive can be accessed by connected users who have permission. This is a great way to save money on hardware. For instance, I use a 1GB Jaz drive on one workstation to back up data from several connected computers, using two different methods. On a daily basis I back up data from every computer to one Jaz disk (each computer has its own directory on the disk). On a weekly basis I back up each computer, in its entirety, to its own Jaz disk. I can collect everything from the workstation that has the Jaz drive attached, or have it sent from each connected computer. For more details about creative and useful methods for backing up, see Chapter 14.

Creating Shares for Peripherals

When we use the words "share" and "peripherals" in the same sentence, we're talking about printers. Most of the other peripherals you'll want to share are CD-ROMs and Zip/Jaz drives, and they're called "drives" instead of peripherals. Sharing printers, however, is one of the most common uses of shares in any network environment.

I'm not going to go into the steps and troubleshooting tips for sharing printers here; you'll have to read Chapter 11.

Creating Shares with Server Manager

You don't have to sit in front of a computer and open Explorer to go through the steps of creating a share. You can use Server Manager to set up shares all over your network (including the server you're sitting in front of).

Open Server Manager (on the Administrative Tools submenu of your Start menu) and select the computer on which you want to create a share. Choose Computer, Shared Directories from the menu bar. When the Shared Directories dialog box opens, you'll see a display of the existing shares for the computer. Choose New Share to bring up the New Share dialog box seen in Figure 7-3.

Enter the share name. You are restricted to 12 characters for a share name when you use Server Manager. (I know; the Share Name box has room for more than 12 characters, but you'll get a beep at the 13th character and won't be able to enter any additional characters.)

Enter the path to the directory you want to share. You must enter the fully qualified path, including the drive letter; you cannot use *directoryname*. And sorry, but there's no Browse button, so you have to know the name of the directory before you begin.

NOTE: Actually, a Browse button wouldn't do you a lot of good, because until a share is established not even an administrator can access a directory or drive on a remote computer through Explorer or Network Neighborhood. However, as a lazy person, I can think of some ways to make this a more productive process. For example, if I were designing Server Manager's New Share process, I'd let an administrator create a share for the hard drive, then make Browse available to see the directories on that drive. After shares had been created for applicable directories, the shared drive could be removed, having outlived its usefulness as a browser. Actually you can perform an end run that does just that. First, create a share for the drive, then open Network Neighborhood or expand the Network Neighborhood object in Explorer. You'll see the names of all of the directories. Then return to Server Manager and create the directory shares you need. A Browse button would just be less onerous.

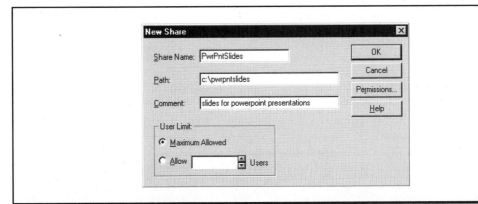

Figure 7-3.   Using Server Manager to create shares saves you the bother of running all over the building

Creating Shares with the Administrative Wizards

Windows NT 4 Server has a feature called Administrative Wizards, found on the Administrative Tools submenu. There are all sorts of nifty administrative things you can do with this program, as you can see in Figure 7-4.

In this case, of course, we'll select Managing File and Folder Access. Like all wizards, this one will ask questions, ask for selections, and provide a Next button to move on to each step.

The first wizard window asks if you want to make folders and files available on this computer or another computer. If you opt to use the wizard for remote computers, you're shown a list of computers on the network. Select the one you want to work with and choose Next.

The Wizard Has Some Behavior Problems

A weird problem with this program rears its head at this point. First of all, if you're following along on your own computer, you're probably aware that there is no help available for this wizard. There's also nothing about the Administrative Wizards in the Windows NT Help system. And almost all of the books about Windows NT 4 ignore this feature. So this discussion of the peculiarities in the Managing Folder and File Access Wizard consists of things I've learned on my own, with no additional assistance or

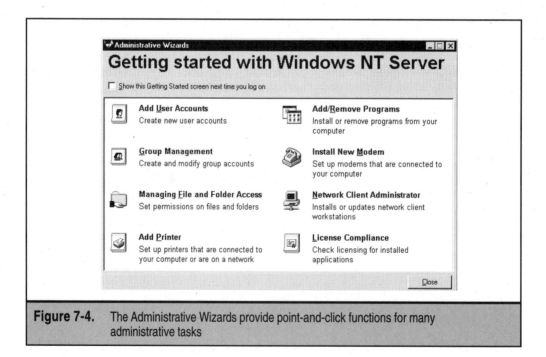

Figure 7-4.   The Administrative Wizards provide point-and-click functions for many administrative tasks

explanations from Microsoft's support team, knowledge base, or troubleshooting wizards. I say that so you'll understand you're not getting expert advice here, just the feedback of one user.

The Wizard and Windows 95 Clients

If the computer you select is a Windows 95 client, when you click Next, it's over. One of two things happens:

▼ A dialog box appears with the following message: "An error occurred while listing shares on the selected computer."

▲ You die of boredom. There's no error message, but there's also no hourglass. Absolutely nothing happens. When you get bored or impatient enough to open Task Manager, you'll see that the task Managing Folder and File Access has a status of Not Running. Click End Task.

There's no particular pattern here. It's not every other time that you get the error message, or every third time (and the rest of the time you wait forever). It seems to be totally a matter of whim. Regardless, it's clear that you can't work with Windows 95 machines from this wizard.

The Wizard and Windows NT Computers

If you select a computer running Windows NT (either Server or Workstation), the next wizard window displays the computer's default administrative share. We'll discuss this administrative share later in this chapter, but for now take my word that in Figure 7-5 you're looking at an icon representing the computer's hard drive (the drive that is the Windows NT 4 boot drive).

Hooray, a way to browse—double-click the administrative share to see a display of all the folders and files on the drive. When the display is presented, the contents of the drive are in alphabetical order, regardless of the type of object. It's not "folders first, then files"; it's totally alphabetical (see Figure 7-6).

Select the folder you want to share. The folder expands to display any subfolders or files, and the bottom of the dialog box displays the path as C$*directoryname*.

Here can occur another whimsical display of erratic behavior from the Managing Folder and File Access Wizard. Sometimes, at this point in the procedure, you get a Dr. Watson error, followed by a shutdown of the wizard. I played with this over and over for some time, and the only clue I have is that I seemed to get the Dr. Watson error whenever Explorer was open on the target computer. That may or may not be a coincidence.

If the good doctor doesn't show up, the next window shows you the current permissions for the folder (see Figure 7-7). By default, an administrator has Full Access permissions, and the group called Everyone has Change permissions. You can use the options in this window to change those permissions, but for now we'll leave them (there's

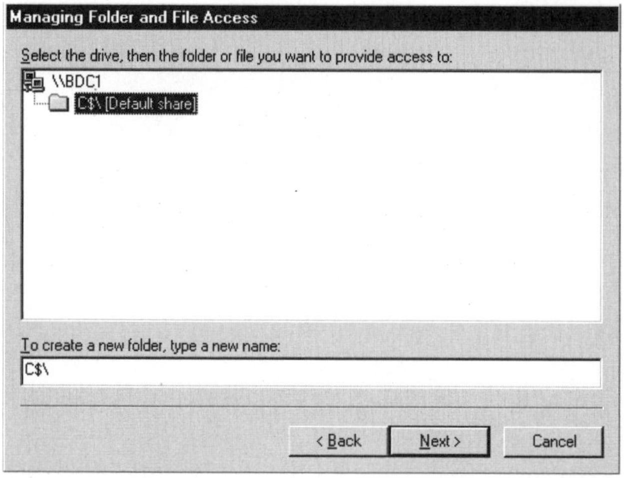

Figure 7-5. The hard drive is accessible for a Windows NT computer when you use the wizard to create shares

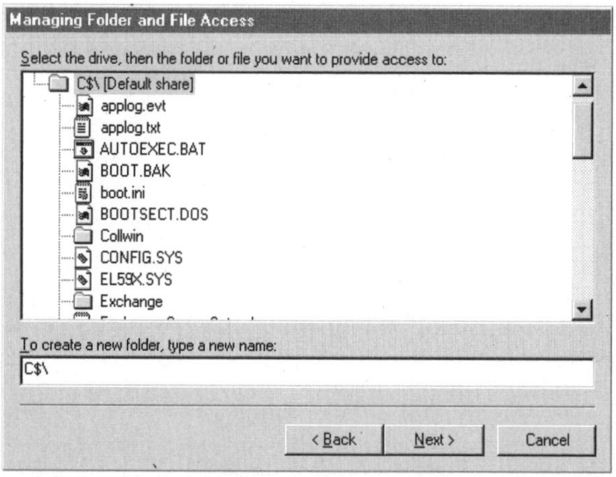

Figure 7-6. The contents of this hard drive are displayed, so it's easy to select a directory to share

Managing Folder and File Access

These are the current permissions:

Name	Permissions
Administrators	Full access
Everyone	Change

You can keep these permissions or change them. What do you want to do?

○ Keep the original permissions

○ Change permissions
   ○ Only I have access and full control
   ○ I have access and full control, everyone else can only read it
   ○ Everyone has access and full control

☑ Apply these permissions to all folders and files within this folder.

[< Back] [Next >] [Cancel]

Figure 7-7. The default permissions for the directory and its contents are usually exactly what you'll need for sharing the directory

rarely a compelling reason to change them). More information about groups and permissions is available later in this chapter, in the section called "Setting Share Permissions."

Choosing Next brings up the important dialog box, the one asking if you're trying to create a share. As seen here, it requires a simple click of the Yes button to create this share.

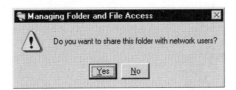

Now you can name the share (12 characters or less, please) and enter an optional description (see "Naming Shares," later in this chapter). You can also indicate which user platform can access this share. The choices are Windows, NetWare, and Macintosh, but the choices are accessible only if those platforms are connected to this network (see Figure 7-8).

Now that all the pertinent information has been delivered to the wizard, you have a chance to check the decisions you made. The summary screen, shown in Figure 7-9, reflects the status of your new share. Click Back and return to the appropriate window if you want to change anything. Click Finish if it all looks right.

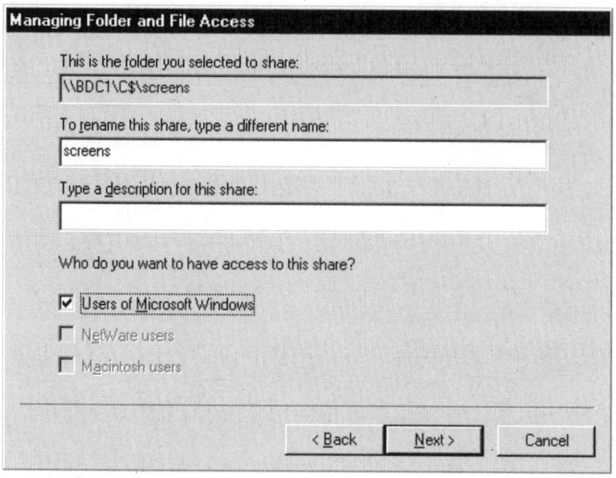

Managing Folder and File Access

This is the folder you selected to share:

\\BDC1\C$\screens

To rename this share, type a different name:

screens

Type a description for this share:

Who do you want to have access to this share?

☑ Users of Microsoft Windows

☐ NetWare users

☐ Macintosh users

< Back   Next >   Cancel

Figure 7-8.   The LAN this computer resides on has no NetWare or Macintosh services, so those choices are grayed out

The wizard, apparently pleased with the success of the operation, displays a dialog box asking if you want to create another share. Answer Yes or No depending on your need (or mood).

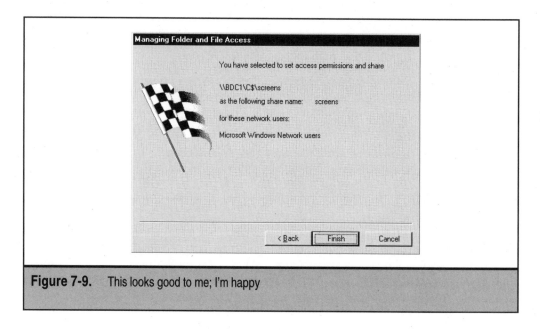

Managing Folder and File Access

You have selected to set access permissions and share

\\BDC1\C$\screens

as the following share name: screens

for these network users:

Microsoft Windows Network users

< Back   Finish   Cancel

Figure 7-9.   This looks good to me; I'm happy

Creating Shares at the Command Line

You can use a command prompt to create a share on the local computer. The command for creating shares is Net Share, and it has the following syntax:

net share *sharename=drive:path* [/users:*number* | /unlimited] [/remark:"*text*"] [/delete]

where:

sharename is the name of the shared resource (if there is a space in the name, use quotation marks)

CAUTION: You are limited to 12 characters for the share name if you create the share with the Net Share command.

drive:path is the full path to the share

/users:*number* sets the maximum number of users who can access the share simultaneously

/unlimited sets the number of users who can access the share simultaneously as unlimited

/remark:"*text*" adds text that is used as a description of the share (the text must be enclosed in quotation marks)

/delete stops sharing of the resource

Enter **net share** with no parameters to display information about the shares on the local computer. Figure 7-10 shows an example of the information that's returned.

Enter **net share** *sharename* to display information about that share (use quotation marks for share names that contain one or more spaces). The system returns information about the share, as seen in Figure 7-11.

NOTE: The Net Share command will not accept a UNC path as a parameter, because the command works only on the local computer.

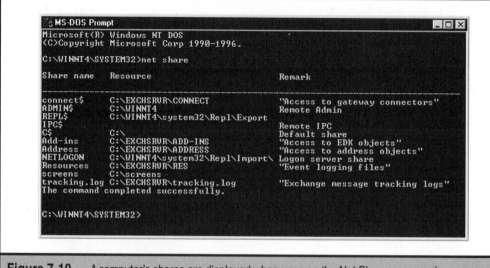

Figure 7-10. A computer's shares are displayed when you use the Net Share command

You cannot set permissions for a shared resource via the command line, although the default permissions are automatically applied. After you've created the share, you can open Explorer, select the share, and reset the permissions. See the section "Setting Share Permissions," later in this chapter.

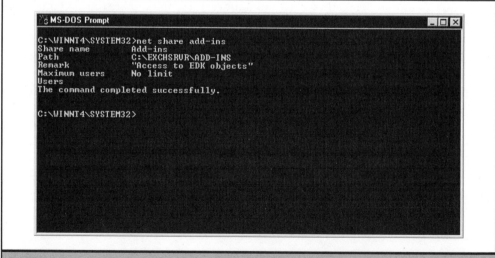

Figure 7-11. The specific information about a local share is available with the Net Share command when you include the share name

NAMING SHARES

When the Properties dialog box opens, the Sharing tab is in the foreground and Windows NT 4 has already filled in the name of the share, using the directory name. Actually, the default name is derived from the last part of the path, so if you're creating a share for \Documents\Legal\Projectx, the default name of the share will be "Projectx."

You may want to change the name to something more descriptive. For example, the share name "PwrPntSlides" will probably work as users search for the slides they need to prepare a company presentation in PowerPoint. But the share name "screens" is a bit enigmatic and should be changed to something more descriptive, such as "Figures" or "ScreenShots" for those users looking for screen shots to be used as figures in technical reference documents. In fact, "Projectx" doesn't work well either, because there could be a lot of different reasons that users need to work on Project x, and there may be a \Projectx subdirectory under several different types of data directories.

It's also a good idea to enter a description of the share, to make it easy for connected users to understand what's in the directory. For drives, a simple explanation of the drive and the computer it's on is the best approach to naming the share—for instance, Accntg or Server4. Use the Comment field to add explanations such as "Accounting Software Server" or "Server on 4th Floor" or whatever it takes to let users know which machine your share represents.

There are some caveats about naming shares:

▼ You can use up to 80 characters in a share name, and you can use special characters such as @, #,!, and spaces, but that usually makes it harder to read and understand the share name. (There is a special use for $, covered later in this chapter.)

■ If you have Windows 3.x clients, they will not see shares unless the share names fall within the 8.3 specification. Windows NT and Windows 95 provide 8.3 translations for long filenames for the DOS Redirector, but they do not perform that service for share names. The DOS Redirector also gets confused and balky over nonalphanumeric characters and spaces. In fact, if you choose a share name that cannot be seen by the DOS Redirector, you'll see this message:

▲ If you have a space in a share name, you will have to use quotation marks to access it in a command or in a path (UNC) reference. I'm much too lazy to do that, so I find it better to use WidgetSpecs instead of Widget Specs or Widget_Specs (typing an underscore is a pain).

There are some additional anomalies with share names, and they're covered later in this chapter, in the section "Troubleshooting Shares."

SETTING USER LIMITS

When you create a share, you're asked to set a limit on the number of users who can access this share simultaneously. You can either permit the maximum allowed number of users (which is the default choice) or specify a number of simultaneous users who can work in this share. Setting your own maximum is a good idea if you feel it's advisable to limit the activity on a given computer. If a shared application uses an extraordinary number of resources—perhaps generating a great deal of I/O action—it might be more productive to limit the users (so the folks who get there can work productively).

The maximum number allowed varies. For a server, it's the maximum number of users for which you've purchased Windows NT licenses. For an NT workstation there's a built-in limit of 10 simultaneous users for a shared resource.

When a user attempts to access a share that already has the maximum number of users, an error message is generated. For Windows 95 clients, the error message is "An extended error has occurred"—not one of the most helpful error messages an operating system has produced. For Windows NT clients, the error message is "No more connections can be made to this remote computer at this time because there are already as many connections as the computer allows." Now that's an error message that explains things!

SETTING SHARE PERMISSIONS

Nobody gets into a share without having permission to do so. Of course, most of the time the reason for creating a share is to make it accessible, so the default permission scheme for a share is "everybody can do whatever they want to." You can, of course, change this, and the reasons for doing so depend on the contents of the share. You can set permissions for individuals, for the groups you've established in User Manager, and also for special groups that exist in Windows NT for the purpose of assigning rights and permissions.

Understanding Special Groups

The groups you see and work with in User Manager (users, guests, and so on) aren't the only groups that exist in a Windows NT environment. There are other groups (also called Identities) that are used for assigning permissions. These special groups are

▼ **Everyone**, which means everyone. It means all users, including guest logons and users from other domains.

■ **Creator Owner**, which represents the user who created a file or a directory.

■ **System**, which represents the operating system. The permissions that are given to System permit the operating system to get its work done. It's usually disastrous to mess around with permissions for System.

■ **Interactive**, which is for the logged-on user who is sitting in front of the computer.

▲ **Network**, which means any user who accesses a directory or a file through the network.

For setting share permissions for groups, we really only concern ourselves with Everyone and Creator Owner. The other groups are either automatically disqualified or automatically qualified when matched against these two groups.

Understanding Permissions

There are four permission levels that can be assigned to a group or individuals for shares:

▼ **No Access**, which means the group or user cannot access the share or any subdirectories or files in the share.

■ **Read**, which gives the group or user the right to view filenames and subdirectory names, move to any subdirectories in the share, run any applications contained in the share, and view the data in the files created by those applications (unless the data file is protected).

■ **Change**, which gives all the rights given to Read, and also grants rights to add files and subdirectories to the share, remove files and subdirectories from the share, and change the data of files (usually by loading the files into applications).

▲ **Full Control**, which gives all the rights given to Change, plus rights to change permissions.

You can set permissions for individual users, groups, and the special identity groups. Right-click the share and use the Permissions button on the Sharing tab to see the Access Through Share Permissions dialog box shown in Figure 7-12.

Permissions for NTFS Systems

The dialog box that appears when you create a share in an NTFS system has an additional tab, Security (see Figure 7-13).

▼ The Permissions button lets you replace the permissions for the files or the subdirectories (or both) in the share.

■ The Auditing button lets you establish or view auditing specifications for the share.

▲ The Ownership button lets you take ownership of the share or view the current owner.

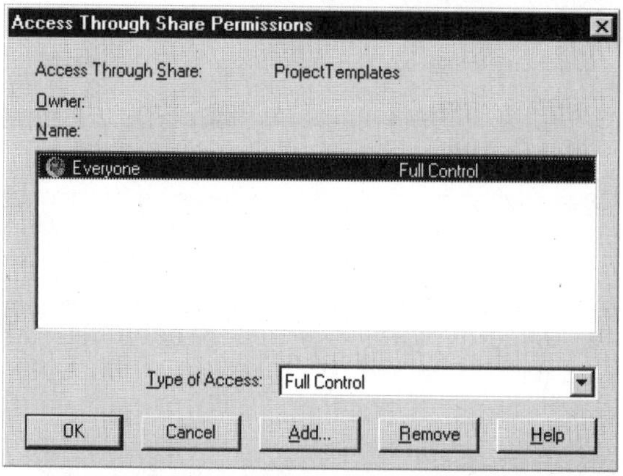

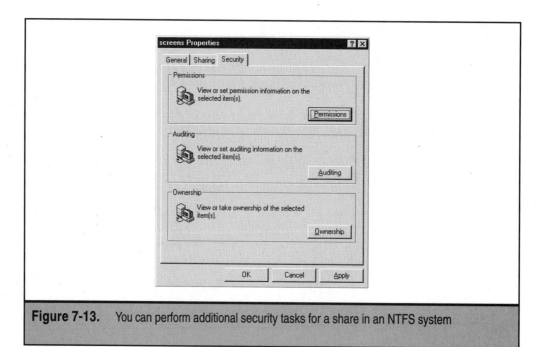

Figure 7-12.   It's easy to set or change permissions with this dialog box

The permissions attached to the files and subdirectories in a shared directory aren't ignored when you set permissions for the share. Both sets of permissions are active, and for any individual user, the rule is that the most restrictive permission applies while the user is accessing the share.

Figure 7-13.   You can perform additional security tasks for a share in an NTFS system

Permissions for FAT Systems

The permissions you set for a share in a FAT system are also, automatically, the permissions for all the subdirectories and files in the share. The only reason to add individuals or groups to the permissions scheme is if you've changed the permissions of the special group Everyone.

HIDING SHARES

There are occasionally good reasons to hide a share from the general user group. There may be confidential work going on, or there may be some temporary project to which you want to limit access.

To hide a share, use $ as the last character in the share name. You can use any share name except for those reserved for the system (see the next section, "Special System Shares").

When a share is hidden, it cannot be seen from Network Neighborhood, nor by expanding the Network Neighborhood object in Explorer. Hidden shares can be accessed by those users to whom you tell the share name in any of several ways:

▼ By mapping the share name to a drive letter in Explorer (check the Reconnect at Logon button to avoid having to do this every day)

■ By mapping the share name to a drive letter with the Net Use command (use the Persistent:Yes parameter to reconnect at the next logon)

▲ By entering the UNC for the share in the Run box of the Start menu

The first two options also provide a way to make the share permanent, which saves the user a lot of work.

One of the advantages of hiding a share is to avoid all of the work needed to specify permissions for the small number of users who require access to the share. It's easier to notify those folks of the share name and let them find their own way there.

If you create a hidden share for a directory whose parent directory is shared, you've defeated your purpose. If the parent directory is available as a share, any user can see all of its subdirectories and access all of the files in those subdirectories, including the directory for which you created a hidden share. Remember, you aren't hiding the directory, you're hiding the share. This means that if you want to have hidden shares you cannot share the drive on which the shared directory resides.

SPECIAL SYSTEM SHARES

Some shares are created by the Windows NT 4 operating system, and these special shares shouldn't be touched. Depending on the configuration of the computer, you may see some or all of the following special system shares:

▼ *Driveletter*$, which exists to allow administrators a way to connect to the root directory of a drive. In Windows NT 4 Server, members of the Administrators,

Backup Operators, and Server Operators groups can see these shares. In Windows NT Workstation, only members of the Administrators and Backup Operators groups can see them. There are no *Driveletter$* administrative shares for drives with removable media (CD-ROMs, floppy drives, and so on).

■ Admin$, which is a shared resource for members of groups, as explained in the previous paragraph. This share is really the path to the Windows NT system root.

■ Ipc$, which is a shared resource for named pipes. These pipes (communication channels) are used to communicate when you are viewing or administering a remote computer.

■ Print$, which is a shared resource used for administering printers remotely.

■ Repl$, which is found on Windows NT Servers that are configured for replication.

▲ Netlogon, which is found on Windows NT Servers to use for processing domain logons.

TROUBLESHOOTING SHARES

There really aren't too many problems with shares, because if you create them properly and set the permissions carefully, they work smoothly and efficiently. However, there a couple of glitches you should be aware of.

Renaming a Shared Directory

If you change the name of a directory that's shared, you destroy the share. You must re-create the share and reconfigure the permissions.

Allowed Length of Share Name Can Be Confusing

Microsoft has some confusing mixed signals and mixed rules about the length of share names. It's pretty simple to understand that if a share name exceeds the 8.3 file specification rule, DOS and Windows 3.x workstations won't see it. However, what isn't widely circulated is the fact that many Windows for Workgroups (WFW) clients won't see a share if the share name doesn't meet the 8.3 specification. I know it sounds ridiculous to say "many," but I've seen WFW clients that could and some that couldn't—and I have absolutely no explanation for that (neither did the tech support person I talked to at Microsoft, who also was aware of this erratic behavior).

TIP: If you create a share name for a directory or drive that exceeds the 8.3 specs, you see a warning. However, for some reason Microsoft did not include that warning when you're creating printer shares. The rule holds, however: the printer won't be seen if it's name exceeds the specifications. It's just that the warning doesn't appear. Bear that in mind.

Technically, WFW clients should see any share name that does not exceed 12 characters when using File Manager. If you create a share using File Manager, you are limited to 12 characters. However, a WFW user can enter **net use drive: ***computername***** *sharename* at a command prompt, using a share name of any length, and connect successfully.

Windows 95 clients also have a problem with share names if those share names exceed 12 characters. A Windows 95 client using Network Neighborhood will not see any share name that exceeds 12 characters. Microsoft's documentation says that a share name in excess of 12 characters will be seen when the Network Neighborhood object is expanded in Explorer—don't believe it! A Windows 95 user can enter **net use drive: ***computername******sharename* at a command prompt, using a share name of any length, and connect successfully.

TIP: The 12-character limit for Windows 95 comes from the fact that technically, while browsing, Windows 95 announces it's an 8.3 client. In fact, it's not, so the combined number of characters available in an 8.3 name is permitted (remember, the period counts as a character). Just one of those useless facts that makes good cocktail chatter.

Unless your network is solidly NT, it's a good idea to keep share names (including names of shared resources such as printers) to a 12-character limit.

WINDOWS
NT
Professional
Library

CHAPTER 8

User Profiles

In Windows NT, the arrangement of the desktop, the software listed on the Start menu, the mouse settings, and other configuration selections can be altered by a user, and those alterations are remembered in that user's profile and loaded whenever that user logs on. If more than one user has access to the same computer, that user will see his or her own, personal configuration because logging on invokes the profile attached to the logon name.

As an administrator, most of your work with profiles involves Window NT Workstation (as opposed to NT Server), because that's where the users are. You have numerous options for dealing with the issue of user profiles, ranging from ignoring them and letting users do whatever they wish to maintaining absolute control over them and prohibiting users from making changes (and a couple of choices in between).

Profiles are automatic with Windows NT 4 and are optional in Windows 95. If you have Windows 95 clients on your network, profiles can be administered in a manner similar to Windows NT 4 profiles, and so Windows 95 profiles are covered in this chapter.

You'll find you can do a great deal of preventive troubleshooting by setting profile policies that limit what users can and cannot do. In this chapter we'll discuss how profiles work and the various ways you can manipulate them.

HOW WINDOWS NT 4 PROFILES LOAD

In the standard Windows NT 4 configuration, information about each user profile is kept in two places: the registry and the user's profile folder on the local hard drive. When Windows starts, the default profile (a profile that is placed on the computer during the installation of the operating system) is loaded at the time the Press CTRL-ALT-DEL to Log On dialog box appears. When a logon name is entered, the registry is searched for the logon name in order to determine whether or not there is a profile for that logon name. If there is, the profile is loaded (it's cached) from the hive stored in the user's profile folder. If the current logon name does not appear in the list of profiles, the default profile stays loaded and is copied to a profile bearing the new user's name.

By default, profiles are stored on the user's local hard drive and are called local profiles. You can also store profiles on a server, which is usually done when you want to control the user's environment (mandatory profiles) or deliver the profile to the user regardless of which computer is being used (roaming profiles). Mandatory and roaming profiles are discussed later in this chapter.

The following settings are contained in a user profile:

▼ Taskbar settings

■ Settings for all software listed under Accessories

■ Explorer settings

■ Help bookmarks

■ Control Panel applet settings

- ■ Printer connections (for remote printers)
- ▲ Windows application settings (if the application is configured to accept and remember individual user settings)

The information is gathered from several places:

- ▼ The registry (via the hive stored on the hard drive)
- ■ The information in the subfolders under the user's profile folder on the hard drive
- ▲ The information in the All Users folders on the hard drive

Profile Information in the Windows NT 4 Registry

When a user logs on, the operating system startup process checks the name in the logon dialog box and then searches the registry in HKEY_LOCAL_MACHINE\SOFTWARE\Microsoft\Windows NT\CurrentVersion\ProfileList to see if there is a profile listed for this user name. For the workstation illustrated in Figure 8-1, there have been multiple users accessing this computer, and system startup has located the current logon name (Kathy Ivens).

TIP: You can't read the subkey and figure out who's who, but if you select a subkey you can learn who that user is because there's a path statement for the user's hive file.

If the logon name does not exist in the profile list, the default user profile is loaded, then copied and saved as the profile for the new logon name (see the section "The Default User Profile," later in this chapter).

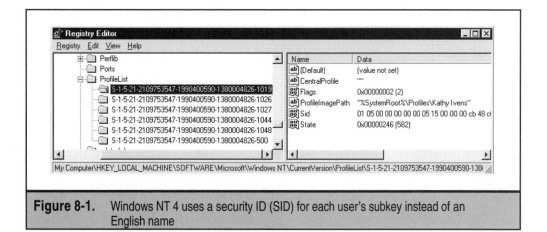

Figure 8-1.   Windows NT 4 uses a security ID (SID) for each user's subkey instead of an English name

If the logon name exists in the profile list, the user's profile is loaded from the registry hive file, Ntuser.dat. That file exists on the user's hard drive in the \%SystemRoot%\ Profiles\Username folder, an example of which is seen in Figure 8-2.

NOTE: Along with Ntuser.dat, each user's profile folder contains a file named Ntuser.dat.log, which is the previously saved version of Ntuser.dat. This backup is made whenever the user makes changes that affect the profile.

The Ntuser.dat file is the registry portion of the current user's profile, and the information comes from HKEY_CURRENT_USER.

Profile Information on the Windows NT 4 Hard Drive

Each user profile has subfolders beneath \%SystemRoot%\Profiles\Username. These subfolders contain specific information about that user's configuration. For instance, the Accessories subfolder shown in Figure 8-3 displays the objects installed for this user that appear on the Start menu. Figure 8-4 is the Start menu itself, and you can see the relationship between the cascading menu items and the subfolders in the user's profile folder.

In Windows NT you can see all user profiles and their configuration settings both in the registry and on the hard drive.

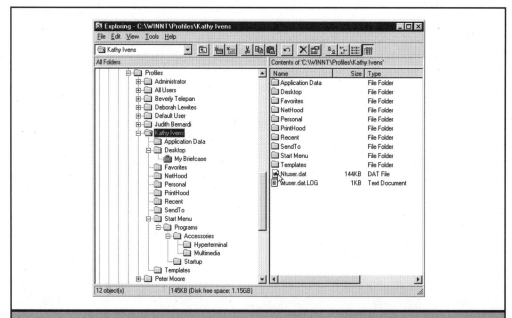

Figure 8-2.   The registry hive for the profile is kept in this user's profile folder on the local hard drive

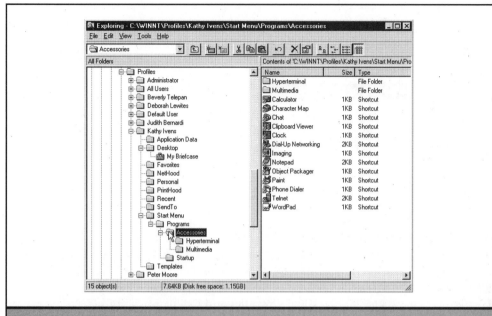

Figure 8-3. The \%SystemRoot%\Profiles\Username\Start Menu\Programs\Accessories folder reflects this user's installation choices

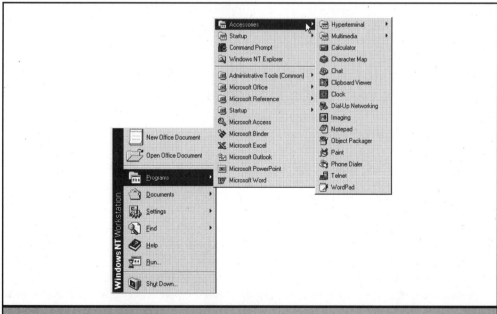

Figure 8-4. The Accessories menu reflects the structure of the user's profile folders—the arrows for additional cascading menus represent additional subfolders

> *NOTE:*   If you enable roaming or mandatory profiles, you can store the profiles on the server. These
> options are covered later in this chapter.

PROFILES IN WINDOWS 95 CLIENTS

Windows 95 does not require logon names or profiles. However, you can enable a logon dialog box to process a logon to your NT network (in fact, you've probably already done that). Unlike Windows NT, Windows 95 allows the user to bypass the logon by pressing the ESC key at the logon dialog box and end up working locally. You can also enable profiles so that multiple users for that computer can customize and save their own workstation settings.

Profile Information in the Windows 95 Registry

When you view the Windows 95 registry to examine profile information, you look in HKEY_USERS. That key has one subkey if profiles have not been enabled, and that subkey contains the default configuration that is offered to all users who have not logged on with a specific logon name. The subkey is named .DEFAULT (notice that there's a period at the front of the subkey name). If profiles have been enabled and the current user has logged on by name in order to load his or her profile, there is a second subkey in the registry with that user's name. The registry shows you only the Default and current user subkeys because the registry is not searched for all known users during logon—instead the hard drive is searched for the current user's profile file and the information in that file is written back to the registry. Each Windows 95 user that has logged on with profiles enabled has a profile folder on the hard drive. This is the opposite of the way Windows NT works with profiles during logon.

Profile Information on the Windows 95 Hard Drive

The profile file (we don't use the term "hive" in Windows 95) for the default configuration is found in \%SystemRoot% and is named User.dat. Any user that is not logged on with a specific logon name (any user can avoid giving a logon name by pressing the ESC key when the logon dialog box appears) makes changes to this file when configuration changes are made. The last version is then saved in a backup file named User.da0.

Once the Windows 95 system is configured for UserName logons and user customization of preferences is enabled, a new subfolder is placed into the \%SystemRoot folder. The new folder is named Profiles, and it contains additional subfolders for each user who has logged on to this Windows 95 computer. There is a User.dat file (and a User.da0 file) in each user's folder. As configuration changes are made, they are written to the logged-on user's User.dat file. The next time this user logs on, the configuration in that file is passed to the registry and the user's configuration options are loaded for the session.

Subfolders beneath the user's profile folder hold specific information about this configuration (see Figure 8-5).

TIP: Windows 95 users frequently enable profiles and logon passwords even if the machine is a stand-alone computer. This is a great way for parents to keep desktops separate from those of their kids on the family home computer (and hide the desktop shortcut and menu listing for the accounting software). Of course, because of the total lack of security in Windows 95, any user can access any folder or file, so the kids can get to the family bookkeeping program as soon as they learn how to use Explorer or My Computer. If you use Windows 95 at home, make sure you password-protect the files you want to keep private (assuming the software you use permits it), because there's no such thing as administrative rights.

THE DEFAULT USER PROFILE

.In Windows NT, the default user profile represents the configuration created as a result of installation decisions (in Windows 95 it represents the current configuration, which may have been changed by any user who bypassed the logon dialog box in order to work locally). The first time a user logs on to the workstation, the default user profile is copied to the user's profile. Then, as changes are made, they are saved in that user's profile. Changes made to profiles are written to both the profile file and the registry.

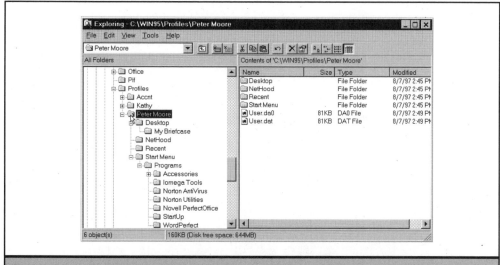

Figure 8-5.   The names of some of the subfolders differ from those in Windows NT 4, but the tree structure of the user profile is similar

Tweaking the default user profile is a good way to ensure that each user who logs on to a workstation for the first time has what he or she needs (or what you, as the administrator, have decided the configuration should be). In Windows NT 4, of course, you cannot log on as "default user," so you have to use other means of tweaking the profile. You can work with the folders in Explorer and the registry. You can also use the Policy Editor to change the default user configuration (see Chapter 10 for information about using the Policy Editor).

Changing the Default Profile in the NT Registry

In Windows NT 4, the default profile is stored in the registry in HKEY_USERS\DEFAULT, as seen in Figure 8-6.

To change the registry settings for the default user profile, follow these steps:

1. Launch Regedt32 from the Run command on the Start menu.

2. Select HKEY_USERS on Local Machine.

3. Choose Registry, Load Hive from the menu bar.

4. In the Load Hive dialog box, move to \%SystemRoot%\Profiles\Default User.

5. Select Ntuser.dat as the file to load.

6. In the Key Name field that appears, enter **ntuser** and choose OK.

7. Make changes to the registry subkeys as desired (an overview of the registry keys follows these instructions).

8. Choose Registry, Unload Hive from the menu bar. You'll be asked to confirm your action, so answer Yes.

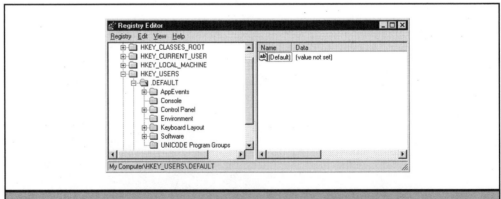

Figure 8-6.   Default registry settings for users who log on to this computer are stored in HKEY_USERS\DEFAULT

TIP: You can add new subkeys if you wish. When you do, you must highlight the new subkey and choose Security, Permissions from the menu bar and make sure that all users have at least Read access to this key. If you fail to do this, the key won't be copied to the user profile when a new user logs on.

The subkeys under HKEY_USERS\DEFAULT determine an enormous amount of the configuration for users. Here is an overview of the contents of this key.

Default User AppEvents Settings

The AppEvents subkey controls the sounds that are associated with system events, as well as sounds associated with installed programs (if the programs establish their events in the registry during installation). It has two subkeys: EventLabels and Schemes.

The EventLabels subkey contains the sounds available on this computer along with their standard associations.

The Schemes subkey lists the actual associations between sounds and events.

Default User Console Settings

The Console subkey controls the characteristics of any text-based window (the command prompt window or the window for a text-based application). You can get an idea of the controls in Figure 8-7.

Figure 8-7. The appearance of the console window is controlled by these registry entries

Default User Control Panel Settings

The Control Panel subkeys represent some of the items users can configure via the applets in the Control Panel. As you can see in Figure 8-8, in addition to the devices and settings you'd expect to see, Windows NT also stores settings for screen savers that were installed during the setup of the operating system.

Default User Environment Settings

The Environment subkey holds user variables used during NT logon. It's the same type of information you loaded via Autoexec.bat when you used DOS or Windows 3.x. Because a great deal of the environment information you formerly put into Autoexec.bat to create the environment is now handled by NT system functions, the data for the default user profile is usually limited to naming the location of the temporary directory (usually %SystemDrive%\Temp or %SystemDrive%\%SystemRoot%\Temp).

For logged-on users, settings for this registry key are changed in the System applet in Control Panel. Two sets of variables are found in an NT 4 system: System Variables and User Variables. The System Variables remain the same regardless of the logged-on user (they're machine based). Users can place additional User Variables into their environment by entering a variable and a value in the Environment tab of the System Properties dialog box.

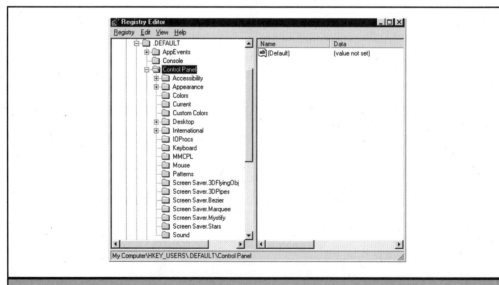

Figure 8-8. To change Control Panel settings for the default profile, you must use the registry, because you cannot log on as the default user in order to use Control Panel applets

Default User Keyboard Layout Settings

This subkey specifies the primary keyboard layout. There are two subkeys: Preload (which contains a pointer to the code page for the keyboard layout) and Substitutes (which has no value in the default user profile, but users can configure their systems for a substitute keyboard layout). This subkey differs from the Keyboard subkey under the Control Panel key, which holds speed and other user settings.

Default User Network Settings

Don't panic if you don't see this subkey in your default user key of the registry. It usually exists only if you upgraded from an earlier version of Windows NT Workstation (you almost certainly won't see it in a Server registry). If you do have this subkey, it probably contains additional subkeys for persistent connections (mapped drives that are connected at logon).

Default User Printer Settings

This is another key you probably don't have in your default user key, but if you do see it (again, due to an upgrade), it contains information about remote printer connections.

Default User Software Settings

This key holds subkeys for system and applications software that has been registered with the registry. As seen in Figure 8-9, the default user profile generally contains little more than a Microsoft subkey.

Default User UNICODE Program Groups Settings

This key contains subkeys for programs that use UNICODE, and each subkey has specific settings for its associated program. I've never seen any entry in the default user section

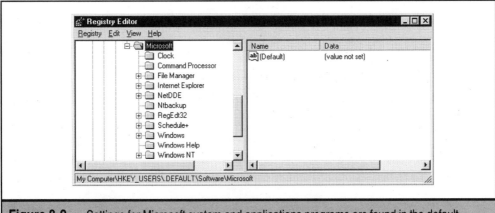

Figure 8-9.   Settings for Microsoft system and applications programs are found in the default user's profile subkey

of the NT Workstation registry for this key (although I have run into default user settings on some servers).

Changing the Default User's Profile Folders

The profile folder for the default user is found on the hard drive in \%SystemRoot%\ Profiles. As seen in Figure 8-10, it has subfolders for a variety of configuration options. Most of the subfolders are empty, but the Programs subfolder usually contains the Accessories cascading menu items, the Startup group (which is usually empty), the Command Prompt, and Explorer.

TIP: I usually copy the Explorer shortcut in the Programs subfolder to the Desktop subfolder, to ensure that all users have access to this handy desktop shortcut.

USING THE PROFILE FOLDERS TO MAKE CHANGES

You can open Explorer (or My Computer) and work directly in the user profile folders to add items to the profile. When you expand \%SystemRoot%\Profiles\UserName, you can see the subfolders that act as containers for additional profile information (see Figure 8-11). Notice that I said additional information, because most of the existing configuration information that is in the registry and the hive is not replicated in the folders on the hard drive. You can think of the basic profile information as being taken for granted, such as the fact that the standard objects (My Computer, Network Neighborhood, and so on) are

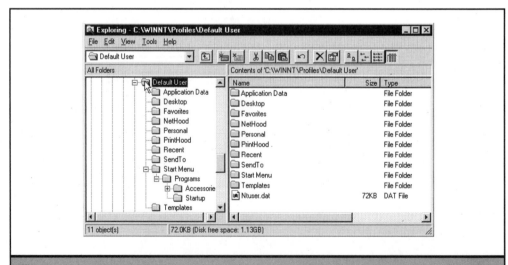

Figure 8-10. You can manipulate the items in the profile folders to add objects to the default user profile

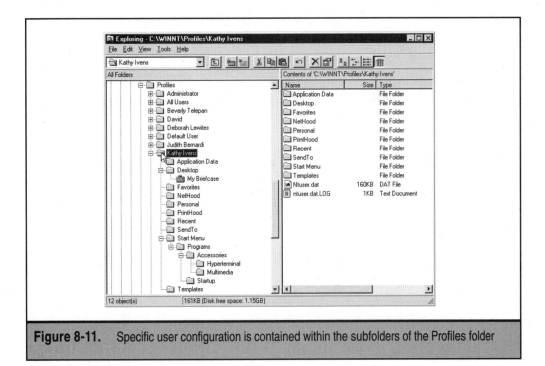

Figure 8-11.   Specific user configuration is contained within the subfolders of the Profiles folder

on the desktop. Changes made by adding or removing folder objects are written to the user hive and registry.

Copy Program Objects to Another User's Start Menu

If a logged-on user installs software and the computer is used by another user, that software doesn't appear on the Start menu for the other user. The odds are that the second user will need the same software and might go through an entire installation process. If the installation folder chosen by the second user is different from the original installation, you could end up with a whole lot of hard drive space being used up (especially if the software doesn't check for existing copies).

If one user has installed programs that you want additional users to have access to, just copy the Start menu items from one user's profile to another user's profile:

1. Open the Programs subfolder of the source profile and right-click the program object.

2. Choose Copy from the shortcut menu.

3. Move to the target Programs subfolder, right-click, and paste.

When the target user next logs on, the item is on his or her menu. This process works for both Windows NT 4 and Windows 95.

TIP: To do the same thing for multiple users, just keep opening subfolders and choosing Paste from the shortcut menu.

Copy Desktop Shortcuts to Another User's Desktop

You can use the same theory to copy shortcuts from one user's desktop to another user's desktop (or to multiple user desktops). Open the Desktop subfolder of the source user and select one, some, or all of the handy shortcuts. Then copy them to the appropriate target Desktop subfolder(s). This process works for both Windows NT 4 and Windows 95.

Be careful about the shortcuts you move—some users create shortcuts to documents or folders they've created for special purposes, and those items aren't needed by other users (in fact, sometimes it's none of their business). It's best to copy only those shortcuts that launch applications or that point to folders that all users access (perhaps folders created to hold documents for companywide projects).

Place Common Programs on Every User's Menu

You can add common program groups to the Start menu of every user's profile automatically. Windows NT 4 creates a special profile folder called All Users, which exists to help administrators create items for the common groups section of the Programs menu. Common groups are menu items that meet all of the following criteria:

▼ They are automatically placed on the Programs menu of every user.

■ They are listed below the separator line that appears on the Programs menu.

▲ They do not appear in the Programs subfolder of any user's profile folder.

The common program group is a powerful administrative tool, because it's a method of making sure that every user of every workstation has access to certain applications. This eliminates the need to have each user go through an installation program for a program that everybody needs. To add a common application to everyone's Programs menu, follow these steps:

1. Right-click the Start button.
2. Choose Open All Users. The \%SystemRoot%\Profiles\All Users\Start Menu subfolder opens on the desktop.
3. Right-click and choose New, Shortcut, and install a shortcut to a program in the folder.

TIP: You can also add a Startup group to the common groups section of the Program menu.

Another method that I think is faster for creating common program items is to move items directly from one folder to another. Follow these steps to complete the process:

TIP: I've found it easier to do this from My Computer, rather than Explorer, because I can open the folders I need and place them side by side to facilitate dragging.

1. Find the user profile that has this program installed (probably yours). If the software is not installed, install it so that it appears in your Programs subfolder, and then begin this process.

2. In My Computer, open your Programs folder (the path is \%SystemRoot%\ Profiles*YourUserName*\Start Menu\Programs).

3. Open \%SystemRoot%\Profiles\All Users\Start Menu\Programs.

4. Drag the icon for the program you just installed from your Programs folder to the All Users Program folder.

This program menu item now appears on the common groups section of every user's program menu. Even though you dragged the icon, moving it instead of copying it, you haven't lost the menu item; you've just moved it to your own common programs list. If you copy it instead of moving it, it will appear on your own Programs menu twice.

Add Program Menu Items Throughout the Organization

Once you understand the process, you can access multiple computers and open the Programs subfolders you need. With a window filled with Programs subfolders from a variety of connected computers (see Figure 8-12), start copying program shortcuts to all users who should have access to those programs (or to the Programs subfolder for All Users if you want to target every user on that computer). Of course, either the programs have to have been installed on each computer's drive or the program shortcuts have to point to a network installation of the software.

NOTE: There is no All Users folder in Windows 95. If you have Windows 95 workstations as targets, you'll have to open each individual user's Programs subfolder on each workstation.

MAKING DIRECT COPIES OF USER PROFILES

You can copy a profile from one user to another, and the copy includes all the information in the profile, the registry settings and the configuration of the profile folders.

Open the System Properties dialog box (either from the Control Panel or by right-clicking My Computer and choosing Properties) and move to the User Profiles tab (see Figure 8-13). Then follow these steps:

1. Select the profile you want to copy and choose Copy To.

2. When the Copy To dialog box opens (as seen in Figure 8-14), enter the path to the target profile subfolder.

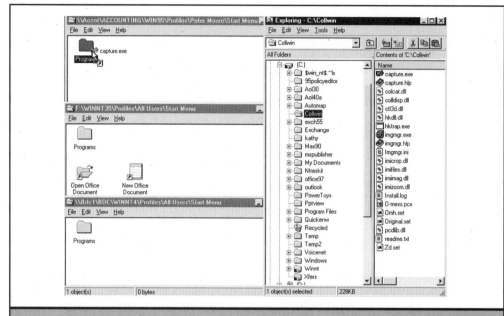

Figure 8-12.   Drag a program shortcut to multiple Programs subfolders—the folders don't have to be open to accept the shortcut

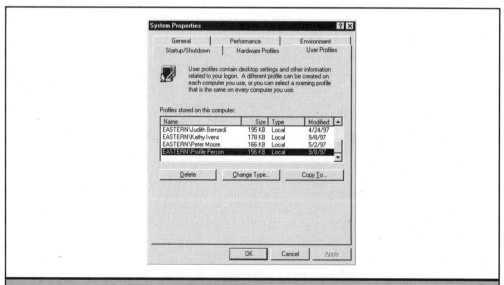

Figure 8-13.   All of the profiles established for users who have logged on to this computer are displayed in the System Properties dialog box

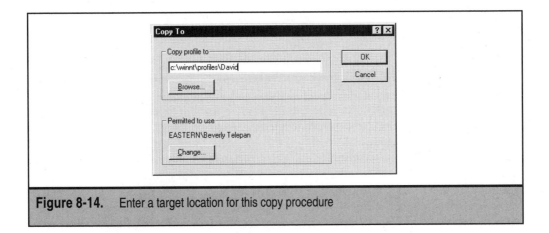

Figure 8-14.   Enter a target location for this copy procedure

3. The user given permission to manipulate this profile is the owner of the original profile you're using. To permit the target user to change settings, choose Change in the Permitted to Use section of the dialog box. The Choose User dialog box opens (if you need to see a list of all of the users in the domain, click Show Users) so you can select the target user.

4. Choose OK.

One nifty way to use this ability to copy profiles easily is to make one user profile that contains exactly what you want all users to have, and then copy that profile to the other existing users. Because these users have already logged on at least once, and as a result already have profiles, it's too late to make the default user profile the perfect profile.

I've actually used the logon name Profile Person (giving myself full administrative rights when I created this user both locally and on the domain).

Now, as this user, create the environment you want to see in the mandatory environment. Create shortcuts, configure the system through the applets in Control Panel, and so on.

After you've created the perfect profile, log on to the computer as the Administrator and copy the perfect profile to the target users through the System Properties dialog box.

In fact, if you have several varieties of profiles you want to give users (perhaps the accounting department should have a profile that's different from that of the research department), create a user for each profile variety and then follow the procedures described here. Whenever you need to adjust one of these profiles, log on as that profile person, make the changes, and copy the profiles to the appropriate users.

USING MANDATORY PROFILES IN WINDOWS NT 4

Mandatory profiles are created by administrators in order to control the settings for individual users, a group of users, or all users. When a user logs on, if a mandatory profile is assigned it is downloaded from the server. No matter what changes the user makes to his or her desktop, the changes are not saved to the mandatory profile, so the next logon is the same as the last logon.

Setting Up Mandatory Profiles

There are several different ways to get to the same place when you want to implement mandatory profiles. The procedures described here are the ones I use. I find them to be thorough and almost foolproof (although I've learned, as all administrators have, that nothing is absolutely foolproof). Follow these procedures when users already exist in your network. It is, of course, much easier to perform all these tasks when you are first installing your network and rolling out Windows NT 4. However, I've never met an administrator who had all the fine-tuning planned and implemented during rollout, and in fact, every case of establishing mandatory profiles that I've seen has occurred on a network with existing users.

To set up a mandatory profile, follow these steps:

1. Create a share on the server (I like to use \users), and give Full Control permissions to Everyone.

2. In User Manager for Domains, open the target user's properties and choose Profile to display the User Environment Profile dialog box seen in Figure 8-15.

3. Enter the path to the server share, using the UNC (universal naming convention). The subdirectory for the specific user does not have to exist (there will be no error message). It will be created automatically when you move the user's profile to the server from the workstation, or when the user next logs on (whichever comes first).

4. Repeat this for all users who will have mandatory profiles.

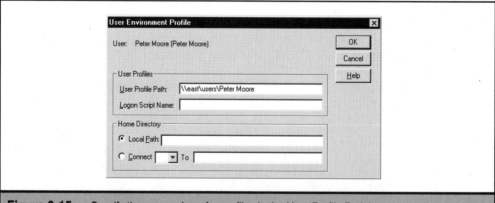

Figure 8-15. Specify the server share for profiles in the User Profile Path box

5. Log on to the workstation as the Administrator and use the User Profiles tab of the System Properties dialog box to copy the appropriate profiles to the network share, as seen in Figure 8-16.

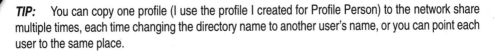

TIP: You can copy one profile (I use the profile I created for Profile Person) to the network share multiple times, each time changing the directory name to another user's name, or you can point each user to the same place.

6. When you choose OK and return to the User Profiles tab, you'll find that the user's profile type is changed to Roaming, as seen here:

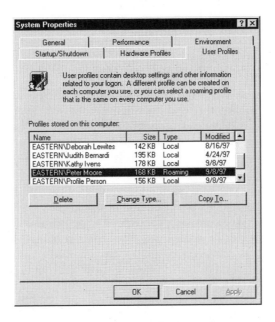

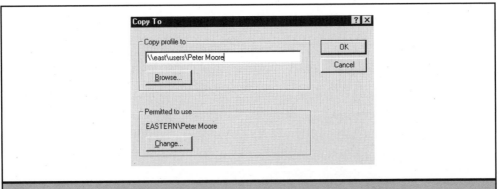

Figure 8-16. Copy the user profile to the user's subdirectory on the network share

7. At the server, open the share you created and select the target user subdirectory. Rename the profile hive file, Ntuser.dat, to Ntuser.man. The .man extension is the only reference you have to make in order to tell Windows NT that this is a mandatory profile.

TIP: Don't worry about the fact that the profile type may change to Roaming on the User Profiles tab. Once the mandatory setup is completed at the server, the profile type will change to Mandatory.

CAUTION: If you are creating the mandatory profile for a user who logs on to the network from a workstation running Windows NT 3.51, when you change the profile path in User Manager for Domains, you must include a filename (usually Ntuser.man).

Understanding How Mandatory Profiles Work

Once you understand that changing the profile file extension to .man automatically creates a mandatory profile, the mind leaps with the possibilities for shortcuts. The first one that occurs to almost everyone is to avoid all the hassle on the server and rename the local profile Ntuser.man. Don't do it; it just won't work. The .man extension does not lock the file or prevent it from being overwritten.

When a user logs on, if his or her logon calls for a mandatory profile, that profile is loaded during logon. It is cached locally. When the user logs off, it is written back locally, along with any changes the user has made to configuration options. The .man extension means that the profile will not be written back to the server; it does not mean that the user can't play around with configuration. In fact, try this experiment to see what happens:

1. Create a local profile for a user with a number of desktop objects—stick a half dozen shortcuts on the desktop.

2. Go through the steps described here to change this user's profile to a server-based mandatory profile.

3. Log on as that user. The desktop should have all of those shortcuts.

4. Delete the desktop shortcuts. In fact, move to the local profile folder and open \%SystemRoot\Profiles\Username\Desktop and remove the desktop shortcuts, just to make sure.

5. Log off and log on as Administrator (or use your normal logon name).

6. Open Explorer and look at \%SystemRoot\Profiles\Username\Desktop for the user you're experimenting with. Notice that the removed desktop shortcuts aren't there.

7. Log off and log on again as the test user.

8. They're baaaack—on the desktop and in the profile folder.

It didn't matter what the user did to the profile, because during logon the mandatory profile on the server was loaded and cached. It is written back locally during logoff. The user cannot write back to the server-based profile. If the local file had been the mandatory file, changes would have been written back, which kills the whole idea behind mandatory profiles.

> **TIP:** Another reason for using the server for mandatory profiles is that most servers use NTFS as the file system, which provides a great deal of security for individual files so users can't access them and change them. Making the local file read-only doesn't work because even beginning users can figure out how to bypass that maneuver. Besides, the file is saved during logoff, so a read-only attribute would create an error message (users frequently panic at error messages and require administrators to run to reassure them).

Incidentally, there are ways to make the system ignore any changes to a local profile without implementing mandatory profiles. These are covered in Chapters 9 (on using the registry) and 10 (on using the Policy Editor).

Troubleshooting Mandatory Profiles

You have mandatory profiles on the server, and everything's been done carefully. It's all set, right? Of course not, because anything that can go wrong will go wrong. Murphy's Law is at its most potent when it comes to computers, especially computers that are part of a network.

Error: The Operating System Was Unable to Load Your Profile. Please Contact Your Network Administrator

This error message usually means that either the server is down or the user does not have read privileges in the subfolder containing the profile. The default profile should be loaded for the user. Notice I said "should be", because a message appears that announces that's what will occur, but I've seen workstations load the local profile instead (which is usually harmless because it is probably the original profile that was copied to the mandatory profile).

If the server is running, check the share for the server-based profiles and make sure that Read permission has been granted to the Everyone group. Also check the root directory for the server and make sure that Read permission hasn't been removed for this user, because all of the subfolders will lose Read permissions if that happens.

Error: After the Logon Dialog Box Goes Away, There Is a Blank Screen, or Wallpaper, with No Taskbar and No Desktop Icons

This is another symptom of the inability of the user to get his or her profile because of a missing server or insufficient privileges. See the previous error and solutions.

I've run into another possible cause for this error message and the preceding error message a couple of times, after administrators reconfigured networks and changed the logon server for certain groups of users. If you've recently reassembled a network leg, make sure your replication scheme includes the share and subfolders that have the mandatory profiles, or move the profiles to the new server yourself.

Error: You Do Not Have Permission to Access Your Central Profile Located at \\server\share\username.man. The Operating System Is Attempting to Log You On with Your Local Profile

This error is specifically the result of Read permissions that are missing (the server is running and the connection is fine). The default user profile will probably load.

USING ROAMING PROFILES

Roaming profiles are incredibly handy, and the first roaming user you should create is yourself. A roaming profile is a server-based profile that loads when you log on, regardless of the workstation you're using. If you change your configuration, it stays changed when you move to another workstation. Your configuration follows you all over the network. This is incredibly handy if you're troubleshooting workstations, since you can have all of your permissions and software tools available. Of course, this assumes the software tools are either installed on the local computer or available through the server. In fact, if you are implementing roaming profiles you should administer your network with one of these rules:

▼ Install applications on every workstation in exactly the same directory so all of your shortcuts point to the same path.

▲ Install applications on a server.

TIP: These rules for setting up workstations are actually a good idea even if you're not planning to implement roaming profiles, because they make administration of a network a whole lot easier. In fact, one of the most efficient ways to set up a network is to put applications on the server as a matter of policy, because tweaking, upgrading, and otherwise manipulating the software is a breeze compared to having to deal with every workstation. When network-based software also requires supporting files on the local drive, be sure every workstation has those files in the same directories.

Creating Roaming Profiles

As with mandatory profiles, there are several ways to approach the task of creating a roaming profile. Here's the method I use, which I find to be reassuringly accurate and efficient:

1. On the server, be sure there's a share with Full Control permissions granted to Everyone.

2. At the workstation on which the user has established a profile, open the Systems Properties dialog box (right-click My Computer and choose Properties, or open the Systems applet in Control Panel).

Who Benefits from Roaming Profiles?

When you are considering the need for roaming profiles, remember that it's not just administrators and help desk personnel who benefit from this feature; there are other circumstances that are eased by roaming profiles. For example, consider the accounting department and the special protocols you might have established. In many companies, printer sharing is a matter of course, and centrally located printers are available that multiple users access. However, the printers that hold checks, purchase orders, or other forms that raise security issues are usually attached to a specific workstation and are not shared. In fact, in many organizations that workstation and its attached printer are behind locked doors. If there are several users who have permission to write checks or create purchase orders, each of them has to travel to that computer and printer to perform the task. These users could benefit from roaming profiles also. As you consider the ways in which the rules and protocols of your organization affect users, you'll probably think of other likely candidates for roaming profiles.

3. Move to the User Profiles tab and select the user profile you want to copy to the server to create a roaming profile. You can use the target user's profile or a preconfigured profile you've created.

4. Copy the profile to the share and include a directory for this user, with the format *servername**sharename**username*, as seen in Figure 8-17. The *username* directory does not have to exist; it will be created automatically.

5. Click OK to return to the User Profiles tab. Choose Change Type, and change the profile type to Roaming.

6. At the server, open User Manager for Domains. Open the target user's Properties and choose Profile. Then enter the path to the server-based profile.

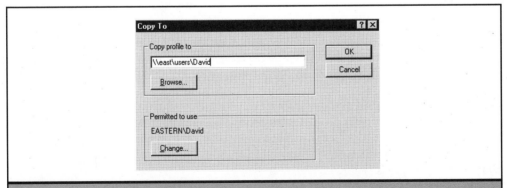

Figure 8-17.   Put a copy of the profile on the server so this user can get to it from any workstation

Changing the Profile Type on Demand (or at Whim)

A roaming user can change the profile type back to a local profile on his or her own "home" computer, which is handy for creating additional configuration options for the home workstation that aren't needed when roaming. If, as an administrator, you don't want users to be able to change the profile type, you have to remove the users' ability to access the System applet in Control Panel. This can be accomplished only if the computer is running NTFS, which provides the ability to configure permissions and settings for specific files. If the computer is running NTFS, you can remove the Read permission from the \%SystemRoot%\System32\Sysdm.cpl file for those users (which removes the System icon from Control Panel).

Troubleshooting Roaming Profiles

Of course, things can go wrong, and roaming users get upset, angry, or confused when that occurs. This section covers some of the most common problems with roaming profiles. Before examining specific problems, however, it's a good idea to look at what the operating system does with roaming profiles.

There is a checklist the operating system follows in an effort to load the appropriate profile and to save changes the roaming user might make to the profile back to the roaming profile. Let's examine what happens when everything goes smoothly before discussing the problems that can occur.

When a roaming user logs on, the system checks to see if the server-based profile is available. If it is, the system checks the date/time stamp of the hive file and then looks for a local profile for this user. Depending on what is found, one of the following events occurs:

▼ If a local profile is found and the date/time stamp of the hive file is later than the date/time stamp on the server-based hive, the local profile is loaded and placed in the cache.

■ If a local profile is found and it is older than the server-based profile, the server-based profile is loaded and cached.

▲ If no local profile is found, the server-based profile is loaded and cached.

When the user logs off, the profile that is in the cache is saved back both to the server and to the local disk (a local profile is created if none had been found during logon). As you can see, this pretty much ensures that the most recent profile is saved on the server. The next time this user logs on from any workstation, this new profile, containing all the changes the user made, is loaded.

Now let's look at some of the problems that administrators can face when running a system with roaming profiles.

The Default User Profile Is Loaded Instead of the Roaming Profile

There are several possible causes for this problem:

THE USER IS DIALED IN OVER A WAN AND THE CONNECTION HAS BEEN LOST FOR SOME REASON
Before the profile could be loaded from the remote server, the connection was lost. Since there is no local profile for this user, the default user profile on this computer is loaded and saved as this user's profile.

Dial-in connections are not as safe or foolproof as cabled connections, and it's not a good idea to deliver roaming profiles over a WAN. If there are times when users are sent to other sites, connected to the user's home site by a WAN, it's a better idea to replicate the user's profile to the remote site server. In fact, if a user is visiting a site fairly often, create the profile on a computer at that site.

THE NETWORK CABLE CONNECTION IS LOST   If the network connection is not working (usually because the server goes down) at the time the logon process would load the roaming profile, the system looks for a user profile. If none is found, the default profile is loaded.

THE USER HAS LOGGED ON TO A DIFFERENT SERVER WHICH DOES NOT HAVE A COPY OF THE ROAMING PROFILE   When a roaming user moves down the hall, around the corner, or onto a different floor of the building, the computer at which he or she settles may log on to a different server. As a result, there is no roaming profile found, nor is there a local profile for this visitor, so the default user profile is loaded. The cure for this is to make sure you replicate your profile folders to all the servers in the system that might get involved in the logon of a roaming user.

THE ROAMING PROFILE HAS BEEN REPLACED BY THE DEFAULT PROFILE   This can sometimes occur as an aftereffect of any of the previous problems with connections to the server that holds the roaming profile. Remember that the profile that's loaded and cached locally is written back to the server. Suppose the server wasn't available during logon and the default user profile was loaded. Then, during the time the user is working on the computer, the server becomes available again. When the user logs off, the operating system writes the profile that's in the cache back to the server, overwriting the server-based profile that is already there.

Personally, I think this is a serious flaw in Windows NT 4, and could qualify as a bug. It isn't difficult to come up with a scheme to stop the operating system from overwriting the server-based profile—in fact I can think of a couple, and there are probably other schemes that haven't occurred to me:

▼ If the cached profile was derived from the default user profile, don't write anything back to the server.

▲ If the cached profile was derived from a local profile for this user, do a time/date check on the original hive, and if it's older than the server-based hive, don't write anything back.

If you think of any other schemes, write to Microsoft.

Profile Changes Made at the Server Aren't Loaded

You can make changes to the server-based profile for a roaming user directly at the server. Perhaps you've added software to the server (or to all of the workstations that the roaming user visits) and you want to add a desktop shortcut or a Program menu item for that software. You can just create the object (or copy it from another profile) and place it in the appropriate profile subfolder on the server. Then the changes don't show up.

To understand what causes this to happen, let's build a scenario that's typical of the circumstances that cause this error.

You made changes to the user's roaming profile today.

Yesterday, the user made a change to the profile locally, and it was written back to the server when the user logged off.

Today the user logged on and the system checked the date/time stamp of the local hive and the server-based hive. Due to yesterday's changes, the local hive file is newer, so it is loaded. The user doesn't see your new items. Then it gets worse—the user logs off and the cached profile is written back to the server. Your changes are gone.

Making changes at the server does not change the date/time stamp of the hive, and this is the cause of this problem.

There is a cure, and it's found in the Windows NT 4 Resource Kit. If you've installed the Resource Kit CD-ROM, find Touch.exe. If you haven't installed the kit, copy the file from the CD-ROM of either NT 4 Workstation or NT 4 Server. The Intel version is found in the \I386\filebat subdirectory.

Touch is a command line program, and the syntax is

```
Touch [-a] [-c] [-f] [-m] [-r file][-t] file
```

where:

-a changes the last access time.
-m changes the last modification time (this is the default change).
-c prevents Touch from creating the file if it doesn't already exist.
-f attempts to change the time stamp regardless of the write permissions attached
  to the file.
-r *filename* sets the time to match the time stamp of another file.
-t lets you set the time manually, using the format *YYYY MM.DD hh mm*
  (time is military).
file is the filename of the target file.

For example, if you enter **touch /t 1997 01 02 11 00 ntuser.dat,** the file Ntuser.dat will have a last modified date of January 2, 1997 at 11:00a.

The ability to understand, manipulate, and troubleshoot user profiles is an important and powerful skill for an administrator. Many of the problems users face (and yell for help on) are caused by inadvertent changes to the profile. In the following chapters you'll learn about even more potent tools for controlling profiles.

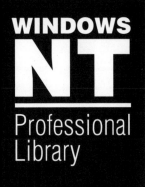

WINDOWS
NT
Professional
Library

CHAPTER 9

Controlling Users with the Registry

The best way to handle troubleshooting is with preventive actions. One quick way to prevent a user from experimenting with the operating system to the point of destruction is to build safeguards against user actions by amending the registry. In addition, you can use the registry to limit user access to programs, to operating system functions, and even to other computers. The registry is a massive database that controls all of the configuration options and settings for a computer. Since there's nothing more painful to an administrator than a user who knows just enough to be dangerous and has enough confidence and courage to experiment, using the registry to rein in that user is often a good idea.

> **TIP:**   It's best to use the registry for controlling user actions if there are only a few users upon whom you need to impose controls. If you want systemwide controls, you should use the Windows NT Policy Editor (or the Windows 95 Policy Editor for your Windows 95 workstations). The Policy Editors are discussed in Chapter 10.

Windows NT 4 provides two editors for hacking the registry, Regedit.exe and Regedt32.exe. They differ a bit in appearance and function, but you can accomplish the registry changes you need in either editor.

As you can see in Figure 9-1, Regedit.exe presents an interface that resembles Explorer. You can expand or collapse keys by clicking the plus or minus signs. There are

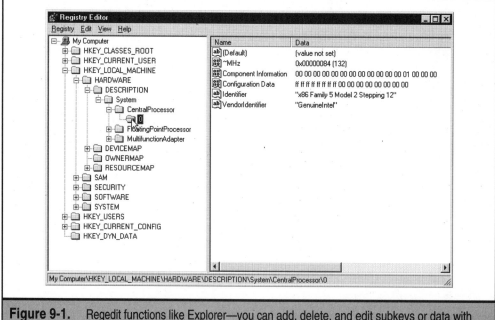

Figure 9-1.   Regedit functions like Explorer—you can add, delete, and edit subkeys or data with right-click shortcut menus

right-click functions and menu commands. I personally find it easiest to work with Regedit for most tasks.

On the other hand, Regedt32.exe functions in a manner reminiscent of the Windows 3.x File Manager. As seen in Figure 9-2, each root key displays in its own window, and clicking a plus sign next to a key does nothing; you must double-click the key to expand it. Also, you have no right-click functions, so you must use the menu bar to perform any actions.

A QUICK OVERVIEW OF THE REGISTRY

The Windows NT 4 directory has five root keys:

▼ HKEY_CLASSES_ROOT

■ HKEY_CURRENT_USER

■ HKEY_LOCAL_MACHINE

■ HKEY_USERS

▲ HKEY_CURRENT_CONFIG

NOTE: The Windows 95 registry has an additional root key, HKEY_DYN_DATA.

Each of these keys expands to subkeys, and some expand into multiple levels of subkeys.

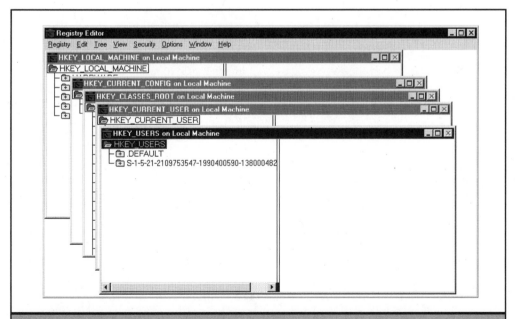

Figure 9-2.   Regedt32 opens a window for each root key, and you use the menu bar to perform tasks

Registry Data Types

Data is registered for the subkeys using a variety of data types:

▼ **REG_MULTI_SZ**, which can contain multiple values, delimited by the ASCII 0 null character. The data is usually a string of text, and the null character makes it easier to read. The information about your system BIOS is an example of this data type.

■ **REG_SZ**, which contains a single string, usually in readable form. Program names are an example of this data type.

■ **REG_EXPAND_SZ**, which contains variable data that is replaced when the key is accessed by an application. (It's similar to the % variable used in a DOS batch file). An example is the notation for the directory you chose for Windows files when you installed the operating system, which is %SystemRoot%.

■ **REG_BINARY**, which is the data type for binary value entries, usually found in entries connected to your hardware configuration.

▲ **REG_DWORD**, which includes 32-bit data (4 bytes long) and can be binary, decimal, or hexadecimal. Most of the time the data is in hexadecimal form with a prefix of 0x (entries that refer to IRQ settings are an example of this data type).

Understanding Alias Keys

Having listed the root keys, I'll now amend my statement by telling you that there are actually only two keys. They are HKEY_LOCAL_MACHINE and HKEY_USERS. All of the other root keys in the registry are either aliases for subsets contained in these two keys or are keys that are created dynamically during system startup by fetching information from one of the two real keys. Changes made to an alias key are also made to the main key (and vice versa).

HKEY_LOCAL_MACHINE contains global information pertaining to system hardware and applications software settings. The information and settings apply to all users who log on to the computer. The root key aliases for HKEY_LOCAL_MACHINE are

▼ **HKEY_CLASSES_ROOT**, which is the alias for HKEY_LOCAL_MACHINE\SOFTWARE\Classes. For both Windows NT 4 and Windows 95, this is where you find information about file associations, drag-and-drop, shortcuts, and OLE/COM.

■ **HKEY_CURRENT_CONFIG**, which differs by operating system. In Windows NT 4 there are two subkeys below HKEY_CURRENT_CONFIG, and each subkey is an alias for a subset of HKEY_LOCAL_MACHINE. The subkey \Software is an alias for HKEY_LOCAL_MACHINE\SYSTEM\ControlSet00n\Hardware\Profiles\000n\Software (the n represents a hardware profile, and data is found in the subkeys if hardware profiles have been enabled for the computer). The subkey \System is an alias for part of

HKEY_LOCAL_MACHINE\SYSTEM\CurrentControlSet. In Windows 95, this key is the alias for HKEY_LOCAL_MACHINE\Config\000*n*.

▲ **HKEY_DYN_DATA**, found only in Windows 95, derives its data from a number of different locations in the HKEY_LOCAL_MACHINE\Config Manager subkey. Its PerfStats subkey is derived from performance information reported by the local system. Both are dynamically created at boot time.

The first-level subkeys of HKEY_LOCAL_MACHINE for Windows NT are

▼ **HARDWARE**, which contains detailed information about the hardware configuration of the system and any locally attached devices.

■ **SAM**, which holds information related to the Security Accounts Manager.

■ **SECURITY**, which is tied to application security information.

■ **SOFTWARE**, which contains information about installed applications.

▲ **SYSTEM**, which contains detailed information about the Current Control Set as well as previously configured Control Sets.

The first-level subkeys of HKEY_LOCAL_MACHINE for Windows 95 are

▼ **Config**, which stores configuration information for system hardware profiles.

■ **Enum**, which enumerates the information found in the Windows 95 Device Manager (in the System applet in Control Panel). There is a separate entry for each class of hardware and an entry for each specific piece of hardware.

■ **Hardware**, which contains serial port and floating-point hardware information.

■ **Network**, which contains the network logon configuration information (network type and the default user name).

■ **Security**, which contains information about network security and remote-access devices.

■ **Software**, which contains information about installed applications. This ranges from default window locations to file associations to the keystrokes that fire the laser guns in your favorite game.

▲ **System**, which contains the Current Control Set configuration information.

HKEY_USERS has two subkeys. One is the \.Default subkey (for the default user configuration), and the other is identified only by a security ID code (SID) for the currently logged-on user. In a Windows 95 computer, the registry might have only a \.Default subkey if specific user profiles have not been established. If specific users exist, the subkey for the current user displays the name of the current user; it is not encrypted like the security ID key in Windows NT 4. There is one root key alias for HKEY_USERS:

▼ **HKEY_CURRENT_USER** is the information from HKEY_USERS*Whatever user you logged in as*. This applies to both Windows 95 and Windows NT 4. (In

Windows 95, if the system logon screen is canceled or nonexistent, HKEY_CURRENT_USER uses the \.Default key).

The second-level subkeys of HKEY_USERS for Windows NT are

▼ **Default**, which contains the default user configuration information.

▲ **SID**, which contains the configuration for that specific user.

Both keys contain the following subkeys:

▼ **AppEvents**, which contains information about the sounds that Windows NT makes when an event occurs, as well as information about desktop themes.

■ **Console**, which contains the current configuration for the appearance of the MS-DOS Command Prompt window.

■ **Control Panel**, which contains configuration data for some of the Control Panel applets and also tracks information about screen savers and sounds.

■ **Environment**, which contains system environment variables.

■ **Keyboard Layout**, which contains information about the current keyboard layout and any other stored keyboard layouts.

■ **Software**, which contains information about the software configuration for the current user. It does not have information about applications installed in the Common Groups section of the Programs menu.

▲ **UNICODE Program Groups**, which stores current user UNICODE information. Windows NT 4 doesn't really use this key, but Windows NT 5 probably will, since UNICODE will be available to developers.

The first two next-level subkeys of HKEY_USERS for Windows 95 (there may be more depending upon your system configuration) are

▼ **.Default**, which contains the default user configuration information.

▲ **USERNAME (substitute the current user name)**, which contains configuration information for the current user.

Both keys contain the following subkeys:

▼ **AppEvents**, which contains information about the sounds that Windows 95 makes when an event occurs, in addition to configuration information for the desktop themes.

■ **Control Panel**, which contains the settings for some of the Control Panel applets. (These are the same settings you found in Win.ini in Windows 3.x.)

■ **InstallLocationsMRU**, which is the Most Recently Used list for application installation programs.

- **Keyboard layout**, which identifies the keyboard layout that is specified in the Current Control Set.

- **Network**, which contains subkeys that identify the current network connections, persistent network connections, and a most recently used list of network connections.

- **RemoteAccess,** which contains configuration information for installed Dial-Up Networking connections.

▲ **Software**, which contains the software configuration settings for the current user.

Using the Registry Safely

The registry is powerful and dangerous. Teeny little changes can render a system unbootable. Thus, there are three important rules you must follow when you decide to hack the registry.

1. Back up the registry before you start.

2. Make only one change at a time.

3. Always obey rule number 1.

You don't have to use your tape backup program to back up the registry; you can do it from the registry editor. In fact, to save time and disk space, you can back up only the key you're going to be hacking.

Backing Up in Regedit

1. Select the root key you're going to be working in.

2. Choose Registry, Export Registry File. Then choose (or create) a directory in which to store the registry file.

3. Name the file (the system will add the extension .reg).

4. To restore the key, choose Registry, Import Registry File. Choose the file you previously saved.

Backing Up in Regedt32

1. Select the window for the root key you're going to be working in.

2. Choose Registry, Save Key. Then choose (or create) a directory to store the registry file.

3. Name the file and add an extension that will remind you that this is a registry dump (.reg is probably the best choice).

4. To restore the key, choose Registry, Restore. Choose the file you previously saved.

CHANGING THE START MENU

You can change the Start menu on both Windows NT 4 and Windows 95 computers, eliminating items you don't want users to access. For example, you may decide you don't want certain users to have access to the Printers folder, eliminating any chance of accidental deletion or reconfiguration of a printer. Or you may want to remove the Run item from the Start menu, to prevent users from running software that's not on the Programs menu.

In order to eliminate or change items on the Start menu, you have to add a new data item to the registry. That data item is actually a negative (such as NoRun for eliminating the Run command), and you invoke it with a data value that is the binary equivalent of "Yes," which is a 1. If you want to return the access to the user, you don't have to delete the subkey; just change the data value to 0.

There are two approaches you can choose from if you want to make changes to the Start menu.

You can work at the target computer, logged in as the user you want to restrict. Depending on the permissions and restrictions you've already established, you may have to open User Manager and give appropriate rights to manipulate the registry as this user. Don't forget to return to User Manager to put things back after you finish your work at the target workstation. If you choose to work at the target computer, you can use either registry editor.

The other approach is to connect to the target computer from another computer (the server or your own workstation). If you choose this method, the target computer must be logged on to the network, with the user you want to restrict logged on. For remote editing of this particular section of the registry, you must use Regedt32.exe. From the

Inconsistencies in Behavior

The first time you make these registry changes, they take effect immediately. If you return the power to the user by changing the data value to 0, or change a 0 back to a 1, a reboot is necessary.

Sometimes, before the reboot, the options remain on the menu, but when the user tries to use the option the system generates an error message explaining the situation:

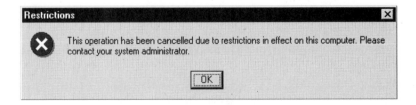

After the reboot, however, the menu item disappears. I have no explanation for this behavior; it doesn't make much sense to me.

menu bar, choose Registry, Select Computer, and select the target machine from the Select Computer dialog box:

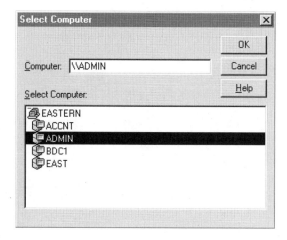

Now follow these steps to reconfigure the Start menu:

1. In the appropriate registry editor, go to HKEY_CURRENT_USER\Software\ Microsoft\Windows\CurrentVersion\Policies\Explorer.

2. In Regedit, right-click in the right pane of the Regedit window and choose New, DWORD Value. When the new item appears in the right pane, enter the name for the new data item that you want to add to this computer (the details for items are described next). Then double-click the entry to bring up the Edit DWORD Value dialog box, and enter the value **1** to turn on the restriction.

   In Regedt32 choose Edit, Add Value from the menu bar, and fill in the Add Value dialog box with the appropriate name (described next). From the drop-down list for Value Type, choose REG_DWORD. Choose OK (or press ENTER) to display the DWORD Editor dialog box, and then enter the value for this restriction (**1** to turn on the restriction).

Here are the specific values you enter for making changes to the Start menu. Remember that in each case, a value of 1 imposes the restriction, and a value of 0 gives the Start menu option back to the user:

▼ **NoClose**, which disables the Shut Down command on the Start menu. (However, the user can still use the Shut Down command in the Logon dialog box).

■ **NoCommonGroups**, which eliminates the menu choices in the common programs group section of the Start menu. Since administrative tools are usually included in this group, there is often good reason to restrict the user in this way.

■ **NoRun**, which removes the Run command.

■ **NoSetFolders**, which eliminates the choices for the Control Panel and the Printers folder from the Settings menu item. They are also eliminated from My Computer and Explorer.

■ **NoSetTaskbar**, which eliminates the Taskbar menu choice in the Settings menu item. The user will also be prevented from right-clicking on the taskbar to set properties (an error message appears when the user attempts this maneuver).

■ **NoFind**, which prevents users from using the Find command on the Start menu. It also prevents the F3 key from being used on the desktop to find files, and the Find command disappears from the Tools menu in Explorer.

▲ **RestrictRun**, which prevents the user from running any application beyond those listed in HKEY_CURRENT_USER\Software\Microsoft\Windows\CurrentVersion\Policies\Explorer\RestrictRun. You must create RestrictRun as a new subkey and enter data values (strings) that list the applications you want the user to be able to run.

Incidentally, when you enter these new restrictive data items, they are also written to the subkey \HKEY_CURRENT_USER\Software\Microsoft\WindowsNT\CurrentVersion\Program Manager\Restrictions. In fact, they may be written to additional subkeys (the registry is full of duplications), but this is the only one I've noticed.

LIMITING ACCESS TO OTHER COMPUTERS

While the peer-to-peer aspects of a Windows NT network can be advantageous (the "point, click, and install" access to printers is such a pleasure compared to setting up shared printers in NetWare, for instance), they also mean that users can get to other

---

Beware of More Strange Things

One of the more interesting side effects I've found to making these particular changes is that occasionally, after you make changes to restrict the Start menu through the local registry, the next time you want to use that registry subkey (HKEY_CURRENT_USER\Software\Microsoft\Windows\CurrentVersion\Policies\Explorer), it's missing. You can see it if you look at the registry with Regedt32.exe from a connected computer; it's just not displayed on the local registry with Regedit.exe.

I've discovered an undocumented fix for this undocumented, intermittent problem: Move to the root key (HKEY_CURRENT_USER) and press F3 to search (or choose Edit, Find from the menu bar, or press CTRL-F). Then search for anything that you know is in the missing subkey (such as NoFind or NoClose or whatever you added). The search is successful and the subkey is back. Picture me shrugging my shoulders.

computers and wreak havoc. Most of the time this isn't intentional (it isn't the norm to find destructive hackers working in front of your corporate workstations). I have, however, seen users expand Explorer and then lose track of where they are as they scroll through Explorer. They sometimes don't realize they're looking at a remote computer below the Network Neighborhood container, so they start deleting folders and files because they think they're looking at their own local drives.

For the most part, you'll want users to be able to reach remote computers. It's a handy way to keep documents together, so that a project leader can have a shared folder on a local drive, and all the other employees who are working on the project can fetch and deliver documents by accessing that folder. In fact, under those circumstances, it's very efficient for all concerned to be able to open a locally installed word processor or spreadsheet program and load a document from that shared folder for editing.

If the number of users who should not be able to see one or more connected computers is small, it's easier to build the blockade wall from the affected users' machines than it is to create complicated permissions on the other computers. And the blockade wall can be erected in the registry of the users you want to restrict.

There are several methods for restricting access to connected drives via the registry. However, users can still reach any connected computer by using the Find command, so this system works only if you remove the Find command from the Start menu (see the preceding section).

Remove the Network Neighborhood Desktop Folder

The quickest way to eliminate any method of accessing a connected computer is to take away the Network Neighborhood folder. To do so, follow these steps:

1. Use the instructions in the previous section to open the local registry or access it from another computer.

2. In either registry editor, go to HKEY_CURRENT_USER\Software\Microsoft\ Windows\CurrentVersion\Policies\Explorer.

3. Add a new item named NoNetHood (it's a REG_DWORD data type).

4. Set the data value to 1.

The Network Neighborhood icon is now removed from the desktop for this user.

Remove Icons from Network Neighborhood

If you have workgroups as well as domains in your system, the icons in Network Neighborhood reflect those distinctions.

In the key HKEY_CURRENT_USER\Software\Microsoft\Windows you can also enter the following, setting a value of 1 to enforce the policy:

▼ **NoEntireNetwork**, which eliminates the icon named Entire Network in Network Neighborhood, limiting the icons to the local workgroup or domain.

▲ **NoWorkgroupContents**, which eliminates those icons that display the computers in the local workgroup.

Again, users who know how to do it can still access these computers with the Find command if it's available.

CAUTION: Some users also may know that you can reach any computer by using the Run command and entering the UNC for any existing computer or share in the Run text box. This action opens a window for the computer or share, regardless of the state of Network Neighborhood..

CUSTOMIZING DESKTOP CONFIGURATIONS

You can control the way a user desktop looks and behaves, and then, if you wish, lock in your settings by preventing further changes. Of course, you could use mandatory profiles for all the users who need this type of control, but those profiles involve more than just desktop settings. If your goal is to stop responding to calls for help about lost shortcuts or to avoid letting a user create so many desktop shortcuts that his eyes glaze when he looks at the desktop, or if you think it's wise to remove the desktop icons that give users entry into configuration processes, just customize the desktop for the users who seem to need these limitations.

Configure the Desktop Appearance

The basic appearance of the desktop can be configured through the Display applet in Control Panel or by directly manipulating the registry. The applet is safer than hacking the registry, of course, but as an administrator you should know where in the registry you can find this information.

In Windows NT 4, the desktop settings for the current user are found in the subkey HKEY_CURRENT_USER\Control Panel\Desktop (see Figure 9-3). A subkey named WindowMetrics holds information about the settings for some of the desktop basics. (In Windows 95, the settings are found in the same key, but fewer items are controlled in this key because many of the settings are contained in the WindowMetrics subkey.)

Incidentally, if you want to change the default settings so that they're applied to users who will be logging on to this computer for the first time, use HKEY_USERS\DEFAULT\ Control Panel\Desktop.

Require a Secured Screen Saver

You can force the use of a password-protected screen saver and set its timing by following these steps:

1. Open a registry editor and go to HKEY_CURRENT_USER\Control Panel\ Desktop. Move to the section where the screen saver data items are, as seen in Figure 9-4.

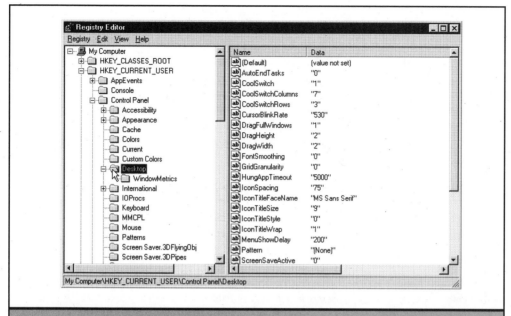

Figure 9-3.   The configuration for the appearance and behavior of the desktop and its icons can be manipulated in the registry

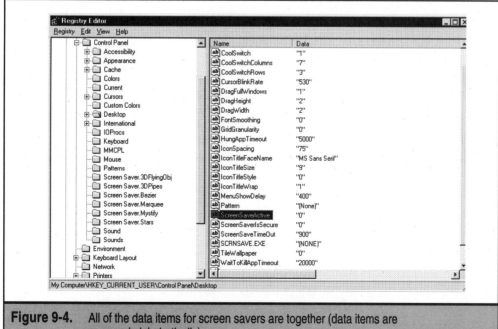

Figure 9-4.   All of the data items for screen savers are together (data items are arranged alphabetically)

2. Select the data item ScreenSaveActive and change the data to 1.

3. Select the data item ScreenSaverIsSecure and change the data to 1.

4. Select the data item SCRNSAVE.EXE and change the data to the filename of the screen saver you want to use.

5. Select the data item ScreenSaveTimeOut and change the data to reflect the number of seconds you want to elapse before the screen saver kicks in.

The next time the user logs on, these settings are in effect. After the elapsed time expires, the screen saver launches. When a mouse click or a key press removes the screen saver, a message displays telling the user the following:

▼ The computer has been locked.

■ The computer can be unlocked only by *<name of logged-on user>* or an administrator.

▲ Press CTRL-ALT-DEL to unlock the computer.

When the user presses CTRL-ALT-DEL, the logon screen is presented. When the user enters the password, the computer is unlocked.

Of course, the user can change everything you did by opening the Display Properties dialog box and changing the configuration for the screen saver. To prevent this, you can remove the Screen Saver tab from the Properties dialog box. See the section "Restricting System Features" later in this chapter.

Allow Users to Manually Launch a Screen Saver

If you do insist on password-protected screen savers, there is frequently a lapse in security because users leave the computer before the screen saver has kicked in. It's pretty difficult to enforce a policy that demands that users sit in front of their machines until they're secure, and it's incredibly annoying to try to cut down the risk by configuring the screen saver to kick in quickly. The solution is to give users a way to bring the screen saver up at will. To do this, you can create a hot key (Microsoft calls it a Shortcut Key) that the user can enter from the keyboard to bring up the screen saver. You can create this on-demand screen saver by following these steps:

1. In Explorer, go to \%SystemRoot%\System32 and find the file for the screen saver you've chosen for the computer (screen saver filenames start with "ss" and have an extension of .scr).

2. Right-drag the file to the desktop and choose Create Shortcut(s) Here from the shortcut menu that appears when you release the mouse button.

3. Right-click on the shortcut and choose Properties.

4. Move to the Shortcut tab, and click in the text box for the Shortcut Key (the current entry for this field should be "none").

5. Type the character you want to use as the hot key. As soon as you enter the character, CTRL + ALT + is appended to the beginning of the text box, as seen here. You can use any key except ESC, ENTER, TAB, PRINTSCREEN, BACKSPACE, or the spacebar.

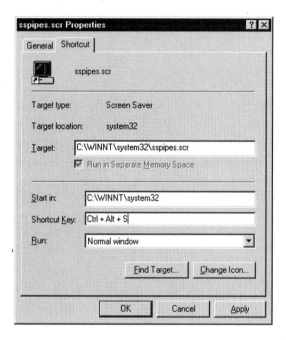

6. Choose OK to close the Properties dialog box.

TIP: Don't try to delete the original entry "none"; you can't. However, as soon as you enter a character, it replaces that original entry. If you use BACKSPACE to delete your hot key, "none" automatically appears again.

Now, to invoke the screen saver at will, just press CTRL-ALT and the character you chose. Or double-click the shortcut. Of course, there's nothing in the registry or any configuration applet that makes the user remember to do this—enforcement is up to you.

Fly the Company Colors on Desktops

If you wish, you can configure the color scheme you want for all the desktops and then make that the official desktop by enforcing its use. There are a couple of ways to do this.

The easiest way is to select the scheme you want and insert it as the data item in HKEY_CURRENT_USER\Control Panel\Current. As you can see, the data item in this subkey is simply the name of the selected desktop scheme.

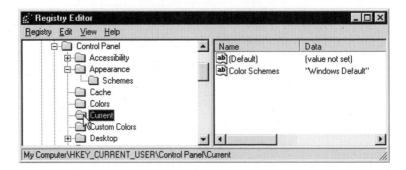

To change the scheme, double-click the data item in Regedit and replace the current data string with the name of the scheme you want to use for this computer. Don't type the quotation marks; they're added automatically. In Regedt32, select the data item and choose Edit, String from the menu bar. Then replace the existing scheme name with your new favorite.

You can also force the user to make this choice by removing all of the other choices from the user's computer. The desktop schemes are offered in a drop-down list in the Appearance tab of the Display Properties dialog box, as shown in Figure 9-5.

The list (and the specific configuration for each of the schemes) comes from the registry, and you can delete all of the choices except the one you want to use. The available schemes are listed in HKEY_CURRENT_USER\Control Panel\Appearance\Schemes and also in HKEY_USERS\DEFAULT\Control Panel\Appearance\Schemes. (The data inside each scheme object is a long string of binary values.) Just delete the data objects for all of the schemes except your official one. Then, when a user looks at the drop-down list of schemes, there won't be any others to choose.

If you design your own scheme, you'll name it, and the name will be written back to the registry, along with the configuration information. To reproduce the scheme on other computers, it's easiest to send out a memo (e-mail of course) and give users explicit instructions to create this scheme.

If your network isn't large and/or you don't want users to perform this task, you can also copy the scheme from your own workstation to every other workstation. It's easiest to do this from your own workstation or from a server, using Regedt32 to call up each computer's registry.

1. Open your scheme data object (in the registry of the computer you used to create it), and select all of the data. Press CTRL-C to copy it to the Clipboard.

2. Open the registry of the first target computer and move to HKEY_CURRENT_USER\Control Panel\Appearance\Schemes (or use the default user if the computer hasn't yet had its first logon).

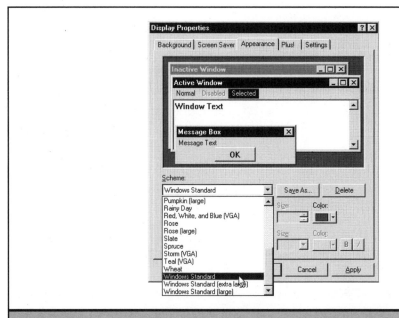

Figure 9-5. There are a large variety of schemes to choose from, or you can design your own

3. Choose Edit, Add Value from the menu bar, and enter the name of your scheme as the Value Name.

4. Choose REG_BINARY as the Data Type.

5. Choose OK to display the Binary Editor, and press CTRL-V to paste the data (don't forget to check the Binary radio button as the Data Format).

6. Repeat this for each target computer.

TIP: You can also use the Clipboard Viewer accessory application to save the data you placed on the Clipboard. Then you can use it at individual computers (fetch it from a connected computer or put it on a floppy disk).

Now your scheme is on the drop-down list on the Display Properties dialog box of each target computer, and the specific configuration data is in the registry.

MANIPULATING THE DEFAULT DESKTOP ICONS

When you install Windows NT Workstation (or Server for that matter), several icons are placed on the desktop by default: My Computer, Network Neighborhood, Recycle Bin, and Briefcase. Depending on your installation options, you may also see Inbox and Internet Explorer. Your Windows 95 workstations probably have the same icons.

To get to the keys for the desktop icons, expand HKEY_CLASSES_ROOT and find the key CLSID. The keys are listed alphabetically, and there are two alphabetical lists, one after the other. The first list is the registered file types, which is really a list of file extensions (notice the period in front of each item). Then, when you arrive at the end of the alphabet for file extensions, there is an alphabetical listing of subkeys representing file class types. Expand the key named CLSID and you'll see a large number of keys and subkeys.

Finding the Desktop Icons

The CLSIDs for the default objects you'll find on desktops are

- ▼ Control Panel {21EC2020-3AEA-1069-A2DD-08002B30309D}
- ■ Dial-Up Networking {992CFFA0-F557-101A-88EC-00DD010CCC48}
- ■ Inbox {00020D75-0000-0000-C000-000000000046}
- ■ My Computer {20D04FE0-3AEA-1069-A2D8-08002B30309D}
- ■ Network Neighborhood {208D2C60-3AEA-1069-A2D7-08002B30309D}
- ■ Printers {2227A280-3AEA-1069-A2DE-08002B30309D}

A Word About Class Identifiers (CLSIDs)

Every type of object that exists in the Windows universe has a unique class identifier (CLSID), and all of the information about handling the object is found in the subkeys under HKEY_CLASSES_ROOT\CLSID. For instance, the CLSID subkey for a file type holds information about the file type's OLE class, along with the location of the file that is used for the implementation of OLE for that file type.

The CLSID key itself isn't English, and it isn't readable by human beings. It's a 16-byte number that is formatted as 32 hexadecimal digits. It's also called a Globally Unique Identifier (GUID), a definition that is literal, because each object has the same GUID on every PC in the world (you can think of it as being an object type's social security number).

If you write software and want to introduce a new object type, you have to create a GUID for it. The Microsoft SDK has a program that takes care of this for you (Uuuidegen.exe). The way GUID creation works is that the first 8 digits are generated at random. The next 4 digits reflect the current date and time on the computer being used to generate the GUID. The last 20 digits are generated using information from the hardware setup of the computer being used to generate the GUID. It would be beyond eerie coincidence if two GUIDs ended up the same, and the odds are so far against it that we can pretty much relax and assume that we won't see duplicates.

- Recycle Bin {645FF040-5081-101B-9F08-00AA002F954E}
- Briefcase {85BBD920-42A0-1069-A2E4-08002B30309D}
- The Internet {FBF23B42-E3F0-101B-8488-00AA003E56F8}
- ▲ Microsoft Network {00028B00-0000-0000-C000-000000000046}

Renaming Desktop Objects

Once you can find the default desktop objects, you can manipulate them. For example, locate the Recycle Bin CLSID, which should look like this:

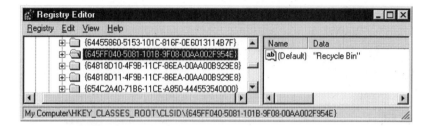

If you want to change the name of the Recycle Bin (you might want to call it a trash can if you're not as concerned about being as environmentally correct as Windows is, or perhaps you want the text under the icon to say "dump your trash here"), double-click the data value entry in the right pane and replace the existing name with your own title.

Changing the Icons for Desktop Objects

Expand the CLSID and check out the data in the DefaultIcon subkey, which looks like this:

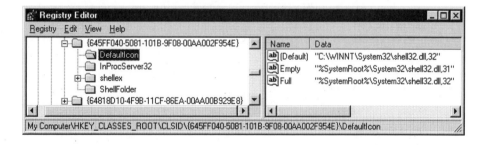

The data item is a path to the object's icon, where:

%SystemRoot% is the name of the directory in which your Windows operating system software resides.
System32 is the subdirectory that holds the .dll file for this object's icon.

Shell32.dll is the name of the .dll file that contains the icon.

31 is the icon number within the .dll file (it's the 32nd icon in this file, because computers start counting with zero).

If you want to change the icon to another icon within this .dll file, change the icon number to the appropriate one.

If you want to change the icon to an icon within a different file, change the path statement (and don't forget to enter the icon number).

There are several .dll files in Windows NT that have system icons, but there's no system application to peek inside them. There are, however, some shareware programs that can display the icons in order, so that you can intelligently change them in the registry. See Appendix C for information about available applications.

Meanwhile, for fast reference, here are the icon numbers for \%SystemRoot%\ System32\shell32.dll:

0 Unassigned file types

1 Document

2 Window

3 Closed folder

4 Open folder

5 5 1/4-inch disk

6 3 1/2-inch disk

7 Removable drive

8 Hard drive

9 Network drive

10 Network drive (disconnected)

11 CD-ROM drive

12 RAM chip

13 Globe

14 Network cable connection

15 Network computer

16 Printer

17 Networked computers

18 Networked computers

19 Small folder and window

20 Small open folder with paper

21 Gears

22 Find file

23 Help

24 Window and hourglass cursor

25 Monitor

26 External removable disk drive

27 Monitor

28 Shared folder

29 Shortcut arrow

30 Larger shortcut arrow

31 Empty Recycle Bin

32 Full Recycle Bin

33 Dial-Up Networking folder

34 Desktop

35 Control Panel folder

36 Start menu folder

37 Printers folder

38 Fonts folder

39 Windows flag

40 CD (music)

41 Green tree

42 Multiple documents

43 Find file

44 Find on networked computer

45 Monitor on computer case

46 Control Panel folder

47 Printers folder

48 Printer image on paper pad

49 Network printer

50 Print to file (3 1/2-inch disk)

51 Alternate full Recycle Bin

52 Alternate full Recycle Bin

53 Alternate full Recycle Bin

54 Document to document

55 Documents going folder to folder

56 Pen writing a label for folder

57 Computer, gears, and open folder

58 Configuration file

59 Text file

60 Window with gears

61 Gears image on paper

62 Font file

63 TrueType font file

64 Window with larger hourglass cursor

65 Are you sure you want to delete these files?

66 Tape backup (hard drive, tape cassette, 3 1/2-inch disk)

67 CD in drive

68 Defrag

69 Printer

70 Network printer

71 Print to file

NOTE: The other subkeys under the Recycle Bin and all the other desktop icons contain data the operating system uses to handle the object; there is nothing you can safely manipulate in those subkeys.

PREVENT USER CHANGES

After you've standardized the configuration of the workstation to match the official company design, you can make sure it stays that way. If you lock the configuration, users can't make any changes. Actually, that's technically not true—they can make all the changes they wish, but the next time they log on, everything is back the way you want it because the changes weren't saved.

This is another restriction setting for which you enter the "negative" item and set the data to 1 for Yes and 0 for No:

1. Go to HKEY_CURRENT_USER\Software\Microsoft\Windows\ CurrentVersion\Policies\Explorer.

2. Add a new DWORD data item and name it NoSaveSettings.

3. Enter the data, using a 1 to invoke this restriction (you can change the data to 0 if you decide you want to allow changes).

RESTRICTING SYSTEM FEATURES

There are a number of system features you can remove so that users cannot reconfigure a system or make system changes that shouldn't be made. To establish these limits, you have to create a new subkey in the registry and then add the data items that match the desired restrictions. Follow these instructions to accomplish this:

1. In a registry editor, go to HKEY_CURRENT_USER\Software\Microsoft\ Windows\CurrentVersion\Policies. You are adding a new subkey under this subkey, so make sure you've selected the Policies subkey.

2. In Regedt32 choose Edit, Add Key from the menu bar to bring up the Add Key dialog box seen in Figure 9-6. Name the key System, and enter REG_DWORD as the class.

   In Regedit right-click on a blank spot in the right pane and choose New, Key to create a new icon in the left pane. As seen here, the new key is named New Key #1 and the name is highlighted, indicating that it is in edit mode. Enter **System** to replace this default name.

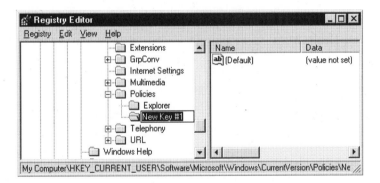

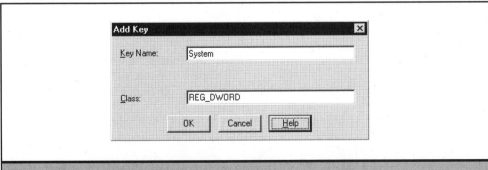

Figure 9-6.   In Regedt32, use the data type for the Class entry

3. To add value items to this new subkey in Regedt32, select the subkey and choose Edit, Add Value from the menu bar. When the Add Value dialog box appears, enter the name and data type of the new value item (see the details that follow about the restrictions you can impose).

   To add value items to the new subkey in Regedit, select the subkey and right-click in the right pane. Choose New, REG_DWORD. Then change the default name that appears to the name of the new value item you want to enter (see the details below about the restrictions you can impose).

You now have a new registry subkey named HKEY_CURRENT_USER\Software\Microsoft\Windows\CurrentVersion\Policies\System, and you can enter data items in this subkey to impose user restrictions. For each restriction you want to impose, enter the value item name and then enter data for each value item, using a data value of 1 to impose the restriction (if you want to lift the restriction, you can change the data value to 0). Here are the data items you can enter to impose restrictions:

▼ **DisableTaskManager**, which prevents the user from launching Task Manager (neither the taskbar right-click access nor Taskmgr.exe program file access will work).

■ **NoDispCPL**, which prevents the user from getting to the Display Properties dialog box.

■ **NoDispAppearancePage**, which removes the Appearance tab from the Display Properties dialog box so that the user cannot change the colors or color scheme of the desktop.

■ **NoDispBackgroundPage**, which removes the Background tab from the Display Properties dialog box, preventing the user from changing wallpaper and background patterns.

■ **NoDispScrSavPage**, which removes the Screen Saver tab from the Display Properties dialog box, preventing the user from making changes to screen saver settings.

▲ **NoDispSettingsPage**, which removes the Settings tab and Plus tab from the Display Properties dialog box, preventing the user from making changes to those configuration items.

There are some additional restrictions you can impose on users by working in the registry key HKEY_CURRENT_USER\Software\Microsoft\Windows\CurrentVersion\Policies\Explorer. Add these data items, giving each a data value of 1:

▼ **NoNetConnectDisconnect**, which removes access to the Map Network Drive and Disconnect Network Drive options in Explorer.

■ **NoTrayContextMenu**, which prevents menus from displaying after a right-click on the taskbar, Start button, clock, or application buttons. (This restriction works only if you've installed SP2 or later service packs.)

▲ **RestrictRun**, which prevents the user from running any application beyond those listed in HKEY_CURRENT_USER\Software\Microsoft\Windows\CurrentVersion\Policies\Explorer\RestrictRun. You must create this new \RestrictRun subkey and enter data values (strings) that list the applications you want the user to be able to run (enter the full path).

SECURING THE REGISTRY

Every administrator can identify at least one user who knows enough to be dangerous and has the courage to experiment. It's important to secure the registry of each user who fits this description. If the computer is running NTFS, you can set permissions to do this, and, in fact, you can set permissions on the registry editors and also on the hive files in the user's profile folder. However, most NT 4 workstations use FAT, not NTFS, so you'll have to come up with an alternate plan.

Change the Registry ACL

Windows NT keeps an Access Control List (ACL) for the registry, which is a database that maintains information about permissions for accessing the keys in the registry. Use the power of the ACL with Regedt32 by following these steps:

1. Select the key for which you want to impose permissions (and therefore restrictions).

TIP: You can make changes to the ACL at any key in the registry; you do not have to work solely with the top keys.

2. Choose Security, Permissions from the menu bar to display the Registry Key Permissions dialog box, seen in Figure 9-7.

3. If you want your permissions to extend to the subkeys below the selected key, select Replace Permission on Existing Subkeys.

4. To delete a group or a user, select the listing and choose Remove.

5. To change the level of permission, select the listing and choose a different permission level from the Type of Access box, which offers these choices:

   ▼ Full Control, which means the user can read, change, and delete the key.

   ■ Read, which means the user can view the key.

   ▲ Special Access, which lets you specify exactly the rights you want to give, by making selections in the text box that lists the available permissions, as seen in Figure 9-8.

6. To add a group or a user, choose Add, which brings up the Add Users and Groups dialog box, seen in Figure 9-9.

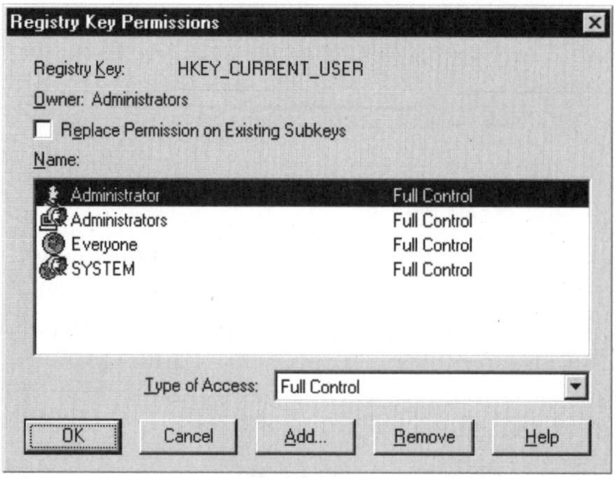

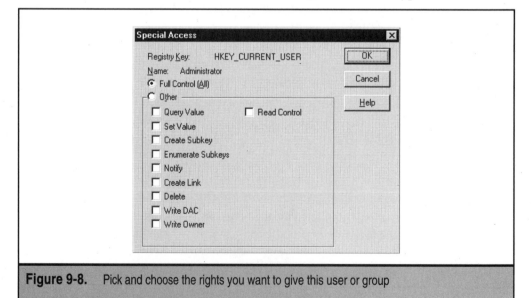

Figure 9-7. You can change, remove, and add permissions for user access of registry keys

7. Select a list from the List Names From box (in this case I chose the domain list), and then choose Show Users if you want to add individual users instead of groups.

8. Select the user or group and choose Add (or double-click on the listing).

9. Choose an access level for this user, choosing one from the Type of Access box.

Figure 9-8. Pick and choose the rights you want to give this user or group

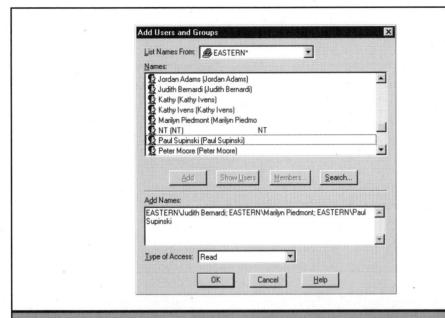

Figure 9-9.   Use the Add Users and Groups dialog box to give additional people permissions to access a registry key

NOTE: The Special Access permission level is not available in the Add Users and Groups dialog box. It can only be assigned to a user or group that has already been added to the permissions list. Therefore, for a new user or group, assign Full Control or Read permission, then select that user when you are back in the Registry Key Permissions dialog box and change the access to Special Access.

10. Repeat this until every user or group you want to give permissions to has been configured. Then choose OK to return to the Registry Key Permissions dialog box. Choose OK again to complete this task.

CAUTION: Do not change the permission level for System, because the operating system and applications must have full access to every registry key.

The Keys You Should Secure

There are some keys that are so important that if a user inappropriately hacks them he or she could destroy the system. In order to make your registry secure, make sure that

The Following Permissions Are Available in the Special Access Dialog Box:

▼ Query Value: the user can read a value entry.

■ Set Value: the user can read and modify a value entry.

■ Create Subkey: the user can create a new subkey.

■ Enumerate Subkey: the user can expand and read the subkeys.

■ Notify: the user can audit notification events for a key.

■ Create Link: the user can create a symbolic link from a key.

■ Delete: the user can delete a key.

■ Write DAC: the user can modify a key's permissions.

■ Write Owner: the user can gain ownership of a key.

▲ Read Control: the user can read a key's security information.

If you set Special Access permissions for a user and you want to make changes, first select that user. The Type of Access list box displays Special Access. Click the down arrow next to this box. You should see two instances of Special Access. One is the selected user's current permissions; the other is the real Special Access choice (it has an ellipsis after its name). The real Special Access choice is the one to choose in order to change the permissions. Afterwards, the user-specific Special Access listing will be updated to match your changes.

the group named Everyone has only limited permissions for these important keys. The maximum level permissions for ordinary users for these important keys are

▼ Query Value

■ Notify

■ Enumerate Subkeys

▲ Read Control

The keys that are considered important to secure are

▼ **HKEY_LOCAL_MACHINE\SOFTWARE\Microsoft\RPC** (and all subkeys)

■ Under **HKEY_LOCAL_MACHINE\SOFTWARE\Microsoft\WindowsNT\ CurrentVersion**, these subkeys:

    \ProfileList
    \AeDebug

\Compatibility
\Drivers
\Embedding
\Fonts
\FontSubstitutes
\GRE_Initialize
\MCI
\MCI Extensions
\Port (all subkeys)
\WOW (and all subkeys)

▲ **HKEY_CLASSES_ROOT** (and all subkeys)

Secure a Registry Against Remote Access

It's possible to edit a registry from another, connected computer. In fact, for administrators, this is a pretty handy technique, and throughout this book I've suggested that you use it.

For certain target computers, however, this might create a problem. I'm thinking in particular of an administrator's workstation or a workstation used for special services such as printing. Procedures are available to prevent unauthorized users from accessing a computer's registry from a remote computer.

When a remote user tries to connect to the Windows NT registry, the operating system performs some tasks:

▼ It looks for a special subkey named HKEY_LOCAL_MACHINE\SYSTEM\ CurrentControlSet\Control\SecurePipeServers\winreg.

■ If the \winreg subkey doesn't exist, any user is permitted to access the registry and manipulate it to the limits set by the ACL.

▲ If the \winreg subkey exists, the ACL for that subkey determines whether the user can access and manipulate any part of the registry.

This means that if you want to secure your Windows NT workstation, you have to create the \winreg subkey and then configure the ACL for it.

NOTE: It's only necessary to create the \winreg subkey in Windows NT Workstation. It is created in NT Server by default (and administrators have Full Control permissions).

To create the \winreg subkey and configure permissions for accessing the registry, open Regedt32 and go to HKEY_LOCAL_MACHINE\SYSTEM\CurrentControlSet\ Control\SecurePipeServers. Then follow these steps:

1. Select the SecurePipeServers key and choose Edit, Add Key from the menu bar.

2. Name the new key winreg.

3. Select the new key and choose Security, Permissions from the menu bar.

4. Configure the permissions for remote users.

Hereafter, only those remote users with appropriate permissions will be able to access this registry. Oh yes—make sure you give yourself full permissions.

The power of the registry has the potential to make an administrator's life easier or harder, depending on how the registry is manipulated and by whom. Getting used to working in the registry is a fact of life for administrators. Securing it against other users is a sanity strategy.

WINDOWS
NT
Professional
Library

CHAPTER 10

Controlling Users with the Policy Editor

W indows NT Server comes with System Policy Editor, which you can use to impose controls and restrictions on some or all of the computers on your network. The Policy Editor changes the registry of the target computer in order to configure the controls you need, but it saves you the trouble of opening the registry and finding the appropriate subkey. In fact, you don't even have to understand the registry. You can use the Policy Editor on a single computer, on a group of computers, or on an entire domain.

The System Policy Editor is on the Administrative Tools menu on Windows NT 4 Server computers. It is not included in the installation of Windows NT 4 Workstation (although it runs perfectly well on NT 4 Workstation). It works with two registry keys: HKEY_LOCAL_MACHINE and HKEY_CURRENT_USER.

NOTE: The Policy Editor does not address any registry item that contains binary data.

This chapter covers the System Policy Editor for Windows NT 4, which you can use to modify policies on any Windows NT 4 computer (whether running Server or Workstation). There is also a Policy Editor for Windows 95 that you can use for the Windows 95 clients on your network. It's not loaded as part of the operating system, but you can find it on the Windows 95 CD-ROM.

HOW THE POLICY EDITOR WORKS

Setting systemwide policies with the System Policy Editor is a four-step process:

1. You create a set of policies.

2. You apply the policies to specific users or to the entire domain.

3. You save the policy as a file in the netlogon share of the PDC/BDC (\%SystemRoot\System32\Repl\Imports\Scripts).

4. Windows NT 4 computers find and adopt the policy file during logon.

TIP: If you want to impose policies on the majority of the users on your network, you'll probably find it easier to create those policies systemwide, across the domain, and then create reversing policies for the few exceptions.

I always work on the PDC when I use the Policy Editor, because saving the policy file to the netlogon share is a local save, and the next replication moves it to the BDCs on the domain. If you're not working on the PDC, use the UNC for your PDC to save your policy files to the netlogon share.

For now, we'll establish policies for the whole domain; then we'll discuss ways to implement policies for specific users and groups.

Open the System Policy Editor and choose File, New Policy from the menu bar. As seen in Figure 10-1, two icons appear in the Policy Editor window:

▼ Default Computer, where you create policy settings that are written to the registry in HKEY_LOCAL_MACHINE.

▲ Default User, where you create policy settings that are written to the registry in HKEY_CURRENT_USER.

You begin setting policies by opening one of the icons (depending on whether you want to create policies for the computer or for the user).

SETTING COMPUTER POLICIES

Double-click the Default Computer icon to see the categories for computer policies (Figure 10-2). The icon for a category is a book, and you expand the book to reach the available policies (sometimes you find books under books, as in the Help system). To begin creating policies, expand any book and drill down to the policy you need.

Some of the policies you can set here match the policies we discussed in Chapter 9. With the Policy Editor, however, we're not opening the registry directly. As we did in the discussion of registry changes to control computers and users, we'll go over some of the more common (and useful) policies here.

Customize Logon

To customize the logon procedure, expand the Windows NT System icon, then expand the Logon icon to see the available policies (see Figure 10-3).

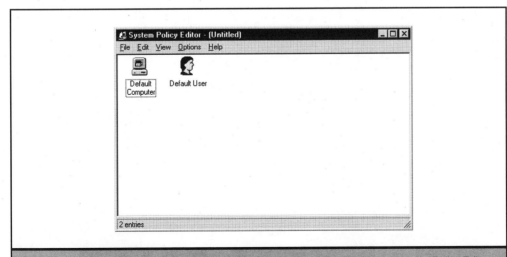

Figure 10-1.   The icons represent the two registry keys you can manipulate with the Policy Editor

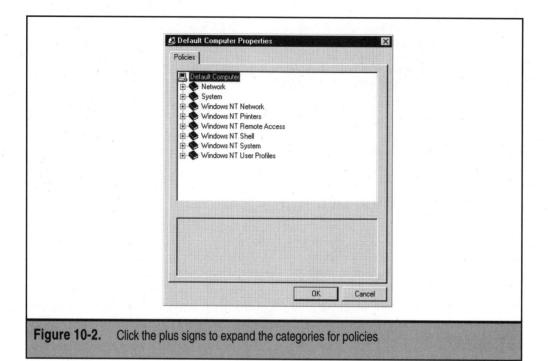

Figure 10-2.   Click the plus signs to expand the categories for policies

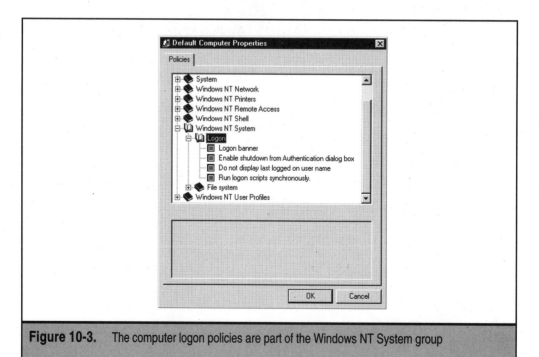

Figure 10-3.   The computer logon policies are part of the Windows NT System group

The first time you use the Policy Editor, all of the available policies have a gray check box. Here's the legend for reading the listings:

▼ Gray check boxes mean that no policy has been specified.

■ Selected check boxes mean that the policy is in effect in this policy file.

▲ Deselected clear check boxes mean that the policy is not in effect in this policy file.

As you click the check boxes, they rotate among the three choices, in the order gray, checked, unchecked.

Create a Logon Banner

If you want to display a message during the logon process, select the Logon Banner check box. As soon as the option is checked, two text boxes open at the bottom of the Policy Editor window, one for the message caption, or title, and one for the message text (see Figure 10-4).

TIP: You can enter many more characters than the text box displays at one time. Just keep typing.

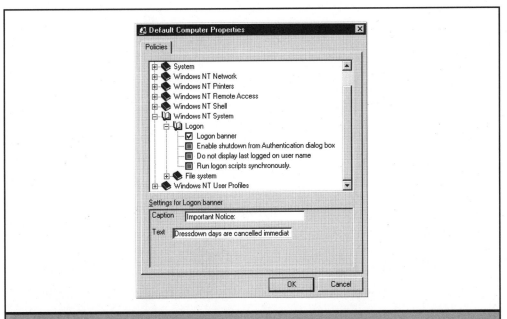

Figure 10-4.   Enter the caption for the title bar of your message window, then enter the text of the message

Enable Shut Down at Logon

By default, Windows NT Workstation has a Shut Down button on the Authentication dialog box. (In fact, besides the text boxes for the user's name and password, there are several buttons: OK, Cancel, Help, and Shut Down). On the other hand, the Windows NT Server Authentication dialog box has the Shut Down button grayed out.

Here are the guidelines for changing this policy:

▼ A checked check box lets all the computers on the domain have access to the Shut Down button.

▲ A clear, unchecked check box removes access to the Shut Down button from every computer on the domain.

Be aware that there is no way to return to the default settings (Workstation=Yes, Server=No). Once you make a change, returning to the Policy Editor and clicking until the check box is gray does not return the computers to their original state. You will have to make a choice of either Yes or No, and then individually configure the computers that you want to have the opposite function. (See "Creating Policies for Groups or Individuals," later in this chapter.)

Hide Last User

If you don't want the Authentication dialog box to display the name of the last logged-on user (displaying it is the default behavior), check the Do Not Display Last Logged On User Name box. This is an added security measure that some administrators use because they're afraid that users might create passwords based on their names, making them easy to figure out if the name is displayed.

Delay Loading the User Shell Until Scripts Are Run

If you are using computer logon scripts, you may want to delay the loading of the user shell until the scripts have finished running. Sometimes logon scripts cause errors or problems, and sometimes they cause a real slowdown in the system when they are running at the same time the shell is loading. Select the Run Logon Scripts Synchronously option to delay loading them.

Note that this option is for the computer, not for the user. The same option is available in the Policy Editor for user configuration. If you enable this option on one policy and not the other (for instance, on the Default Computer policy but not on the Default User policy), the Default Computer policy takes precedence.

Set File System Policies

The File System section of the Policy Editor allows you to set the following policies for files on a computer:

▼ **Do not create 8.3 filenames for long filenames**.   There are some situations in which you don't want long filenames automatically translated to 8.3. Make sure that the computer is only running software that can handle long filenames.

■ **Allow extended characters in 8.3 filenames**.   This policy is useful mainly for those computers that are using something other than the standard code page.

▲ **Do not update last access time**.   Windows NT tracks access time and date. If you don't need this information (usually you don't), you can speed up file access by eliminating this function. This has no effect on updating file saves.

A number of other policies are available for the computers on your network. You should examine all of the available policies for computers, although you'll probably find that, except for the policies covered here, most of them are appropriate for individual computers, not for the domain.

SETTING USER POLICIES

There are many more user policies available than computer policies. Open the icon for the Default User to see the categories, as shown in Figure 10-5.

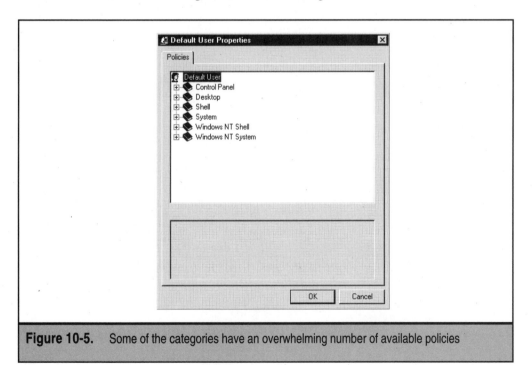

Figure 10-5.   Some of the categories have an overwhelming number of available policies

It would take too many pages to list all of the available policies for users, so I'll limit the discussion to some of those that are commonly used restrict users. This seems to me to be in keeping with the theme of this book, troubleshooting. I've always found that restricting users from messing around with system functions means that I can congratulate myself for good troubleshooting—preventive actions are the best form of troubleshooting.

Shell Restrictions

Expand the Shell book, then expand the Restrictions book, to see the limitations you can place on user activity, as seen in Figure 10-6.

Here's a brief overview of some of the choices:

▼ **Remove Run command from Start menu**, which prohibits users from running applications that aren't on the Program menu.

■ **Remove folders from Settings on Start menu**, which means that when the user points to the Settings item, no folders are displayed on the submenu.

■ **Remove Taskbar from Settings on Start menu**, which removes the Taskbar folder from the submenu of the Settings menu item.

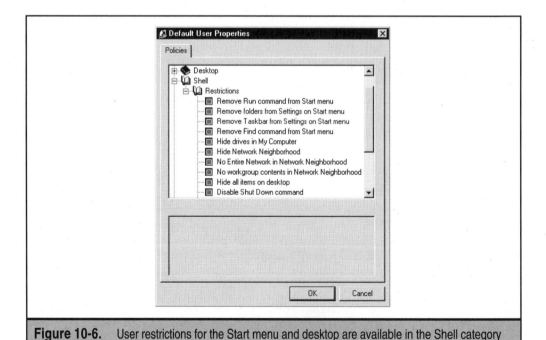

Figure 10-6.   User restrictions for the Start menu and desktop are available in the Shell category

■ **Remove Find command from Start menu**, which prevents the user from finding files and computers from the Start menu.

■ **Hide drives in My Computer**, which removes the drive icons from the My Computer folder. This keeps users away from all of the drive utilities and tools that are available, some of which can be dangerous.

■ **Hide Network Neighborhood**, which eliminates that icon from the desktop. This prevents users from browsing and manipulating other users' computers. This is one of those restrictions that probably needs to be enforced on only a limited number of users (and you know who they are).

■ **No Entire Network in Network Neighborhood**, which limits the icons to the local computer and the server.

■ **No workgroup contents in Network Neighborhood**, which means that only computers on the domain are displayed.

■ **Hide all items on desktop**, which creates the ultimate clean desktop. The Start menu and its contents remain available.

■ **Disable Shut Down command**, which eliminates that command from the Start menu.

▲ **Don't save settings at exit**, which prevents any user changes to the workstation's configuration from being saved. The changes are made and remain in effect while the user is logged on for that session, but the next reboot produces the original configuration.

System Restrictions

Expand System, then expand Restrictions to see a couple of powerful controls you can impose.

The Hide Network Neighborhood Restriction Has a Bug

When the Hide Network Neighborhood policy is in effect, users can still click the Map Network Drive icon on the My Computer toolbar or on the Explorer toolbar to show connected drives and gain access to them. In addition, the commands Net View and Net Use still let users see and access connected computers. The same is true for the other choices that restrict the display of computers in Network Neighborhood.

To make sure that you're really keeping users away from connected computers, you must also select Hide Drives in My Computer. This stops the functions for the Map Network Drives icons and also stops the Net Use command from functioning.

Incidentally, after you do this, the Net Use command does not return an error message when a user attempts to execute it. In fact, it says "Command completed successfully." However, as soon as the user tries to access the connected resource, an error message reports that the device is not ready.

Keep Users Away from the Registry

Choose **Disable Registry editing tools** to disable the users' ability to muck around in the registry. This one doesn't have to be explained.

Limit the Windows Applications Users Can Run

Choose **Run only allowed Windows applications** to limit the software users can run to those applications you specify. When you check this option, the bottom of the Properties window changes to display a Show button. Click it to open the Show Contents dialog box, which lists the allowed applications, if any.

    To begin an allowable applications list, click Add and enter the application filename in the Add Item dialog box (see Figure 10-7).

Problems and Bugs with Limiting Applications

There are a couple of side effects to limiting the Windows applications users can run. You have to be aware of them, and solve them, if you're going to use this restriction.

Include Systray.exe in Your List

There's a tray that holds some of the objects on the taskbar, such as the time display and the volume control for the sound card. This tray is placed there and controlled by a system application named Systray.exe. The operating system launches this application after logon.

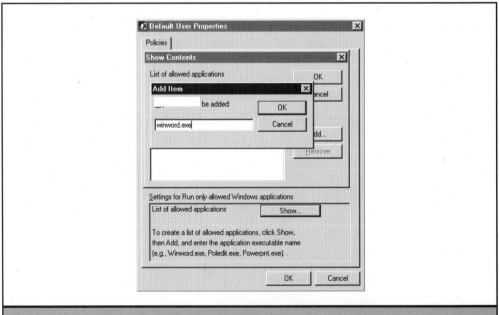

Figure 10-7.   Add the filenames of allowed applications to restrict users to those packages

When you restrict Windows applications by creating a list of allowable software, if you don't include Systray.exe, the user sees the following error message after logon: "This operation has been canceled due to restrictions in effect on this computer". After that the desktop and taskbar load but the tray objects don't.

To give the user the tray objects, be sure to include Systray.exe in your list of allowed applications.

DOS Applications Are Affected Too

There's a bug in the **Run only allowed Windows applications** restriction. The bug is that the limitation doesn't apply only to Windows applications. It affects any MS-DOS program shortcut. Apparently, Windows sees a shortcut as a Windows program, regardless of the target application for that shortcut.

Microsoft says it is preparing a fix for the bug (I guess it was either fix it or change the name of the restriction), but as of this writing it isn't ready. In the meantime, here's the workaround:

1. Create a batch file that launches the MS-DOS application.

2. Create a shortcut for that batch file.

3. Put the batch file on your list of allowed applications.

4. Put the target MS-DOS application on your list of allowed applications, just to be safe.

Microsoft Office Applications Can Always Run

The applications included in Microsoft Office can bypass the shell name space, which controls the running of applications. Instead, they use the utilities Msinfo.exe and Msinfo32.exe. This eliminates them from being monitored or affected by this system policy restriction. The only way to stop a user from accessing Office applications is to make sure that they aren't installed on the computer.

CREATING POLICIES FOR GROUPS OR INDIVIDUALS

When you first create a policy, the Default Computer and Default User icons appear in the software window, which means that your policies are applied to the entire domain. You can, however, change the target. When you first start, don't double-click the Default Computer or Default User icon. Instead, move to the Edit menu and follow these guidelines:

▼ Choose Add User to display the Add User dialog box. Enter the name of the user you want to target, or click Browse to see the Add Users dialog box, from which you can select one or multiple names (see Figure 10-8).

■ Choose Add Computer to display the Add Computer dialog box. Click Browse to see a list of domain computers, and double-click the target computer. Choose OK to place an icon for that computer on the Policy Editor window. To add more target computers, repeat the process (I cannot figure out a way to add multiple computers in one pass).

▲ Choose Add Group to display the Add Group dialog box. Click Browse to see a list of the administrative groups in your domain, and select those you want to target.

When you have finished making your selections, the icons for your targets appear in the window, as seen here:

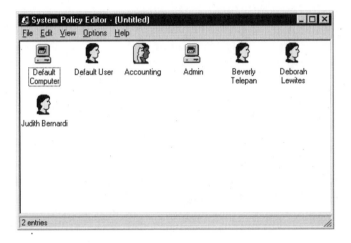

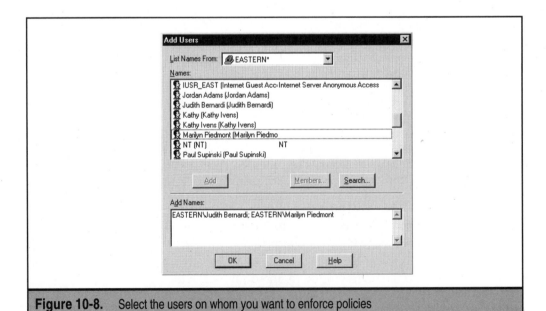

Figure 10-8.   Select the users on whom you want to enforce policies

Double-click the icon you want to work on, and select all the policies you need for that target. It's okay to leave the Default Computer and Default User icons in the window, because as long as you don't open them you're not configuring policies for them.

COMING SOON

Microsoft is currently testing a couple of new policies that will be included in the next version of this application. As a sneak preview I'll present them here (you can call Microsoft and ask for the hotfix if you don't want to wait for the next service pack).

Hide GoTo

Once you remove drives from My Computer and Explorer, using the NoDrives system policy, users can still access the drives by clicking GoTo on the Tools menu in Explorer. This option hides the GoTo command.

Hide View, Options Menu Item

There is currently no way to stop users from viewing all files or extensions of known file types in Explorer. Letting hidden files show makes it very easy for users to manipulate them. For instance, users could change the attributes of hidden files and then delete them, or reconfigure known file types to change their associations. Having a policy to restrict this view is probably an excellent idea for many administrators.

If you call Microsoft and get the fix for these missing policy restrictions, they will both be available in the Windows NT Shell, Restrictions category.

WINDOWS
NT
Professional
Library

PART IV

Troubleshooting Peripherals

WINDOWS
NT
Professional
Library

CHAPTER 11

Troubleshooting Printing

A ny Windows NT computer that has a printer attached can act as a print server for all of the Windows NT and Windows 95 computers on the network. In fact, a Windows 95 computer can also act as a print server.

It's a good idea to have an overview of Windows NT 4 printing, because it can sometimes be easier to troubleshoot a problem if you know what's supposed to happen.

UNDERSTANDING PRINTING IN WINDOWS NT 4

Printing in Windows NT 4 is basically a kernel process, with a series of processes involved in getting a print job to the printer.

Don't forget that Windows NT 4 is a protected-mode operating system, meaning that there's no direct access to hardware. When you print, you're printing to a virtual printer (some people call it a logical printer). The virtual printer controls the printing process and ultimately sends the print job to the physical printer. The configuration options you select when you are setting up a printer's properties are applied to the virtual printer. Of course, the options you select must match the capabilities of the physical printer.

Windows NT 4 approaches the relationship between virtual printers and physical printers in a very flexible way, providing you with a great deal of creativity as you set up printing services for the network. You can have any of three relationships between the virtual and physical printers.

A one-to-one relationship is a configuration in which print jobs are sent to a single virtual printer, which sends the print jobs to the single physical printer. This is the usual setup, and it works well when all users who use the same printer have the same basic printing needs.

A one-to-many relationship is a configuration in which all print jobs are sent to a single virtual printer, which passes the jobs to multiple physical printers. Those physical printers must be the same (or capable of emulating the same printer by accepting the same codes and instructions) and must be attached to the same computer. This process is called *printer pooling*, and it's used to spread the printing load in a high-volume environment or to ensure that there's a backup available if a printer fails in a mission-critical environment.

A many-to-one relationship is a configuration in which print jobs are sent to multiple virtual printers, all of which send jobs to the same physical printer. This is useful when you need different virtual configurations for the same physical printer. A couple of good reasons to set up multiple virtual printers for a single physical device are

▼ Some users need separator pages for their print jobs.

▲ Some users are printing enormous, graphic-filled documents that should take advantage of the delayed printing feature so they are printed overnight.

DECIDING ON PRINT SERVERS

Most of the time administrators choose a computer running Windows NT 4 Workstation to use as a print server. This choice usually makes a great deal of sense. It's actually more productive to purchase additional printers and use NT Workstation computers to service the printing needs of even a very large network. Most servers are providing important services to users and shouldn't have to assume the additional burden and overhead of providing print services.

It's possible to use a workstation as a print server while letting a user have that workstation for his or her tasks. The user should not be one who compiles programs, works in complicated graphics applications, or does complicated searches on databases. A workstation used primarily for word processing or some other less intensive task would be a good candidate for a print server. In addition, the hardware requirements for running Windows NT 4 Workstation are less than those required for Server, so it's not inappropriate to think about buying computers for the sole purpose of acting as print servers (or using the computers you're replacing with more powerful machines). They don't need CD-ROMs or backup devices, they can use a small, cheap monitor, and they don't need a lot of RAM.

However, there are some other limitations in the use of Windows NT Workstation as a print server:

▼ There is a limit of 10 simultaneous users, and they must all be on the same LAN.

■ You cannot run print services for Macintosh.

■ You cannot run print services for NetWare.

▲ Spooling priority is lower on NT Workstation than it is on NT Server. This may slow down the printing process a bit.

Don't forget that Windows 95 computers (which require even less RAM) can also act as print servers.

THE COMPONENTS INVOLVED IN PRINTING

A number of components are involved in providing printing services in Windows NT 4, and print jobs can have problems in any of them. Understanding the components and what they do can help you track down the source of problems.

The Spooler

The spooler is a group of .dll files that implement a number of tasks when a print job is dispatched by a user. The spooler performs the following tasks:

▼ Keeps track of the association between a printer and its port

■ Assigns priorities to print jobs waiting in the queue

■ Keeps track of the configuration of the physical printer (such as the number of trays and the amount of memory installed)

■ Sends the print job through the software processes involved in printing

▲ Sends the job to the physical printer

When the actual work is performed, the spooler receives the print job and stores it on disk. The sending application considers the job "printed," and the user has full use of the application to continue working. In the background, the spooler passes the job to the various print processes (the number and type of processes depend on the specifics of the print job) and eventually on to the physical printer.

The spooler is implemented as a service by Windows NT 4, and you can see its configuration in the Services applet in Control Panel (see Figure 11-1). By default, it has an automatic startup. You can stop and start the Spooler service if you need to by using the appropriate buttons in the Services Applet.

You can also stop and start the spooler by entering **net stop spooler** or **net start spooler** from the command line.

The Spool Files

By default, the disk files used by the spooler are contained in \%SystemRoot%\System32\spool\printers. Each spooled print job results in two files:

▼ The spool file, which is the print job and has a file extension of .spl

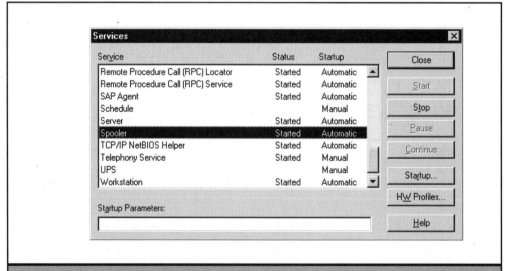

Figure 11-1. If you have overwhelming printing problems you can stop the Spooler service, but don't forget to notify users

▲ The shadow file, with a file extension of .shd, which contains the information needed to print the job (things like the priority, the name of the sending user, and the name and location of the physical printer)

The collection of spool files in the spooler directory is called the *queue*. Every computer that has an installed printer, whether it's attached locally or remotely, uses the same default location for the queue. If a print job is sent to a remote printer, the local spooler accepts the files and then ships them to the remote computer. In the end, the disk files sit on the computer that has the printer attached, waiting to be sent to the physical printer.

Problems with Disk Space and Large Queues

A computer acting as a print server can accumulate an enormous queue. If the files threaten to crowd the disk too much, you can move the queue to another drive on the same computer (if one exists). Otherwise, you'll have to make some other arrangements, such as using the computer only as a print server without installing any software, or replacing the drive with a larger one (or both).

If you are moving the queue to another drive on the computer, it's not merely a matter of creating the new directory on the new drive; you have to hack the registry to make sure the spooler knows where the queue is located. To accomplish this, follow these steps:

1. Create the new directory for the spooler files on the other drive (the path must exist before you can enter it into the registry).

2. If the file system on the drive is NTFS, be sure that the group Everyone has at least Write permissions (by default, the Everyone group has Full Control permissions, so it's easiest not to change the permissions).

3. Open a registry editor and go to HKEY_LOCAL_MACHINE\SYSTEM\ CurrentControlSet\Control\Print\Printers.

Queues and Queues

For those of us who spent years with NetWare printing, or who have experience with OS/2, the word "queue" conjures up a totally different meaning than the one it has in Windows NT 4. The queue in NetWare and OS/2 is the software interface between applications and physical printers. There is a one-to-one relationship between a queue and a printer.

In OS/2, when a print job is sent, the job is intercepted by the OS/2 spooler/queue (it's a combined concept), which passes the job to the physical printer. There's a one-to-one relationship between the software entity and the physical printer.

In NetWare 3.x (and also NetWare 4.x if you use a queue instead of a virtual printer), the concept is the same as in OS/2, except that there's a lot more work to setting up the queue.

4. When you select the Printers subkey, you can see the DefaultSpoolDirectory data item for the spooler. You also see additional subkeys for each printer installed on the computer (see Figure 11-2).

5. Modify the data value to reflect the path to the new location.

When you reboot the computer, the new spool file is the default.

The Printer Drivers

Another printing component is the printer driver, which translates the data and codes contained in the document to a form that is understood by the printer. Windows NT 4 uses the printer driver for three discrete tasks and therefore looks at the printer driver as an entity with three discrete parts. Those parts are

▼ The printer interface drivers

■ The graphics drivers

▲ The characterization data files

Windows NT 4 uses these components as follows:

▼ Interface drivers are used to let users configure the printer options. There are two drivers: Rasdui.dll for raster printers and dot-matrix printers and Pscrptui.dll for PostScript printers. Both drivers are found in \%SystemRoot%\System32\spool\drivers\w32x86.

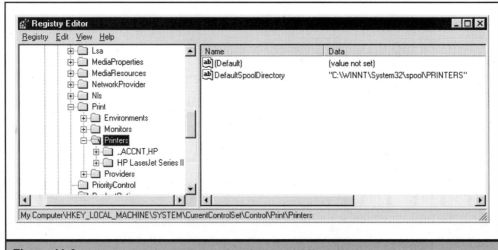

Figure 11-2. You cannot change the location of print spool files without changing the registry

- Graphics drivers are used to render images. There are two graphics drivers, also found in \%SystemRoot%\System32\spool\drivers\w32x86: Rasdd.dll for raster printers and dot-matrix printers and Pscript.dll for PostScript printers.

▲ Characterization data files are configuration files for the printer. They have the information about the manner in which the printer expects to receive data and codes. These files are provided by the printer manufacturer, and during the printer installation process they are transferred to \%SystemRoot%\System32\spool\drivers\w32x86. Most of the manufacturer-supplied drivers are found on your Windows NT 4 media; if they aren't there, you must obtain them and use the Have Disk option to install the printer. For raster printers, the files are referred to as minidrivers and are implemented as .dll files. For PostScript printers, the files are PPD (PostScript Printer Description) files.

NOTE: Minidrivers are source-code compatible across platforms and processors. PPD files are binary compatible across platforms and processors.

Along with the .dll files and the printer drivers, the \%SystemRoot%\System32\spool\drivers\w32x86 subdirectory also holds the help files that are used during printer installation. When you are using the dialog box for configuring a printer, these are the files that provide the text for the "What's This" help pages. They are Rasddui.hlp and Pscrptui.hlp.

The Print Provider

The print provider is responsible for matching your configuration options to the job that's being sent to the printer. There are two print providers, one for local printing and one for remote printing.

The local print provider (Localspl.dll) is found in \%SystemRoot%\System32 and operates only when a print job is sent to a local printer. It performs these chores:

▼ It writes the two files to the spooler (the job file and the shadow file).

- It processes the configuration item for a separator page, if there is one.

- It determines which print processor is needed to take care of the job's data type and passes the job along to that print processor (see "The Print Processor," later in this chapter).

▲ It passes the print job to the print monitor for the target port (see "The Print Monitors," later in this chapter).

The remote print provider wakes up when a Windows NT 4 computer sends a print job to a remote print server. There are actually two remote print providers: Win32spl.dll for Windows print servers and Nwprovau.dll for NetWare print servers. Both files are in the \%SystemRoot%\System32 directory.

If the print job is going to a Windows print server, the print provider turns the file over to the print router (discussed next). If the print job is going to a NetWare server, the job is sent to the NetWare redirector, which passes the job to the NetWare print server.

The Print Router

The print router sits between the client and the print server (even if the print server is also the client because the job is going to a local printer). It is implemented with Winspool.drv, which is in the \%SystemRoot%\System32 subdirectory.

The print router has two important jobs:

▼ It has to find the printer the print job needs.

▲ It has to make sure there's a printer driver for that printer on the print server.

After the print router has located the printer, it searches the print server to make sure there's an appropriate driver for the printer. If it does not find a driver, it sends one. If the print server is not the same computer as the sending computer (in other words, if it's not a local print process), it copies the spooled print file from the local hard drive to the spooler of the print server.

The Print Monitors

Another component in the Windows NT 4 printing process is the print monitor. This component controls the port and the communications between the port and the spooler. It performs these specific tasks:

▼ Accesses the port and sends the job to the port

■ Releases the port at the end of a print job

■ Notifies the spooler when the port is released so the spooler can delete the job from the queue and send the next job

▲ Monitors the printer to see if errors are being returned

NOTE: If the printer returns an error message to the print monitor, the print monitor sends notification of the error to the spooler. The spooler re-sends the print job. If the error prevents printing, an error message is sent to the client window. Frequently this is an "out of paper" message, but sometimes it's more serious.

A number of print monitors are included with Windows NT 4.

The Local Print Monitor

The local print monitor is named Localmon.dll, and it is in the \%SystemRoot\System32 subdirectory. It controls local ports, but it defines the term "local ports" in its own way. To the local print monitor, every item in the following list is a local port:

▼ The locally attached parallel port(s)

■ The locally attached serial port(s)

■ A file (the print monitor prompts for a name if you select this port for a print job)

■ An explicit filename (every job sent to that filename overwrites the last print job sent there)

▲ A UNC designation for a remote printer connection

Test Network Printing with the Local Print Monitor

There's another device that the local print monitor sees as a port, and it is named NUL. This is a "test" port. It exists not to print hard copy but to test your network printing processes. To use the NUL port for testing, follow these steps:

1. Set the printer to use the NUL port by selecting NUL from the Ports tab of the printer Properties dialog box.

2. Pause the printer.

3. Send a job to the printer from a connected computer.

4. Open the printer object; you should see the job listed.

5. If the job isn't listed, there is a problem with printer setup, and you will have to check the setup at both ends.

6. If the job displays, everything is fine. Resume printing. Nothing prints; the job disappears into la-la land.

If a NUL port doesn't exist for the printer, follow these steps to create it:

1. Open the printer's Properties dialog box and move to the Ports tab.

2. Choose Add Port, which brings up the Printer Ports dialog box, seen in Figure 11-3.

3. Select Local Port as the port type, then choose New Port.

4. The Port Name dialog box opens, as seen here. Enter **NUL** and choose OK.

5. Close the Printer Port dialog box to return to the Properties dialog box. The NUL port is installed and is selected for use (Figure 11-4).

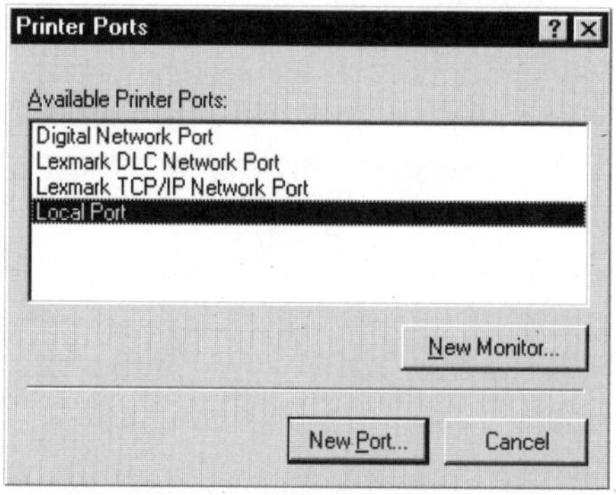

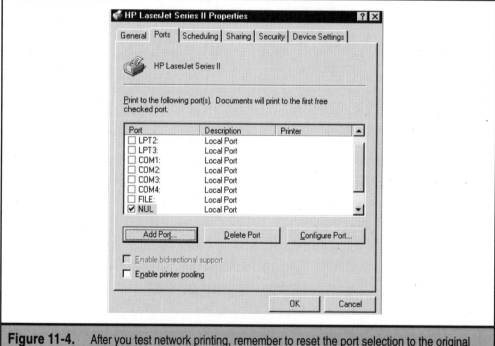

Figure 11-3.   All of the port types that are available for installation are displayed in the Printer Ports dialog box

Figure 11-4.   After you test network printing, remember to reset the port selection to the original configuration

Proprietary Print Monitors

There are several proprietary print monitors you can install for use with Windows NT 4; these are available on the CD-ROM.

▼ The Digital Print Monitor (Decmon.dll) is provided for Digital Network Ports you select for DEC PrintServer devices.

■ The HP Print Monitor (Hpmon.dll) is provided for JetDirect adapters and printer-based NICs.

■ The Macintosh Print Monitor (Sfmmon.dll) is for printing over the AppleTalk protocol. This monitor can be installed in any Windows NT computer for sending print jobs over AppleTalk, but only Windows NT Servers can receive these print jobs. To use the Macintosh Print Monitor you must install AppleTalk in your Network Protocols in the Control Panel.

▲ The LPR (Line Printer Remote) Print Monitor is part of the protocols that have been developed for TCP/IP. (It can be used to provide print services for Unix clients.) Actually, LPR is the client side of the protocol, and it runs via an executable file (Lpr.exe), which provides the LPR services. Those services, in turn, supply the print monitor (Lprmon.dll). On the receiving, or print server, end, LPD (Line Printer Daemon, a Unix term) is the required protocol, and it is provided via Lpdsvc.dll. No processing is available with Lpdsvc.dll, so the sending application must send files in the format expected by the printer. To use the LPR Print Monitor, you must install Microsoft TCP/IP printing services in your Network Services in the Control Panel.

The Print Processor

The Windows NT 4 print processor, Winprint.dll, is located in the \%SystemRoot%\ System32\spool\prtprocs\w32x86 subdirectory. Its function is to take the print job from the spooler and render it, if necessary. *Rendering* is the process of translating the data in the print job into a form that the physical printer can understand and accept. The print processor does not make the decision about whether or not rendering has to be applied; that decision is made by the spooler. If rendering is necessary, the spooler notifies the print processor of that fact when the job is passed to the print processor.

Whether a print job needs rendering or not depends upon the data type sent by the client application when matched against the information expected by the physical printer. That data type is derived from the configuration of the virtual printer (which uses information available in the printer driver).

Data Types

There are five data types generally found in printers configured for Windows NT 4 (I'll just list them here and then later discuss how they're used):

▼ RAW

■ RAW [FF appended]

■ RAW [FF auto]

■ TEXT (usually used for PostScript printers and plotters)

▲ NT EMF (enhanced metafiles)

The data type is established in the Properties dialog box for the printer. By default, most printers specify RAW as the data type, and generally there's no reason to change that.

But (there's always a "but" because things are never simple) most Windows applications pay absolutely no attention to the default data type configured for the selected printer. It is most common for Windows applications to send a job to the printer with the data type specified as NT EMF.

Next we'll talk about the processes involved in printing, and you'll see how the data type is manipulated and dealt with as the print job heads for its final output form.

THE PROCESSES IN NETWORK PRINTING

There are a slew of processes involved in printing to network printers, and problems can arise during any portion of the implementation of these processes. (I'm not covering local printing, because printing problems are much less common there.) Let's go over them briefly, assuming that a couple of processes have already been accomplished: a printer has been installed and configured on the print server and a printer has been installed as a network printer on the client computer. The remaining processes involved in printing are

▼ A user creates a print job in an application.

■ The user sends the print job.

■ The various components and processes that are part of Windows NT printing perform appropriate manipulations on the print job. The job is then sent to the network printer (actually to the print server that is connected to the network printer).

■ The print server ships the print job to the physical printer.

▲ The physical printer reads the data and codes and then produces a printed document.

The User Creates a Print Job

If a user is working in Windows software, the odds are that some of the components of the printing processes are being used well before the user even thinks about printing a document. A printer driver for the currently selected printer is loaded into memory when the application launches. This provides the information needed to produce a WYSIWYG interface.

The User Sends the Print Job

When the user does decide to print the document, a number of things occur. The application uses the Windows NT Graphics Device Interface (GDI) to generate an output file. The graphics engine in the Windows NT print services (Gdi32.dll) looks at the commands in the GDI and creates a translation that can be understood by the Windows NT print processes and also by the printer driver for the selected printer. Most Windows applications use the GDI to generate NT EMF data for the print job. (And by the way, it's the GDI that provides the WYSIWYG interface.)

The Local Spooler Works on the Print Job

The local spooler examines the print job, checking the data type. If the data type needs some manipulation, a note is attached that says, "Dear Print Processor: When you get this, render it properly so the printer can understand what you're sending" (okay, it's a not a real note and that sentence doesn't really appear, but that's the essence of what happens). The local spooler then passes the job to the Windows NT print processor.

The Print Processor Works on the Print Job

The print processor takes the following actions on data types:

▼ If the data type is RAW, no action is necessary; the job is ready for the printer.

■ If the data type is RAW [FF appended], the client application has sent a document for which the spooler was unable to determine whether or not a form feed code is present at the end of the job (to make the last page eject). The print processor checks this and adds one if necessary.

■ If the data type is RAW [FF auto], the print job is definitely missing an ending form feed and the print processor must add one.

■ If the data type is TEXT, the print processor uses the information in the appropriate printer driver to render the job into printer commands that will be accepted by the printer.

▲ If the data type is NT EMF, no work is performed by the print processor (the GDI did all the work before spooling the job).

After any rendering is performed, the print processor checks the location of the physical printer that is the target of this print job and sends the job to the spooler on the appropriate print server. To find the location, it uses the print router.

The Print Router Finds the Printer and Checks Printer Drivers

The first thing the print router does is find the target printer. After it locates the printer, it examines the printer driver that exists on the attached computer. If everything is fine and dandy, the print router delivers the job to the local spooler. If the job is intended for a network printer, the print router then copies the job from the local spooler and sends it to the printer server's spooler. If the correct printer driver is missing, or if the date of the driver on the sending computer is earlier than the date on the server, a new driver is sent to the client and loaded. The client then sends the job back to the router, which delivers it to the local spooler. If the job was intended for a network printer, the print router immediately copies it from the local spooler to the print server spooler.

TIP: If no printer is found, the client receives an error message ("printer not found") and everything stops. The client must select a different printer and start the process again.

The Print Server Gets the Job

When the print job is placed in the spooler on the print server, the print monitor is notified that a job is in the spooler (see "The Print Monitors," earlier in this chapter). The print job is shipped to the physical printer.

The Printer Gets the Job

The printer receives the print job and processes it, using all of the information that's been gathered, manipulated, and checked by all of the Windows NT 4 print processes. It prints. Whew!

Troubleshooting Data Type Problems

Sometimes the print processor incorrectly manipulates the data type, causing printing problems. You can almost always correct this by changing the default data type in the printer's Properties dialog box.

Line Printer (LPR) Problems

If you're using LPR, you may see one of these errors:

▼ The code for the printer's language (PCL or PostScript) prints out.

■ Extended characters included in the text print incorrectly.

▲ The physical printer's factory default font (usually Courier) is used. If you play with the controls on the printer to change the default font, the factory default font continues to print.

Earlier in this chapter, in the section "Proprietary Print Monitors," I said that one of the unique things about LPR printing is that no data manipulation takes place. If you see one of the problems just listed, it means there was some manipulation of the data type; these things do happen even if they're not supposed to. In fact, all of the problems listed here indicate that a data type of TEXT was assigned to the print job. As I also said earlier, at the receiving end (LPD), there is no power to make any changes to the data type, so the incorrect data type cannot be repaired.

The workaround is to reconfigure the LPR client to send the commands that result in a data type of RAW.

Last Page Ejection Problems

There are only two problems that can occur with last page ejection:

▼ The last page ejection doesn't work and the last page doesn't print.

▲ The last page ejection works too well and an extra page is ejected at the end of the job.

Some applications send a form feed at the end of the job; some fail to do so. It's the combination of what the application does and what the data type is that causes the problems.

If the last page fails to eject, it means the application does not send a form feed command at the end of a print job. Therefore, you have to take one of these steps:

▼ Reconfigure the client application to append a form feed to print jobs.

▲ Change the default data type value to RAW [FF Auto] or RAW [FF Appended] to force the print processor to deal with the problem.

If you're getting an extra page ejection after the print job, you have a couple of workarounds:

▼ Reconfigure the application to stop sending a form feed.

▲ Reconfigure the data type in the printer.

I hate to be so vague in that last choice, not telling you exactly what change to make, but there are certain things you have to look at before you can decide which data type to use as the new default for the printer. It's not the same as a missing form feed, where you can change the data type and let the print processor take care of the problem. The print processor can only add a form feed; it can't remove one.

▼ If all of the applications are sending form feed commands, set the default data type to RAW.

▲ If some applications send form feed commands but others don't, set the default data type to RAW [FF Auto].

A Stuck Print Job Cannot Be Deleted

If a print job gets hung in the spooler and you try to delete the job and cannot, the jobs behind the stalled job are stalled as well. In earlier versions of Windows NT, this required a reboot of the system, but with Windows NT 4, you can stop and then start the Spooler service. Unfortunately, this eliminates all of the jobs in the spooler, so after you restart the Spooler service you'll have to notify all users to re-send their print jobs. Don't let the stalled job return until you try to figure out what was wrong with it.

A Reinstalled Printer Doesn't Print

If you have to remove a printer from a system and then later reinstall it, you may find that the printer will not accept print jobs and gives you configuration error messages whenever you try to send a print job. This is caused by corrupted or incompatible files in the printer directory. You need to refresh the files. Delete the files from the \%SystemRoot%\System32\spool\drivers\w32x86 folder (on Intel processor machines), and then reinstall the printer.

PRINTING FROM DOS

There are a number of similarities in the way you install printers in Windows NT 4 and Windows 95, and in fact it's quite common to see networks with printers attached to computers with either operating system.

One difference, however, is that when you are installing a printer in Windows NT 4, there's no opportunity to tell the system that you want to be able to use the printer for DOS applications or for printing from the command line (that option is available when you install a printer on a Windows 95 computer).

If the printer is locally connected, you won't have a problem, because LPT1 is recognized by the operating system. As long as your DOS software is configured to print to LPT1, or you use LPT1 as the target when you're printing from the command line, the operating system will cooperate.

None of this is true if the printer is on a remote computer. Any effort to print from DOS or the command line in Windows NT 4 will generate an error message because there isn't any printer to receive the data stream that's sent to LPT1. To print from DOS to a network computer, you have to redirect the printing manually.

Windows NT 4 sees a printer as just another share and uses the standard command for manipulating shares (Net Use) to access the share.

The redirection command is **net use lpt1 ***computername**printersharename*. The command redirects printing for the current session. If you want to make the redirection permanent, so it's available the next time you log on, use the parameter **/persistent:yes**. The persistent connection is stored in the registry for the current user, not for the computer. This means the connection is persistent for this user; it will be not be available if a different user logs on to the computer. To get rid of a persistent printer connection, enter **net use lpt1 /delete**.

If you want to be able to print from DOS to multiple network printers, configure the DOS software for additional LPT ports, then use the command line to redirect those ports to the appropriate network printer.

TROUBLESHOOTING CONFIGURATION TASKS

There are a few configuration tasks (besides getting the data type right) that either present problems or cause problems later. We'll discuss some of them in this section.

Using Separator Pages

Separator pages (also called banners, especially by those of us who spent a lot of time administering NetWare networks) are a little more complicated to configure and implement than they are in NetWare (which just asks if you want one or not).

Separator pages are configured in the printer's Properties dialog box. Click the Separator Page button on the General tab to get started. The Separator Page dialog box opens, as seen here, asking for the name of the file you want to use for the separator page.

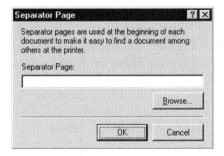

Notice that I said the file you want to use, not the file you want to print. The separator file isn't printed; it's just a series of instructions that are sent to the local print provider. The local print provider has an interpreter for the codes that appear in the file.

By default, all separator files print the user name, the date, and the job number. However, you can edit the file to change the information that's printed, or you can create your own. If you are going to try to make one, it's best to copy an existing file and use it as a template.

All of the separator files are in the \%SystemRoot%\System32 directory. There are three separator files, each of which has a specific use:

▼ For PostScript printers, use Sysprint.sep.

■ For PCL printers use Pcl.sep. This file will also switch the target printer from PostScript to PCL if the printer is dual-language.

▲ For dual-language printers that you want to switch to PostScript for this print job, use Pscript.sep.

As an example, the Pcl.sep file reads as follows:

```
\
\H1B\L%-12345X@PJL ENTER LANGUAGE=PCL
\H1B\L&l1T\0
\H34
\B\S\N\4
\I\4
\U\D\4
\E
```

Each line in this file is an escape code. You can modify or delete these codes or insert your own. Table 11-1 contains the function for each escape code.

\N	User name
\I	Job number
\T	Time the job prints
\Hnn	A printer-specific control sequence (nn is a hex code)
\Wnn	Width of the page in columns (characters beyond that width are truncated)
\B\S	Prints text in single-width block characters (continues until \U)
\E	Ejects a page
\n	the number of lines to skip (zero moves to the next line)
\B\M	Prints text in double-width block characters (continues until \U)
\U	Turns off printing of block characters

Table 11-1. Escape Codes for PCL Separator Files

To add the configuration option for separator files to a printer installed on a Windows NT computer, you can open the printer Properties from any computer on the network. However, if you try to do this for a printer installed on a Windows 95 computer you won't be successful. What's frustrating is that you can open the Properties dialog box and make the configuration changes without seeing any error messages. However, no separator pages will ever print. Windows 95–connected printers must be configured for separator pages from their local computer.

If only some of your users need (or want) separator pages, you should copy the target printer to create a second identical virtual printer. Set the printer up for sharing and give it a name that indicates it's configured for this option ("banner printer" probably isn't a bad idea). Configure the separator page option and then instruct those users to use that printer.

Pooling Printers

For important, busy, or mission-critical print servers, the ability to switch print jobs over to another printer when the first printer dies is a wonderful luxury. Printer pooling provides this service. The Ports tab of a printer Properties dialog box has an option for enabling printer pooling. A printing pool is made up of multiple identical (or compatible) printers that are connected to the same computer. The printers must be able to understand the same codes and instructions, and they must be on separate ports (see Figure 11-5).

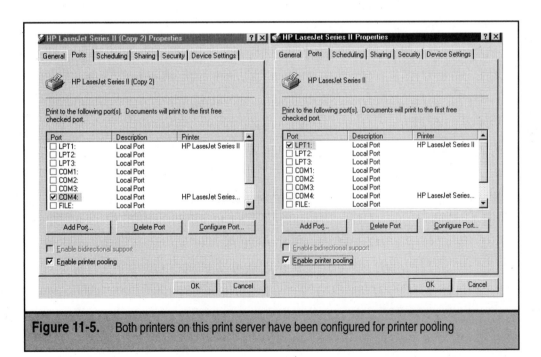

Figure 11-5.   Both printers on this print server have been configured for printer pooling

To move a print job, open the Properties for the dead printer and change the port to the location of the healthy printer. Then open the job list and restart the job. Remember to restart, not resume. You want the whole job reprinted to the new computer.

Handling Mismatched Print Jobs

A mismatched job is one in which the options called for in the print job don't match the currently available options for the printer. For example, a print job that calls for legal paper or an envelope in a one-tray printer may be mismatched with the printer's current configuration.

You can configure a printer to hold mismatched jobs on the Scheduling tab of the printer's Properties dialog box. Once the option is selected, the spooler will match the document's printer codes against the setup of the physical printer. If there's a mismatch, the spooler will hold the job in the queue, pushing other jobs ahead of it. At some point, when it's convenient, you can change the physical printer to match the job, configure the Properties to match the change, and print the job.

If you don't tell the printer to watch out for mismatched jobs, the mismatched job holds up the entire queue until somebody notices an error message (if you're lucky enough to get one) or notices the printer's blinking lights (and probably a message on the front panel asking for a manual feed of paper).

Spooling Efficiently

The Scheduling tab of the printer Properties dialog box also has options for spooling (see Figure 11-6).

The two major spooling options are to spool documents or send them directly to the printer. For a shared printer, you really have no choice; you have to spool documents. Actually, there's rarely a good reason not to spool documents. If you don't, the user has a long wait before the software operates at an efficient productive level. Spooling gets the printing out of the way quickly so the user can go back to work fast.

Once you've opted for spooling, you have two methods for spooling print jobs:

▼ Start printing after the last page is spooled, which has as an advantage the fact that the entire document is available to the printer before printing starts. Sometimes, for a busy shared printer, there's a deluge of data arriving and there may be a delay in printing while the spooler receives and processes the rest of the file. This is rare, however, and the delay is usually not terribly long.

▲ Start printing as soon as the first page arrives, which helps the user get back to full productivity in the sending application.

In addition, you can opt to print spooled documents first (see the configuration choices at the bottom of the Scheduling tab). This option can often make the printer a more productive device. What it means is that the spooler gives priority to any document that has finished spooling when it is deciding what to print next. Print job priority is ignored in this approach, because any low-priority document that has completed spooling will be printed before any high-priority document that is still spooling. In

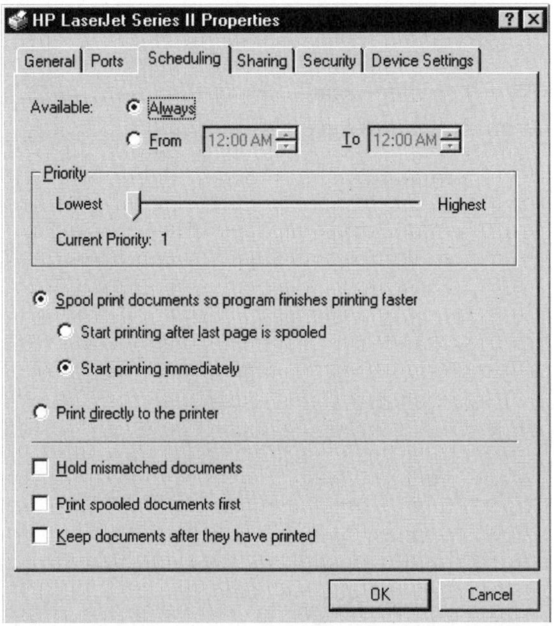

Figure 11-6.   The Scheduling tab has options for a great deal more than scheduling, and spooling options can affect the efficiency of your printing operations

addition, if there are a lot of documents in the process of spooling (and none finished spooling), the spooler will set a print priority by placing the largest document first in line, then the next largest, and so on (print job priorities are ignored).

AUDITING PRINTERS

If you need to track printing operations and any administrative events connected to printing, you can audit the printing process. To accomplish this, you really have to take two steps: turn on auditing as a feature, and specifically configure auditing for the printer(s).

To turn on auditing for a computer, follow these steps:

1. Open User Manager and choose Audit from the Policies menu.
2. When the Audit Policy dialog box appears (Figure 11-7), select Audit These Events. This makes the items in the event list accessible.
3. For printing audits, select File and Object Access and then choose whether you want to audit success, failure, or both.
4. Choose OK when you have made your selections.

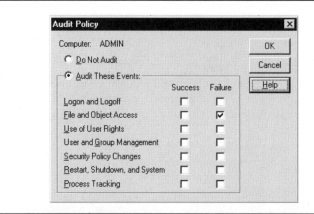

Figure 11-7. You must turn on auditing for the appropriate type of event before you can establish specific auditing on your computer

TIP: There's rarely a good reason to audit successes, and doing so makes the audit log enormous. Unless you have some need to know every single thing that occurred, stick to the failures because that's where your problems probably are. Later, if you think you're not gaining enough information, you can return to the configuration and change the audit options.

Now that auditing has been established for the computer, you can set up auditing for the printers on the computer. To do that, take these steps:

1. Open the Properties for the printer and move to the Security tab.

2. Select Auditing to display the Printer Auditing dialog box, which is illustrated in Figure 11-8.

3. Choose Add to specify groups and users you want to audit. The Add Users and Groups dialog box appears, allowing you to choose the users you need. Click OK when you have finished adding names.

4. Back at the Printer Auditing dialog box, select the events you want to track. Choose Success, Failure, or both.

Any events that fall under your auditing options are reported to the Security log in the Event Viewer.

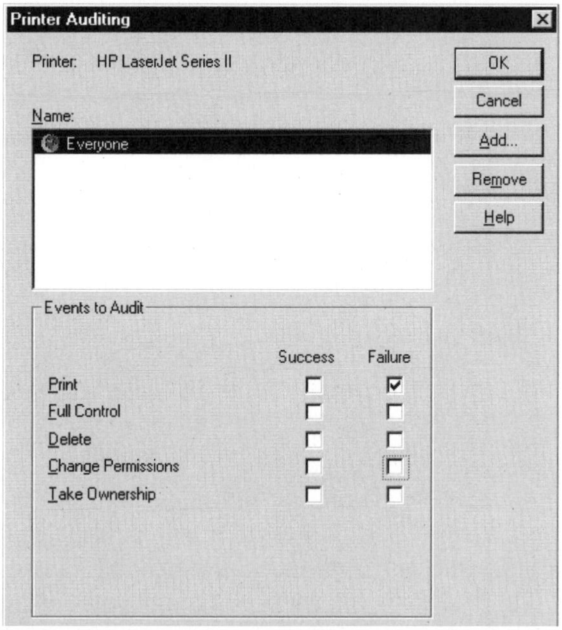

Figure 11-8. Start with a simple audit; you can always come back and add more items

TIP: For shared printers I usually choose Network as the group to audit, since that group is defined as anyone who connects to the printer from a remote computer. That's frequently where the problems are.

WINDOWS
NT
Professional
Library

CHAPTER 12

Troubleshooting Modems and RAS

Troubleshooting Remote Access Services (RAS) can be one of the most frustrating troubleshooting jobs you'll have with Windows NT. The confluence of Windows NT, RAS, modems, phone lines, remote modems, remote systems, and—most important—remote users makes troubleshooting very complex. And while I always find it's extremely satisfying to solve some of these tricky problems, I've learned that it frequently takes quite a bit of time and patience to solve remote access problems.

To troubleshoot RAS successfully, you need to proceed through the troubleshooting process step by step. While sometimes you will encounter a problem that you can quickly home in on and address, most of the time you need to be methodical in eliminating possible sources of trouble one item at a time. At a high level, you need to examine and eliminate the following sources of trouble:

▼ Is RAS functioning? Was it working previously, and is it still working for other users or applications?

■ Is the Windows NT RAS computer communicating with the modem?

■ Are the installed network protocols working correctly, and is their configuration correct?

■ Has there been a hardware failure in the RAS server, its communication ports, or its modems?

■ Has there been a hardware failure in the remote user's modem, system, or COM ports?

■ Is the phone line working properly, both at the local RAS server connection and at the remote user's location?

■ Is the remote user's system properly configured for RAS, for the RAS network connection, and for the modem?

▲ Has the remote user made some operational mistake or misinterpreted the situation? For instance, is he or she using the wrong phone number or not logging in to the network properly?

These questions are just the beginning, but their breadth shows you how many factors can be involved in troubleshooting RAS problems, and why it can often be difficult to quickly solve RAS problems, particularly for remote users, because you cannot bring your training and experience to bear in observing the problem firsthand.

In this chapter you learn about troubleshooting RAS, about the tools available to help you do the job, about specific problems encountered when troubleshooting RAS, and some tips in working with remote users to troubleshoot RAS.

USING PERFORMANCE MONITOR TO TROUBLESHOOT RAS

Performance Monitor, discussed in Chapter 15, contains some important performance counters that are helpful in solving RAS problems, or just for monitoring the health of your RAS server and its connections. There are two performance objects that contain counters applicable to RAS: RAS Port and RAS Total. (These performance objects appear only when RAS is installed, by the way.) The RAS Total performance object contains performance counters that show the status of all RAS ports on the system combined; it is helpful in monitoring the overall health of the RAS server and in comparing total RAS activity with the activity on specific ports. The RAS Port performance object, on the other hand, contains counters that monitor specific RAS ports on the system. Use the Instance window in the Add to Chart dialog box of Performance Monitor to select the specific port you want to monitor. The actual performance counters in RAS Total and RAS Port are the same; they apply either to all ports combined or to a specific port, respectively.

Following is a description of the available counters and how you can apply them to RAS troubleshooting:

▼ **Alignment Errors** Use this counter to see how often the data received by the RAS server was not what was expected due to an alignment error in the stream of bits from the remote system. Generally, errors in this counter are caused by poor-quality telephone connections or electrical interference on the cable leading from the modem to the RAS server's COM port (which can be eliminated by using good-quality shielded cable and keeping cable length to less than 50 feet for RS-232C cables).

■ **Buffer Overrun Errors** This counter shows the number of errors caused when the RAS server could not process incoming information as quickly as it was received. Data tends to be received in bursts, and the system buffers incoming data so that it can process the data smoothly. When the data buffers are overrun, it's because the system is not clearing the buffers as quickly as data is being received. When you see these errors, consider installing a faster processor or more RAM, or look at other general-purpose performance counters to find the actual bottleneck in the system.

■ **Bytes Received** This counter simply counts the total number of bytes received, either in total (RAS Total) or for a specific port (RAS Port). It can be useful in load-balancing the system or in planning for upgrades in the number of ports on the system.

■ **Bytes Received/Sec** You typically want to correlate the number of bytes received per second with any error counts experienced. Doing so can help you to learn whether the problem is related to the load on the system. Sometimes RAS servers work fine when they have nominal loads, but at maximum load errors start cropping up because the system's resources are being overwhelmed. When correlating this performance counter, compare it to Alignment Errors and Buffer Overrun Errors.

- **Bytes Transmitted** This counter, used in combination with Bytes Received, allows you to measure the ratio of downstream and upstream data requirements. One place where this ratio becomes useful is in evaluating whether to use ADSL (asynchronous DSL) or SDSL (synchronous DSL) for your remote users or sites.

- **Bytes Transmitted/Sec** This counter, used along with Bytes Received/Sec, allows you to see how the server is being loaded, and can also correlate with any error counters that are appearing. It is possible to have errors that correlate with only one of either Bytes Received/Sec. or Bytes Transmitted/Sec.

- **CRC Errors** A corrupt frame causes CRC (Cyclic Redundancy Check) errors. It means that the CRC value for the data received (similar in concept to a checksum value) is not what the received CRC says it should be. Causes include an improperly operating modem, a poor cable, and poor telephone line quality.

- **Frames Received and Frames Transmitted** Frames Received and Frames Transmitted (two different performance counters) are similar to Bytes Received and Bytes Transmitted, in that they show the amount of data being sent and received over the RAS connections.

- **Frames Received/Sec. and Frames Transmitted/Sec** Again, similar to Bytes Received/Sec and Bytes Transmitted/Sec, these counters can be used to show instantaneous communications load on the RAS server.

- **Percent Compression In** This counter shows how efficiently data is being received. The value varies, depending on the types of data being received; highly compressed binary data, such as .zip, .jpg, or .gif files, cannot be compressed any further, while text data is easily compressed and will register higher values in this counter.

- **Percent Compression Out** Use this counter to see how efficiently the RAS server is compressing data being sent out. It will vary depending on the load on the RAS server and the types of data being transmitted.

- **Serial Overrun Errors** Serial overrun errors are caused when the computer cannot keep up with the amount of data being received by the serial ports. It can indicate IRQ saturation on the RAS server, so check the server's IRQ load with the System performance object and see if the errors correlate. If so, consider installing different serial ports (perhaps with better UARTS), using a higher-throughput bus instead of ISA, or upgrading other server resources that are not letting it keep up with the data being sent (processor, RAM, or other bottlenecks).

- **Timeout Errors** When the remote system isn't sending data as quickly as it should, a timeout error occurs. It generally indicates a performance problem or some other trouble with the remote system.

- **Total Connections** This counter shows the current number of RAS connections and should be correlated with any error counters. It is possible to have problems that correlate more closely to the number of connections than to the amount of data being sent and received. For example, six 9,600 bps RAS connections have a different impact on the system than one 57,600 bps connection, even though the maximum amount of data is about the same. If this becomes the case, you'll want to examine hardware problems related to processing multiple connections, such as having more than one port active, a saturated bus, or interrupt conflicts with other devices.

- ▲ **Total Errors and Total Errors/Sec** Use these counters to keep a watchful eye on your RAS server. They are the sum of all of the error counters.

TIP: You may want to use Performance Monitor to create alerts on the Total Errors and Total Errors/Sec. counters so that you don't have to monitor them manually on a regular basis. Chapter 15 describes how to do this.

USING SPECIAL REGISTRY SETTINGS TO LOG RAS

To diagnose tricky problems, you can enable detailed logging of aspects of the RAS system. These log settings are enabled by modifying the system's registry. (All of the standard warnings and disclaimers apply; be careful when doing this!)

The first special log is called RasMan Logging. It lets you look for problems between the RAS server and its modems. In the log you see what commands are being sent to the modems and how the modems reply. You look at this data to see whether the modems are operating correctly and whether the server is using the right command sets for the modems you've installed.

To enable RasMan Logging, follow these steps:

1. Open a registry editor and go to HKEY_LOCAL_MACHINE\SYSTEM\ CurrentControlSet\Services\RasMan\Parameters.

2. Open the Logging item (it's a DWORD item).

3. Change the Data to 1.

4. Restart the system.

When the system is restarted, a log file will be created in the \%SystemRoot%\System32\RAS\ directory. The file created is called Device.log. It will contain the commands sent to the modems as well as the replies received (such as OK or ERROR). It is a text file viewable with Notepad or WordPad.

Another useful log to look at when encountering problems is the PPP transaction log. You enable it by finding the following key in the registry editor: HKEY_LOCAL_MACHINE\SYSTEM\CurrentControlSet\Services\RasMan\PPP.

Modify the Logging value so that its DWORD data is 1, and then restart the system. A logging file called Ppp.log will then be created in the \%SystemRoot%\ System32\RAS\ directory. In it, you can view and monitor PPP errors or problems.

Another useful log to create is not enabled in the registry editor but rather in the Modems dialog box in the system's Control Panel. Select one of the modems shown in the Modems dialog box and open its Properties dialog box. Go to the Connections tab and click the Advanced button. In the Advanced Connection Settings dialog box, select the check box labeled Record a Log File. Click OK to close the dialog box. A log file called Modemlog.txt will then be maintained in the \%SystemRoot%\ directory, showing activity between the specific modem and the RAS services.

TROUBLESHOOTING MODEMS AND PORTS

Modem troubles are problematic to track down and solve, for several reasons. First, there are two modems involved in any particular dial-up RAS connection, and it can be time-consuming to find out which of the two is causing the trouble. Second, remote users often use the least-expensive modems available, not realizing that such modems are often subject to many problems. Third, even the best modems often do unexpected things and need to be completely reset to work properly after a previous connection. Indeed, modems can be a real pain in the RAS.

Consider the following topics when troubleshooting apparent modem problems:

▼ **Make sure that the RAS server's modem is listed in the Windows NT HCL.**
Modems not found in the hardware compatibility list (HCL), while they may work properly, have not been certified by Microsoft to do so. RAS can be demanding of modems, so it's a good idea to use modems that have passed Microsoft's RAS modem testing process.

■ **Make sure the remote user is using an acceptable modem.** With some companies selling "100 percent compatible" modems (that never are) for half or less of what reputable modem manufacturers' products cost, the user's modem is often a problem. Find out if the modem is certified with the operating system they're using.

■ **Try resetting the modems on both ends.** External modems can be reset simply by cycling their power, while internal modems will require that the system be shut down, *and its power turned off*, to perform a real reset. (Similarly, to reset a serial port, a restart is not enough; the power to the system must be cycled.)

■ **Make sure the remote user has properly installed the modem driver.** Have the remote user go into the Modems Control Panel dialog box and check the installed driver. Small differences in the modem's model numbers can result in big problems. In a pinch, have the user remove the modem's driver and reinstall it from the Windows original media.

- **Try a different modem on either end, if they simply can't communicate.** Modems can and do go bad, and sometimes in surprising ways (for instance, they may work well with one sort of remote connection, but work poorly with a different sort of connection). There are times when replacing the modem, even with another of the same type, can yield positive results.

- ▲ **Use HyperTerminal to communicate with the modem.** Try using HyperTerminal to issue simple modem commands to the appropriate COM port to see if the modem responds. For example, ATZ resets the modem and should result in an OK from the modem. ATH1 will pick up the phone line from the modem (you should see the OH light come on for an external modem, and you should hear a dial tone for both internal and external modems), and ATH0 hangs up the phone line. If the modem won't respond to HyperTerminal, it won't respond to RAS, so using HyperTerminal as a troubleshooting tool can save you some time.

If the modems are working properly but the problem remains, your next bet is the serial port and cable for both the RAS server and the remote computer (depending on which of the two works with other connections). With regard to cabling, check to make sure the remote user's cable from the serial port to the modem is correct (this only works, of course, if the user has never connected to any remote computer). The user may have purchased a null-modem cable by mistake, which will not work with a modem. If you suspect cable trouble, it's best to replace the cable. Good-quality serial cables are inexpensive and are easily replaced.

Diagnosing serial port problems is more difficult. You first need to determine whether the problem has always existed or has just developed. After learning that, consider the following ideas:

- ▼ **Serial port problems often occur because of IRQ conflicts.** You cannot have two devices using the same IRQ simultaneously, and it's a bad idea to share IRQs for sequential access, even if the IRQ is guaranteed to be shared exclusively. Moreover, the standard IRQ assignments for COM1 to COM4 contain overlaps: COM1 and COM3 share IRQ 3, while COM2 and COM4 share IRQ 4. Because of this, you cannot use COM1 and COM3—or COM2 and COM4—simultaneously. In addition, if there is a NIC in the computer, check to see if there could be a conflict there. Many NICs are set to IRQ 3 by default, and most system administrators move the IRQ in order to use COM ports. Remote users with external modems may just install a NIC with the default settings, not realizing the consequences.

TIP: Run Windows NT Diagnostics to see what IRQs are assigned to each COM port under Windows NT. For Windows 95, check the Device Manager in the System Properties dialog box to see a listing of all IRQ assignments in the system.

- **Check the serial port's settings.** Particularly when using an add-on serial port, make sure its settings are all correct.

- **Check internal modem settings.** Internal modems include their own COM ports, and their COM ports may conflict with other COM ports installed in the system. For instance, you cannot have an internal modem set to be COM1 when there is a COM1 port on the motherboard that is still working. The answer is either to choose a different COM port for the internal modem or to disable or reassign the built-in COM port.

- **COM ports must be sequential.** You cannot have any gaps in the COM port numbers in the system. An internal modem set to be COM4 when there is no COM2 or COM3 will not function properly.

- **Check to make sure that some other program isn't trying to use a particular COM port simultaneously.** Some older communications programs may not properly release the port so that it can be used by RAS. A common problem is a non-TAPI-compliant fax application that is seizing the COM port in order to await incoming faxes. The remote user will have to quit any such application in order to use the COM port to make a dial-up connection. Remember that some users may not even realize the fax application is running, if it loads on startup.

- **Try testing the serial port.** You might consider using a serial loopback plug and some sort of third-party diagnostics program. Many computers come with software to test the serial ports with a loopback plug. Check the documentation that came with the system or the serial port to find out where to get an appropriate loopback plug or how to wire one yourself.

- ▲ **Try replacing the serial port.** You might have to try disabling a motherboard-based serial port in favor of an add-in card with serial ports to make sure there isn't a problem with the built-in serial ports on a system.

TROUBLESHOOTING PHONE LINES

Troubleshooting telephone lines is often bothersome. Because each individual connection will use different connections at the telephone company's central office (CO) , or may be carried over different long distance lines, a problem that surfaces once in a while can be tough to duplicate long enough to properly diagnose. Furthermore, a clean line can suddenly and intermittently degrade with static or crosstalk and then clear up again just as mysteriously.

You should check for phone line problems when you see the following symptoms:

▼ Slower than expected connection speeds

■ Sudden degradations (or simply unexpected fluctuations) in the speed of the transmitted or received data

■ Remote user having a connection abruptly terminated without warning (a blinking carrier detect [CD] light on an external modem is a great clue that the phone line has degraded suddenly)

▲ Inability to connect to the RAS server, particularly on a sporadic basis

To sort out telephone line problems, look into the following troubleshooting activities:

▼ Try calling in to the RAS modem, particularly from the remote site having the problem, with a standard telephone. Not only can you then confirm that the remote modem is answering the call correctly, but if you are experienced with how modems should normally sound, you may be able to detect line static. Keep in mind that static may be occurring only in the point-to-point connection; the remote user may not experience static when calling other voice telephone numbers. If the problem occurs only when the user is connected to the RAS server, but you've eliminated the RAS server's phone line as a possible source, you can have the local RBOC (Regional Bell Operating Company) conduct a point-to-point line quality check.

■ If the problem with phone line quality seems to involve multiple remote users, it is almost certainly on the side of the RAS server. Have your local telephone company test the lines. You may have to upgrade the lines to be data-certified, typically for a small additional monthly charge per line, in order to get the phone company to guarantee the clarity needed for high-speed modem connections.

▲ International connections are often subject to delays in how quickly signals move between sites due to satellite delays. Whenever possible, request that the involved long distance carrier flag the long distance lines as being landline based. Some carriers charge extra for ensuring that calls are routed through fiber-optic lines, while others will do so for no additional charge. (Of course, it also depends on whether the long distance carrier has any landlines available for use; many don't.)

Diagnosing phone lines is tricky because you can't control all the factors involved and can't even really tell what's happening between the remote site and the RAS server. However, if you can work through various examples and counterexamples to completely isolate the problem, you can then work with the RBOC to come up with solutions.

COMMON RAS PROBLEMS

There are a number of other problems commonly seen with RAS. Checking though the following sections may help you save time in identifying and resolving a particular problem. While there are certainly many problems that can occur that aren't described here, you'll find the most common problems—and their solutions—in the following sections.

The Modem Cannot Be Initialized

Seen when the RAS server cannot properly reset the modem or get it to respond correctly, this problem will generate the following error in the System log in the Event Viewer:

```
Error 692: Hardware failure in port or attached device
```

Most often this is caused by the modem not responding as expected. To resolve the problem, first try completely resetting the modem (remember that an internal modem needs the computer's power cycled in order to reset fully). Then check to make sure you're using the right driver for the modem and that the modem is listed on the Windows NT HCL. You might also check to see if a newer driver is available for the modem.

TIP: It sounds obvious, but this error can also occur when the modem is turned off!

This particular error message can also occur when the serial port in the system has failed. Again, the first thing to try is resetting it completely. Check that the cable to the modem has not become loose.

Finally, read "Troubleshooting Modems and Ports," earlier in this chapter, for more advice on correcting this error message.

The Modem on the RAS Server Answers, but No Connection Is Made

This is a common problem with several possible sources. You'll first want to test the modem and port that the remote user is attempting to use by trying to connect yourself from another remote machine that is known to be working.

TIP: It's always a good idea to set up another computer on the network with the necessary Dial-Up Networking software and hardware, as well as its own telephone line, to test specific RAS ports if remote users report trouble. Having such a resource available makes narrowing down the problem to a server-side problem or remote-side problem a snap.

Next, make sure that both the RAS server and the remote system have the correct modem drivers installed. Then have the remote user try to connect at a slower speed, like 9,600 bps or even 2,400 bps. The goal with this maneuver is to isolate the phone line;

poor-quality lines may not allow connections to be made at the top modem speed but may work fine at slower speeds.

Try to use the exact same model of modem on the RAS server side as on the remote computer side. As a general rule of thumb, modems from the same manufacturer will tend to connect more reliably and will also negotiate a best possible speed with each other more successfully than two different models or makes of modems.

Have the remote user change some of the Dial-Up Networking settings. Have the user disable modem compression, hardware-based flow control, and modem error-checking features in the Modems property dialog boxes (you can find these settings on the Connection tab by clicking on the Advanced button found there).

A Remote User Connects but Cannot Log In

There are several things to try when this occurs. First, you must ensure that the user account the user is attempting to log in with has been enabled for remote connections to the RAS services. You can find the check box that enables this access by using the Remote Access Admin tool in Windows NT.

A tricky problem that can cause these symptoms can occur when the remote user is using Windows NT Workstation. To check this, have the remote user follow these steps:

1. Open the Dial-Up Networking Phonebook.

2. Edit the properties for the connection they've defined.

3. Move to the Security tab.

4. Select the Accept Only Microsoft Encrypted Authentication check box.

5. Clear the Use Current Username and Password check box.

After making these changes, have the user again try to connect.

Sometimes a user's logon name is located in a domain that is different from the one in which the RAS server is a member. If such is the case, the two domains must have a trust relationship in order to authenticate the user. Also, the remote user has to specify his or her home domain to log in to, rather than the RAS server's domain.

Finally, if the RAS server performs authentication for some users, but the user attempting to connect is authenticated through a different domain, make sure the user specifies his or her home domain instead of the RAS server's domain.

RAS Protocol Connection Errors

Remote callers may see one of the following three error messages:

```
Error 629: The port was disconnected by the remote server.

Error 733: The PPP control password for this network protocol is not
available on the server.
```

```
Error 734: The PPP link control protocol terminated.
```

These errors often occur when the protocol the remote user is attempting to use is not configured correctly or there is some other protocol violation. To resolve these errors, have the remote user ensure that he or she is trying to use a connection protocol supported by the RAS server.

Next, if the remote user is using TCP/IP and is expecting the RAS server to provide an IP address, but the RAS server isn't configured to do so, the user will experience this kind of error.

Finally, if using NetBEUI, the remote computer may be attempting to use a NetBEUI network name that matches one already connected to the network, which NetBEUI doesn't allow.

RAS Won't Connect to an ISP

Windows NT Workstation machines use RAS to dial out to Internet service providers. Users dialing out might encounter problems that you will be called on to resolve. There are several RAS settings that could be the cause. Check the following:

▼ **Disable LCP extensions.** Some older systems don't support LCP extensions for PPP connections. Try opening the Phonebook settings, moving to the Server tab, and clearing the Enable PPP LCP Extensions check box.

■ **Disable IP header compression.** Another problem seen with older PPP servers is an inability to support Van-Jacobson compression (also known as VJ Header Compression or IP Header Compression). This setting is found in the Properties dialog box for the TCP/IP networking protocol.

■ **Try disabling other protocols.** You might try disabling all protocols other than TCP/IP when trying to connect. Ensure that other protocol support is disabled in the DUN or RAS properties for the connection you're attempting.

▲ **Use plain-text passwords and logon names.** Some ISPs don't support encrypted passwords when connecting. Under Windows NT 4, open the Phonebook entry, move to the Security tab, and select the Accept Any Authentication Including Clear Text option button.

If these suggestions fail to resolve the problem, you should try a manual logon to see if doing so sheds any light on what's happening. Under Windows NT 4, edit the Phonebook entry, switch to the Script page, and select the Pop Up a Terminal Window option button. After the carrier detect signal is received from the remote system, a terminal window appears in which you can try logging in manually. You may see error messages during this process that help you find the source of the problem.

A Remote User Connects but Cannot Access the Network

You may see this problem, in which the remote user connects successfully but then cannot see any printers, shares, or folders on the network, when the logon name and password with which the user connected doesn't match the one he or she used to log on to their *local system* originally.

When a remote user connects to a RAS server, the logon name and password the user enters is used only for access to the RAS server. Thereafter, the logon name and password with which the user logged on to the local system takes control when opening network resources.

If this happens, have the remote user remain connected to the RAS server but log off from the network (right-click on the appropriate domain or server in Network Neighborhood and choose the command from the shortcut menu). Then have the user open the server or domain by double-clicking on it, at which point there will be a prompt to log on again. The user can provide the correct user name and password to access the network resources. Another option is to have the remote user create a new local account and password that matches the one the network requires. The network will then automatically validate the user for access to network resources. Finally, have the user employ the Net Use command (specifying the domain and /User parameter) to force a new logon to the network.

Using an Unlisted Modem for a RAS Server

It is strongly recommended that you only use modems listed in the Windows NT HCL for a RAS server. Sometimes, though, you have no choice and must use some other modem. There are some things you can try to improve your chances of success when doing this:

▼ Check with the modem's manufacturer for Windows NT and RAS compatibility. The company may have done its own testing for Windows NT and RAS compatibility and chosen not to participate in the Microsoft-sponsored testing that makes up the HCL. It may also have Windows NT modem drivers and RAS scripts available.

■ You can try to use a modem driver that is emulated by the non-HCL modem. Windows NT also lists some generic Hayes-compatible modem drivers that might work (of course, they won't take advantage of any of the modem's enhanced features).

▲ You can sometimes use Windows 95 .inf files under Windows NT when no Windows NT .inf file is available. Try this as a last resort (or as the next-to-last resort, the last resort being getting new modems).

NOTE: Like most sound cards, most modems claim 100 percent compatibility with some modem standard, and just as similarly, they are almost never 100 percent compatible. All modems are not created equal, even if their manufacturers say they are!

A Remote User Can't Connect to a Local and Remote NetWare LAN

As a remote user, you cannot be connected locally to a NetWare LAN (via Ethernet or some other LAN connection) and also connect to a different NetWare LAN via a RAS server. The problem is due to limitations in how Novell designed the architecture of IPX/SPX.

There are two possible solutions. First, the remote user can disconnect from the local NetWare LAN before forming the RAS connection. Second, you can install the Windows NT Gateway Services for NetWare, which provides services to a NetWare LAN on the RAS server side, but does so in a way that doesn't conflict with the NetWare client software. What happens is that the Gateway Services provide NetWare LAN access but do so by emulating Windows NT networking services and running over NetBEUI. When a user is connecting to a RAS server running the Gateway Services for NetWare, make sure he or she uses NetBEUI to connect and not IPX/SPX.

Windows NT Can't Communicate with Serial Ports

Changes in the way that Windows NT 4 works with serial ports can be incompatible with the way a system's BIOS expects the operating system to access its serial ports. If everything worked fine under Windows 95 and Windows NT 3.51, but not under Windows NT 4, suspect a BIOS problem. A flash memory upgrade of the BIOS will usually take care of this. If you experience similar trouble, contact the manufacturer of your computer system and ask about a BIOS upgrade.

Problems with Windows NT 4 Service Pack 2

Service Pack 2 for Windows NT 4 introduced some RAS problems not seen with base-level Windows NT 4 or Service Pack 1. The problem occurs when you are using a system running Service Pack 2 and connecting to an ISP for an Internet connection. The easiest solution is to install Service Pack 3 or later. You can also download a specific fix for this problem without installing a later Service Pack from the Microsoft Web site. This RAS-only fix for Service Pack 2 can be found by using FTP and accessing the following directory: ftp://ftp.microsoft.com/bussys/winnt/winnt-public/fixes/usa/NT40/hotfixes-postsp2/ras-fix.

Windows NT 4 Service Pack 2 also contains memory leaks in the RAS subsystem. If you're using RAS, you don't want to use Service Pack 2 and should install a later Service Pack.

No More Static IP Addresses!

When you configure TCP/IP for RAS, you can assign a pool of static IP addresses from which the RAS server can assign addresses to remote users automatically. Sometimes you might run out of these addresses, even when the pool is much larger than the total possible number of connections using the pool. This is due to a bug and has been addressed in the latest (post SP2) Service Packs.

Problems After Upgrading from Windows NT 3.51

You will sometimes see this error after upgrading from Windows NT 3.51:

```
Error 633: The port is already in use or not configured for Remote
Access dial out.
```

This happens when the Unimodem driver installed with Windows NT 3.51 is retained after upgrading to Windows NT 4 because the driver is in use (by a non–Unimodem service or driver) in the NT 3.51 RAS configuration. The underlying program seizes control of the Unimodem driver and won't let go.

To correct this problem, you need to remove any non–Unimodem drivers and then install the driver that comes with Windows NT 4. First, though, you can check to see if the wrong driver is running. Open the Network Control Panel, move to the Services tab, and open the Remote Access Service properties. The Type column will show the name of the driver being used by RAS; if it says Modem (Modem.inf), you're using the wrong one. Remove the item from the RAS properties dialog box, and then add the Unimodem driver for the affected COM ports and restart the system.

WORKING WITH USERS

You'd think that solving the myriad technical problems that can go wrong with RAS would be the most difficult part, right? Well, actually not. By far the most challenging problem in solving RAS problems is in working with the remote users who are having trouble. It's important to brush up on the following skills:

▼ Being an effective interviewer

■ Being supportive of the user while working through the problem

■ Being able to extract specific information from the remote user without appearing to be interrogating them

▲ Being able to maintain a good working relationship over the telephone

In order to be an effective interviewer, you need to be able to sort out the user's conclusions from the actual facts you need to know. Many users will report conclusions, not understanding that what they're seeing may indicate something else entirely. For example, they may report that the server is down, when in reality their modem is turned off. It would be nice to instead have people that simply reported, "I'm seeing an error 692 when trying to connect to the RAS server," but it just won't happen. (If wishes were fishes . . .) At any rate, the first rule is always to elicit the actual facts of what's happening from the user, form your own opinion about what the circumstances might suggest, and then proceed accordingly.

Be careful not to exacerbate the user's frustration. By the time a user calls you, there's already a high level of frustration extant. You can easily make his or her mood worse. One way to do this is to rapidly ask different questions. If you do this, the user is going to feel like an attack victim, and you're going to lose your ability to work smoothly for a resolution of the problem. Instead, you'll get better results if you reassure the user during the process in nonpatronizing ways and work through the problem carefully. In the long run, you'll solve the presenting problem more quickly if you keep this in mind.

TIP: When you work with computer problems frequently, it becomes very easy to minimize their importance to or impact on the users. Be careful not to do this. If you keep in mind the idea that what's important is what the person *thinks* is important, you'll be much more successful in working with computer users when they have trouble.

You'll sometimes run into users who think they know more than they actually do. While their interest in the technology is laudable, they can present unique challenges to those trying to work with them to solve problems. Avoid getting into a technical contest with them, and if you need to correct them or suggest something different than what they say, be extremely careful. (This is always a good rule; nobody likes having their ego messed with!) One idea is to say things like, "Yes, I thought the same thing the first time I saw this problem, but it turned out to be . . ." Using catchphrases like this lets you gracefully redirect the user to more productive troubleshooting avenues.

Many people who use computers still do not understand the vocabulary properly. Just because a user can say, "It seems like my serial port is using an incorrect IRQ" doesn't mean he or she has any idea of what that means. It's a good idea to ask questions about what they're actually seeing and hearing to gauge their levels of understanding.

NOTE: As an amusing aside that illustrates the above point, there are many users who think that their system units are called hard disks or hard drives because support people look at the blinking light on the front of the case and say things like, "Boy, your hard disk sure is busy." They don't realize that the light merely indicates one of the components of the system unit, so they start calling the entire computer the hard disk.

Finally, be methodical when interviewing users about the problems they experience. Be sure to find out when the problem started, what else happened to the computer since the function last worked (if it ever worked), and what other problems they may have recently experienced. Also be sure to have them walk through the steps that led to the problem one at a time. If you follow these suggestions, you'll solve many more problems much faster than otherwise.

WINDOWS
NT
Professional
Library

PART V

Securing Computers

CHAPTER 13

Windows NT
Server Safety

If you gather a group of system administrators in a room, at some point the topic of conversation will turn to server crash protection and fault tolerance. Keeping servers safe and secure is an enormously important topic and a nerve-racking responsibility.

You have to run your network with the belief that the worst possible thing that could happen will happen, that the worst series of incredibly awful coincidences will occur. And then, acting on that belief, you have to do what you can to protect yourself. This means counting on disasters that are as bad or as weird as your imagination can conjure up. It also means planning for recovery from those disasters. Don't hesitate to spend the money it takes to provide total redundancy if your entire enterprise would grind to a halt because a couple of servers went down at the same time.

Even with all that planning, when disaster occurs, you have to repair everything. The trick is having the tools, the configuration, and the procedures in place to ensure that the repair process works.

The other primary concern is security—not necessarily an invasion by Internet hacks, but the security of the files on your server. This means that files that should be limited in their exposure are, files that should not be modified aren't, and users are able to access the files they need without having access to files they should never get near.

AN OUNCE OF PREVENTION

There are a number of items that should appear on your "protect myself against problems" checklist. Let's go over a few that owe their presence in this section to the fact that I've heard so many administrators say, "If I'd only thought to . . ."

Protect the Power Supply

All servers should be on an uninterruptible power supply (UPS). Even if a sudden power loss doesn't totally trash your drive (or the surge as power is restored doesn't fry your system board), you may have to go through all the problems of a restart after the operating system isn't shut down properly. Frequently this includes having to repair a damaged boot sector, deal with lost or corrupted database files, and a host of other possible problems. Although some of these problems aren't fatal, the down time certainly affects your operation.

Use NTFS

Protecting your files is a two-part protocol: You have to protect files from the damage that could accrue from a crash, and you have to protect files from the damage that users can inflict. To give the best possible effort to both mandates, servers should be formatted for NTFS, not FAT.

NTFS attempts to recover corrupted files (and does a fairly good job of it most of the time), and it is far more robust than FAT. Unlike FAT volumes, an NTFS volume doesn't go to pieces in the face of a minor disaster. The worst that could happen is that you might have to run (r)MDBOchkdsk /f /r(r)MDNM to recover from a server that shut itself down (or was shut down by the power company because no UPS was attached).

Use DiskSave to Copy the MBR and Boot Sector

DiskSave is one of the gems in the Windows NT 4 Resource Kit. You can use it to save the Master Boot Record (MBR) and/or boot sector as binary image files. Then, if the MBR or boot sector becomes corrupted, you can restore the file. (This utility is for Intel machines only.)

The MBR holds the code that the BIOS uses to read the partition table and then move to the partition that holds the operating system. If the MBR is damaged, the computer won't boot. The problem announces itself as a black screen after POST, or you may see error messages about an invalid partition table or a missing operating system.

The boot sector holds the code that loads the operating system (or the multi-boot loader). If it's corrupt, you may see a Stop:0x0000007B during boot, or the machine may just hang at the point before it loads Ntldr (which displays the bootup selections).

After your heart starts beating again, you just have to reach for your DiskSave files.

DiskSave is a command line utility, and it resides in the directory in which you installed your Resource Kit. It does not run in a Windows NT 4 command session; it runs from real, true DOS. Here's how to get started with DiskSave:

1. Create a real DOS bootable floppy disk. I keep a set of disks from DOS 6.2 around and boot to Disk 1 (the plastic tab is removed from my original DOS disks to prevent accidental writing or virus infection). Then I format a new-out-of-the-box floppy disk, using the command (r)MDBOformat a:/s(r)MDNM, or sometimes, if I don't feel like waiting, I use the command (r)MDBOsys a:(r)MDNM (while I'm at it, I usually copy Format and Fdisk from the original disk to the new one, just in case).

2. Put this floppy disk into drive A of your NT computer, and use Explorer to copy DiskSave to the floppy disk.

3. Boot the NT computer to this disk.

4. At the A\>: prompt, enter (r)MDBOdisksave(r)MDNM.

DiskSave starts up. It's text based, but there's a title bar at the top of your screen that says Microsoft DiskSave. The menu reads as follows:

F2 - Back up the Master Boot Record

F3 - Restore Master Boot Record

F4 - Back up the Boot Sector

F5 - Restore Boot Sector

F6 - Disable FT on the Boot Drive

ESC - Exit the program

To save the Master Boot Record, press F2. The system displays the message "Enter a fully qualified path & filename." Enter (r)MDBOa:*filename*.**dsk(r)MDNM (I usually use a descriptive filename, such as mbr010698.dsk).**

To save the boot sector information, press F4. The same system message appears, so enter a filename and save this file to drive A (again, a filename of bs*date* is a good idea).

The files are each 512 bytes, and they are image files.

When you have a startup failure due to the corruption of the MBR or the boot sector, boot to this floppy disk and run DiskSave. Use the Restore options to put the image file you saved back on the hard drive. Magic!

Use the F6 menu item (Disable FT on the Boot Drive) when the computer won't boot from a mirrored drive. DiskSave looks for the bootable partition (the partition marked Active). Then it looks at the SystemType byte to see if it has the high bit set. (Windows NT sets the high bit of the SystemType byte if the partition is a member of a fault-tolerant set.) Disabling this bit basically breaks the mirror.

Implement Virus Protection

Viruses continue to be a prevalent, dangerous problem, and MBR and boot sector viruses are the ones that drive us nuts. It's one thing to have a macro virus or another virus that does mischief to a running computer, because you merely launch a virus checker on the spot and take care of the problem. Being unable to boot a computer because of a virus is scary and sometimes fatal.

The viruses that infect the MBR and boot sector generally run independently of the operating system and actually do their work before the operating system loads. This debunks the myth that drives formatted for NTFS or HPFS are not susceptible to viruses. Virus damage is the most common reason for a computer that won't boot because the MBR or boot sector are corrupted.

There are a number of steps you can take to protect a mission-critical server from viruses:

▼ Don't expose the server to the Internet.

■ If you ever use a floppy disk, be sure to remove it before shutting down the server. The risk of virus infection from an inserted floppy disk during bootup is well documented.

■ Configure the BIOS to disable booting from the floppy disk, or at least change the order of drive seeking to boot drive C first.

■ Configure the BIOS to enable system password protection if it's available.

■ Don't run downloaded software on the server until you have run it on another computer and checked it for viruses.

▲ Keep virus protection software on the server and run it frequently.

USING FAULT TOLERANCE

A great preventive scheme for protecting important servers is to implement fault tolerance, the most important of which is RAID.

Using RAID

Windows NT 4 supports RAID levels 0, 1, and 5 (RAID stands for redundant array of inexpensive disks, and there are six levels of RAID available, from level 0 to level 5).

- ▼ Level 0 RAID is disk striping.
- ■ Level 1 RAID is disk mirroring.
- ▲ Level 5 RAID is block striping (parity blocks that are distributed over multiple drives).

NOTE: Backup services and UPS services are also considered a form of fault tolerance.

The key to RAID is striping, which enables data blocks to be interleaved across multiple drives. The drives have to have the same performance and storage characteristics. Each drive in a RAID system operates independently of the other drives, so data transfer is parallel. This means if you have three drives, data is transferred in one-third the time it would take for a single drive to receive the data.

The reliability is achieved by using one disk for storing a check byte, which is built so that if a drive fails, its data can be reconstructed.

NOTE: If you implement RAID level 0, you get only the striping feature; there is no redundancy. This improves performance quite a bit, but doesn't do much for data safety and the ability to keep a server up and running when a drive fails. Since there is no check byte in level 0 RAID, there's no provision for reconstruction of data.

Using Mirroring

If you implement RAID level 1, you have disk mirroring. (Microsoft's implementation of mirroring does not include striping, although the original specifications for level 1 RAID do.) The mirror disk has an exact copy of the data on the primary disk.

Mirroring is the simplest, least expensive form of redundancy and is good protection against disk failure for smaller networks. The big problem with mirroring is the shared controller (that's like asking for Murphy's Law regarding controller failure to implement itself). Disk duplexing is mirroring with separate controllers, and it is worth the extra expense.

Configuring Fault Tolerance

It's a good idea to go over the way you configure fault-tolerant setups, so that if you're considering it you can see what it involves.

To configure disk mirroring, follow these steps:

1. Open Disk Administrator (on the Administrative Tools menu of the Program menu).

2. The Disk Administrator window displays the computer's disks. On the first disk, choose the partition you want to mirror.

3. Hold down the CTRL key and click the partition on the second disk you want to use for mirroring.

NOTE: The second disk partition must be at least as large as the first disk.

4. Choose Fault Tolerance, Establish Mirror from the menu bar.

5. Acknowledge the message that indicates you are mirroring the partition by choosing Yes.

6. In the Disk Administrator window, you should see that both the partitions have the same drive letter (and they're purple). This means the mirroring is complete. Exit Disk Administrator, and choose Yes to confirm the changes you made to your disks.

At this point you'll see a series of messages:

▼ You're prompted to restart your computer—choose Yes.

■ You're told to update the Emergency Repair Disk (ERD)—follow through.

▲ You're told you should restart your system—do it.

When you're up and running again, log on and immediately open Disk Administrator. The labels in the mirrored partition are red (which means the mirrored set is being regenerated). If you select the mirror (the secondary partition), its status says "Initializing"; then, when mirroring is running, the status says "Healthy." Everything is running correctly.

To configure RAID level 5 (disk striping with parity), you need at least three disks. You'll create your striped set by choosing a partition from each disk. If those partitions aren't of equal size, Disk Administrator will create a striped set with parity, using equal-sized partitions that are based on the smallest partition you have. There is a minimum size of 5MB, but your partitions are sure to be much larger than that.

CAUTION: The system and boot partitions cannot be part of your striped set.

Follow these steps to configure RAID level 5:

1. Open Disk Administrator and select the partition on the first disk that you want to use for your striped set.

2. Holding down the CTRL key, click on the partitions on the other disks that you are making part of your striped set (there must be at least two other disk partitions).

3. Choose Fault Tolerance, Create Striped Set With Parity. Then choose the size of your striped set.

4. Click OK. The striped partitions have the same drive letter (and they're green).

5. Exit Disk Administrator.

You'll see the same series of messages as those described for creating a mirrored set in the previous section—do the same things.

Recovering from Fault-Tolerance Partition Failures

It'll break. A disk, the mirror, one partition in a striped set—something will break. And you'll have to fix it.

Let's start by repairing a broken mirror set. To fix a mirror, you have to break it first. We'll go over the general steps (the particular condition of your disk and mirror may affect your procedures).

1. Open Disk Administrator and select the primary partition in the mirror set.

2. Choose Fault Tolerance, Break Mirror from the menu bar. There's a confirmation message, so choose Yes. The formerly mirrored partition now displays the next available drive letter.

3. Choose Partition, Commit Changes Now from the menu bar. There's a confirmation message, so choose Yes.

4. Make sure the working part of the mirror set is assigned the drive letter that was used by both parts of the mirrored set. The other (not working) disk should get the next available drive letter.

5. If there's another disk in the computer, make a new mirrored set. If not, exit Disk Administrator.

Now you can go out and buy a disk, install it, and create a new mirrored set.

Regenerating a striped set with parity really means replacing the disk. Even though your system keeps running, performance is definitely affected. Replace the bad disk and then regenerate the striped set with parity by following these steps:

1. Open Disk Administrator and select the striped set with parity.

2. Choose free space on the new disk that is at least the same size as the other disks in the striped set.

3. Choose Fault Tolerance, Regenerate from the menu bar.

4. Exit Disk Administrator and restart the server.

When the operating system restarts, it generates itself onto the new member of the striped set.

SECURITY AND SAFETY

The security and safety of your folders and files is an ongoing problem because you have to let users get at the files. (How many administrators have said, "I'd have a perfect system if I could keep users away from the files"?)

The efficiency of your security protocols is directly proportional to the care you exercise in assigning rights and permissions.

> **TIP:**   An important security strategy is to keep mission-critical servers in a physically secure area. Locked doors, limited keys to those doors, a vicious growling dog—whatever it takes to keep people away from the server, do it. Use a password-protected screen saver on the server (most of the time the screen saver is up, since most servers don't have an operator at the keyboard all day).

Control Share and File Permissions

Files inherit the share status of the directory in which they are located. You can set specific file permissions that are different from those of the directory, but a user who has no access to a directory share cannot get to any files in the directory, no matter how you've changed the file permissions.

If your user group is large, you need a philosophy, a logical approach to permissions, or you'll find yourself operating in chaos. Individual users want specific access to individual files, then other users want access, and it grows and grows. Create logical groups and give permissions to the groups. Then move users in and out of groups as their jobs require access changes.

It is as dangerous to the efficiency and productivity of your company to tighten permissions too much as it is to the security of your company files to be too loose.

Users Log On and Shell Does Not Start

A default set of permissions for Administrator and the system on %SystemRoot% causes problems for any non–Administrator user who logs on. You have two methods of approaching a fix for this:

▼   Give Everyone at least RX permissions.

▲   Create discrete permissions for the groups and users you want to permit to log on.

Open the Directory Permissions dialog box on the Security tab for \%SystemRoot% (Figure 13-1) and make the following changes:

1. Give Everyone (or the specific groups and users you've selected) at least RX permissions.

2. Deselect the Replace Permissions on Subdirectories option.

3. Deselect the Replace Permissions on Existing Files option.

Shell Does Not Start for Any Logon

It only takes one or two overenthusiastic clicks of a mouse to shut everybody (including Administrators) out of a logon. (I once shut myself out of my registry and couldn't get back in to let myself back in.) Many times I've seen permission problems in \%SystemRoot% that were really the result of permission problems on the whole volume. Some people actually eliminate the Administrator account or tighten its permissions too much. The ripple effect is overwhelming.

There's really no guaranteed cure for this situation, but depending on the way you've established permissions throughout the network, you may be able to change the permissions from another computer. If that doesn't work, you're out of luck. You'll need to reformat the drive and reinstall the operating system (you cannot just reinstall the operating system because you can't get Write permission).

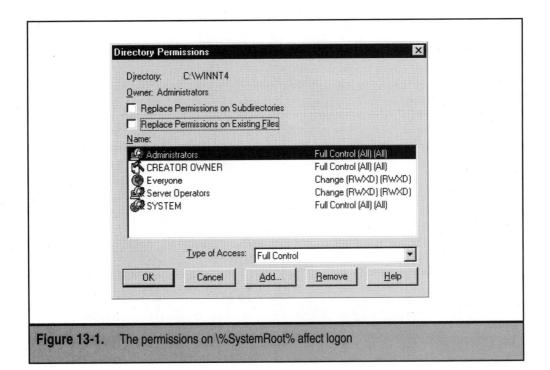

Figure 13-1.   The permissions on \%SystemRoot% affect logon

Print Jobs Not Removed from Print Queue

On a print server, you may notice that jobs from remote users are not deleted after printing and the queue gets enormous. If you track this, you'll probably find that print jobs initiated by Administrators and Print Operators print normally (the print job disappears after it's finished). This means that someone has changed the permissions for the Creator Owner account so that only Print is permitted (or the Creator Owner account has been removed).

You cannot remove the default Manage Documents permission from the Creator Owner account. Instead, go to the printer Properties dialog box and move to the Security tab. Choose Permissions, select the Creator Owner account, and make sure the permission level is Manage Documents. While you're there, be sure the Administrator account is present with full control.

Quota Software Locks Permissions

If you see an error message when you want to view or change NTFS file or directory security, you may be able to change permissions, but the changes will disappear. The error message displayed is "The security information for <path> is not standard and cannot be displayed. Do you want to overwrite the current security information?"(r)MDBO (r)MDNMResponding Yes and making the changes is fruitless; the next time you view the permissions they're back the way they were.

This is almost always the result of quota software that has been inappropriately configured. By "inappropriately" I mean that the quota locks have been set too high in the tree. When parent directories have quotas and reach their limit, the subdirectories are locked also. For example, you may have imposed quotas on a parent directory that has child directories for individual users. When the parent directory locks, you cannot manipulate security for any of the child directories. The quotas should have been imposed on the child directories.

Remove the quota lock on any parent directories, and apply quotas only on child directories for which such action is appropriate.

NOTE: Windows NT 5 supports features such as the ability to edit security information and impose deny access control limits. (I just wanted to give you a look into the future.)

Task Manager Gives Security Error

Users who do not have Administrator rights may see an "Access Denied" error message when they try to end a process with Task Manager. When Task Manager ends a process, it does so by calling TerminateProcess (Win32 API), which will not terminate a process that is running under a different security context than the security level of the user issuing the call to TerminateProcess. (Windows NT services and system processes, of course, frequently have higher levels than logged-on users.)

The workaround is to install the Kill utility from the Resource Kit, which will kill a process irrespective of security levels.

Using Kill.exe

The Kill program in the Windows NT 4 Resource Kit is a handy utility to keep on the computer of all users who can be trusted to employ it (which means users who can discriminate about which processes can be killed safely).

When you use Kill, you can specify a process ID (PID), a process name (including a partial name), or the process title on the title bar of its window (if the process has a window). The syntax is (r)MDBOkill [/f] (**PID** | **pattern**)(r)MDNM, where:

/f forces the process to end instead of letting it terminate itself (without /f, the Kill command is really a request that the process terminate).
PID is the process ID.
pattern is the process name or part of a name (wildcards work).

To obtain the PID, you can use Tlist or Pulist, also in the Resource Kit.

NOTE: There's information about Kill.exe in Chapter 16.

Using Tlist.exe

Tlist is a utility for viewing a task list from the command line. It returns the ID, name, and window title (if there is a window) of every process running on the computer. The syntax is (r)MDBOtlist /t(r)MDNM, where:

/t requests that the display be sorted by child/parent relationships.

Using Pulist.exe

This command line utility performs the same tasks as Tlist.exe, but works on remote computers in addition to the local computer. When it is run on a local computer, it displays the user name for each process (if the user name is available). The syntax is (r)MDBOpulist [**server**](r)**MDNM.**

Control Ownership

The owner of a folder or file has the right to change the permissions on that object. It's a good idea to troll through your servers and take ownership so that you, as the administrator, can control permissions. Once you take ownership, the previous owner can no longer manipulate the permissions. To grab the ownership of an object, follow these steps:

1. In Explorer, right-click the target file or folder and choose Properties from the shortcut menu.

2. Move to the Security tab.

3. Choose Ownership to display the Owner dialog box, which displays the current owner.

4. Choose Take Ownership, then confirm the change in ownership.

Implement Strong Encryption

There's a Windows NT Server 4 System Key hotfix that gives you the ability to use strong encryption techniques that increase the protection of account password information stored in the registry.

Windows NT Server stores user account information (including a derivative of the user password) in the registry. The information can be protected by access controls and made accessible to members of the Administrators group.

If you feel the need for more security than that provides, you can gain an additional level of security that prevents Administrators from accessing passwords through registry programs.

The file is available from Microsoft at ftp://ftp.microsoft.com/bussys/ winnt-public/fixes/usa/nt4/hotfixes-postSP2/sec-fix.

The way this hotfix works is by encrypting the password data, using a 128-bit cryptographically random key (called a password encryption key). Only the private password information is strongly encrypted, not the whole account database. Any system that uses this option has a unique password encryption key (which is itself encrypted with a System Key). Strong password encryption can be used for both Server and Workstation.

Using strong encryption of account passwords adds additional protection for the SAM portion of the registry. Copies of the registry information in the \%SystemRoot%\repair directory that were made using the Rdisk command will contain the strong encryption, as will copies on system backup tapes.

The System Key is defined with the command (r)MDBOSyskey.exe(r)MDNM, which can be run only by members of the Administrators group. This program initializes (or changes) the System Key, which is the master key that protects the password encryption key.

You have three options for implementing the System Key:

▼ Use a random, machine-generated key as the System Key, and keep that key on the local computer, using a complex obfuscation algorithm. This gives you the strong encryption of registry password information and still permits an unattended system startup.

■ Use a random, machine-generated key that is stored on a floppy disk. That floppy disk is required for system startup. There's a user prompt for insertion of the floppy disk after the startup sequence begins and before the system is available for logon.

▲ Use a password (chosen by the administrator) to derive the System Key. The operating system will prompt for that password when the system has begun startup but before the system is available for logon.

If the password is lost, forgotten, or corrupted (if it's disk-based), the system won't start, and the only way to overcome the problem is to restore the registry to its state before strong encryption was installed. Be sure to keep a copy of the last Rdisk -s backup around.

> **CAUTION:**   Once strong encryption is enabled, it cannot be disabled by the strong encryption program (there's only an "enable" choice in the dialog box).

Audit Folder and File Access

You can audit directory and file access if you want to keep a close eye on all security-related activity on a server. To enable auditing for directories and files, follow these steps:

1. In Explorer, move to the target directory or file.

2. Right-click and choose Properties.

3. Move to the Security tab and choose Auditing. The Directory Auditing dialog box appears if the target is a directory. The File Auditing dialog box appears if the target is a file.

4. Choose Add to see the Add Users and Groups dialog box.

5. Select the domain from which the users and groups are being selected.

6. Choose Show Users to display the user accounts in the domain.

7. Select each group or user you want to audit and choose Add to place the names in the Add Names list box.

8. Choose OK when you have finished selecting groups and users.

9. Select the check box in the Success and/or Failure columns for each of the events you want to audit.

10. Choose OK.

If the target is a directory, you can specify the way in which directory auditing applies to subdirectories and files. Choose Replace Auditing on Subdirectories to apply the directory auditing selections to the subdirectories. If you've made audit selections for the subdirectories, the directory audit selections will supersede them.

> **TIP:**   Do not audit write failures on files that have only Read and Execute access. This creates a spurious Security Event from Explorer (Microsoft is working on the problem).

A PEEK AT THE FUTURE

Some interesting developments are being displayed at technical shows, and they're aimed at making the data on network servers safer and more secure. Here's a brief peek at what you'll be seeing (and perhaps purchasing) soon.

Adaptec FileArray

Adaptec, Inc. is planning a staged rollout of a new file array technology. FileArray uses hardware and software to process I/O requests in an accelerator card instead of the computer's processor. This frees the server's CPU to process user requests. The controller actually handles part of the I/O stack and file system, which means the path to that system is shorter (traditionally, RAID searches the entire I/O stack to find and process each I/O request). You can think of this as a controller that controls the file system in addition to drives.

This new controller is loaded! It contains RAM, NVRAM, an Intel i960 processor, two UltraFast Wide SCSI chips, and a DEC bridge chip (it links the SCSI chips). The software interface has wizards for creating logical volumes, assigning partitions, and assigning failover disks.

Computer Associates Identica

CA is getting ready to release storage management software that provides fast failover when a server crashes. It's based on replication (data duplication instead of data mirroring).

Administrators can select the data designated to participate in this system, and any change in that data is automatically duplicated on a second server. The replication system is designed for speed (CA claims 4.5MB per second). Administrators identify the primary and secondary servers, and when a primary server fails, the failover takes less than 1 second. The secondary server becomes the primary server, even adopting its computer name.

Software controls for restoring data on a failed server can be used without taking the computer offline (or forcing users to log off). Any changes in data during the down time are automatically replicated on the now-running primary server.

As complicated as all this redundancy seems to configure and maintain, it makes the difference between a company that can keep rolling after a disaster and a company that will lose thousands or millions of dollars due to lost data and down time. There's really no choice.

WINDOWS
NT
Professional
Library

CHAPTER 14

Backing Up

One of the most important administrative tasks is ensuring that all the important information on the network is backed up. That includes data saved to workstations in addition to the information on servers. There are a variety of schemes you can use to accomplish this; I'll go over some of the more trustworthy plans in this chapter. This is not a full instructional chapter about using Windows NT Backup (this is, after all, a book on troubleshooting). I will, however, provide an overview of the important issues surrounding the built-in backup software. I'll also discuss some of the common problems encountered.

However, before I begin I have to tell you about my rule, my mantra, my deepest belief about backing up. I've made signs of this rule and posted them all over clients' offices. Here it is:

The purpose of backing up is not to make the backup procedure quick and efficient. The purpose of backing up is to make the restore procedure quick and efficient.

COUNTING ON CALAMITY

Backup strategies need to be planned before they're implemented. You have to start with the worst-case scenario and make sure your schemes cover you. Start with the premise that backing up each server to tape every night isn't enough of a plan.

Your original media for the operating system (and for the backup software if you're using a third-party application) should be stored somewhere safe, preferably off-site. In fact, if you have duplicates of these original software packages, store them in separate off-site facilities. If you have a major disaster and have to rebuild your system from scratch, you cannot restore your tapes until you've installed the operating system.

Archives are another backup-related matter. Old company data files, no longer in active use, may be needed in the future. This is another candidate for duplicate off-site storage.

Believe it or not, you're better off saving archives on floppy disks than on tape. Of course if you have a CD-ROM burner, that's the best and most efficient medium. Tape doesn't last long; you can only count on it for a couple of years. The deterioration process for tape starts as soon as you use it and keeps going even if you never again put the tape into a tape drive. It's the nature of magnetic tape (people in the television business have learned this lesson the hard way).

For the same reason, replace the tapes you're using for regular backups on a frequent basis.

The ideal way to plan for a real disaster is to purchase identical computers for the entire network. At the very least, make all of the servers identical, then all of the workstations (which don't have to be identical to the servers). Restoring tapes from one computer to another (working) computer is a fast recovery method but doesn't work if the computers don't have the same equipment and configuration (the registry gets very upset). If you can't manage that (it's probably too late), try to make sure all of the backup equipment on all of the servers is the same brand and model.

UNDERSTANDING NT BACKUP TYPES

Windows NT Backup is a fairly robust application, capable of providing the protection you need. There are also third-party backup applications that are approved for Windows NT 4.

After you have selected the files you want to back up, the Backup Information dialog box offers a choice of backup protocols. The software provides five types of backups. I'll describe each in turn.

Normal Backup

A normal backup backs up all of the files that are selected, no matter what the current state of the archive bit is on any file. When the backup is completed, the archive bit of every file is cleared to indicate that the file has been backed up.

Copy Backup

A copy backup backs up all selected files, regardless of the state of the archive bit on a file. When the backup is complete, the software does not change the archive bit of any file, but leaves everything the way it was when the backup started.

Incremental Backup

An incremental backup looks at all of the selected files and backs up only those that have changed since the last backup of any type (only those on which the archive bit exists). When the backup is complete, the archive bit for all backed up files is cleared.

Incremental backups are frequently used on a daily basis to supplement a weekly normal backup. Although this makes backing up faster, it can make restoring a lot of work. You have to restore the last normal backup, then restore each incremental backup in the correct order. If your normal backup is performed on Friday, a Thursday crash can be onerous to fix.

Personally, I think the best use of incremental backups, especially for large installations with a lot of data being produced, is between nightly normal backups. Run an incremental backup at 11 A.M. and 3 P.M. and do a normal backup at night. If something awful happens, you've only lost a couple of hours of work.

Differential Backup

Like an incremental backup, a differential backup checks the selected files, looking for those with the archive bit set, indicating the file has been changed since the last backup. However, when the backup is completed, the archive bits are not reset and everything stays the way it was. The advantage of a differential backup over an incremental backup for nightly use is that the backup is cumulative, since the archive bit isn't reset. This means there are fewer tapes to use if you have to restore.

Daily Backup

A daily backup looks at the date stamps of all of the selected files and backs up only those that were created or modified today.

BACKING UP WORKSTATIONS

Many workstations are self-contained for software, and the data is saved locally. In fact, the majority of the networks I've seen have had word processing and other non-database work configured totally for workstations—software and data. That's an efficient way to keep productivity high because there really isn't all that much document sharing going on in the corporate world and there's no particular reason not to give a user the advantages of working locally. (Some Windows software requires so many .dll and other supporting files to be installed on the local machine that you might as well go ahead and install the entire program.)

But you have to worry about backing up the work that's performed at those workstations. Almost no users cooperate with requests to back up data files nightly to diskette. It just doesn't happen.

Copy Workstation Files to Servers

One of the best solutions for backing up workstations is to move the data to a server that's scheduled for regular backups. In fact, it's not a bad idea to have a server dedicated to this chore.

You can create any of several schemes to receive and hold files from workstations on a server. Start by creating a subdirectory on the server for each workstation. Then use some automated way to move the files. Do not explain to users how to do this with Explorer, because they won't bother. Create an easier scheme so it will actually get done. The best idea is a batch file. Here's the one I use for a workstation named Admin, which is backing up to a server named Accnt. There is a share named Admin on Accnt for this purpose.

```
net use i: \\accnt\admin
xcopy c:\my documents\*.* i:\my documents /s/e/h/i/r/c
xcopy c:\outlook\*.* i:\outlook /s/e/h/i/r/c
xcopy c:\program files\*.* i:\program files /s/e/h/i/r/c
xcopy c:\regback\*.* i:\regback /s/e/h/i/r/c
xcopy c:\winnt\*.* i:\winnt /s/e/h/i/r/c
exit
```

This works because data for all software is sent to a folder named My Documents. Incidentally, I don't have the software installed in the Program Files directory (I use discrete directories for software), but all those shared files and other important support files get put into Program Files automatically. If the workstation crashes I'll have to reinstall the software before restoring the backup, but I prefer that to taking up a lot of disk space on the server (which is collecting backups from other workstations). I do include the Winnt directory because I don't want to reconfigure the entire system after a reinstall of the operating system. The Regback directory holds exported files from the registry, so the registry is being backed up to the server. (Of course, that means the user has to remember to back up the registry via an export file, or an administrator has to do it remotely.)

There's a shortcut on the desktop to this batch file, so all the user has to do is double-click before leaving the office.

Incidentally, if you don't recognize them, Table 14-1 explains the Xcopy switches I'm using in this batch file.

The one possible danger in the switches used for this batch file involves the /c switch, which continues to copy if an error occurs. I've tried running the batch file without it, and most of the time the errors were innocuous or affected only one file. However, the users were faced with answering a query regarding the error when they returned to the office in the morning, and then the batch file proceeded for another twenty minutes while the users were locked out of the workstation. I found that nonproductive enough to put the /c switch back. Major errors such as "cannot read from drive C" or "cannot write to drive I" don't permit continued processing, so you'll know if you have a significant problem.

/s	Copies subdirectories
/e	Copies subdirectories even if they are empty
/h	Copies hidden and system files
/i	Assumes the target name is a directory if it doesn't exist and the source is more than one file
/r	Overwrites read-only files
/c	Continues to copy if an error occurs

Table 14-1.   Xcopy Switches for the Backup Batch File

> **TIP:** The Windows NT Server resource kit contains a utility named Scopy. This works like Xcopy but preserves file permissions for NTFS (if you have workstations running NTFS).

Data-Only Backup for Workstations

For many companies, a data-only backup of workstation files is a perfectly sound idea. There are plenty of workstations on the network, and a dead machine doesn't create a calamity. The user just moves to another workstation that can access the same software. As long as the data files are available, the user can go right back to work.

You can use the same scheme discussed in the previous section (move the files to a server that's going to be backed up) or use some other target for data-only backups from workstations.

If there are Zip or Jaz drives available on the network, you can use them for backing up workstations and use the larger tape drives for backing up servers. You can use removable drives that are connected to servers or to selected workstations and share them. The advantage of this method is that, for workstations, most of the use of the Restore function is to restore a file that was inadvertently deleted. That's a lot easier to do from a drive than it is from a tape.

If the procedure is a data-only backup, a Zip or Jaz drive can hold data from quite a few workstations. And the individual workstation users don't have to do anything; you can write a batch file that goes out and collects the data from each workstation and copies it to the removable drive. The workstation documents must all be in one parent subdirectory (other subdirectories can exist under the parent if the user likes to keep data separated by type). Create a directory for each workstation on the removable drive and write a batch file similar to the one described earlier, switching the source and target drives. For instance:

```
net use i: \\admin\my documents
xcopy i:\*.* c:\admin /s/e/h/i/r/c
net use j: \\wkstnX\my documents
xcopy j:\*.* c:\wkstnX /s/e/h/i/r/c
```

The workstations must be running with a user logged on to access the share.

Problems with Copy Instead of Backup

There is a significant problem with using Xcopy instead of standard backup software. The problem is that the target directories keep growing. Xcopy does not use a "delete and replace" approach; it just keeps adding new files without deleting the files on the target that have been deleted on the source. Every once in a while you have to clean everything out and start again.

If your target is a network server, open Explorer and then open each workstation subdirectory. Use CTRL-A to select all the contents (which may be a group of subdirectories), and press DEL (or SHIFT-DEL to bypass the Recycle Bin).

If the target is a removable drive, I personally find it easier to right-click on the drive in My Computer and choose Format from the shortcut menu. A short format takes only a few seconds. Then I have a batch file that creates the subdirectories on the removable drive for each source workstation, so I'm ready for the next backup:

```
md d:\admin
md d:\ wkstnX
more of the same for each directory that should exist on the target drive
```

The subdirectories under each workstation's directory, of course, are created during the Xcopy procedure.

TROUBLESHOOTING PROBLEMS WITH NT BACKUP

Problems occur occasionally with Windows NT Backup software; most of them are quite easy to fix.

Skipped Files

Windows NT Backup will not back up open files. It will try again in 30 seconds, but if the file is still open it is skipped. There are third-party software applications for backing up Windows NT that are able to back up open files. Incidentally, the reason that open files aren't backed up by Windows NT Backup (and by some commercial backup applications) isn't that an open file cannot be accessed, because it can. It's because there's a philosophy that says if an open file is backed up, the user who is currently working with the file may be changing something, and the backed up version won't match the final file. My own philosophy is that a backed up file that is mostly correct is better than no backup at all. If the file in use is an executable file, restoring it won't work, but you can reinstall the software from the original media. If it's a data file, my philosophy is better than NT Backup's philosophy.

Problems with Remote Drive Backups

If you are backing up a mapped remote drive, you may see the following error message indicating that you lack the permission to perform this task:

```
You do not have permission to access portions of data. Please see the
owner or administrator to get permission.

Directory X:\directoryname
```

This is a bug in Windows NT 4, and it is fixed in Service Pack 3. If you haven't installed SP3, you can get a quick fix for the bug by downloading it from ftp://ftp.microsoft.com/ bussys/winnt/winnt-public/fixes/usa/nt40/hotfixes-postSP1/NTBackup-fix.

It is also possible that you'll see an "access denied" error when you try to access directories under the remote share you've connected to, if the drive is formatted as an NTFS drive. This occurs because the permissions for subdirectories aren't inherited by the logged-on backup operator. You will have to go into all of the subdirectories and specifically give this user Read rights on all the files. This is a bug; Microsoft was working on a fix at the time of this writing.

Be aware that when you give these permissions, you give the user access to those files for any reason, not just for backup.

Hardware Problems

When hardware problems occur with NT Backup, many times they are resolved by troubleshooting the SCSI configuration. The following list gives solutions for some of the more common error messages.

▼ **Tape drive is not recognized.** This error message is almost always an indication that there's a problem with the SCSI bus. Most of the time you'll find that the termination scheme is incorrect (or missing), or the cables are improperly attached to the tape drive. Sometimes it's just a bad cable, which is a common problem with SCSI devices.

TIP: I once read an article that said that the cables on a SCSI device had to have differing lengths, that you could not have two cables of the same size. I have never been able to learn whether this is true or not, but just in case it's accurate, you may want to check the cable lengths for all of your SCSI devices.

■ **Error writing to tape.** This message can just as often be a problem with the SCSI adapter as a problem with a bad tape.

■ **Fatal error on drive 1.** This error message is almost always the result of incompatible hardware or a firmware level that isn't supported by Windows NT 4. The hardware involved can be either the tape drive or the SCSI controller. Read the HCL to see what you can learn, and if your firmware level is below the supported level, contact the manufacturer.

■ **Fatal translation error on tape in drive 1.** This message is almost always the result of an incorrect SCSI termination (although sometimes it can be a compatibility problem with the firmware level, so you'll want to check that too).

■ **Tape drive error detected: A SCSI tape device has been detected, but the tape driver has either not been installed, or failed to start. Make sure that the appropriate driver has been installed using the Tape Devices option in Control Panel.** This message just means that you haven't performed the proper installation procedure for your tape drive. Windows NT Backup sees the tape device, but there are no drivers. Device drivers for tape devices are not installed during the setup of Windows NT. You must go through a complete setup for a tape device after you've installed the operating system.

■ **Unknown firmware error.** This error message is directly connected to the tape device (instead of the SCSI adapter). The firmware level is incompatible, and you have to contact the manufacturer.

■ **Tape drive error detected: A tape device has been detected, and the tape driver started. However, the tape device is not responding. Check that tape device power is on and cables are properly connected.** This message has several possible causes. There may be an incorrect firmware level for the tape drive or the SCSI adapter, or the CMOS settings may not have SCSI Disconnect enabled.

■ **Tape device reports an error on a request to change physical block size. The tape device reported an error on a request to read the tape. Hardware failure.** This usually means your tape device is not supported by your SCSI adapter. You may be able to obtain a firmware upgrade (for either device or both) to solve the problem.

▲ **Cannot load catalog from tape.** During Restore, this error message indicates a problem with compatibility, involving either the SCSI adapter or the driver for the SCSI adapter. While it's really annoying that this problem didn't stop the backup but isn't permitting the restore, this happens fairly often. Always do a test backup and restore before trusting your backup device to a real backup.

Problems with Specific Tape Devices

There are some known problems with particular brands of tape devices. I'll present them here, in alphabetical order, so you can see if you should worry.

Cheyenne ARCServe cannot use Windows NT drivers, even though Windows NT 4 is happy to install its own drivers for this device when you install the tape device. Use the manufacturer's instructions to load the ARCServe drivers.

An **Exabyte EXB-8200** tape device connected to an IBM SCSI controller can cause the backup process to halt before it is finished. The error message "Fatal error on Drive 1" might appear. This problem occurs with IBM SCSI controllers having revision dates prior to 1992. Contact IBM. Unfortunately, the error message appears late; the backup process will seem to start correctly and you'll go home. Of course, when you return in the morning you'll find you don't have a backup.

MINIQIC devices have a setup problem if they're connected to a SCSI controller that uses Aic78xx.sys.. After you choose Hardware Setup in NT Backup, select the MINIQIC device, and choose OK, the SCSI bus may stop working. The operating system tries to restart with a SCSI Reset command, but after sending the command a few times, it gives up. This is fixed in SP3. Incidentally, if the same SCSI controller is used for the boot drive, the system totally shuts down and gives you the dreaded blue screen with a STOP.

QIC floppy controller drives can have a compatibility problem, depending on the speed of the unit. Some of these drives operate at 500 kbs and other operate at 1 mbs. You need to determine which speed your QIC drive uses. To do that you have to load the driver (open NT Backup, install the unit, and leave NT Backup running) so you can peek in the registry with the driver open.

Use a registry editor to look at HKEY_LOCAL_MACHINE\Hardware\Devicemap \Tape\Unit 0. Look at the FDCType data item and compare it with Table 14-2 to see the throughput figure.

Now that you know the throughput, here are the requirements for QIC floppy-based drives:

▼ QIC117 Standard = Floppy drive controller requirements

■ QIC-40 = 500 kbs or higher

■ QIC-80 = 500 kbs or higher

■ QIC-3010 = 500 kbs or 1 mbs

▲ QIC-3020 = 1 mbs

On **Seagate** CTT8000-A (ATAPI) tape drives, the LED activity light on the tape drive stays lit after you exit NT Backup. In fact, it stays lit forever, until you remove and reinsert the tape. The problem is that the ATAPI drives don't understand the Rewind command that NT Backup issues at the end of the backup session. This has not yet been fixed by Microsoft.

Sony 7000 4-millimeter digital audio tape (DAT) drives may display the error message "Tape drive error" during cataloging. This means the device has older firmware; contact Sony for a compatible firmware version.

Registry Value	Floppy Controller Type	Controller Throughput Available
FDC_NORMAL	Any NEC 768 compatible	250 kbs 500 kbs
FDC_ENHANCED	Supports the version command	250 kbs 500 kbs
FDC_NATIONAL	National 8477	250 kbs 500 kbs 1 mbs
FDC_82077	Intel 82077	250 kbs 500 kbs 1 mbs
FDC_82077AA	Intel 82077AA	250 kbs 500 kbs 1 mbs
FDC_82078_44	Intel 82078 44-pin version	250 kbs 500 kbs 1 mbs
FDC_82078_64	Intel 82078 64-pin version	250 kbs 500 kbs 1 mbs
FDC_UNKNOWN	Type unknown	250 kbs 500 kbs

Table 14-2. Registry Entries to Determine Throughput of Floppy Drives

Catalog Errors

The catalog of the backup tape is extremely important (for restoring), and errors that affect it must be resolved. The following are some of the more common errors.

▼ **Error: The backup set is not completely cataloged.** This error appears if the catalog file on your hard drive has incomplete information. Sometimes, closing NT Backup and restarting it can fix the problem. If it doesn't, you must locate the catalog file on your drive and rename it (or delete it) and recatalog the tape.

■ **Catalog information: Unable to load catalog data from tape** or **Catalog error: Error writing a catalog file, check available space.** If you see either of these error messages, it means you are trying to restore a tape to a drive that is too full to accept the information. You'll have to free up some space. It doesn't matter if you're restoring existing files; you still need more room. The extra space is needed by the catalog files, which are stored on your drive in a compressed format but have to be expanded in order to begin the restore.

▲ **Error: Cannot load catalog from tape.** This usually means you have a compatibility problem with a SCSI adapter or its driver. This is one of those frustrating scenarios in which the backup seems to go fine, and the problem appears only when you try to restore the data (when you are in a big hurry and are operating in panic mode anyway). Always test tape devices with a backup and restore before trusting your backup procedures to the device.

WINDOWS
NT
Professional
Library

PART VI

Using Troubleshooting Tools

WINDOWS
NT
Professional
Library

CHAPTER 15

Using Windows NT Tools

Like a master mechanic who solves problems with complex machinery, a master computer troubleshooter needs to maintain a comprehensive toolbox with which to diagnose and treat complex computer problems. Fortunately, Windows NT comes with a number of tools that offer considerable power in tracking down and fixing most problems.

In this chapter you will learn about the myriad tools that can be used to solve problems on Windows NT systems. Taking the time to master these tools, including knowing all their features and abilities, will go a long way in helping you solve problems quickly and comprehensively.

PERFORMANCE MONITOR

There are two reasons to examine the performance of the system when troubleshooting. First, trouble often manifests itself as poor or degraded system performance, and being able to examine the performance of the system closely can help you find the component of the system that is causing the trouble. Second, sometimes performance problems are in and of themselves problems that need to be addressed. Performance problems are rooted in bottlenecks in the system. While performance problems may not have arisen suddenly, and therefore are not an indication that something is broken, they may be sapping productivity. When troubleshooting Windows NT, you should be able to address components that aren't working correctly as well as components that aren't working optimally.

Windows NT comes with a powerful program called Performance Monitor. Performance Monitor examines performance objects and counters built into Windows NT and reports on their values in several different formats. Because of Windows NT's preemptive multitasking nature, you can examine its performance data while the system continues running normally, with minimal impact on the performance of the system.

Performance Monitor can monitor performance in four different ways:

▼ **Chart View** lets you visually inspect the status of different performance counters, using line graphs.

■ **Alert View** shows you the status of alerts that you've set up in the system. Alerts perform some action when selected performance counters meet criteria you have set.

■ **Log View** lets you see the status of performance logs you have created. The logs record performance counters for later playback.

▲ **Report View** lets you create reports based on different performance counters, for viewing or printing.

In the following sections you will learn how to use each of these four different modes of Performance Monitor. After learning about the four different Performance Monitor views, see the section titled "Important Performance Objects and Counters" for an overview of the most significant performance counters to keep an eye on.

Preemptive Multitasking—How Performance Monitor Stays Covert

Windows NT is a preemptive multitasking system, which means the operating system closely controls which program thread runs at which time. Because the multitasking system is scheduled, with different priority levels for each thread, the system can appropriately apportion processor time among the different running threads. For example, say you have two running threads, one that maintains a link to a host system and another that updates the system time on the taskbar's display. Obviously, the host thread needs to be able to do work at a moment's notice, regularly and reliably, and you certainly wouldn't want the time display thread to interrupt the more important work.

When a thread is started, the program that starts it tells the system the priority level at which the thread should run. There are four priority classes: Real Time, High, Normal, and Low. Within each class, there are 16 priority levels, numbered from 1 to 16. If there are two threads at the same class and priority level, each program will be given an equal opportunity to use the system's processor.

In the example just given, the thread that maintains the link to the host system will probably have a Real Time or High priority class, ensuring that it can always run when it needs to, while the thread that updates the display of the clock will probably have a Low priority class, ensuring that it doesn't run to the detriment of higher-priority threads. (However, a Low priority thread will still typically run once a second or so, which is an eternity of time to the system.)

Windows NT Performance Monitor runs at a High priority level so that it responds to your commands quickly, but the underlying performance counters and objects run at a low priority level, ensuring that the very act of monitoring the performance of the system doesn't actually detract from the performance being measured. Provided you're not actively using Performance Monitor's commands and dialog boxes while you're trying to measure performance, you'll be able to get a true picture of what's going on with the system.

Charting System Performance

Performance Monitor's default mode visually charts the performance of the Windows NT system, using line charts that correspond to performance counters you have selected. When you first start Performance Monitor, no counters are shown; you see the blank Performance Monitor screen shown in Figure 15-1.

To add a counter to the chart's display, click the Add Performance Counter button on Performance Monitor's toolbar, or choose Edit, Add to Chart. Either command displays the Add to Chart dialog box shown in Figure 15-2.

You select the appropriate performance object in the Object drop-down list box, and then choose from the listed performance counters within that object in the Counter list. Examples of performance objects include Processor, Memory, Process, and Thread.

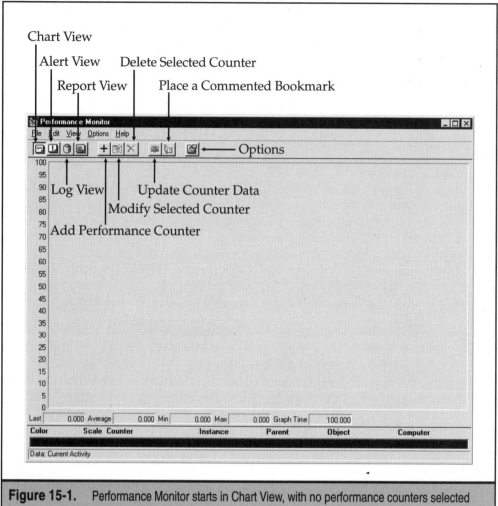

Figure 15-1. Performance Monitor starts in Chart View, with no performance counters selected

The default selected performance object is Processor, and the default selected performance counter is % Processor Time. This counter shows the percentage of total processor time that the processor is actually doing work. To select this counter for display, make sure it is selected in the Counter list, and then choose from the available display options beneath the Counter list (Color, Scale, Width, and Style). Then click the Add button to display the counter in the Chart View. The Add to Chart dialog box remains on the screen so you can choose additional counters to add to the chart. Click the Done button to close the dialog box. Figure 15-3 shows Performance Monitor displaying the % Processor Time counter in Chart View.

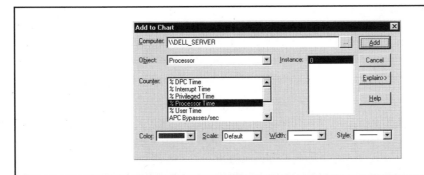

Figure 15-2.   The Add to Chart dialog box displays all performance objects and counters, from which you select the ones to be monitored

TIP: To see what any of the performance counters do, select one in the Counter list and then click the Explain button. This expands the display of the Add to Chart dialog box and shows an explanation of the selected performance counter's function.

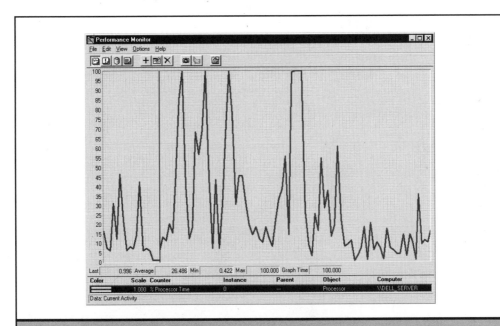

Figure 15-3.   Performance Monitor displaying a single counter in Chart View

In addition to the visual display of the performance counter, the status bar displays some of the counter's numeric data. You can view the last, average, minimum, and maximum values that have been charted for the selected counter (you select each counter using the list at the very bottom of the Performance Monitor window). Graph Time refers to the number of seconds represented on the chart.

Modifying or Deleting the Display of a Counter

You can easily modify the way each of the charted performance counters is displayed. You often need to do this when you have many performance counters being charted and find it difficult to distinguish among them on the chart. You can also modify the formatting of some of the charted counters to make them stand out more, which makes it easier to pay close attention to more important counters.

To change the display of any of the charted performance counters, double-click on the performance counter you want to change in the performance counter list at the bottom of the Performance Monitor window. This displays the Edit Chart Line dialog box, which is identical to the Add to Chart dialog box shown previously in Figure 15-2, except that you can only change the display formatting of the counter; the dialog box options that let you select performance objects and counters are grayed out and inaccessible.

To delete a performance counter, select the counter in the legend area of the Performance Monitor window and press the DEL key.

Changing Chart Options

There are several options you can set to modify the way the chart works. Click the Options button on Performance Monitor's toolbar to display the Chart Options dialog box, shown in Figure 15-4. The available options are shown in Table 15-1.

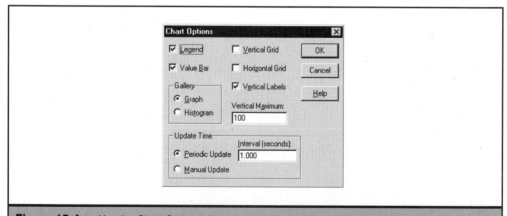

Figure 15-4. Use the Chart Options dialog box to change the display characteristics of the chart

Option	Effect
Legend	Displays the status bar and list of counters.
Value Bar	Displays the status bar (also called the value bar).
Vertical Grid	Displays a vertical grid in 5 percent increments.
Horizontal Grid	Displays a horizontal grid in 4-second increments.
Vertical Labels	Displays labels on the vertical axis.
Gallery	Toggles between the graph display and the histogram display. The histogram display is a real-time bar chart, with one bar per counter.
Vertical Maximum	Sets the vertical maximum value of the chart.
Periodic Update	Updates the information at the times specified in the Interval field; the default is once per second.
Manual Update	Causes the chart to update information only when the Update Counter Data toolbar button is clicked.

Table 15-1. Settings in the Chart Options Dialog Box

Using Chart View to Find Problems

There are two different ways you might use Chart View to spot problems, depending on the type of problem you're searching for. If the problem is sporadic, occurring only when some action is performed on the system, you can start Performance Monitor, add the performance counters that you think may be related to the problem, and then perform the action that leads to the problem. Then, after completing the action, view the Performance Monitor display to see how the different counters performed while the problem occurred.

You can also view the chart while the problem is occurring, although you should be aware that the act of moving Performance Monitor from background to foreground will cause a short spike in processor utilization and possibly cause some memory pages to be moved to and from the paging file, which may cloud your results.

On the other hand, if the performance problem is consistent, you can just leave Performance Monitor running in the background, checking it occasionally after periods in which the system was sluggish or seemed to be experiencing the problem. Over time, you can get an understanding of which system component is bottlenecking the system and then take appropriate action—replace the component, install an upgraded component, seek updated drivers for the component, or look into changing the demands of the software so that the bottleneck is avoided.

Creating Alerts

Performance Monitor includes an Alert View that lets you set criteria on selected performance counters and then displays an alert when a counter exceeds the threshold you set. Alerts can also be set to run a program if an alert occurs, which could be a program that sends a page to a system administrator or sends out a network broadcast message to certain administrative users on the system.

Use the View menu's Alert command to switch Performance Monitor into Alert View. Then click the Add Counter button on the toolbar to display the Add to Alert dialog box shown in Figure 15-5.

To set an alert, select the counter you want to monitor. Then select either the Over or Under option button and fill in a value in the field provided. An alert will be generated when the counter exceeds the value you supply. You can also elect to run a program when an alert occurs by entering the program name into the Run Program on Alert field and then selecting either First Time or Every Time.

TIP: If you set an alert to page someone when an alert occurs by using an external program for that purpose, consider the type of alert when choosing between the First Time and Every Time options. For example, if you set an alert on free disk space falling below a certain value, you don't necessarily want the paging application to continue to generate pages every second, which is how often the alert will repeat (this is not a great way to make friends with the person you're paging). Instead, you would just generate a page the first time the counter exceeded the value.

Unfortunately, you cannot set multiple alerts on a single performance counter. So, for example, you cannot have an alert occur if disk free space falls below 100MB and another alert that occurs if it falls below 50MB. You can have as many alerts as you want, but only one alert per counter. Figure 15-6 shows Alert View with a number of example alerts displayed.

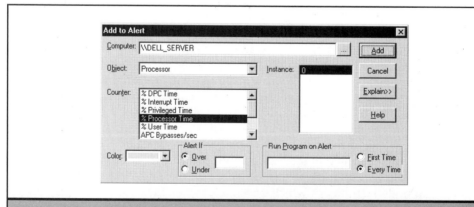

Figure 15-5. The Add to Alert dialog box lets you choose a performance counter and then set a criterion on that counter. When the counter exceeds the criterion, an alert event is logged into the Performance Monitor's Alert View display

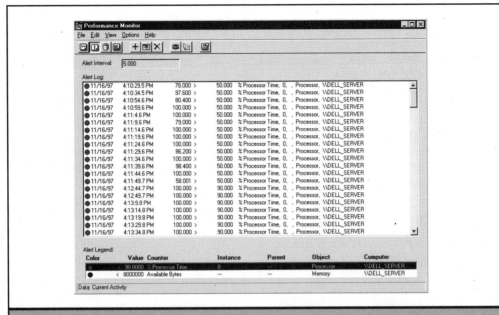

Figure 15-6. Alert View in Performance Monitor, along with a series of example alerts

Setting Alert View Options

Just as you did with Chart View, click the Options button on the toolbar to access Alert View's options, which you can see in Figure 15-7.

You can choose the Switch to Alert View option to cause Alert View to become visible whenever an alert occurs. Performance Monitor must be running, of course, and any other view you are looking at will be preempted by Alert View. You can also choose Log Event in Application Log to generate a log entry viewable with Windows NT's Event

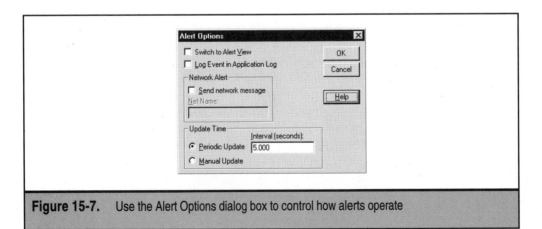

Figure 15-7. Use the Alert Options dialog box to control how alerts operate

Viewer. If you want to send a pop-up message over the network to a specific computer when an alert occurs, choose the Send Network Message option box, and then type the network name of the computer to which you want the alert message sent. Finally, you can use the Update Time section to control how often Performance Monitor checks to see whether an alert has occurred.

NOTE: To view the network names defined for a particular computer, type **net name** at the computer's command prompt. You can add alias names with the command **net name name_to_add /add.** Furthermore, the messenger service must be running on the recipient computer in order for it to receive alert messages. To ensure that it is active, type **net start messenger** at a command prompt on the recipient system.

Logging Performance Activity

There are times when you want to view a chart of different performance counters but can't view it in real time for some reason. For instance, you may want to step some application through a long series of steps, but you don't want to spend time switching back and forth from Performance Monitor (not to mention the confusing numbers that would be displayed). Or you may need more time in which to study a complex chart of performance counters (there's no way to "pause" Performance Monitor in Chart View, except by turning off its automatic update feature through the Options dialog box). In times like these, you use Performance Monitor's Log View feature to create a log of performance information. After going through the sequence of events that you want to monitor, you stop the log and then view its information at your leisure.

To start a log file, first use the Log command in the View menu. Then assign performance objects to the log file. All counters within the assigned performance objects will be stored in the performance log (when you play back the log, you only have to view the counters you want within each object). Click the Add Counter button on the toolbar to assign performance objects with the Add to Log dialog box, shown in Figure 15-8.

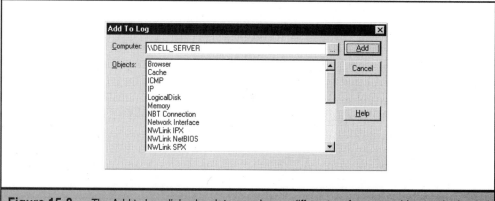

Figure 15-8.   The Add to Log dialog box lets you choose different performance objects to be logged

TIP: You can CTRL+click the performance objects you want in the Add to Log dialog box before clicking the Add button to add them all at once.

After selecting the objects, you then select a log file. Click the Options button in the toolbar to display the Log Options dialog box (see Figure 15-9). Assign a filename, or use an existing log file to append additional information to it. You can then choose how frequently the performance information should be written to the log file with the Update Time section of the dialog box. More frequent updates give you more information but will also make the log grow more quickly. After completing the dialog box's fields, click the Save button to save the choices, or click the Start Log button to both save the choices and start the log simultaneously. When you're done recording the log, display the Log Options dialog box again, and click the Stop Log button.

To view the log's data, follow these steps:

1. Switch to Chart View in Performance Monitor.

2. Pull down the Options menu and choose the Data From command. You see the dialog box shown here:

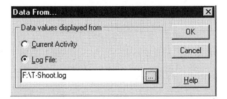

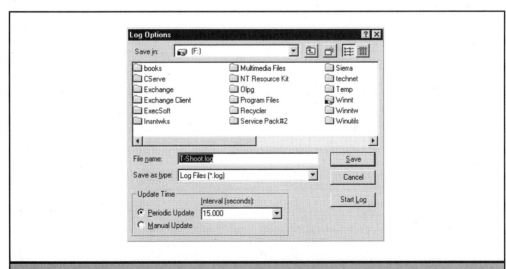

Figure 15-9.   The Log Options dialog box lets you choose a filename for the log file

3. Choose either the Current Activity or Log File option button. If you choose Log File, select the filename into which you recorded the log data. Choose OK.

4. Click the Add Counter button to display the Add to Chart dialog box, and select from the available performance objects and counters. You can only select counters from objects that were recorded in the log file.

5. Performance Monitor then displays the log data, as shown in Figure 15-10.

Notice how the data in Figure 15-10 is compressed: the Graph Time variable is set to 225 seconds. You can control the time period that is displayed. This lets you "zoom in" on the recorded data to examine it more closely. Pull down the Edit menu and choose the Time Window command to view the Input Log File Timeframe dialog box shown in Figure 15-11. You use this dialog box to select the start and stop time within which to view the logged performance data. Drag the two slider controls in the dialog box to select a time period. As you drag the slider controls, two vertical lines indicate how the time period selected corresponds to the data.

Saving Performance Monitor Settings

You can save the settings you've created in Performance Monitor for later use. Since it can be time-consuming to add counters each time you start Performance Monitor, instead set it up once, save the settings, and then launch Performance Monitor with those settings to save lots of time.

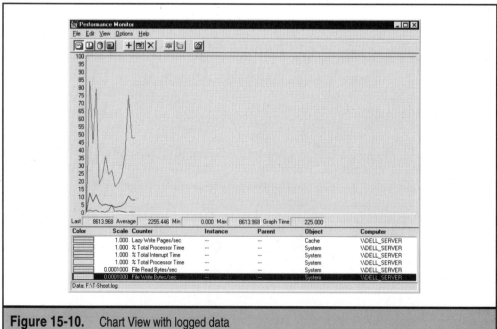

Figure 15-10.   Chart View with logged data

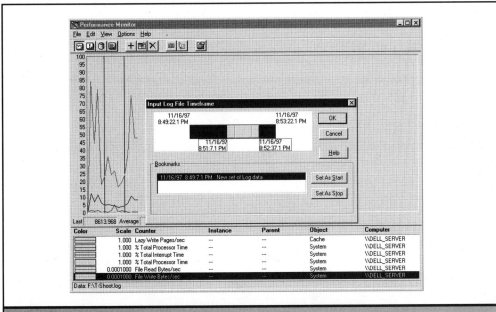

Figure 15-11. The Input Log File Timeframe dialog box lets you choose the time window to examine

When you use the Save As command in the File menu, a file is saved that remembers the counters you were working with. A different file must be saved for each different Performance Monitor view, and the extensions of each saved file correspond to the view in question. Each file has an extension of .pm?, where ? can be "c" for Chart View, "a" for Alert View, "l" for Log View, and "r" for Report View. You can create desktop shortcuts to these saved files; double-click on the saved file, and Performance Monitor starts with those settings loaded.

Creating a Performance Report

Performance Monitor can also generate overview reports of the different performance counters in the system. Often, such reports are used to provide information on relatively static data, such as free disk space and the like, but the report display also shows variable data, although only the most recent information appears at any given time. Figure 15-12 shows an example report in Performance Monitor.

You have limited formatting options in the Performance Monitor reports. You cannot, for example, change the formatting of the values displayed, nor can you reposition them on the display. (Despite its name, Report View isn't really designed for creating attractive printed reports.)

Use the Add Counter button to add counters to Report View, just as you do in any of the other modes. You can also use the Settings button to change how frequently the data shown in the report is updated.

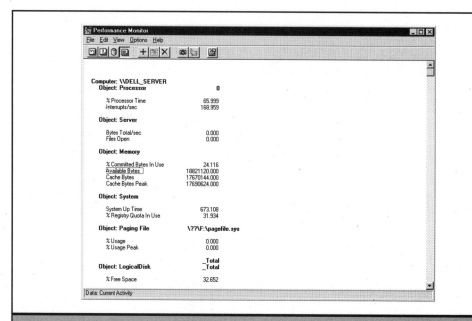

Figure 15-12. Report View can give you a nice overview of the status of a Windows NT computer

Important Performance Objects and Counters

Quite a few performance objects and counters, of varying usefulness, are available in Performance Monitor. The two tables shown here list the key performance objects and counters that are often useful to watch, particularly when measuring performance. Table 15-2 contains a list of the basic performance objects available, while Table 15-3 shows you some of the key performance counters you might want to monitor in different situations.

TIP: Certain disk-based performance counters are not enabled by default in Windows NT, but they can offer more detailed performance data on how well the system's disk subsystem is running. On slower Windows NT systems, such as 486-based systems, these counters may slow the overall system by about 5 percent. On Pentium systems, they should not cause an appreciable impact. To enable the enhanced disk-based performance counters, open a Command Prompt window and type the command **diskperf –y**. To enable the disk counters for use with a stripe set, use the command **diskperf –ye.** (Stripe sets are discussed in the section "Disk Administrator," later in this chapter.) In either case, you will be prompted to restart the system, after which the counters will function and be available in Performance Monitor. To turn the counters back off, open a Command Prompt window and type **diskperf –n** and restart the system again.

In addition to the information displayed in these tables, certain applications install additional performance objects and counters into Windows NT that can be viewed with Performance Monitor. See the documentation for the application in question for information on its performance objects and counters.

Performance Object	Description
Browser	Network browser activity
Cache	Cache Manager statistics (includes both disk and network cache)
Logical Disk	Disk partition activity
Memory	Memory activity, including virtual memory paging
NetBEUI	NetBEUI performance activity, when NetBEUI is installed
NWLink IPX	IPX activity, when IPX is installed
NWLink NetBIOS	NetBIOS over IPX activity, when NetBIOS is installed
NWLink SPX	SPX over IPX activity, when IPX is installed
Objects	Object counts (events, semaphores, threads, etc.)
Paging File	Usage counters for the paging file
Physical Disk	Physical disk drive activity
Process	Process-specific performance counters
Processor	Performance counters for each individual processor
Redirector	Network redirector activity
Server	Server activities
Server Work Queues	Backlog of server activity requests
System	Computerwide activity counters
Telephony	Telephony activity
Thread	Thread-specific performance counters

Table 15-2. Default Performance Objects in Windows NT

Performance Object	Performance Counter	Description
Cache	Copy Read Hits %	Measures the efficiency of the cache in terms of satisfying application requests from data already cached. A higher percentage indicates that more data is being found in the cache, and therefore fewer disk accesses are being required. To improve this number, free up system memory so that the system can create a larger cache (which it will do automatically if appropriate).
Cache	Copy Reads/sec	Measures the volume of data being read from the cache. Use this counter in concert with Cache: Copy Read Hits %.
Cache	Data Map Hits %	Displays the efficiency with which requests from the cache for file system meta-data (directory information, folder information, etc.) are satisfied.
Cache	Data Maps/sec	Displays the volume of data being moved to satisfy application requests for file system meta-data. Higher numbers indicate more frequent directory read and write activity.
Cache	Data Flushes/sec	Displays the number of times the write cache has been flushed to disk per second.
Logical Disk	% Disk Read Time	Shows the percentage of system time that the system is busy reading data from the disk. You can use the Instance window in the Add Counter dialog box to select a particular drive letter.

Table 15-3. Important Performance Counters

Performance Object	Performance Counter	Description
Logical Disk	% Disk Time	Shows the percentage of system time that is being spent reading from or writing to a logical disk (a partition).
Logical Disk	% Disk Write Time	Shows the percentage of system time that is being spent writing to a logical disk.
Logical Disk	% Free Space	An excellent counter for use in an alert. Shows the percentage of free space on a selected logical disk.
Logical Disk	Avg. Disk Queue Length	Counts the average length of the queue of logical disk requests.
Logical Disk	Avg. Disk sec/Read	Indicates the average amount of time needed to fulfill logical disk read requests. Consider using this counter with the same application and making use of different disk drives to find the drive that performs the best or that is having a problem.
Logical Disk	Avg. Disk sec/Write	Indicates the average amount of time to fulfill logical disk write requests.
Logical Disk	Current Disk Queue Length	An instantaneous number showing the current length of the disk request queue for a particular logical disk.
Logical Disk	Disk Bytes/sec	Displays the number of bytes being read or written per second on a selected logical disk.
Logical Disk	Free Megabytes	Handy for alerts, this counter displays the number of free space on a logical disk (in MB).

Table 15-3. Important Performance Counters (*continued*)

Performance Object	Performance Counter	Description
Memory	% Committed Bytes in Use	Shows the percentage of the allocated paging file that is in use. When over 75 percent, consider increasing the size of the paging file.
Memory	Available Bytes	Shows the current amount of free working memory. This number rarely drops below 4MB, because Windows NT starts managing its use of RAM more aggressively when this counter hits 4MB.
Memory	Cache Bytes	Shows the size of the system cache. The system will adjust the size of the cache automatically as needs and opportunities dictate. The only way to force this number to increase is to free up system memory by closing programs, stopping services, or adding RAM to the system.
Memory	Cache Bytes Peak	Shows the peak size of the system cache.
Memory	Page Reads/sec	Displays the quantity of page reads from the system paging file. Note that each page read might contain multiple pages, so you cannot correlate this number with the amount of data being paged.
Memory	Page Writes/sec	Shows the quantity of page writes to the system paging file.
Memory	Pages Input/sec	Shows the number of pages being read from the paging file per second. Each page is 4KB on Intel systems.
Memory	Pages Output/sec	Displays the number of pages being written to the system paging file.

Table 15-3. Important Performance Counters (*continued*)

Performance Object	Performance Counter	Description
Memory	Pages/sec	Shows the number of pages (both read and write) being moved from or to the system paging file.
NetBEUI	Bytes Total/sec	Lists the quantity of bytes being received or transmitted using NetBEUI.
NWLink IPX	Bytes Total/sec	Lists the quantity of bytes being received or transmitted using IPX.
NWLink	Bytes Total/sec	Shows the quantity of bytes being received or transmitted using NWLink (NetBIOS).
NWLink SPX	Bytes Total/sec	Shows the quantity of bytes being received or transmitted using SPX.
Paging File	% Usage	Displays the overall utilization of the system paging file.
Paging File	% Usage Peak	Shows the peak utilization of the system paging file.
Physical Disk	% Disk Read Time	Displays the percentage of system time being spent reading from a physical disk.
Physical Disk	% Disk Time	Shows the percentage of system time being spent reading from or writing to a physical disk.
Physical Disk	% Disk Write Time	Displays the percentage of system time spent writing to a physical disk.
Physical Disk	Avg. Disk Queue Length	Shows the average length of the disk queue (one queue entry per application disk request).
Physical Disk	Avg. Disk sec/Read	Gives the average time to take care of a physical disk read request.
Physical Disk	Avg. Disk sec/Write	Gives the average time to take care of a physical disk write request.

Table 15-3.   Important Performance Counters (*continued*)

Performance Object	Performance Counter	Description
Physical Disk	Current Disk Queue Length	Displays the current length of the disk queue for a specified physical disk.
Physical Disk	Disk Bytes/sec	Shows the number of bytes being read from or written to a physical disk.
Process	% Processor Time	Lists the percentage of time the processor is busy doing work for a specific process.
Process	Page File Bytes	Shows the number of bytes being stored in the system paging file for a specific process.
Process	Private Bytes	Shows the number of bytes allocated by a specific process.
Process	Working Set	Gives the amount of physical RAM used by a specific process.
Processor	% Processor Time	Useful when more than one processor is installed in a system. Shows the percentage of time that a specific processor is busy doing work.
System	% Total Processor Time	Shows the total amount of time that all processors are busy doing work. High numbers may indicate the need for more processors, assuming the applications can make use of them.
System	% Total User Time	Shows the percentage of time the processor runs code at the User level ring of the processor (this level consists of all nonprivileged code running and has nothing to do with network users or local users).

Table 15-3. Important Performance Counters (*continued*)

Performance Object	Performance Counter	Description
System	% Total Privileged Time	Shows the percentage of time the processor runs code at the Privileged level ring of the processor.
System	File Read Bytes/sec	Displays the number of bytes being read from the file system, across all physical and logical disks.
System	File Write Bytes/sec	Displays the number of bytes being written to the file system, across all physical and logical disks.
System	Processor Queue Length	Shows the number of requests waiting in the processor queue. Numbers in the 2 to 4 range are fairly normal and usually not cause for concern.

Table 15-3.   Important Performance Counters (*continued*)

EVENT VIEWER

Another very important tool to consult when troubleshooting is Event Viewer. Windows NT keeps a set of logs of significant events in the system. The log files are kept in the \%SystemRoot%\System32\config directory and are named Sysevent.evt, Secevent.evt, and Appevent.evt for System, Security, and Application events, respectively. The System event log displays important system information, the Security log shows selected audited security events, and the Application log shows whatever messages the server applications are programmed to report.

Figure 15-13 shows an example of Event Viewer with the System log displayed. Notice that each event has an icon to the left of its listing. To make it easier when you're looking at your screen, the icons are color coded: red Stop icons indicate serious problems, yellow Warning icons indicate less severe problems, and blue Information icons indicate informational messages.

Start Event Viewer by selecting it in the Administrative Tools folder in the Start menu's Programs folder. By default, system events are displayed, with the most recent event at the top of the list. Double-click on any event to see the detailed information about the event, as illustrated in the lower right window in Figure 15-13. Once the Event Detail window is open, use the Previous and Next buttons to look quickly through the detailed

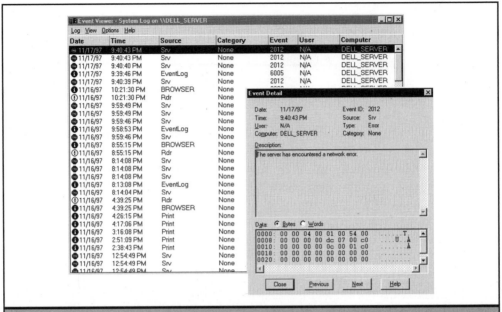

Figure 15-13. Event Viewer shows detailed information about system, security, and application events. System events are displayed in this figure.

events. To see other types of events, pull down the Log menu and choose System, Security, or Application.

NOTE: In order for event logs to be updated by the system, the Event Log service must be running. If logs don't seem to be collecting data, check to make sure that nobody has disabled that service in the system.

If a large number of events are recorded, you can filter the list to make it more manageable and perhaps help you find the data you need. Open the View menu and choose Filter Events. You see the Filter dialog box shown in Figure 15-14. Use the available fields to select which events you want to view, and click the OK button to display only those events.

You can change how events are kept by the system. Access the Log menu and choose Log Settings from the menu. You see the Event Log Settings dialog box shown in Figure 15-15. In this dialog box, you can control the maximum size of each of the three main event logs. First, use the Change Settings For drop-down list box to select the event log with which you want to work. Then you can set a maximum size for the log and control how events are overwritten (or not) when the log becomes full. Each file grows in 64KB increments, up to the maximum selected. The default is 512KB.

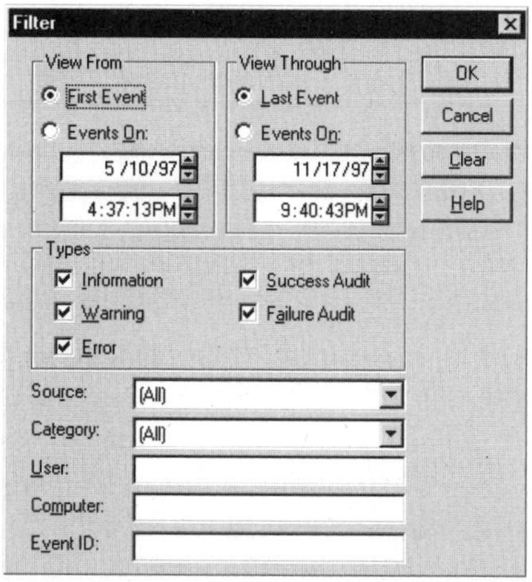

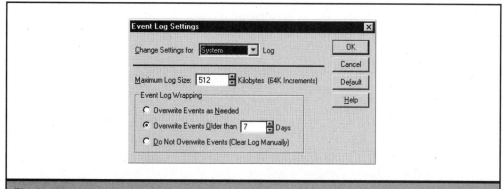

Figure 15-14.   Use the Filter dialog box to show only events of interest

TIP: You can check the size of the event log files occasionally to get some feel for how quickly your logs are growing. Different logs will grow at different rates, depending on the level of logging that the system is set to perform. If you are logging file accesses, for instance, the Security log may grow quite large very quickly. In general, the System log will grow the fastest if you are not auditing many events, and the Application log's growth is the slowest (although this depends on what applications are running on the server and their respective log settings).

Figure 15-15.   Check the Event Log Settings dialog box to control how events are overwritten in the logs when the logs become full

Event logs typically need to be reviewed and cleared on a regular basis. How frequently you need to do this depends on how you've configured the server and its applications, and how busy the server is. To start, you should check the logs frequently to find out how often important information is recorded. Over a short period of time you'll learn how often you should check and clear the system's event logs. After checking the logs, you can erase all the recorded events, and you have the option of saving the logs before you clear them. To clear and save an event log, follow these steps:

1. Open the Log menu and choose Clear All Events.

2. You are prompted to save the log file before clearing it. If you choose to do so, you next see a standard Save As dialog box that lets you choose a name for the saved event log file.

3. After you save the log file, you are warned that clearing the log is irreversible. Acknowledge the message and the log is cleared.

Event Viewer can save the event logs into three different formats. Files saved in .evt format can be used only with Event Viewer (you can open them with the Open command in the Log menu). Files saved in .txt format are plain ASCII text files viewable with any text editor. Files saved in .csv format are comma-separated files suitable for importing into a database or spreadsheet application. No additional information is recorded into these files that you can't see in Event Viewer, but the two other formats (.txt and .csv) can be useful for reporting or other analyses that can't be performed in Event Viewer.

AUDITING

One of the nicest features of Windows NT is that it includes the ability to audit security events in the system. You establish how you want events logged, and they are then displayed with Event Viewer in the Security log. You can log things like successful attempts to open a particular file, failed attempts, failed logons, and so forth. There are three resources that you can audit: user activity, disk activity (on NTFS-formatted drives), and printer activity. Sometimes this audit information can prove useful in solving problems with the system.

Auditing User Activity

You establish audits of user activity using User Manager for Domains. After opening the program, access the Policies menu and choose Audit. You then see the Audit Policy dialog box shown in Figure 15-16. You first need to enable auditing by selecting Audit These Events. You can then use the available option boxes to select which user activity events will be audited. As a rule of thumb, you will want to audit certain failure events, such as failed logons, failed file accesses (attempts to open a file to which the user doesn't have privileges), and security policy changes. Auditing successful events may be desirable in some cases, but you should consider carefully whether you will be swamped with too much information if you audit success events.

Event Viewer and Event Logs: No More Server Log Books?

Event Viewer and the event logs in Windows NT are very helpful tools, and they make it much easier for an administrator to keep track of important system information. However, they do not take care of all of the logging that one should do for any Windows NT Server (or any server for that matter). It is imperative that you also maintain a physical log for each server under your care. Doing so will drastically speed recovery and aid troubleshooting. While maintaining a physical log is not a fun chore, when your system is having trouble you'll find that a detailed physical log of the system is worth its weight in gold.

A good server log book should contain a number of elements, including the following:

▼　A description of the hardware for the system, including any serial numbers, model numbers, or part numbers that are installed in the system.

■　If possible, a copy of the invoice for the system, or at least the packing list

■　Contact information for technical support, both for the hardware of the server and for any key applications installed onto the server.

■　A log book that records significant events on the server. This should include any hardware configuration changes, significant software configuration changes (such as changing how disks are partitioned or how protocols are installed), any errors or other problems that occurred with the system, as well as how they were resolved, and any routine maintenance or testing performed on the system.

▲　If possible, it's a good idea to keep any CD-ROMs or diskettes needed to rebuild the server from scratch. Also include any diagnostic utilities that are designed for the server in question. And don't forget the Windows NT Emergency Repair Disk!

Not only is such a server log book useful if you are the only one maintaining the system, but it becomes even more important if several people maintain the system. The time you and others spend keeping the log book updated is worth it.

Auditing File and Directory Activity

File and directory audits can be enabled only for NTFS-formatted drives. To enable and set the audit rules, right-click on the drive, folder, or file to be audited and choose Properties from the shortcut menu. Move to the Security tab and click on the Auditing button. You then see an Auditing dialog box like the one shown in Figure 15-17. It is important to understand that the auditing settings apply to each object on the partition in question. You can have different auditing settings for individual drives, folders, and files. You can also apply a particular set of auditing rules to an entire directory structure

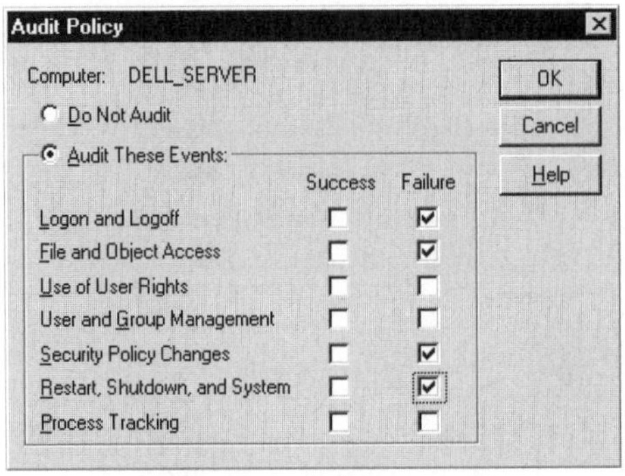

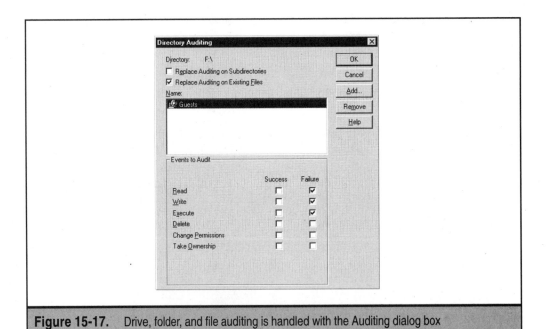

Figure 15-16. User Manager for Domains contains the Audit Policy dialog box, with which you can enable user activity auditing

or to an entire set of files within a directory. But the important thing is that each object has its own private auditing settings. Moreover, these auditing settings apply to each user and group specifically. You can elect to audit everyone's access by using the Everyone group to assign the audit settings, or you can choose other groups or users to audit

Figure 15-17. Drive, folder, and file auditing is handled with the Auditing dialog box

differently. You can define as many sets of auditing rules as you require. For instance, you might audit Take Ownership successes and failures for the Everyone group, but audit only Delete successes and failures for a specific user. The auditing policies in Windows NT are extremely flexible and powerful.

To add an auditing rule, click on the Add button. You then see the Add Users and Groups dialog box shown in Figure 15-18. Select the group or user to which you want to assign auditing rules and click OK. Remember that you can use the Members button to see the membership in a group, or the Search button to find a user in a large list.

After choosing a user or group and clicking the Add button, the names are added to the Add Names list at the bottom of the dialog box. After you have added all of the names you want to audit, click OK to return to the Auditing dialog box. You can then select each user or group in the Name window (refer to Figure 15-17) and click the appropriate Success and Failure check boxes to select which events you want to audit. Of particular importance in the Auditing dialog box are the Replace Auditing on Subdirectories and Replace Auditing on Existing Files check boxes. By using these two check boxes, you can apply an auditing rule to an entire set of subdirectories, as well as to all of the files in the subdirectories.

After you click OK in the Auditing dialog box, all of the auditing rules you defined are applied to the selected directories and files. If you are changing auditing rules on a large set of directories and files, this process may take quite some time. (Fortunately, it is cancellable if you make a mistake, and you see a status dialog box showing the subdirectories and files that are being set as the process proceeds.)

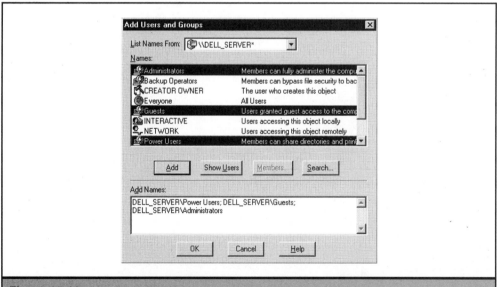

Figure 15-18.   The Add Users and Groups dialog box lets you choose exactly which users will be audited for the drive, folder, or file object in question

Auditing Printer Activity

Just as you can audit drive, folder, and file activity, you can also audit printer activity. Functionally, you set up printer auditing in the same way as drive, folder, and file auditing. Open My Computer, open the Printers folder, right-click on the printer in question, move to its Security tab, and click the Auditing button. The only difference for printer auditing is that there are different types of events to audit. Also, you do not have to be using NTFS-formatted partitions in order to perform printer auditing; FAT-formatted partitions still provide printer auditing under Windows NT. Figure 15-19 shows the Printer Auditing dialog box and the events you can audit.

NT DIAGNOSTICS

Windows NT comes with a tool called Windows NT Diagnostics. Unlike other diagnostic software you may be accustomed to, Windows NT Diagnostics is more of a reporting tool than a testing tool. In fact, it doesn't perform any testing of the system, but rather provides a convenient and quick way to view a variety of important troubleshooting information about the system. Figure 15-20 shows the Version tab of Windows NT Diagnostics.

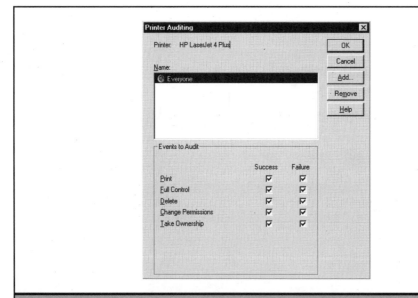

Figure 15-19. The Printer Auditing dialog box lets you establish auditing for different types of printer events

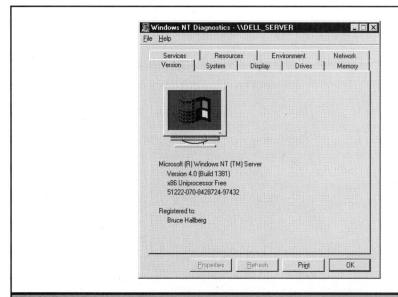

Figure 15-20.   Windows NT Diagnostics is found in the Administrative Tools folder and provides a wealth of important system information about the Windows NT system

The information available from the Windows NT Diagnostics application is extensive.

▼ **System**   The System tab, shown in Figure 15-21, displays the overall system identifier and the version of the HAL being used, as well as important BIOS version information and—for when Intel announces those pesky processor errata—the processor stepping level. (A processor's stepping level is analogous to Windows NT build or Service Pack numbers.)

■ **Display**   The Display tab shows you the configuration of and data about the video display system. Figure 15-22 shows an example of the Display tab.

■ **Drives**   The Drives tab (see Figure 15-23) provides a wealth of information about the partitions (also called drives) in the system. By expanding one of the drive categories, selecting a drive, and clicking on the Properties button, you can see detailed information about the file system the drive is using. This can also be handy to see what size clusters any FAT-formatted drives in the system are using.

■ **Memory**   The Memory tab of Windows NT Diagnostics (my favorite tab) really lets you see how memory in the system is being used. Not only can you view details about the physical memory installed, but you can see how many memory objects exist at any given time, how the paging file is being utilized by the system, and how much memory is being consumed by the Windows NT kernel. Figure 15-24 shows an example of the Memory tab.

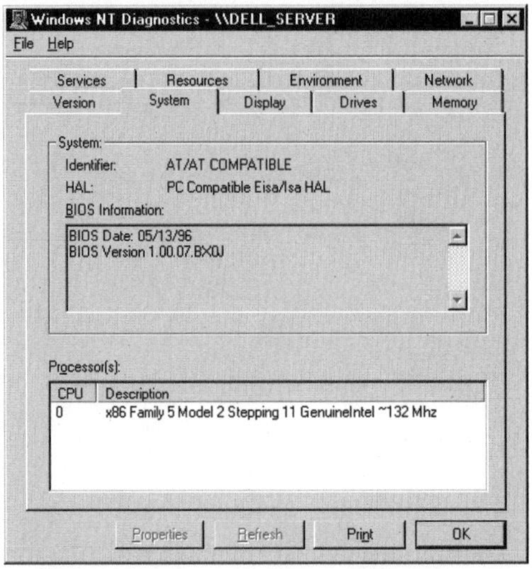

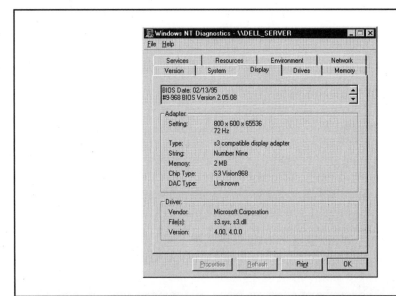

Figure 15-21. Use the System tab to see how the hardware in the system is identified, the BIOS version, and the processor stepping level

Figure 15-22. Use the Display tab to see what version of video driver the system is using, as well as what type of video is installed

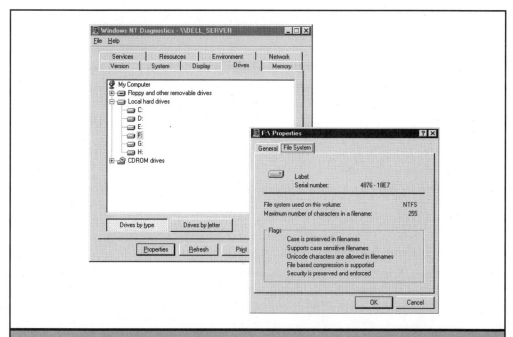

Figure 15-23. Use the Drives tab to see information about each drive's file system

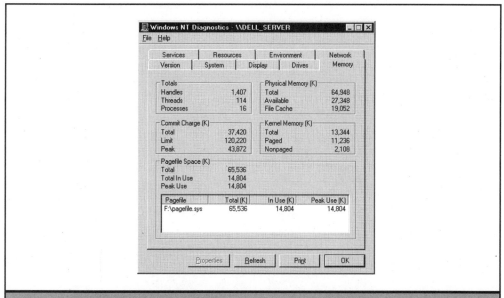

Figure 15-24. The Memory tab shows a wealth of information about system memory

- **Network** On the Network tab (see Figure 15-25), you can see detailed information about the various network settings of the Windows NT system. By clicking on the buttons at the bottom of the window, you can see just about every important network setting that affects the system.

- **Environment** When you select the Environment tab, you can see all of the environment variables in effect at any given time. This is similar to typing the Set command at a command prompt. Remember to look at both the System variables and the Local User variables, as both are operable, and the Local User variables may be different, depending on the settings for the logon account you're using. See Figure 15-26 for an example of the Environment tab.

- **Resources** When you're faced with a hardware problem, you often need to check the resources used by all of the installed hardware devices. The Resources tab (see Figure 15-27) is designed for this purpose. You can see the IRQ, I/O port, DMA, memory, and device assignments in the system with this tab, all in one easy-to-view location.

▲ **Services** Finally, the Services tab, seen in Figure 15-28, shows you the Windows NT services and devices and their status. Select any of the services or devices and then click on the Properties button to see its dependencies and general information. You can also see the filename that is providing the service or device support to Windows NT.

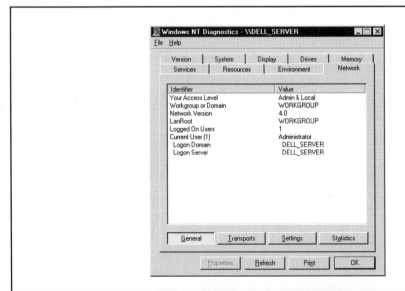

Figure 15-25. Having a network configuration problem? Check the Network tab first to see how the system's networking components are configured

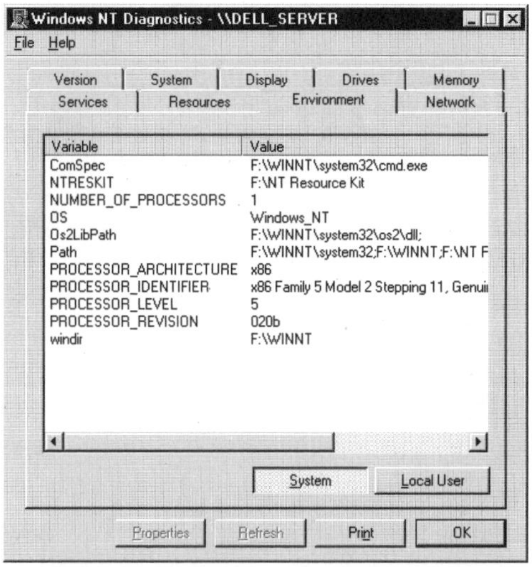

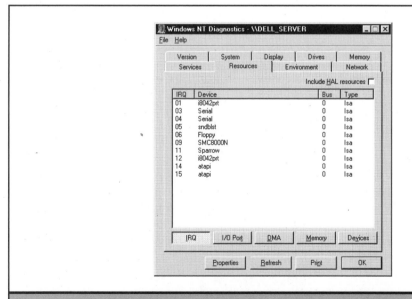

Figure 15-26. Environment variables, useful for debugging command files, can be viewed with the Environment tab

Figure 15-27. Use the Resources tab to track down conflicts or problems with peripheral resource assignments

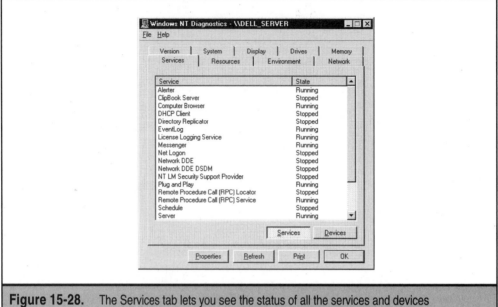

Figure 15-28. The Services tab lets you see the status of all the services and devices in the system

DISK ADMINISTRATOR

Disk Administrator is a program that manages the partitions on a Windows NT system (see Figure 15-29). It lets you create, modify, and delete partitions.

Disk Administrator also lets you create mirrored disks and stripe sets. *Mirrored disks* are exactly what their name implies: Two disks contain the data of just one disk, but the data is repeated—or mirrored—on each disk. That way, if a disk fails, the remaining disk can carry on as if nothing had happened and you can replace the failed disk as soon as practical.

A *stripe set* lets you spread data across multiple disks in order to improve performance. For example, when you have a stripe set made up of four physical hard disks, the data is automatically spread among the different disks. Because the data is on multiple disks, you also have multiple heads working when data needs to be read from or written to the stripe set. Stripe sets are significantly faster than single disks. You can create stripe sets with or without parity. A stripe set with parity sets aside one of the disks to store information that can be used to rebuild the stripe sets if one of the disks fails. Without parity, if you lose a single disk in a stripe set, you lose all of the data on all of the disks (now there's a nightmarish thought).

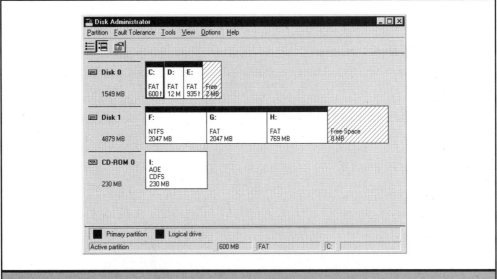

Figure 15-29.   The main Disk Administrator window displays information about disks

Disk Administrator doesn't really help you in troubleshooting your system. While it can tell you when a disk has failed, it's better to keep an eye on Event Viewer, where such information is also displayed. Instead, Disk Administrator comes into action when you have a failure from which you need to recover. For example, if you have a stripe set with parity and one of the disks fails, the system keeps running normally, after recording the event in the System log. As soon as you can manage, take down the server and replace the disk. After startup you can use Disk Administrator to partition the new disk, and then rebuild the stripe set using the new disk in place of the failed disk. Similarly, Disk Administrator can be used to remirror disks when the mirrors break.

CHAPTER 16

Using Resource
Kit Tools

The Windows NT Server 4 Resource Kit CD-ROM is chock-full of useful—and fun—utility programs. This chapter covers some of the diagnostic and management tools included in the Resource Kit CD-ROM, many of which will help you in troubleshooting Windows NT Server, or in managing it more effectively. Table 16-1 provides an overview of the Resource Kit tools discussed in this chapter.

Name	Description
Auto Logon	Allows a Windows NT Server computer to automatically log on using a specified user name and password on startup.
C2 Configuration Manager	Helps configure Windows NT Server for C2-level security compliance.
Command Scheduler	A graphical interface to the AT command line utility.
Time Zone Editor	Lets you change details about Windows NT's time zone settings.
Run Application as Service	Allows the configuration of an application to run as a Windows NT service.
Process Viewer	Shows detailed information about running processes on the system.
Shutdown Manager	Lets you perform timed shutdowns of NT Server.
TechNet CD Sampler	A sample of what you get with the TechNet CD-ROM subscription service. Includes useful technical papers and notes.
Online Documents	A comprehensive reference of Windows NT Server technical information.
Crystal Reports for Windows NT Server 4 Resource Kit	A special version of Crystal Reports that generates reports from the Windows NT event logs.

Table 16-1.   Resource Kit Utilities Discussed in This Chapter

Name	Description
Quick Slice	Shows an abbreviated graphical display of processor time slice allocations.
Disk Probe	A disk editor similar in concept to Norton Disk Editor for DOS.
WinDiff	Graphically compares files in two directories for byte-level differences.
Text Viewer	Browses directories to view text files in a graphical environment.
Netclip	Lets you view the contents of another computer's Windows Clipboard over the network.
Batch file utilities	A collection of utilities useful for creating automated batch files.
Scripting languages	Two powerful Windows NT scripting languages are available: Perl and ReXX, either of which will meet virtually any scripting needs you might have.
KiXtart95	Similar to a full script language, this is a powerful tool for automating Windows 95 logon processes.
Floplock	Use this utility to keep non-Administrators from accessing a Windows NT computer's diskette drives.
Soon	Similar to the AT command, the Soon command lets you automatically repeat commands at regular intervals.
Timserv	Don't let your server's time be off by even a nanosecond! Use this utility to automatically synchronize your server with super-accurate external sources, such as the NIST atomic clock.
Sysdiff	Sysdiff lets you automate the installation of additional applications when rolling out Windows NT Workstation.
Kill	A Windows NT version of the old Unix favorite, Kill lets you kill processes from the command line.

Table 16-1.   Resource Kit Utilities Discussed in This Chapter (*continued*)

Name	Description
Perfmtr and Pmon	Use these two command line utilities to quickly see performance counter data on the system.
Timethis	You can use the Timethis command to find out how long complex command files or programs take to process.
Quickres	This handy utility lets you quickly and easily change your video settings.
Showdisk	The Showdisk utility works at a command prompt to show you how the disks in the system are configured.
Diruse	Diruse can be used to easily show and report on how much space any set of directories (such as user home directories!) on your system consumes.

Table 16-1.   Resource Kit Utilities Discussed in This Chapter (*continued*)

There are many other useful and helpful utilities on the Resource Kit CD-ROM. These include applications such as 3DPaint, Desktop Themes for Windows NT, PERL and ReXX programming files, and more. You should spend some time browsing the Resource Kit CD-ROM to discover all of its contents, because you'll definitely find lots of utilities you'll want to try.

Auto Logon

Picture this: Your Windows NT Server has automatically restarted due to a power outage and subsequent restoration, and has booted itself. However, the machine's purpose is to run a database server program that doesn't start as a service, but rather starts when the administrator logs into the system. You, being the administrator, are unaware that the system restarted overnight and hasn't yet loaded the database server program (which is relied on by everyone in the Accounting department) when you decide to run a few errands on the way in to work. You arrive, late, to find that the entire Accounting department staff has been sitting on their thumbs for an hour or two because the accounting system isn't working. You check the server room, quickly realize what happened, and log on to Windows NT Server. The database server loads itself, and all is again right with the world.

Except, of course, that there are still a bunch of annoyed users, all of whom know that you were late to the office and that it had a significant impact on all of them. You can expect your boss to bring this little incident up at your next meeting.

An unavoidable snafu? Not if you had set up the system to automatically log on when it started in situations such as the one described.

In cases where the server is located in a locked room and you aren't concerned about it being logged in all the time with a particular user name—such as when that user account runs an important program, like our fictional database server—you can set up Windows NT to log on to an account automatically when it starts. Included in the Resource Kit is a utility that sets this up for you, called Auto Logon. You can find it in the Resource Kit 4 folder, in the Configuration subfolder. Running it activates the dialog box shown in Figure 16-1.

After starting Auto Logon, simply enter the password needed for the account with which you are currently logged on and click the OK button. Henceforth, the system will automatically log on using that account. Notice that you cannot specify an account, but rather must use the logon name that you're currently using.

Auto Logon works by making a couple of registry changes that you could otherwise do by hand, if you were so inclined. Two values are created in the registry key HKEY_LOCAL_MACHINE\SOFTWARE\Microsoft\Windows NT\Winlogon.

The first value is called DefaultUserName, a REG_SZ value. In this value is stored the text string of the account name under which you want automatic logon to function (in this case, it is "Administrator"). The second value is called DefaultPassword, again a

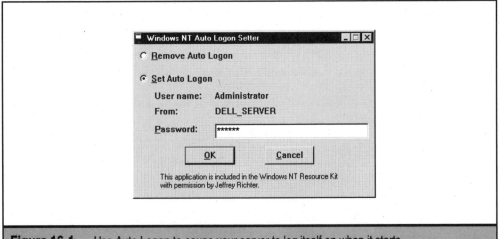

Figure 16-1.   Use Auto Logon to cause your server to log itself on when it starts

REG_SZ value. This second value contains a string (in plain text) of the password needed to log in with the account.

> **CAUTION:**   Before enabling automatic logon using either the Auto Logon utility or the registry changes discussed here, make sure that you carefully consider the security implications of such a change, given your site's requirements and the physical security of the server.

Wait; you're not quite finished. Go into User Manager and make sure this password doesn't require changing (it's almost guaranteed that the day it must change is going to be the next day you're late to work). Enable the Password Never Expires option.

C2 Configuration

When Windows NT was first being designed, Microsoft made a lot of noise about how the operating system would be certified at the U.S. government C2 security level, as defined by the Orange Book (a book published by the National Computer Security. Center [NCSC] with a cover that is, well, orange). In a nutshell, C2 security means that the system implements Discretionary Access Control (DAC), in which users are granted certain security rights and are then trusted to assign their own rights to others. (This is different from Mandatory Access Control [MAC], in which a system administrator must grant all security privileges on the system, no matter what.)

A default installation of Windows NT Server does not meet C2-level security. Certain changes must be made in the system in order to configure Windows NT Server to match the configuration at which C2 security was achieved in tests by the NCSC.

Included in the Resource Kit is a utility that examines the system and lets you know what aspects of the system do not meet C2 security, and then can assist you in making the necessary changes. You run C2 Configuration Manager, found in the Configuration subfolder in the Resource Kit 4 folder, to access this program, shown in Figure 16-2.

You can double-click on each of the C2 Configuration parameters shown in the window in Figure 16-2 to learn what needs to be done for the items. Typically, the utility will offer to make the necessary changes for you.

Before setting Windows NT Server up to match the tested C2 configuration, you should carefully weigh your actual security needs against the loss of utility that implementing all of the changes will bring. Of particular note, you cannot configure Windows NT Server for C2-level security if networking is enabled; the networking protocols used by Windows NT Server (TCP/IP, IPS/SPX, NetBEUI, etc.) are not secure enough for C2-level security. Furthermore, the machine must have no removable media drives enabled (such as a floppy diskette drive or CD-ROM), and a number of other changes must be made, all of which will decrease the capabilities of the system.

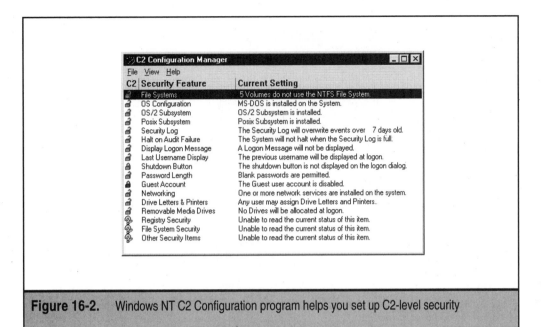

Figure 16-2. Windows NT C2 Configuration program helps you set up C2-level security

Instead, it's a good idea to run the C2 Configuration program and implement the changes that seem appropriate for your site. It provides a good summary of the overall state of the system's security configuration and should be looked at as an informational tool rather than as a mandate to follow all of its recommendations.

Command Scheduler

As a Windows NT Server administrator, you often need to schedule programs to run at regular intervals. For example, you might want to configure a backup program or batch file to run on a regular basis without intervention. Under Windows NT Server, you normally do this with the AT command (see Appendix A for more information).

However, the syntax for the AT command is somewhat cryptic, and a graphical utility that allowed you to access its power would be useful. Included in the Resource Kit is just such a utility, called WinAT. With it, you can not only set up a series of scheduled commands, but you can also manage the scheduled commands on other Windows NT computers on the network.

Running Command Scheduler (aka WinAT) displays the window shown in Figure 16-3. In the window, you can view all of the presently scheduled events on the connected system.

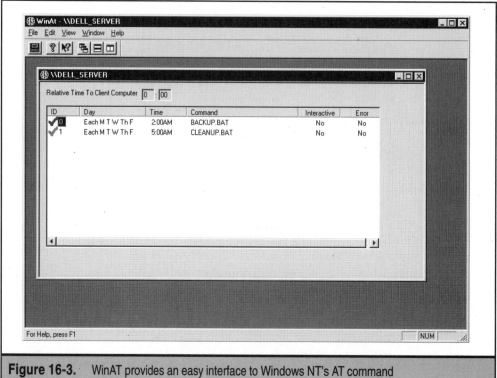

Figure 16-3. WinAT provides an easy interface to Windows NT's AT command

To add a new scheduled command, pull down the Edit menu and choose Add. You can also edit an existing command by double-clicking on it. In either case you see the dialog box shown in Figure 16-4, in which you can choose the appropriate settings.

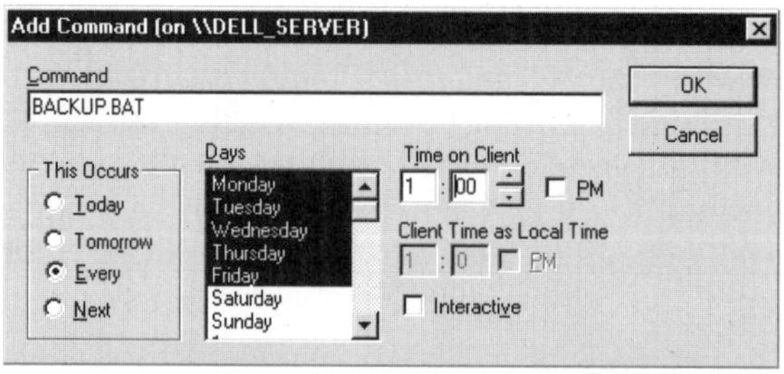

Figure 16-4. The Add Command dialog box lets you determine how a command is scheduled

Time Zone Editor

Use the Time Zone Editor, found in the Configuration subfolder of the Resource Kit 4 folder, to view and edit time zone information on the system. Figure 16-5 shows the Time Zone Editor open, with the Edit Time Zone dialog box active for the Pacific time zone. Using the Edit Time Zone dialog box, you can affect any aspect of the time zone settings, including the offset from Greenwich Mean Time (GMT) and the start and stop times for daylight saving time within that time zone.

TIP: Time zones are not only important for determining when daylight saving time should start and stop, but are vital when e-mail and scheduling entries (such as with Schedule+ or Outlook) are passed between people in different time zones. In one case that I saw, a user had set the time zone to Singapore/Hong Kong time in order to keep an eye on that time zone, and then had changed the clock on the computer to the correct local time (while the time zone was still set to Singapore/Hong Kong time). This wasn't a problem until the user had to view other people's schedules in Schedule+. Since Schedule+ calculates appointment times for multiple users based on the GMT offset and the time zone, this incorrect setting caused considerable problems for the user.

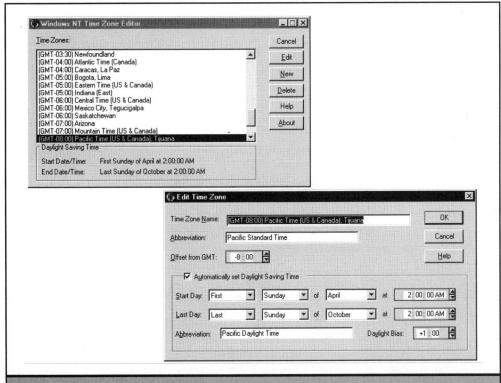

Figure 16-5. Use the Time Zone Editor to control the settings for any of the time zones in Windows NT

Run Application as Service

There are times when it's very efficient to run certain applications as Windows NT services rather than as applications. Remember, services in Windows NT can start even when no user has logged on to the system locally, while applications must be started by a logged-on user. Additionally, since a service can be started at system startup time and doesn't need to be restarted for each user that logs on to the system, you can reduce overhead for background processes that everybody who logs on to the system would want to run or processes that would need to be running no matter who is logged on to the system.

To load an application as a service, follow these steps:

1. Open a Command Prompt window and change to the directory into which you installed the Resource Kit.

2. Execute the following command: **instsrv** *ServiceName* **C:***ResourceKitDirectory***\\Srvany.exe**.

For *ServiceName*, substitute whatever name you want to name the application startup service, such as AppAsService, and for *ResourceKitDirectory* substitute the directory name in which Srvany.exe is located, which should be the same directory into which you installed the Resource Kit.

TIP: You can install the Srvany.exe service multiple times if you like, as long as each occurrence uses a different ServiceName parameter. You then repeat the following steps for each instance you installed.

After issuing the command, you can open the Services dialog box to confirm that the service was installed.

You can now specify, in the registry, the details for the application that Srvany.exe will start as a service.

1. Open a registry editor and locate the following key: HKEY_LOCAL_ MACHINE\SYSTEM\CurrentControlSet\Services*ServiceName*, where *ServiceName* is the name you specified earlier in step 2.

2. Create a subkey named Parameters.

3. Within the Parameters key, create a REG_SZ value named Application. The value of the key should be equal to the fully qualified pathname of the application you want started as a service.

4. If necessary, you can also create a value called AppParameters (also of type REG_SZ) and as its value indicate any startup parameters needed by the application. Moreover, you can also create a value called AppDirectory (type REG_SZ) that contains the startup default directory for the application that will be started as a service.

After completing these steps, ensure that the Srvany.exe service you installed is set for automatic starting. Then restart the system. You can also use the Services Control Panel applet to manually start and stop the service.

CAUTION: When you stop the service manually, the application running as a service is abruptly forced closed and will not have an opportunity to complete any pending operations, such as file stream flushes and the like. Accordingly, be careful when stopping any applications running as services.

Process Viewer

Imagine that your Windows NT Server is not processing some actions as quickly as you think it ought to. You would like to find out what processes and threads are running on the system (and what resources they are consuming), but you don't really have a good way to do that. While you can theoretically use Performance Monitor to view information on a process- and thread-specific basis, Performance Monitor is cumbersome to use in this fashion.

Instead, you will have much better luck understanding what is going on under the hood by using a Resource Kit utility called Process Viewer. With Process Viewer you can browse all of the running processes on the system, along with any associated threads. You can see the priority for each process and thread, and how much memory they are consuming. Figure 16-6 shows the main dialog box of Process Viewer (you can find Process Viewer in the Diagnostics subfolder of the Resource Kit 4 folder).

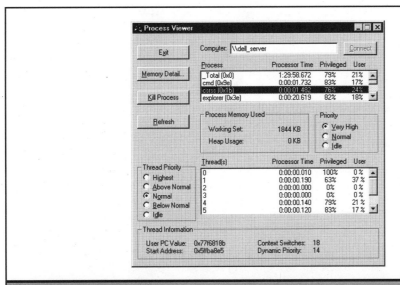

Figure 16-6.   Process Viewer is a real Swiss Army knife when you need detailed process and thread information

As you select each process listed in the upper list box, you see all of the threads owned by that process in the lower list box. (Remember, even though each process has an overall priority level, processes don't actually do any work; threads do all the work. Therefore, each process should have at least one thread—thread 0.)

Using the available option buttons, you can set the priority level for any process or thread in the system. Be very careful when doing this, however, as you can make the system unstable or unresponsive by setting a thread's priority level too high.

You can also terminate any of the listed processes in much the same way that you'd do so in Windows NT's Task Manager. More important, however, you can view detailed memory information on any process. Figure 16-7 shows an example of the memory allocations for a process, which you see when you select a process and click on the Memory Detail button.

Shutdown Manager

Sometimes you need to take down a server, even while users may be accessing it. You need some elegant way to inform the users of the precipitate action you're taking, so they have a chance to save their work before the system shuts down. One way to do this is to

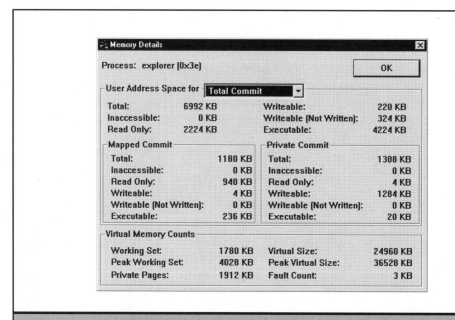

Figure 16-7.   Wondering how an application is using the system's memory? You're certain to find the information you need in the Memory Details dialog box.

send console messages from the server to all the logged-on users, and then keep an eye on the system until they log out so that you can proceed with the shutdown and perform whatever other work you need to do on the system.

In the Resource Kit you'll find a handy utility that will automatically inform any connected users of the impending shutdown and will then carry out the shutdown after a delay that you specify. Found in the Management subfolder in the Resource Kit 4 folder, Shutdown Manager is shown in Figure 16-8.

Using Shutdown Manager is straightforward. First, select the computer that you want to shut down (the default is the computer from which you run Shutdown Manager). Then choose the appropriate options (Kill Applications Without Saving Data, which affects the local computer only, and Reboot After Shutdown). Finally, edit the message text if you wish, and enter the number of seconds to wait before the shutdown occurs.

The message that the users see is informative and keeps them updated on the remaining time until shutdown. The Caution dialog box they receive can be put into the background so that they can safely save their work and log off of the system. Figure 16-9 shows an example of the message users see when you use Shutdown Manager.

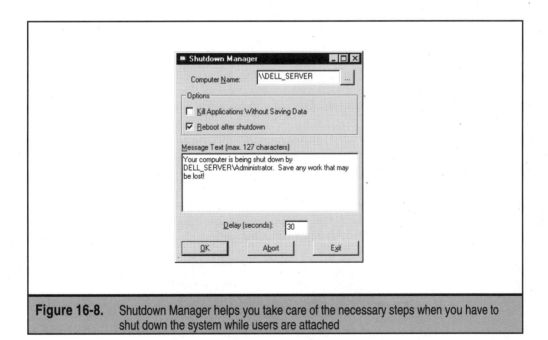

Figure 16-8.   Shutdown Manager helps you take care of the necessary steps when you have to shut down the system while users are attached

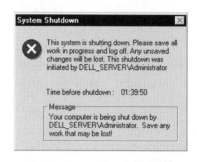

Figure 16-9. A useful dialog box appears on attached computers when you use Shutdown Manager

TIP: If needed, you can use the Abort button on the Shutdown Manager dialog box to stop the process. It's very handy if you get a call telling you this action will stop the payroll from being processed!

TechNet CD Sampler

TechNet is a subscription service that regularly updates you with CD-ROMs containing the Microsoft Knowledge Base, along with important white papers and technology briefings concerning Microsoft products. A sampler of TechNet is included with the Resource Kit, and unlike some samplers, this one provides some pretty useful information.

You can start the TechNet CD Sampler from within the Microsoft Reference folder in Windows NT's Programs menu. Figure 16-10 shows the TechNet CD Sampler with a sample article open.

To search the sampler for information, access the Tools menu and choose Query. In the dialog box shown in Figure 16-11, type a query and click the Run Query button. Figure 16-12 shows the result of the query; as you can see, the sampler contains a wealth of information on working with auditing and RAS.

TIP: Plan on spending at least several hours browsing the TechNet CD Sampler. There is an incredible amount of information within it, and learning to navigate it, as well as knowing what it contains, can save you valuable time when you need a quick answer to a real-life problem.

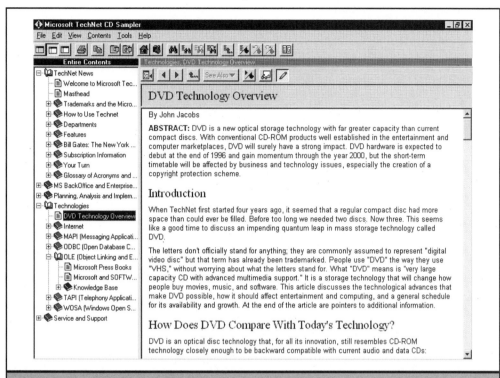

Figure 16-10. The TechNet CD Sampler includes valuable Microsoft product information

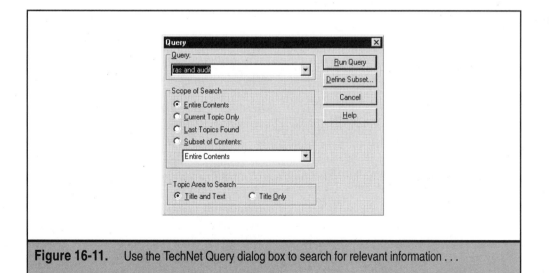

Figure 16-11. Use the TechNet Query dialog box to search for relevant information . . .

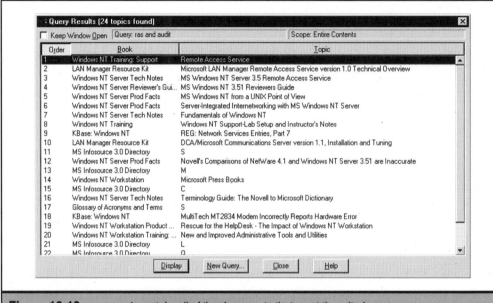

Figure 16-12. . . . and presto!—all of the documents that meet the criteria appear

Online Documents

The TechNet CD Sampler isn't the only valuable information tool included with the Windows NT Resource Kit. You can also find a number of detailed online documents for Windows NT in the Online Docs subfolder within the Resource Kit 4 folder. You can choose from the online help files listed in Table 16-2.

Name of Help File	What It Contains
Adapter Card Help	Contains detailed setup information for most adapter cards certified for use with Windows NT. Includes jumper and dip switch settings, such as the screen shown in Figure 16-13.
Audit Categories	Includes detailed information about what can be audited on a Windows NT Server system, how to control auditing, and how to work with audit information.

Table 16-2. Summary of Online Help Documents on the Resource Kit CD-ROM

Name of Help File	What It Contains
Hardware Compatibility List	The Windows NT Hardware Compatibility List (HCL), which should be consulted before purchasing hardware for use with Windows NT.
Windows NT Messages	A detailed listing, with explanations, of all Windows NT message codes. This is your secret decoder ring for messages you might see in the Windows NT Event Viewer.
Windows NT Server Internet Guide	A complete guide on setting up Windows NT Server as an Internet server.
Windows NT Server Networking Guide	A complete guide to networking with Windows NT Server.
Windows NT Server Resource Guide	Technical and management information about planning, implementing, and managing Windows NT Server. This is an online version of the guide you receive with the Windows NT Server Resource Kit.
Windows NT Workstation Guide	Similar to the Windows NT Server Resource Guide, this help file contains the information for Windows NT Workstation.

Table 16-2.   Summary of Online Help Documents on the Resource Kit CD-ROM (*continued*)

Crystal Reports for Windows NT Server 4 Resource Kit

Crystal Reports, published by Seagate Software, can be used to report on a variety of data from many different sources, such as Excel files, any database with an ODBC driver, Exchange Server data, and so on. Included in the Windows NT Resource Kit is a limited rendition of version 5 of Crystal Reports that lets you create and generate reports based on data in the Windows NT event logs. You can use Crystal Reports to prepare and print

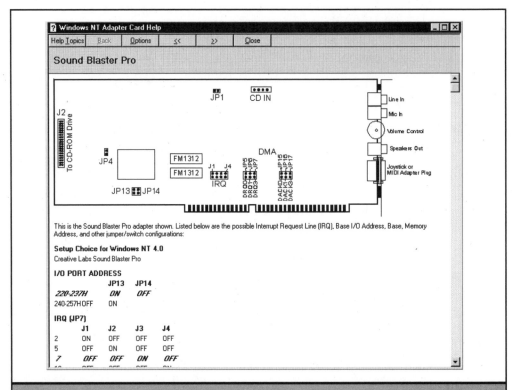

Figure 16-13. A sample from the Adapter Card online document, this page shows detailed setup information for a SoundBlaster Pro card

regular event logs for a Windows NT server in an attractive, useful format. Figure 16-14 shows an example of one of the included report formats that provides information from a Windows NT Server System log file.

The easiest way to try Crystal Reports is to use one of the built-in report formats included with the Resource Kit version. After starting Crystal Reports (run the Crw32.exe file found in the \Program Files\Seagate Software\Crystal Reports for Windows NT Resource Kit folder), access the File menu's Open command. You'll see a number of usable report formats. Open each one in turn and print a sample to get a feel for the information available.

After you open a report format, the system can display the report format with sample data, or the report itself in an editable format. To show real data, follow these steps:

1. Open the Database menu and choose Log On Server.

2. In the resulting Log On Server dialog box, choose any NT Current Event Log and click OK. You see the Select Current Event Log dialog box.

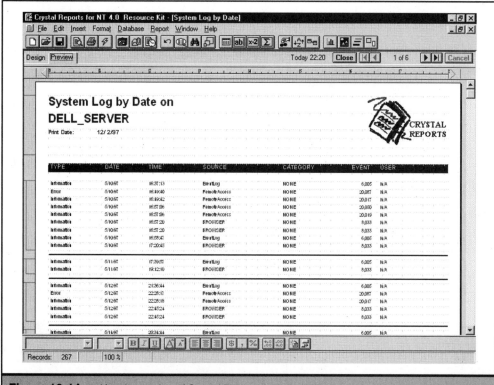

Figure 16-14. Use the version of Crystal Reports included with the Resource Kit to generate reports on Windows NT Server's event logs

3. In the Select Current Event Log dialog box, type the name of the server in the Computer(s) field, or browse the available list to choose the server manually. Choose OK.

4. Open the File menu and choose Print Preview. You will again have to choose the Current Event Log server and click OK, after which you will see the generated report using live data.

5. To drill down in the report, access the Report menu and choose Zoom.

Quick Slice

Quick Slice (found in the Diagnostics subfolder of the Resource Kit 4 folder) quickly displays all of the running processes on the system, along with a graph showing their current processor usage. You can double-click on any of the displayed processes to see more detailed information about its associated threads, as well as their CPU usage. The nice thing about Quick Slice (see Figure 16-15) is that it is much faster at displaying

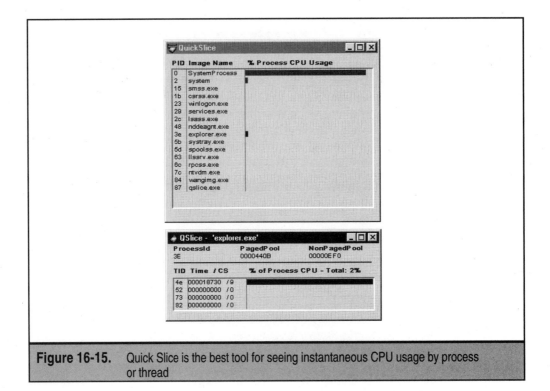

Figure 16-15. Quick Slice is the best tool for seeing instantaneous CPU usage by process or thread

instantaneous information than Performance Monitor (which is a better tool when you need to see trends in CPU usage).

Disk Probe

If you've been working with computers for a while, you probably remember with fondness Norton Disk Editor, a tool that was extremely useful for exploring and changing actual physical data on DOS disks. Included with the Windows NT Resource Kit is a similar tool for reading, editing, and modifying physical data on disks or logical drives under Windows NT. You can find Disk Probe in the Disk Tools subfolder of the Resource Kit folder.

CAUTION: Editing raw data on a system's disks can cause irreparable loss of data or inability to access the data. You should never perform sector-level editing of disks except with specific instructions, and only after you have a complete backup of the system in question. Editing physical structures on a disk is extremely dangerous!

Disk Probe, shown in Figure 16-16, initially opens with no physical disks or logical disks selected for editing. To view (and, if necessary, edit) physical data, follow these steps:

1. From the Drives menu, choose either Physical Disk or Logical Disk (depending on which class of structures you want to edit). An Open dialog box appears.

2. Double-click on the physical disk or logical drive you want to work on. The information appears in the Handle section of the dialog box.

3. Set the options for the Handle (in particular, make sure that Read-Only is selected if you just want to browse data without risk of causing problems), and click the Set Active button. Then click the OK button to close the dialog box.

4. Open the Sectors menu and choose Read. A Read Sectors dialog box appears in which you indicate which sectors you want to read into memory for display or edit. Select the sectors of interest and click OK.

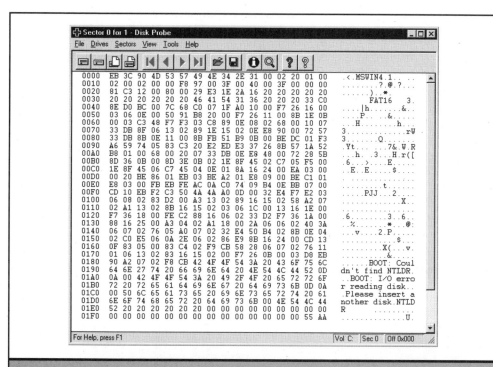

Figure 16-16. Disk Probe, a tool with which you should exercise extreme caution, can view and edit physical data on disks

5. Use the navigation buttons on the toolbar to move through the displayed sectors.

You can also search the physical disks for data by choosing Search Sectors from the Tools menu. You will be given an opportunity to set a range of sectors to search, as well as the data you want to locate.

WinDiff

WinDiff, which is actually called File and Directory Comparison in the File Tools folder of the Resource Kit, is a terrific tool for comparing files, either two files or all of the files in two different directories. Not only is WinDiff terrifically fast, but it can also graphically show you the exact differences between the compared files.

After starting WinDiff, open the File menu and choose either Compare Files or Compare Directories. Figure 16-17 shows the results of comparing a Windows NT 4 Workstation directory with a Windows NT 4 Server directory.

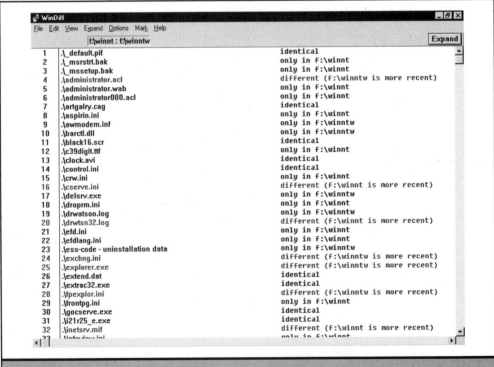

Figure 16-17.   The results of comparing Windows NT Server and Windows NT Workstation files

You can select any of the listed files and click the Expand button in the upper right corner of the WinDiff window to see a detailed comparison of the two files. WinDiff is intelligent about matching up data between the two files, so that extra data in one file doesn't throw the entire comparison off. In Figure 16-18 you can see the results of comparing two text files, one of which had some text added prior to the comparison.

WinDiff is an invaluable aid when you need to know how an application is modifying files in a directory structure (which can be helpful in troubleshooting a variety of problems). You can, for instance, copy all of the files in a directory to another directory, perform some action with an application against those files, and then use WinDiff to compare the before and after directories to see how the application changed the underlying data.

For instance, many applications write simple password data into one of their files in a readable—or at least easily decodable—format. The problem is that you don't know where the application stores its passwords. By using WinDiff and copies of the files before

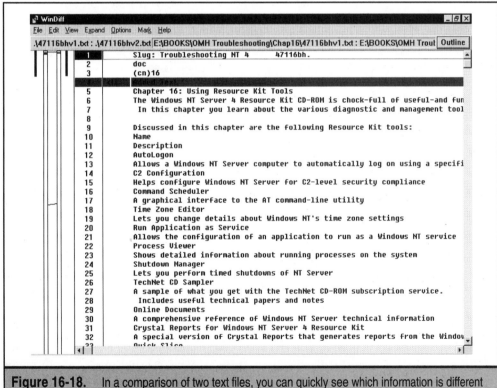

Figure 16-18. In a comparison of two text files, you can quickly see which information is different in the two files—in this case just the text "Added Text"

and after changing the application password, you can discover in what file and in what format the application's passwords are stored. If you have to unlock an application that some user has mistakenly locked up, and no other tools are available, using WinDiff along with a hex editor can sometimes let you perform tricks to get past an application's security.

For example, you may have an application in which a user set a password and then lost or forgot it, or left the company (talk about a familiar scenario!). Some application vendors won't help you unlock the data in such circumstances. Well, you can beat that! Install a fresh copy of the application onto another computer or into another directory, make a copy of its files, and then set a new password. By comparing the freshly installed set of files with the set that only had its password set, you can find out where the application stores its password, and if you're really fortunate the application will use plain text or some code that you can discover after a few trials. Note that this approach won't work if the application vendor uses any kind of sophisticated password encryption scheme. However, a simple encryption scheme is usually easy to figure out.

One network administrator, a friend who contributed some of his knowledge to this book, faced this problem with a well-known accounting application. The software company changed its security scheme from plain text passwords stored in the data file, but the new scheme simply added hex 30 to each byte of the password and then swapped the bytes around in a simple 2 by 2 scheme (byte 1 became byte 2 and vice versa, byte 3 became byte 4 and vice versa, and so forth). It took him a while to hack the system when a user locked up a file with a forgotten password. Now he uses WinDiff, and everything is straightened out quickly. On the other hand, he says, it's now so easy to cure the problem with WinDiff that he misses the feeling of accomplishment he used to get from spending hours and hours (and days and days) solving the problem. However, his system is no longer shut down as a result of these problems and the resulting time needed to do a manual hack.

Text Viewer

Text Viewer is a utility that lets you browse through directories and rapidly view the files in a text format. It's very useful for browsing HTML or text files when you need to become familiar with each file's contents. As shown in Figure 16-19, using Text Viewer is very intuitive: Simply use the folder window at the left to find the folder with the contents you want to browse, and then double-click on a file to display its contents in the view window to the right.

Netclip

This GUI program (Netclip.exe) lets you access the Clipboard of a connected computer. With it, you can drag and drop (or cut and paste) data between Windows NT 4 computers. You can take data you're working on and paste it onto the Clipboard of Bob down the

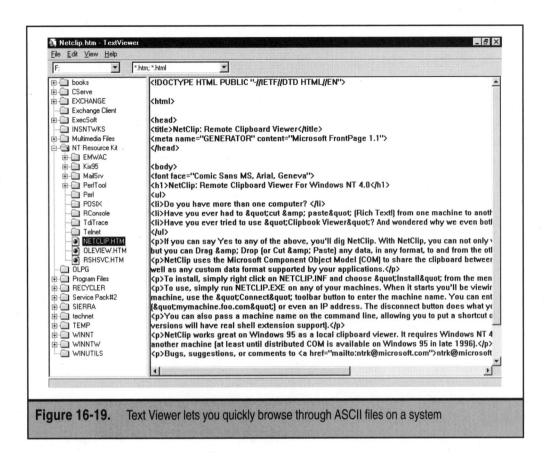

Figure 16-19. Text Viewer lets you quickly browse through ASCII files on a system

hall, so he can paste it into his document immediately. You can view the Clipboard on Sally's computer and take it for your own document. The data can be of any type. Netclip uses the Microsoft Component Object Model (COM) to work its magic. You can find Netclip.exe in the \i386\Netadmin folder on the Resource Kit CD-ROM.

Batch File Utilities

The Resource Kit includes quite a few DOS-based utility programs that are useful for building batch files. Along with the purely batch-oriented tools, you can also find versions of some Unix commands, such as cat or ls. Table 16-3 describes the batch file tools and Unix-style utilities available.

Utility Name	Function
Associate.exe	Registers or unregisters filename extension associations.
Autoexnt.exe	Wouldn't it be nice to have an Autoexec.bat file available for Windows NT? With this utility, you can build just such a tool, and the best part is that the batch file will run before anybody has logged on to the computer.
Choice.exe	Use this utility to prompt for and accept choices during batch file execution.
Clip.exe	With Clip.exe you can redirect the output of a command line program (using its StdOut display interface) to your Clipboard. For example, run **dir	clip** to place a copy of the directory listing onto the Windows Clipboard.
Forfiles.exe	In many situations you need to process a particular command against an entire set of files. With Forfiles you could, for instance, use the Type command on multiple files, even throughout entire subdirectories.
Logtime.exe	You use Logtime to log the current system time into a file called Logtime.log, along with any descriptive text you want to add. Using this utility you can, for instance, find out how long a complex series of backup operations takes, or how long any other series of batch file commands take to process.
Munge.exe	Munge will perform a quick search-and-replace operation on a set of files you define using wildcards. This is extremely useful when you need to perform such operations on large sets of text files, for instance.

Table 16-3.   Batch File and Unix-Style Utilities Included in the Resource Kit

Utility Name	Function
Now.exe	The Now command echoes the current system time. You can use it within batch files to log various times. For instance: now > events.txt DoSomethingElse now >> events.txt DoSomethingElseAgain now >> events.txt Notice the use of the single and double redirection characters to create and then append to the Events.txt file.
Setx.exe	Setx lets you quickly set environment variables for both the computer and user environment spaces. Settings made with Setx go beyond the current command session, unlike the Set command. However, they will apply only to future command sessions and not the current session.
Sleep.exe	Causes a sleep period in batch file execution.
Timeout.exe	Causes a pause in batch file execution, which a user can override by pressing a key.
Whoami.exe	Displays the current user account and domain to which you are logged on.
Ls.exe	The Unix command ls, which displays files in a variety of formats, somewhat similar to Dir.
Cat.exe	The Unix file concatenation utility cat is similar to the Type command with one key difference: wildcards are accepted.
Mv.exe	The Unix file move utility.
Cp.exe	The Unix file copy utility.
Vi.exe	The Unix vi file editing utility. (Great if you know how to work it; otherwise have some Maalox handy.)

Table 16-3. Batch File and Unix-Style Utilities Included in the Resource Kit (*continued*)

Scripting Languages (Perl and ReXX)

Even with the utilities described in the preceding section, batch files are woefully inadequate for more sophisticated scripting projects. There are, however, two excellent alternatives that offer you powerful choices in building scripts under Windows NT: Perl and ReXX.

Perl is based on the scripting language made popular under most versions of Unix, while ReXX was popularized by IBM and is available for a wide variety of platforms (in other words, not just for OS/2). You should explore Perl if you are experienced with Unix or are familiar with C programming (Perl behaves somewhat like C). ReXX, on the other hand, is easier to master if your programming background includes languages such as BASIC, SQL, and batch file programming.

For both language interpreters, launch your session by typing the name of the language followed by the script file name. For example, **rexx *somerexxscript*.rexx** will execute the named ReXX script.

Windows 95 Logon Script Processor

KiXtart 95, included in the Windows NT Server Resource Kit, is yet another, and different, scripting language. It's very useful for automating logon processing under Windows 95. Similar to ReXX or Perl in functionality, KiXtart allows you to build complex logon scripts, with such language features as:

- ▼ Conditional branching (IF-THEN-ELSE)
- ■ DO and WHILE loops
- ■ Subroutines and GOTO statements
- ■ Registry control functions
- ■ String processing functions
- ▲ String and integer variables

Read the file Kix32.doc, found in the \i386\filebat\kix95\win32 directory, for complete documentation.

Floppy Diskette Lock Utility

In some environments it's desirable to keep users from accessing a computer's diskette drives. Usually, security reasons drive such a policy. Using the Floplock service available in the Resource Kit, you can disallow access to the diskette drives on the system unless the logged-on user is a member of the Administrators or Power Users groups on the system.

To enable this service, use the command **instsrv floppylocker c:***reskit***\\floplock.exe**, replacing *reskit* with the directory into which you installed the Resource Kit (or where the Floplock.exe program file is stored).

Schedule Commands to Run "Soon"

The AT command (with or without the WinAT graphical interface) is a great tool for scheduling commands, but it's lousy if you want to set up commands to repeat at regular, frequent intervals. For instance, to build a set of AT commands that would run every 15 minutes is all but impossible. Instead, you can use the Soon.exe utility to set up such chores.

The Soon.exe utility is somewhat similar to the AT command in syntax (in fact, it utilizes the same Windows NT service as the AT command), but it lets you set an amount of time relative to the current time in which to run a particular command. You can use this to your advantage to schedule regular command operations. For example, consider the following batch file, named Regular.cmd:

```
soon 900 regular.cmd
SomeProgramInstructionHere.exe
```

In this example, you run the Regular command file the first time manually. It immediately schedules itself to run again in 900 seconds (15 minutes) and then performs the action you want performed. When the 15 minutes has elapsed, Regular.cmd runs again automatically, with no user intervention required.

Super-Accurate Server Timekeeping

Recently an event occurred that really brought home the impact that accurate server time can have on an organization. The main server in a company had mysteriously had its clock set back about 5 minutes. All of the users, of course, had their local computer's time set by the server when they logged in. It turned out in this particular company that lots of people used their Windows 95 display time in the lower right corner (as well as Schedule+ reminders) to know when they needed to be at appointments within the company. So for a day (until someone realized what was going on), about half the company was five minutes late for meetings, appointments, and the like. (Good thing the system time wasn't further off!)

You can avoid such occurrences by using the Timeserv utility included in the Resource Kit, which automatically synchronizes Windows NT Server's time with an external source, such as the National Institute of Standards and Technology's atomic clock located in Colorado, and you can perform these synchronizations over your normal Internet connection, or over a dial-up RAS connection.

To install Timeserv, first edit the Timeserv.ini file located in the Resource Kit directory. Within the file you will find the instructions for editing it. Then issue the following command, which installs and activates the service that performs the time synchronizations: **timeserv -automatic**.

Automating Windows NT Workstation Rollouts

There are ways to automate the installation of Windows NT Workstation, but there aren't any easy ways to also automate the installation of various application programs that you always install on each workstation.

However, you can use the Sysdiff utility in the Resource Kit to automate the installation of additional software when rolling out Windows NT Workstation. Conceptually, Sysdiff works like this:

1. You complete the installation of Windows NT Workstation.
2. You run **sysdiff /snap** to take a "snapshot" of the current configuration of the client computer.
3. You install the necessary additional applications onto the machine.
4. You run **sysdiff /diff** to create a *difference file*.

After following these steps, you use the command **sysdiff /apply** *difference_filename* to apply the changes to the new machine automatically, without having to run all of the individual application installations again.

Before attempting this, you should read the complete documentation available on Sysdiff in the Resource Kit help files.

Killing Pesky Processes

If you're used to Unix, you probably miss the Unix kill utility at times. While you can perform process killing with the Windows NT Task Manager, many times you'll want to kill a process at the command line.

Use the Pstat command (also in the Resource Kit) to discover the Process ID number of the process you want to kill, and then issue the command **kill** *pidnumber* to terminate the selected process.

Quick Performance Statistics

When working at a command line, particularly when developing command line software, it's often useful to get quick performance statistics on how the system is behaving and how your program is affecting it. To do so, run the command Perfmtr, which provides a text-based periodic display of the main performance counters in the system. Figure 16-20 shows an example of the Perfmtr command in action.

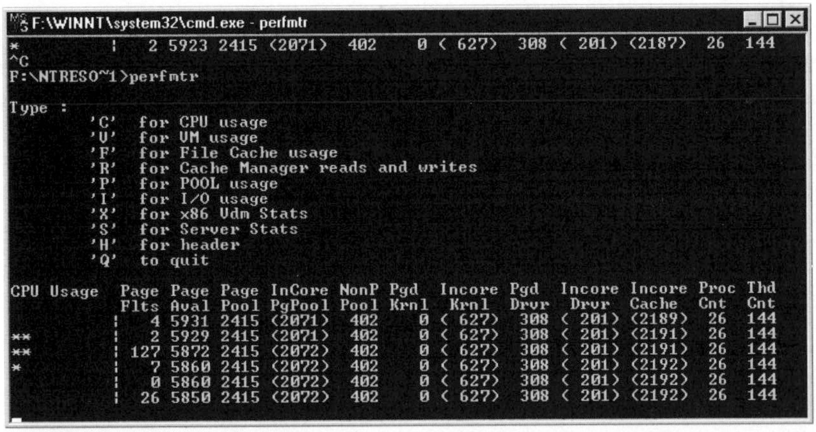

Figure 16-20. As you can see, when you run Perfmtr you can press any of the indicated keys to see different performance information

Another quick-and-dirty performance viewing utility in the Resource Kit is called Pmon, which updates only when it receives a keypress. Pmon is a useful way to see how different processes running on the system are consuming CPU time and memory space, as well as systemwide resource usages. Figure 16-21 shows an example of Pmon.

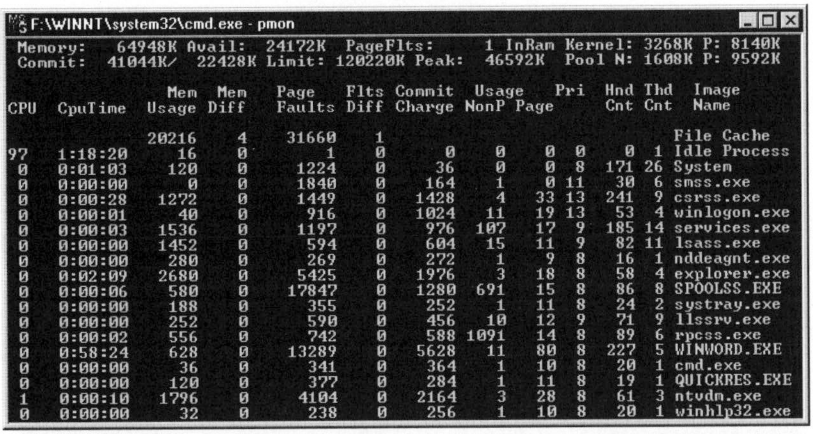

Figure 16-21. Use Pmon when you want quick process-specific performance data

Quick and Easy Benchmarking

Many times you need to construct "do-it-yourself" benchmark tests on the system, particularly when working with command line utilities. A utility in the Resource Kit called Timethis is perfect for such jobs.

To use Timethis, simply issue a command such as the following: **timethis** *somecmdfile_or_program*.

At the end of the program or command file's execution, Timethis will display summary information showing how long the operation took to complete.

Fast Screen Display Property Changes

Every now and again we encounter a program that runs best in one particular screen geometry, which usually isn't the one in which we normally run our systems. It can be a real pain in the neck to have to use the Display Property settings constantly to switch video display modes (especially with Windows NT's mandatory 15-second display of a test pattern). If this happens to you, use a Resource Kit utility called QuickRes, which lets you quickly and easily change your display settings on the fly.

Running QuickRes places an icon on your taskbar, near the usual clock display. Clicking on this icon displays a pop-up menu listing all of the possible video modes on your system. Select one from the menu, and your video mode changes instantly. Figure 16-22 shows an example of the QuickRes menu.

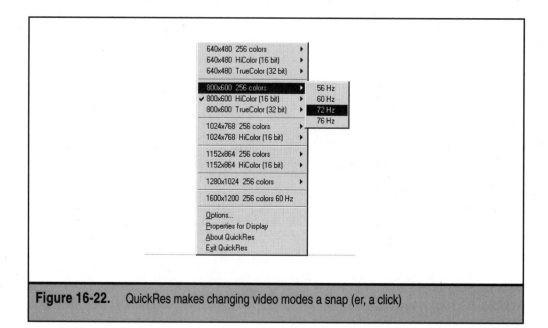

Figure 16-22.   QuickRes makes changing video modes a snap (er, a click)

View Disk Details

Another handy command line utility is one called Showdisk, which displays detailed disk status and configuration data for each physical disk in your system. Simply run Showdisk at a command prompt, and you see the display shown in Figure 16-23.

Show Directory Space Usage

Without a third-party utility, it's difficult to discover how space on a server is being used. Sure, you can open the Properties dialog box for each folder you want to see and then wait for the total space displayed on a folder's Property dialog box to be fully updated, but that's extremely time-consuming and also doesn't generate any kind of useful report.

Instead, use a utility called Diruse, which can report on directory space usage for all subdirectories in any particular directory hierarchy. You can, for instance, point Diruse to the root of your user's home directories, and it will display how much space is being consumed in each directory. Subdirectory contents are counted toward the total but are not displayed individually. So if you have a main folder called HomeDirs in which each user has a HomeDir (named after their user name), the Diruse command will show you how much space each user is taking up in their entire home directory and its subdirectories.

A number of options are available with Diruse. Type **diruse /?** for a complete listing of the options.

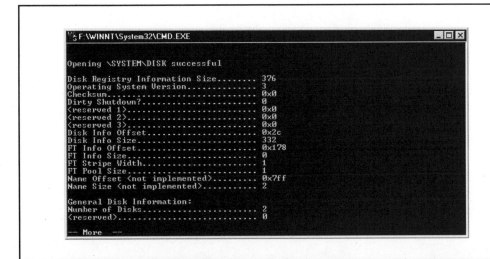

Figure 16-23.   Showdisk displays disk configuration data, including the state of any fault-tolerant partitions

Find time to explore the Resource Kit and grab the utilities that will make your life easier. While a number of Resource Kit utilities have been discussed in this chapter, there are many others that you may also find useful from time to time.

And if you don't have the Resource Kit, order it immediately. There's no excuse for an administrator or other Windows NT professional not to have all the tools available in the kit. They're invaluable!

CHAPTER 17

PowerToys—Tools You'll Love

If you're the kind of power user that's always trying to squeeze a little more performance out of your operating system, you're not alone. As a matter of fact, some of the programmers on Microsoft's Windows Shell Development Team felt the same way, and did something about it. They created the Windows 95 PowerToys, which includes a number of handy tools for optimizing both Windows 95 and Windows NT. Some tools work only with Windows 95, and others with both Windows 95 and Windows NT. Those that work with both operating systems are the ones we'll cover here.

You should be aware that although the PowerToys were developed by Microsoft programmers, they are not "official" Microsoft products. Therefore, they are not supported by Microsoft, which means you can't call for support.

Where I've managed to figure out the relationship between the PowerToy and a registry entry that's changed as a result of implementing the toy, I've indicated it.

DOWNLOADING AND INSTALLING THE POWERTOYS

The first thing you need to do is get PowerToys. Since they are readily available on the Microsoft Web site, www.microsoft.com/windows95/info/powertoys.htm, obtaining them is a simple matter of connecting, downloading, and saving the file(s) to your hard disk. You can either download the entire PowerToys set or download specific applications separately.

The following PowerToys applications are Windows NT 4 compatible:

▼ **Desktop Menu** Places an icon on your taskbar that provides access to the contents of your desktop via a menu.

■ **Explore From Here** Adds a shortcut menu item that enables you to open a new Explorer window from any folder (the current folder is the root).

■ **Find X** Customizes the commands available on the Find menu.

■ **Send To X** Adds new commands to the Send menu.

■ **Shortcut Target Menu** Allows you to right-click a shortcut and see the properties for the target instead of the shortcut.

■ **Tweak UI** Includes tons of options to customize your user interface.

▲ **Command Prompt Here** Adds a shortcut menu item to open a DOS prompt from any folder.

Begin by creating a new folder on your hard drive. Then download the desired files to the new folder. If you download the Powertoy.exe file, double-click it to extract all of the PowerToys files. If you download the tools separately, you'll have to double-click each compressed file to expand it. In either case, you'll note that each tool has an .inf file. To install a PowerToy, right-click the associated .inf file, and choose Install from the shortcut menu.

USING TWEAK UI TO CUSTOMIZE THE INTERFACE

Of all the PowerToys, Tweak UI is by far the most comprehensive and the most fun. There are so many great things you can do with it. However, since it actually changes your registry settings, you must have administrative rights to use it.

The Tweak UI installation creates an applet in the Control Panel, which you use to access all of the Tweak UI features (Figure 17-1).

Mouse Settings

The first tab in the dialog box contains options to change your mouse settings. Unless you have a special mouse driver installed, the mouse applet you find in the Control Panel does not offer you the variety of options found in the Tweak UI tab. Also keep in mind that these settings are user settings and will affect only the currently logged-on user.

Menu Speed

The Menu Speed option controls the speed with which cascading menus open as you move your mouse over them. To have them open quickly, increase the speed by moving the slider to the left; move the slider to the right to slow them down. To test the results of any changes you make, place your mouse pointer over the test icon and right-click. A test shortcut menu with submenus opens. Move your mouse over the submenu items to see the speed with which they now open.

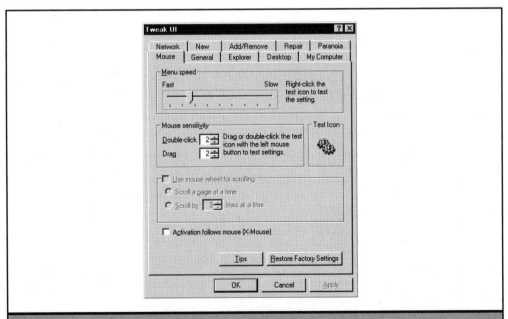

Figure 17-1. The Tweak UI dialog box needs ten tabs to handle all the available options

Your changes are written to the registry in HKEY_CURRENT_USER\Control Panel\Desktop. The new entry is named MenuShowDelay. In my registry, the original setting was 400 and my current setting is 10 (I hate to wait for submenus).

Double-Click Sensitivity

You can adjust the sensitivity for double-clicking, changing the maximum delay between the first and second click. The delay you specify indicates how long you can pause between mouse clicks and still have them interpreted by the system as a double-click rather than as two separate clicks. The lower the setting, the more tolerant the system will be about waiting for your second click. The higher the setting, the more nimble you'll have to be to have the system interpret your clicks as a double-click. Again, you can use the test icon to see the results your changes to the settings have upon your mouse.

The changes take effect immediately and are written to the registry in HKEY_CURRENT_USER\Control Panel\Mouse in the data items named DoubleClickHeight and DoubleClickWidth.

Drag Sensitivity

If you find yourself inadvertently dragging objects when you really mean to click on them, you'll probably want to adjust the drag sensitivity. This setting determines how far you must move the mouse while holding the button down before the system decides you are attempting to drag an object. The higher the setting, the farther you must move the mouse with the button down to drag. If you find that when you are working in Explorer, subfolders are mysteriously disappearing from their original locations and appearing in their parent folders, you probably should adjust the drag sensitivity. Use the test icon to check the changes you make to this setting.

Registry changes are written to HKEY_CURRENT_USER\Control Panel\Desktop in the data items named DragHeight and DragWidth.

Use Mouse Wheel for Scrolling

This option is available only if you have a mouse wheel. Enabling this option allows you to use the mouse wheel to scroll data. By using the suboptions, you can set it to scroll a page at a time or a specified number of lines at a time.

Registry changes are sent to HKEY_CURRENT_USER\Control Panel\Desktop in the data item WheelScrollLines.

Activation Follows Mouse

This X-Mouse feature works within the operating system to cause the window over which your mouse moves to become the active window. With this setting turned on, you no longer have to click on a window to make it the active window. Simply move your mouse over it. This is extremely handy if you have multiple windows open and are moving data from one window to the next. Unfortunately, it does not work within applications, only in the operating system. Therefore, it doesn't work on multiple documents open in your word processor.

Registry changes are effective immediately, in HKEY_CURRENT_USER\Control Panel\Mouse in the ActiveWindowTracking item, which is a DWORD value type (0 is off, 1 is on).

General Settings

The General settings tab is divided into three sections: Effects, Special Folders, and Internet Explorer (Figure 17-2). Like the Mouse settings, the General settings affect only the user currently logged on.

Effects

The first of the Effects settings is for Window Animation. Selecting this option enables the animation effect that takes place when you change a window size (minimizing, maximizing, and restoring). When this option is turned off and you use any of the resizing functions, the changes appear instantaneously, without "trails" of movement.

The registry change adds the data item MinAnimate to HKEY_CURRENT_USER\ Desktop\WindowMetrics. Deselecting the option sets the value to 0; reselecting it sets the value to 1.

The next Effect setting is Smooth Scrolling, which controls the animated scrolling in Explorer and other tree-based windows such as Regedit. Although the option is called Smooth Scrolling, it has nothing to do with the scroll bar movement. Instead, it controls

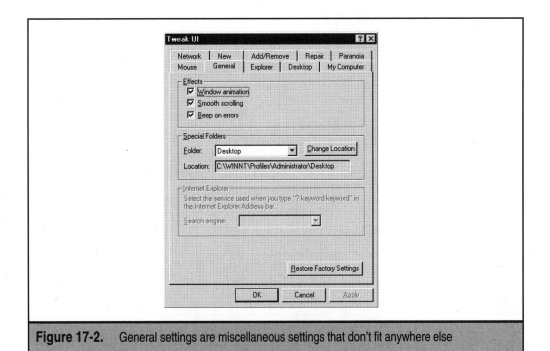

Figure 17-2. General settings are miscellaneous settings that don't fit anywhere else

the way subfolders appear and disappear when you expand and contract them. With Smooth Scrolling enabled, they slide in and out. With the option disabled, the subfolders appear and disappear instantly, without any sliding effect at all.

The registry change adds the data item SmoothScroll to HKEY_CURRENT_USER\ Control Panel\Desktop. It's a binary value type, so if Smooth Scrolling is deselected the value is 00 00 00 00. If you reselect it, the value is 01 00 00 00.

The last Effect setting is Beep on Errors. To be notified by a sound (a beep, by default) each time an error occurs, enable this option. To turn off the error sound alert, disable the option. If you choose to enable it, you can customize the sound that is played by opening the Sounds applet in the Control Panel and selecting a new sound.

The registry change is written to HKEY_CURRENT_USER\Control Panel\Sound, with a data item of Beep that has a value of "yes" or "no," depending on your selection.

Special Folders

During the Windows NT installation, a number of special folders are created, including the Desktop folder, the My Documents folder, and others. The Special Folders option allows you to change the location of these folders. Why you might want to do this is beyond me, but if you do, here's your opportunity. Select a special folder from the Folder drop-down list (Figure 17-3). Then click the Change Location button to open the Browse for Folder dialog box, and select a new location for the special folder. Click OK to move the folder to its new location. The Location text box indicates the current location of the special folder selected.

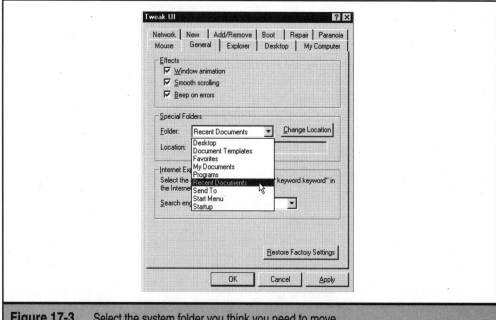

Figure 17-3.   Select the system folder you think you need to move

The changes are written to the registry in HKEY_CURRENT_USER\Software\ Microsoft\Windows\CurrentVersion\Explorer\Shell Folders, changing the existing information for the folder.

Internet Explorer

If you have Internet Explorer 3.0 or higher installed, this option is available; otherwise it is disabled and grayed out. You can use this option to choose the default search engine that launches when you type a question mark followed by a search word in the browser address bar. From the Search Engine drop-down list, select your preferred search engine (Figure 17-4). If you wish to use one that's not listed, choose Custom and type the URL for your favorite search engine in the dialog box that appears.

This change is written to the registry in HKEY_CURRENT_USER\Software\ Microsoft\Internet Explorer\Main in the data value named Search Page.

TIP: Even if you don't use this option, isn't it nifty to learn that you can enter **? word** in Internet Explorer's URL box to launch a search (that's faster than going through the steps to open a search program and enter your search word). My copy of Netscape Navigator (3.01) doesn't have this feature.

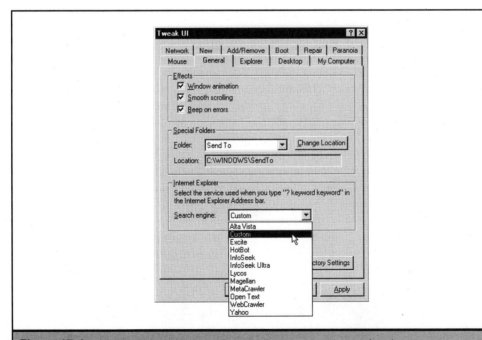

Figure 17-4.   Choose a search engine from the list, or enter your own favorite

Explorer Settings

The Explorer tab refers to the general Windows user interface, not the Windows Explorer application (the interface for Windows NT 4 and Windows 95 is actually officially named Explorer). The Explorer tab contains three sets of options, Shortcut Overlay, Startup, and Settings (Figure 17-5).

Shortcut Overlay

Every time you create a shortcut, the new icon that appears on your desktop contains a small arrow indicating that this is a shortcut icon rather than an original application icon. You can use this option to change the type of arrow that appears, eliminate the arrow altogether, or create your own custom overlay to designate a shortcut icon. Selecting Custom brings up the Change Icon dialog box seen in Figure 17-6, where you should be able to find an icon you like better than the arrow. Be sure you select something small, so you don't cover over the shortcut icon. After you make your selection, check the After icon on the Explorer tab to see what your shortcuts will look like.

The registry changes appear in HKEY_LOCAL_MACHINE\Software\Microsoft\ CurrentVersion\Explorer, where a new subkey named ShellIcons is added. The value data is the path to TWEAKUI.CPL,X where X is the icon for the arrow (which may no longer be an arrow, of course). Note that since the changes are recorded in HKEY_LOCAL_MACHINE, rather than HKEY_CURRENT_USER, this option is systemwide and affects all users.

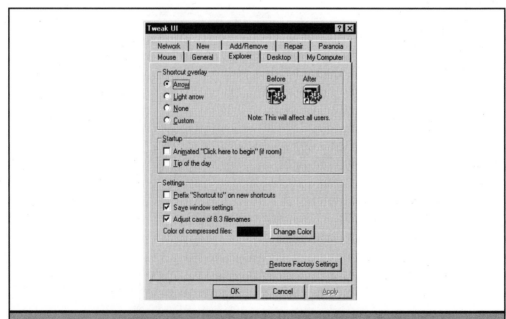

Figure 17-5.   Some of these options should have been built into the operating system configuration options

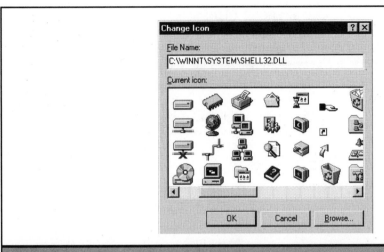

Figure 17-6. Choose an icon to replace the arrow on shortcuts

Startup

If the animated "Click here to begin" message drives you nuts when you log on, eliminate it by deselecting the first option, Animated "Click Here to Begin" (If Room).

If you would like Windows to present you with a tip every time you log in, select the Tip of the Day option. Turning tips on and off creates a data item named DisplayInitialTipWindow (the values are 0 for off and 1 for on) in the subkey HKEY_CURRENT_USER\Software\Microsoft\Windows\CurrentVersion\Explorer\Tips.

TIP: The tips themselves are in HKEY_LOCAL_MACHINE\Software\Microsoft\Windows\ CurrentVersion\Explorer\Tips, and you can remove or change existing tips, or write your own.

Settings

At last you can get rid of the "Shortcut to" prefix automatically added to the title of every shortcut you create. Since the little arrow already designates a shortcut, the prefix is overkill as far as I'm concerned, and it's a pain to edit every title to remove the prefix. Now all you have to do is deselect Prefix "Shortcut to" on New Shortcuts to keep the prefix from appearing on all shortcuts created from that point forward. Unfortunately, it doesn't remove the prefix from existing shortcut titles, so you'll still have to do those manually.

You also might want to use the Save Window Settings option, which stores the setting for each folder so that the next time you log on the previous settings are retained. In addition, any folders that were open when you shut down will open when you log on again.

Registry changes are saved in HKEY_CURRENT_USER\Software\Microsoft\ Windows\CurrentVersion\Policies\Explorer in a data entry named NoSaveSettings. Since the data item is a negative, changing the option creates a binary data value of 00 00 00 00. The default option (don't save settings) is 01 00 00 00.

Adjust Case of 8.3 Filenames

Filenames that appear in Windows NT 4 in uppercase are changed to mixed case when you select this option and view the files in Explorer or My Computer.

Color of Compressed Files

Selecting this option causes Explorer to display compressed files and folders in a different color (the default is blue), which you can choose by clicking Change Color.

The Desktop Tab

The Desktop tab (Figure 17-7) allows you to play around with the system desktop icons. I can't think of any reason for using the options on this tab; I certainly wouldn't use them. If you do decide to manipulate the desktop icons, be sure to read the warnings in the Tweak UI help file.

▼ Select or deselect the check box to determine whether the icon remains on the desktop.

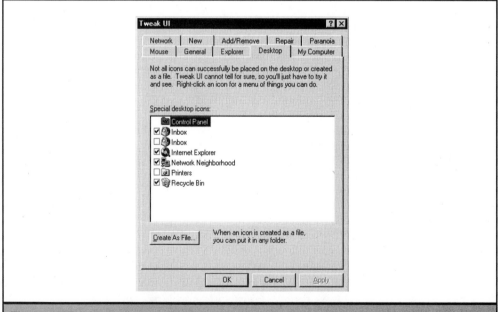

Figure 17-7.   There's no check box for the Control Panel, so you can't make it a desktop icon

■ Rename an icon by right-clicking on it and choosing Rename from the shortcut menu.

▲ Select the icon and choose Create As File to create the icon as a file that can be placed in any folder in your system (you'll be asked to name the file).

The My Computer Tab

Use this tab to hide any drive you'd like to hide from My Computer. While the entire alphabet is displayed on this tab (Figure 17-8), it's unlikely you'd need to use all of them (unless a user went on a mapping frenzy and mapped every single folder on every single computer on the network). Removing a drive letter means that any drive mapped to that letter won't be seen in My Computer, and the user won't be able to access that mapped share.

Registry changes are saved in HKEY_CURRENT_USER\Software\Microsoft\Windows\CurrentVersion\Policies\Explorer. A new data item named NoDrives is placed in the data pane.

The Network Tab

The Network tab contains one option: Log On Automatically at System Startup (see Figure 17-9). While this is certainly a handy feature, it also has a serious downside. If you automate your logon, anyone can log on to the network as you. It's probably best to use this feature only for print servers and other computers that have a special use, so you don't have to stand around and wait through the logon process to get them up and running.

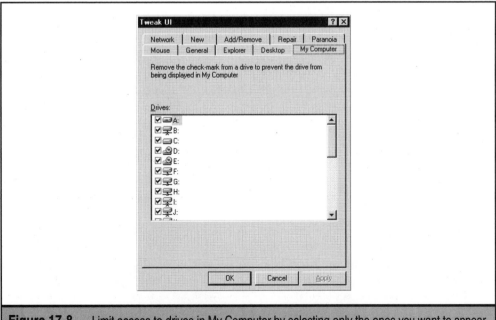

Figure 17-8.   Limit access to drives in My Computer by selecting only the ones you want to appear

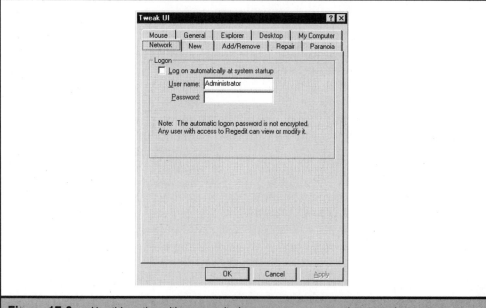

Figure 17-9.   Use this option with care, as it gives anyone access to the network as you

Registry changes are recorded in HKEY_LOCAL_MACHINE\SOFTWARE\ Microsoft\WindowsNT\CurrentVersion\WinLogon. Automatic logon is stored in the data item AutoAdminLogon, which has a value of 1 if enabled and 0 if not. Your password is stored in the data item DefaultPassword, and the data value is the password itself, in plain English that anyone can read.

The New Tab

The New tab controls the document types that appear on the New shortcut menu that appears when you right-click on the desktop and select New (see Figure 17-10). The same menu appears when you choose File, New in the Windows Explorer.

To remove a document type from the New menu, deselect it in the New settings window. To add a new document type to the New menu, drag a file of the desired type from Windows Explorer across the scroll bar of the Tweak UI tab.

Registry settings are changed in HKEY_CLASSES_ROOT*file_extension_subkey*\ ShellNew.

The Add/Remove Tab

Finally! An easy way to get rid of application listings in the Add/Remove Programs applet in Control Panel. If you uninstall an application without using the Add/Remove Program applet, you end up with an orphan listing no longer associated with an application. Tweak UI cleans up the list. Go to the Add/Remove tab (Figure 17-11) to get started.

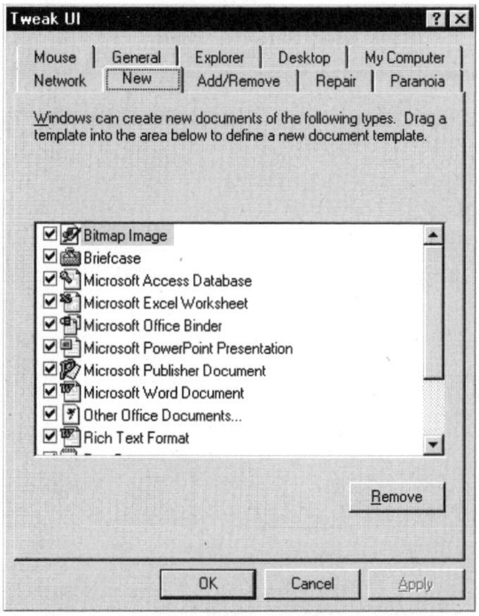

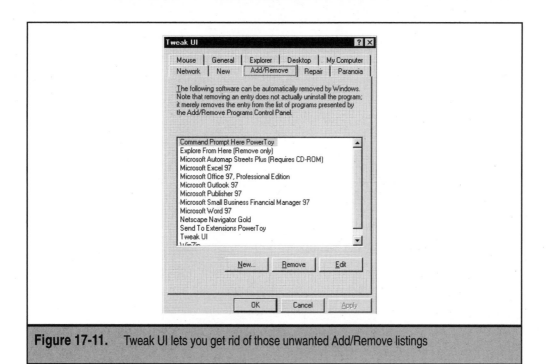

Figure 17-10. Customize the New document shortcut menu by dragging and dropping files onto the Tweak UI tab

Figure 17-11. Tweak UI lets you get rid of those unwanted Add/Remove listings

To remove an entry from this tab, highlight the listing and click Remove. Tweak UI asks you to confirm; choose OK to continue or Cancel to reconsider. Keep in mind that removing the entry does not affect the program itself, only the listing in the Add/Remove dialog box.

If you have software installed that has an uninstall routine, but it does not appear in the Add/Remove dialog box, you can add it yourself, by clicking New and entering a description and the command (including the path) to run the uninstall.

If you move an application's uninstall program, you can indicate the new path by selecting the listing and clicking Edit. Make the necessary changes to the path in the Command line.

Changes to the registry are written to HKEY_LOCAL_MACHINE\Software\ Microsoft\Windows\CurrentVersion\Uninstall, where each application that has registered an uninstall program has its own subkey.

The Repair Settings Tab

Housekeeping is one of those jobs that you always swear you're going to do, but never quite manage to get to. With the Tweak UI Repair tab (Figure 17-12), the job of cleaning up Windows NT becomes a little bit easier.

The first button on the Repair tab is the Rebuild Icons button. When you change icons or delete applications, your system frequently ends up with unused or incorrect icons. Rather than slog through them individually, you can let Tweak UI straighten them out.

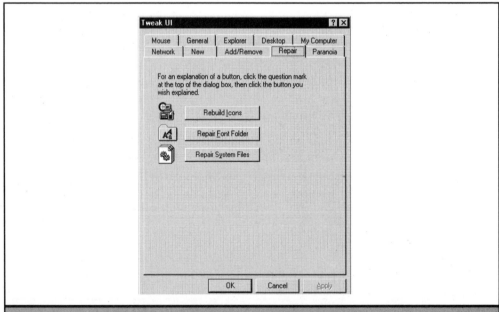

Figure 17-12. You can clean up your NT 4 system without even breaking a sweat

Just click the Rebuild Icons button, let Tweak UI do all the work, and reboot when it finishes.

Repair Font Folder restores the Font folder to proper working condition (for some reason, the extra functions available on the Font folder disappear occasionally).

When you install new applications, system files often get replaced. Sometimes they are overwritten incorrectly, which can result in system errors. Repair System Files restores the file by comparing the existing system file to an original stored in the hidden SysBckup folder. Of course, for this to work, the SysBckup folder must still be on your system with the copies of the original system files still intact.

The Paranoia Tab

One of the nice things about Windows NT is that it makes your life a little easier by keeping track of things you do. So the next time you want repeat an action or return to a document, you don't have to start from scratch. Unfortunately, it not only tracks your activity for you, but also for anyone else who has access to your machine. Who wants anyone peering over their shoulder? Go to the Paranoia tab (Figure 17-13) to set your options, and no one will know where you've been.

The Covering Your Tracks section of the Paranoia tab allows you to clear many of the history logs that Windows maintains, just by logging on. Simply place a check mark next to the appropriate option.

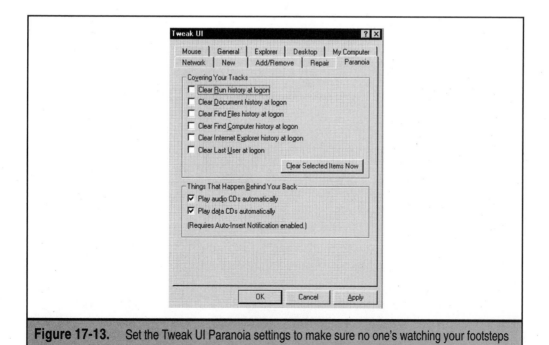

Figure 17-13.   Set the Tweak UI Paranoia settings to make sure no one's watching your footsteps

The Things That Happen Behind Your Back options allow you to enable and disable the automatic playing of both music and data CDs without going into the Device Manager and turning Auto-Insert on and off. In order for it to work, however, Auto-Insert must be turned on.

The registry entry for the CD is located in HKEY_LOCAL_MACHINE\System\ CurrentControlSet\Services\Cdrom, with a data item named Autorun and a DWORD value of 1 for on and 0 for off.

PLAYING WITH THE OTHER POWERTOYS

Tweak UI may be the most comprehensive of the PowerToys, but there are also some great little utilities that may do only one job but do it so well you'll be delighted.

DeskMenu

Place your desktop at your fingertips with this simple yet powerful utility. After you install and run DeskMenu, it puts a desktop icon on your taskbar tray that gives you instant access to your entire desktop on a shortcut menu (Figure 17-14). You can even minimize all windows and undo the minimize from the menu.

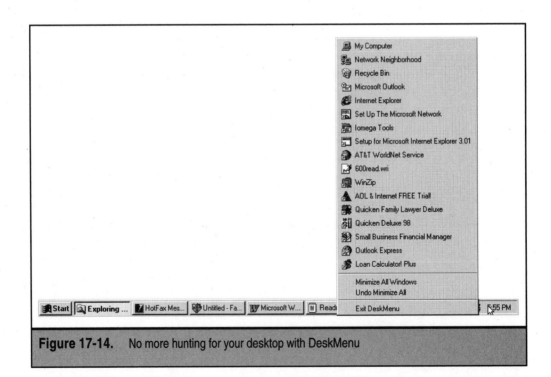

Figure 17-14.   No more hunting for your desktop with DeskMenu

To run Deskmenu, double-click Deskmenu.exe. To access the desktop shortcut menu, right-click the new desktop icon that appears on the taskbar near the clock.

Explore From Here

This PowerToy will be a welcome addition to your tool chest. It allows you to select any folder in Explorer and then open a new Explorer window, using the selected folder as the root for the new Explorer view. This makes it so easy to move files between folders! It's especially handy if you spend a lot of time in Explorer scrolling through your own drive and also scrolling through another drive that's all the way down under Network Neighborhood. Now, instead of traveling all that distance on the scroll bar, you have two windows near each other.

To install Explore From Here, right-click Explore.inf and select Install. To use the utility, right-click a folder and select Explore From Here. A new Explorer window opens with the selected folder at the top of the left pane.

Find Extensions

Not enough find options in your Find command? No problem. Just install the Find Extensions and you'll have a lot more choices the next time you access Find from your Start menu. Right-click Findx.inf and choose Install from the shortcut menu. To utilize the new Find features, select Find from the Start menu and choose one of the new options (Figure 17-15).

The new Find options include:

▼ **Find On the Internet** With Internet Explorer 3.0 or higher, you can search the Internet for key words.

■ **Find In the Knowledge Base** Use this option to search Microsoft's online database of troubleshooting tips.

■ **Find Address** If you've installed Exchange, you can search your Personal Address Book.

▲ **Find E-mail Message** For Exchange only, find e-mail based on your search criteria.

Command Prompt Here (DosHere)

If you're an old timer (in computer years!) like me, you'll love this utility. I still drop to the command line to perform many tasks. When it comes to renaming or deleting groups of files with common criteria, DOS beats Windows hands down every time. The Command Prompt Here utility gives you quick access to a DOS prompt at the directory you selected. No more of that **cd** stuff at the command line (and no more typing those ~ characters).

To install this nifty utility, right-click Doshere.inf and select Install from the shortcut menu. To use it, right-click on a folder and choose Command Prompt Here.

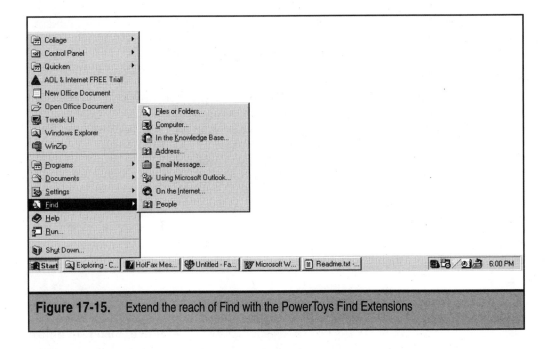

Figure 17-15. Extend the reach of Find with the PowerToys Find Extensions

Send To Extensions

Send To makes the handy Send To option on the Windows Explorer shortcut menu even handier by adding more options. To install Send To, right-click Sendtox.inf and select Install. When the installation is complete, right-click a file or folder in the Windows Explorer to see the new, enhanced Send To menu (Figure 17-16).

Among other things, Send To adds an item called Any Folder, which allows you to send files and folders to any folder on your system or network without having to cut, paste, or drag. Choose the file(s) or folder(s) you want to send, right-click, and choose Send To, Any Folder. A dialog box appears, and all you have to do is indicate whether to copy or move the selected items, enter the target path, and click OK. Note the following:

▼ You need to specify the complete path to which the selected file is to be copied or moved.

■ If the path doesn't exist, it's created.

▲ If you enter a folder name without a path, the folder is created under the current folder.

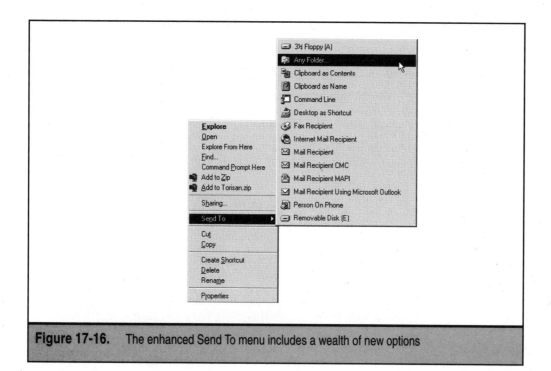

Figure 17-16.   The enhanced Send To menu includes a wealth of new options

REMOVING POWERTOYS

All of the PowerToys can be uninstalled from the Add/Remove Programs applet. In fact, since they're so easy to uninstall, you really ought to install any of the PowerToys that seem the least bit interesting. You'll probably come to depend on several of them, and you can just dump the others.

WINDOWS
NT
Professional
Library

PART VII

Appendixes

APPENDIX A

Command Reference

Even with a powerful GUI operating system, going to the command line is frequently useful and occasionally required. Whether you need to write batch files, manipulate groups of files, or perform some administrative task, there are going to be times when it's just faster and easier to be at a command prompt.

This appendix is not a complete list of every command available in Windows NT 4, but I did try to cover the commands most administrators and users seem to use.

CONVENTIONS

The following conventions are used to indicate command syntax:

▼ Italic is used for variables such as filenames.

■ Square brackets [ ] surround optional items that can be used with a command.

■ Curly brackets { } surround lists of items.

■ A pipe | separates items in a list when one item can be included with the command.

■ An ellipsis in square brackets [...] means you can repeat the previous item, separating items with spaces.

▲ An ellipsis preceded by a comma in square brackets [,...] means you can repeat the previous item, separating items with commas or semicolons, not spaces.

Command Symbols

The command prompt allows you to issue multiple commands on a single line with the use of some special symbols. There are also some symbols that permit you to create command lines that act conditionally based on the results of a previous command. Table A-1 covers those symbols.

To group multiple commands, simply separate them with a single ampersand. For example, **dir & type \autoexec.bat** will execute both commands, one after the other.

You can also use double ampersands (&&) and double pipe symbols (| |) to process multiple commands conditionally on a single line—for example, **type c:\badfilename && dir**. Since the file c:\badfilename does not exist, the Dir command will not execute.

However, if you enter **type c:\badfilename | | dir**, even though badfilename doesn't exist, the Dir command still executes.

WINDOWS NT COMMANDS

The commands included here are presented alphabetically. Each command has a description, the syntax (some commands have multiple syntaxes available), the command options, and any notes I thought were important.

Symbol	Effect
>	Redirects the output from one command into another command, into a file, or into a device
>>	Appends the output from one command to another command, to a file, or to a device
<	Redirects data from a file into a command
&	Separates multiple commands on a single line
( )	Groups commands together
; and ,	Separate parameters from one another
^	Lets you use a special command symbol literally
&&	Causes the following command to execute only if the preceding command is successful
| |	Causes the following command to execute only if the preceding command is not successful

Table A-1. Special Symbols Available on the Command Line

append

Opens files stored in other directories as if they were in the current directory.

Syntax:

append [;] [[*drive*:]*path*[;...]] [/x:{on \| off}][/path:{on \| off}] [/e]

Options:

;	Cancels the appended directories.
[*drive*:]*path*	Specifies the drive and directory that you want to append to the current directory. Use semicolons to separate multiple directories.
/x:{on | off}	Controls whether the DOS subsystem searches appended directories for executable programs called by the program you're running. /x:on means that appended directories are searched for executable files, /x:off means appended directories are not searched for executables. Use /x:on the first time you use the Append command after system startup.

/path:{on | off}   Specifies whether a program searches appended directories for a data file if the path is included with the filename. The default is /path:on.

/e   Creates an environment variable named Append, which contains the list of all appended directories. This switch must be used the first time you use Append after system startup. The variable can be viewed when you use the Set command.

assoc

Displays or modifies associations for file extensions.

Syntax:

assoc [.*ext*[=[*filetype*]]]

Options:

.*ext*   Specifies the file extension to associate with a specified file type.

filetype   Specifies the file type to associate with the file extension.

Entering **assoc** with no options will display the current extension assignments. Enter **assoc .*ext*** (substitute an extension) to see the associations for that extension. You can delete associations by entering **assoc .*ext=*.**

at

Schedules commands or applications to run at a given time. (I love this command; it's so useful.)

Syntax:

at [*computername*] [[*id*] [delete [/yes]]]

at [*computername*] *time* [/interactive] [/every:*date*[,...] | /next:*date*[,...]] "*command*"

Options:

computername   Lets you specify a remote computer (the default is the local computer).

id   Every scheduled command has an identification number assigned. You can use the ID number to delete scheduled commands.

/delete	When used with an ID parameter, deletes the scheduled command. When used without an ID, deletes all scheduled events.
/yes	Forces a Yes answer to queries from the system when deleting events.
time	Specifies the time when the command should run (use *hh:mm* in 24-hour notation).
/interactive	Lets the job run interactively.
/every:*date*[,...]	Runs the command on specific day(s). Use the abbreviations M, T, W, Th, F, S, and Su. Specify particular days of the month using the numbers 1 through 31. You can enter multiple dates by separating them with commas. If the date is omitted, the current day of the month is used.
/next:*date*[,...]	Causes the command to run on the next occurrence of the specified day or date.
"*command*"	Specifies the program or batch file that you want run at the scheduled time. Use the absolute path, including the drive letter (or use the UNC for remote computers).

Notes:

▼ No options displays all currently scheduled commands.

■ The Schedule service must be running in order for At to function (you probably have to start it manually in the Services applet in Control Panel).

▲ If the command you want to run is not an executable file, precede the command with **cmd /c**. For instance, **cmd /c type file.ext > c:\capture.txt** .

attrib

Lets you view or change file attributes.

Syntax:

attrib [+r | -r] [+a | -a] [+s | -s] [+h | -h][[*drive:*][*path*] *filename*] [/s]

Options:

[*drive:*][*path*] *filename*	Specifies the target file or directory
+r	Sets the read-only attribute
-r	Clears the read-only attribute
+a	Sets the archive attribute

-a	Clears the archive attribute
+s	Sets the system attribute
-s	Clears the system attribute
+h	Sets the hidden attribute
-h	Clears the hidden attribute
/s	Processes files in the current directory and any subdirectories that match the given file specification

backup

Backs up files. You can use either hard or floppy drives as the destination, or go from one floppy to another.

Syntax:

backup *source dest-drive*: [/s] [/m] [/a] [/f[:*size*]] [/d:*date* [/t:*time*]] [/l[:*drive*:][*path*][*logfile*]]

Options:

source	Gives the specification of the files you want to back up.
dest-drive:	Indicates the target drive.
/s	Includes all subdirectories in the backup.
/m	Selects only files that have their archive attribute set (they've been modified since the last backup), and also turns off the archive attribute of the backed-up files.
/a	Appends the selected backup files to an existing backup set.
/f[:*size*]	Forces a destination floppy disk to be formatted at the size (in kilobytes) you specify. The values for *size* are 160, 180, 320, 360, 720, 1200, 1440, and 2880.
/d:*date*	Selects only files modified on or after the specified date.
/t:*time*	Selects only files modified on or after the specified time.
/l[:[*drive*:][*path*][*logfile*]]	Creates a log file of the backup.

cacls

Displays or changes the access control lists (ACLs) of files.

Syntax:

cacls *filename* [/t] [/e] [/c] [/g *user:perm*] [/r *user* [...]] [/p *user:perm* [...]] [/d *user* [...]]

Options:

filename	Specifies the target files.
/t	Modifies the ACLs of specified files in the current directory and all subdirectories.
/e	Edits the ACL instead of replacing it.
/c	Continues the work instead of stopping on errors.
/g *user:perm*	Grants access rights to the specified user. The *perm* parameter can be R (Read), C (Change), or F (Full Control).
/r *user*	Revokes a user's access rights.
/p *user:perm*	Replaces a user's access rights. The *perm* parameter can be set to N (None), R (Read), C (Change), or F (Full Control).
/d *user*	Denies access to the named user.

chdir (cd)

Changes the current directory. When used without options, it displays the current drive and directory.

Syntax:

chdir [/d] [*drive*:][*path*] [..]

or

cd [/d] [*drive*:][*path*] [..]

Options:

/d	Changes the current drive and the current directory
[*drive*:][*path*]	Specifies the drive and directory to which you want to change
..	Moves to the parent directory

chkdsk

Checks the integrity of a disk and displays a status report; can also repair errors on a disk.

Syntax:

chkdsk [*drive*:][[*path*] *filename*] [/f] [/v] [/r]

Options:

none	The current drive is checked.
drive:	The specified drive is checked.
[*path*] *filename*	Checks for fragmentation.
/f	Repairs any errors that are found. To use this option, Chkdsk must be able to lock the disk. If it can't, it offers to perform the repair during the next system startup.
/v	Displays a verbose listing of all files checked.
/r	Locates bad sectors and recovers readable information on a locked disk.

cmd

Invokes the Windows NT Workstation command processor.

Syntax:

cmd [[/c | /k] [/q] [/a] [/u] [/t:*fg*] *string*]

Options:

/c	Executes the command and then stops
/k	Executes the command and then continues
/q	Turns echoing off
/a	Outputs ANSI characters
/u	Outputs Unicode characters
/t:*fg*	Lets you set the foreground and background colors for the command processor you invoke, using the Color command
/x	Turns on extensions to Cmd.exe to give you more control over the command processor
/y	Turns off extensions to Cmd.exe
string	Specifies the command you want carried out

color

Lets you set the foreground and background colors for the command prompt.

Syntax:

color *bf*

Options:

bf   Two hexadecimal digits that contain the foreground and background color selection; *b* specifies the background color and *f* specifies the foreground color. Use the following values for the color selections:

0 Black

1 Blue

2 Green

3 Aqua

4 Red

5 Purple

6 Yellow

7 White

8 Gray

9 Light blue

A Light green

B Light aqua

C Light red

D Light purple

E Light yellow

F Bright white

comp

Compares the contents of two files or sets of files byte by byte.

Syntax:

comp [*first_set*] [*second_set*] [/d] [/a] [/l] [/n=*number*] [/c]

Options:

first_set	Specifies the first set of files to be compared
second_set	Specifies the second set of files to be compared
/d	Uses decimal format to display any differences (the default is hex)

/a	Displays differences as ASCII
/l	Shows the line number in which a difference is detected instead of the file offset
/n=*number*	Restricts the process to a specific number of lines
/c	Looks for differences in a case-insensitive manner

compact

This command works only on NTFS systems and cannot be used on volumes that have been compressed with DriveSpace or DoubleSpace. Shows the compression level of files and directories and can also change the compression level.

Syntax:

compact [/c | /u] [/s] [/i] [/f] [/l] *filename*

Options:

/c	Compresses a directory or file
/u	Uncompresses a directory or file
/s	Applies the chosen action (/c or /u) to all subdirectories
/i	Ignores errors
/f	Forces compression for a file that is left in a partially compressed or uncompressed state as a result of a crash
filename	Specifies a directory or file

Notes:

Invoking the command with no options displays the compression state of the current directory and files.

convert

Dynamically converts a drive from FAT to NTFS while maintaining the data on the drive.

Syntax:

convert [*drive*:] /fs:NTFS [/v] [nametable:*filename*]

Options:

| *drive*: | Specifies the drive to be converted. |
| /fs:NTFS | Specifies NTFS as the destination file system type. |

/v	Selects verbose mode so any messages are displayed during conversion.
/nametable:*filename*	Translates unusual filenames. If you have trouble converting files with unusual filenames, you can create a name translation table in the root directory of the target drive, and then specify that filename.

Notes:

You cannot convert the current drive. If the command can't lock the drive, it will offer to convert it the next time the system is started.

copy

Copies files, and can also be used to combine files. When more than one file is copied, Windows NT displays each filename as the file is copied.

Syntax:

copy [/a | /b] *source* [/a | /b] [+ *source* [/a | /b] [+...]] [*destination* [/a | /b]] [/v] [/n] [/z]

Options:

source	Gives the file specification of the source file(s).
destination	Gives the file specification (or only a drive or drive\directory) of the destination files.
/a	Copies files in ASCII mode (copying stops when an end-of-file [EOF] marker [CTRL+Z] is found). Use /a at the beginning of the command (before *source*) to use ASCII mode for all files until a /b switch is encountered.
/b	Copies files in binary mode (the default mode).
/v	Matches the target with the source.
/n	Forces Copy to create short filenames at the destination.

Notes:

You can combine files with the copy command by using the "+" character. For example, **copy file1+file2 file3** creates file3 with the contents of file1 plus file2. When combining, copy uses ASCII mode by default (which terminates copying of each file at any EOFs). To ignore EOFs, use the /b parameter.

date

Displays or sets the system date.

Syntax:

date [*mm-dd-yy*]

Options:

mm-dd-yy   Specify *yyyy* for a 4-digit year.

del/erase

Deletes/erases files.

Syntax:

del [*drive:*][*path*] *filename* [; ...] [/p] [/f] [/s] [/q] [/a[:*attributes*]]

erase [*drive:*][*path*] *filename* [; ...] [/p] [/f] [/s] [/q] [/a[:*attributes*]]

Options:

[*drive:*][*path*] *filename*	Gives the file specification of the files to be erased.
/p	Prompts for confirmation before erasing the specified file.
/f	Forces read-only files to be erased.
/s	Causes subdirectories to be included for the file specification.
/q	Runs the command in quiet mode to avoid confirmations.
/a:*attributes*	Controls target files based on their attributes. You can also use a hyphen to exclude files with a specified attribute. For instance, **del *.*/a:-a** will not erase files that have the archive flag set.

Notes:

Del and Erase work identically. Both are internal commands. Deleting files from the command line bypasses the Recycle Bin.

dir

Displays the contents of a directory.

Syntax:

dir [*drive:*][*path*][*filename*] [; ...] [/p] [/w] [/d] [/a[[:]*attributes*]] [/o[[:]*sortorder*]] [/t[[:]*timefield*]] [/s] [/b] [/l] [/n] [/x]

Options:

[*drive:*][*path*]	Specifies the drive and directory.
Filename	Restricts the display of files to those specified by *filename*.
/p	Pauses the display after each screen fills and waits for a key to be pressed.
/w	Displays files using a wide format, which lists only filenames.
/d	Uses the wide format, but sorts files by column.
/a[[:]*attributes*]	Restricts the display to only those files specified by attributes. Use /a to see any files with special attributes set. Attributes allowed are d (directories), r (read-only), h (hidden), s (system), and a (archive). Precede the attribute with a hyphen to display files that do *not* have that attribute set.
/o[[:] *sortorder*]	Lets you sort the display of files. Allowed *sortorder* values are n (name), e (extension), d (date), s (size), and g (directories first, then files). Precede any of these values with a hyphen to reverse the sort order.
/t[[:] *timefield*]	Specifies which time is shown in the display. Values are c (creation date), a (last access date), and w (last write date).
/s	Applies the command to subdirectories.
/b	Displays only filenames.
/l	Causes the display to use lowercase letters.
/n	Forces the long version of each filename to appear to the right of each file's display.
/x	Changes the order of the output display so that short names are shown to the immediate left of the long filenames.

Notes:

Enter the command with no options to display the contents of the current directory.

diskcomp

Compares the contents of two disks, byte by byte.

Syntax:

diskcomp *drive1 drive2*

diskcopy

Copies one diskette to another, making an exact duplicate of the source diskette on the destination diskette.

Syntax:

diskcopy *drive1*: *drive2*: [/v]

Options:

drive: Specifies the drive letter of the source and destination diskettes

/v   Verifies after writing

diskperf

Enables and disables the system disk performance counters.

Syntax:

diskperf [-y | -n] [*computername*]

Options:

-y   Turns on the system disk performance counters at the next system boot

-n   Turns off the system disk performance counters at the next system boot

computername   Controls the disk performance counters on a remote computer

Notes:

Entering the command with no options reports whether the disk performance counters are enabled or disabled.

doskey

Doskey recalls DOS commands to repeat them or edit them. It also provides the ability to create command macros.

Syntax:

doskey [/reinstall] [/listsize=*size*] [/macros:[all | *exename*]] [/history] [/insert | /overstrike] [/exename=*exename*] [/macrofile=*filename*] [macroname=[*text*]]

Options:

/reinstall	Clears the command history.
/listsize=*size*	Controls the maximum number of commands held.
/macros	Displays a list of all defined macros.
all	Displays all executable-based macros.
exename	Macros attached to the specified executable are displayed.
/history	Displays all commands stored in the buffer.
/insert | /overstrike	Mutually exclusive parameters that control whether editing default is in overstrike or insert mode.
/exename=*exename*	Specifies the executable file in which the macro runs.
/macrofile=*filename*	Specifies a file containing macros, which are installed automatically.
macroname=[*text*]	Defines a new macro. *Macroname* is the name of the macro that, when typed at the command prompt, executes the commands listed in [*text*]. Leave the [*text*] portion blank to erase the macro.

dosonly

Ensures that only MS-DOS programs are called from a Command.com prompt.

Syntax:

dosonly

Notes:

If you use a Command.com prompt instead of Cmd.exe, the Dosonly command ensures that only MS-DOS programs can be run from that prompt. This command is provided to make sure that TSRs cannot be interfered with.

find

Finds a specified string within one or more text files.

Syntax:

find [/v] [/c] [/n] [/i] *"search_string"* [[*drive*:][*path*]*filename*[...]]

Options:

"search_string"	Contains the characters you want to find. Enclose the search string in quotation marks.
[drive:][path] filename	Specifies the filenames to be searched.
/v	Displays all of the lines in the searched text files that do not contain the search string.
/c	Displays a count of matching lines, not the contents.
/n	Puts the line number in front of the found text.
/i	Makes the search case-insensitive.

forcedos

Forces a program to start in the MS-DOS subsystem.

Syntax:

forcedos [/d *directory*] *filename* [*parameters*]

Options:

/d *directory*	Specifies the directory.
Filename	Names the program (use the full path if the program is not in the current directory).
Parameters	Used to specify any parameters that need to be passed to the program.

format

Formats a disk.

Syntax:

format *drive:* [/fs:*file-system*] [/v[:*label*]] [/a:*unitsize*] [/q] [/f:*size*] [/t:*tracks* /n:*sectors*] [/1] [/4] [/8]

Options:

drive:	Specifies the drive that has the disk you want to format.
/fs:*file-system*	Specifies the file system to be used.
/v:*label*	Sets the volume label for the formatted disk.
/a:*unitsize*	Controls the allocation unit size for NTFS formats. *Unitsize* can be 512, 1024, 2048, or 4096.

/q	Performs a quick format (the root directory and the file table are erased). This is not a full format; use this parameter to quickly erase a previously formatted disk.
/f:*size*	Controls the size of the disk that is formatted. *Size* represents kilobytes and can be 160, 180, 320, 360, 720, 1200, 1440, 2880, and 20.8 (for optical disks).
/t:*tracks*	Specifies the number of tracks formatted on the disk.
/n:*sectors*	Specifies the number of sectors formatted per track.
/1	Formats a single-sided disk.
/4	Formats a 5.25-inch, 360KB, DSDD disk in a 1.2MB drive.
/8	Formats a 5.25-inch disk with 8 sectors per track for use on systems running early versions of MS-DOS (up to 2.0).

ftype

Displays and controls file types used for associations.

Syntax:

ftype [*filetype*[=[*command*]]]

Options:

filetype	Specifies the type of file for which you want to display associations
command	Specifies the command to use when a file of *filetype* is launched

Notes:

Entering the command with no options displays all defined and associated file types.

help

Displays help on a particular command.

Syntax:

help [*command*]

Options:

command	Specifies the command for which you want help

Notes:

Entering *command* /? is exactly the same as entering **help [*command*]**.

install

Loads Windows NT memory-resident programs.

Syntax:

install=[*drive*:][*path*] *filename* [*command-parameters*]

Options:

[*drive*:][*path*] *filename*	Specifies the name of the program to load
command-parameters	Specifies parameters you want to pass to the program

label

Sets the volume label for a disk.

Syntax:

label [*drive*:] *label*

Options:

drive:	Indicates the drive that holds the disk for which you want to assign the label
label	Specifies the label you want to assign

mkdir (md)

Creates a directory.

Syntax:

mkdir [*drive*:] *path*

or

md [*drive*:] *path*

Options:

drive:	Specifies the drive on which you want to create a directory

> *path*   Indicates the complete path name you want to create

move

Moves files from one directory to another (the command we would have paid big bucks for in the old days of DOS).

Syntax:

move [*source*] [*target*]

Options:

source   Gives the path and name of the files to be moved

target   Gives the destination path to which the files will be moved

net accounts

This command is used to maintain the user account database. You can use it to modify password and logon requirements for all user accounts. When entered without options, it displays current settings for the password, logon limitations, and domain information for the logged-on account.

Syntax:

net accounts [/forcelogoff:{*minutes* | no}] [/minpwlen:*length*] [/maxpwage:{*days* | unlimited}] [/minpwage:*days*] [/uniquepw:*number*] [/domain]

also:

net accounts [/sync] [/domain]

Options:

/forcelogoff:{*minutes* | no}   *Minutes* gives the number of minutes a user has before being automatically logged off when valid logon hours expire. No is the default value and specifies that forced logoff will not occur.

/minpwlen:*length*   Specifies the minimum number of characters required for a password. The range is 0 to 14 characters (the default is 6).

/maxpwage:{*days* | unlimited}	Specifies the maximum number of days a password is valid. The unlimited option specifies that no limit is imposed. (/maxpwage cannot be less than /minpwage. The range is 1 to 49710, and the default is 90 days.)
/minpwage:*days*	*Days* specifies the minimum number of days that have to elapse before a user can change a password. A value of 0 specifies no minimum time. The range is 0 to 49710; the default is 0 days. (/minpwage cannot be greater than /maxpwage.)
/uniquepw:*number*	Specifies that the user cannot reuse a password for the number of changes specified by *number*. The maximum value is 8.
/sync	Synchronizes the account database.
/domain	Performs the specified action on the domain controller instead of the current computer.

net computer

Adds or deletes computers from the domain database. This command can be used only on Windows NT Server.

Syntax:

net computer *computername* {/add | /del}

Options:

computername	Gives the name of the computer to be added or deleted
/add	Adds the computer to the domain
/del	Deletes the computer from the domain

net config

Displays the configurable services that are running and allows changes to settings for those services. The specific commands for Server or Workstation (the two services that can be configured with this command) are discussed next.

Syntax:

net config [*service* [*options*]]

Options:

service   Specifies a service that can be configured (Server or Workstation)

Notes:

Entering the command with no options displays the configurable services that are running.

net config server

Displays or changes settings for the Server service. This command affects only the server on which it is executed.

Syntax:

net config server [/autodisconnect:*time*] [/srvcomment:*"text"*] [/hidden:{yes | no}]

Options:

/autodisconnect:*time*	Specifies the number of minutes an account can be inactive before it is disconnected. The range is 1 to 65535 minutes. The default is 15. -1 is never.
/srvcomment:*"text"*	The message in *"text"* specifies a comment that is displayed along with the server on Windows NT screens and the Net View command. The message can consist of up to 48 characters and must be enclosed in quotation marks.
/hidden:{yes	no}	Determines whether a computer name is hidden in listings of servers.

net config workstation

This command displays and changes settings for the Workstation service.

Syntax:

net config workstation [/charcount:*bytes*] [/chartime:*msec*] [/charwait:*sec*]

Options:

/charcount:*bytes*	Specifies the bytes of data that are collected before data is sent to a communications device. If /chartime is set, Windows NT relies on the value that is satisfied first. The range is 0 to 65535 byes; the default is 16 bytes.

/chartime:*msec*	Specifies the number of milliseconds that Windows NT collects data before sending it to a communications device. If /charcount is set, Windows NT relies on the value that is satisfied first. The range is 0 to 65535000 milliseconds; the default is 250 milliseconds.
/charwait:*sec*	Specifies the number of seconds Windows NT waits for a communications device to become available. The range is 0 to 65535 seconds; the default is 3600 seconds.

Notes:

Entering the command with no options displays the current configuration for the workstation.

net continue

Reactivates a Windows NT service that has been suspended by Net Pause.

Syntax:

net continue *service*

Options:

service	Any of the following paused services:
	File Server for Macintosh
	FTP Server
	LPDSVC
	Net Logon
	Network DDE
	Network DDE DSDM
	NT LM Security Support Provider
	Remoteboot
	Remote Access Server
	Schedule
	Server
	Simple TCP/IP Services
	Workstation

net file

Use this command to list ID numbers of files, to close a shared file, and to remove file locks. When used without options, Net File lists the open files on a server as well as their IDs, path names, user names, and number of locks. (This command works only on computers running the Server service.)

Syntax:

net file [*id* [/close]]

Options:

id	Specifies the identification number of the file.
/close	Include this option to close an open file and remove file locks. This command must be typed from the server on which the file is shared.

net group

Adds, displays, or modifies global groups on servers. Enter the command without parameters to display the group names on the server.

Syntax:

net group [*groupname* [/comment:"*text*"]] [/domain]

net group *groupname* {/add [/comment:"*text*"] | /delete} [/domain]

net group *groupname username* [...] {/add | /delete} [/domain]

Options:

groupname	Specifies the name of the group to add, expand, or delete. This parameter is also included when user names are to be added to or deleted from a group. Supply the group name alone to see a list of users in a group.
/comment:"*text*"	This switch adds a comment of up to 48 characters, as specified by *text*. Enclose the text in quotation marks.
/domain	Performs the operation on the primary domain controller of the current domain. Without this switch the operation affects only the local computer.
username [...]	Specifies one or more user names to be added to or removed from a group. Multiple user name entries must be separated by a space.

/add	Adds a group to a domain or adds a user name to a group.
/delete	Removes a group from a domain or removes a user name from a group.

net localgroup

Modifies local groups on computers. Enter the command without parameters to list the local groups on the computer.

Syntax:

net localgroup [*groupname* [/comment:"*text*"]] [/domain]

net localgroup *groupname* {/add [/comment:"*text*"] | /delete} [/domain]

net localgroup *groupname name* [...] {/add | /delete} [/domain]

Options:

groupname	Specifies the name of the local group to add, expand, or delete. Supply a group name without parameters to list users or global groups in the local group. If the group name includes spaces, enclose the name in quotation marks.
/comment:"*text*"	This switch adds a comment of up to 48 characters, as specified by the text in quotation marks.
/domain	Performs the operation on the primary domain controller of the current domain. Otherwise, the operation is performed on the local computer. By default, Windows NT Server computers perform operations on the domain. This option is effective only when executed on a computer that is a member of a domain.
name [...]	Specifies one or more user names or group names to be added to or removed from the local group. Multiple entries must be separated by a space. Include the domain name if the user is from another domain.
/add	Adds the specified group name or user name to a local group. User and group names to be added must have been created previously.
/delete	Removes a group name or user name from a local group.

net name

This command adds or deletes a messaging name (a name to which messages are sent) at a computer. Use the command without options to display the names accepting messages at this computer. A computer's list of names comes from three places: message names, which are added with this command; the computer name, which is added as a name when the Workstation service is started and cannot be deleted; and a user name, which is added at logon and cannot be deleted.

Syntax:

net name [*name* [/add | /delete]]

Options:

name	The user account that is to be added to the list of names that will receive messages. The name can have up to 15 characters.
/add	Adds a name to a computer. (/add is optional because typing **net name** *name* works the same as **net name** *name* **/add**.
/delete	Removes a name from a computer.

net pause

Use this command to suspend a Windows NT service or resource. After pausing a service, you can use the Net Continue command to resume it.

Syntax:

net pause *service*

Options:

service	Specifies the service to be paused

net print

Use this command to list print jobs and shared queues. For each queue, the command lists jobs, showing the size and status of each job, and the queue status.

Syntax:

net print *computername**sharename*

net print [*computername*] *job*# [/hold | /release | /delete]

Options:

computername	Indicates the name of the computer sharing the printer queue(s).
sharename	Specifies the share name of the printer queue.
job#	Gives the identification number assigned to a print job. Each job executed on a computer is assigned a unique number.
/hold	Assigns a hold status to a job so that it will not print. The job remains in the queue until it is released or deleted.
/release	Removes the hold status on a job so that it can be printed.
/delete	Removes a job from a queue.

net send

This command sends messages to other users, computers, or messaging names on the network.

Syntax:

net send {*name* | * | /domain[:*domainname*] | /users} *message*

Options:

name	Specifies the user name, computer name, or messaging name to which the message is sent. If the name contains blank characters, enclose the name in quotation marks.
*	When substituted for *name*, sends the message to all of the names in your group.
/domain[:*domainname*]	Specifies that the message should be sent to all users in the domain. If *domainname* is specified, the message is sent to all of the names in the specified domain or workgroup.
/users	Sends the message to all users connected to the server.
message	Specifies the text of the message.

Notes:

The Messenger service must be running on the receiving computer to receive messages. You can send a message only to a name that is active on the network.

net session

This command lists or disconnects sessions between the computer and other computers on the network. When used without options, it displays information about all sessions running on the computer that currently has the focus.

Syntax:

net session [*computername*] [/delete]

Options:

computername	Lists the session information for the named computer.
/delete	Ends the session between the local computer and *computername*. All open files on the computer are closed. If *computername* is omitted, all sessions are ended.

Notes:

This command works only when executed on servers.

net share

This command is used to share a server's resources with network users. Use the command without options to list information about all resources being shared on the computer. For each shared resource, Windows NT reports the device name(s) or path name(s) for the share, along with any descriptive comment that has been associated with the share.

Syntax:

net share *sharename*

net share sharename=drive:path [/users:*number* | /unlimited] [/remark: "*text*"]

net share *sharename* [/users:*number* | /unlimited] [/remark:"*text*"]

net share {*sharename* | *devicename* | *drive:path*} /delete

Options:

sharename	Specifies the name of the shared resource. Typing the command with a share name displays information only about that share.
devicename	Names the printer(s) (LPT1 through LPT9) shared by *sharename*. Used when a printer share is being established.

drive:path	Specifies the absolute path of a directory to be shared. Used when a directory share is being established.
/users:*number*	Indicates the maximum number of users permitted to access the shared resource simultaneously.
/unlimited	Specifies no limit on the number of users.
/remark:"*text*"	Adds a comment about the share. Enclose the text in quotation marks.
/delete	Stops sharing the resource.

net start

Use this command to start services or restart services that were stopped by the Net Stop command. Enter the command **net start** without options to list running services.

Syntax:

net start [*service*]

Options:

service   Specifies the service to be stopped.

The following services can be stopped with this command:

Alerter

Client Service for NetWare

Clipbook Server

Computer Browser

DHCP Client

Directory Replicator

Eventlog

FTP Server

LPDSVC

Messenger

Net Logon

Network DDE

Network DDE DSDM

Network Monitoring Agent

NT LM Security Support Provider

OLE

Remote Access Connection Manager

Remote Access ISNSAP Service

Remote Access Server

Remote Procedure Call (RPC) Locator

Remote Procedure Call (RPC) Service

Schedule

Server

Simple TCP/IP Server

SNMP

Spooler

TCP/IP NETBIOS Helper

UPS

Workstation

The following services are available only on Windows NT Server:

```
File Server for Macintosh (NT Server only)
Gateway Service for NetWare (NT Server only)
Microsoft DHCP Server (NT Server only)
```

```
Print Server for Macintosh (NT Server only)
Remoteboot (NT Server only)
Windows Internet Name Service (NT Server only)
```

net statistics

This command can also be entered as **net stats**. It displays the statistics log for the local Workstation or Server service. Used without parameters, it displays the services for which statistics are available. The stats include computer name, date and time of last statistics update, and detailed information about sessions. Use **net statistics /?** to get the list of statistics.

Syntax:

net statistics [workstation | server]

Options:

server   Displays the Server service statistics

workstation   Displays the Workstation service statistics

net stop

This command is used to stop Windows NT services.

Syntax:

net stop *service*

Options:

service   A Windows NT service that can be stopped. See the Net Start command for a list of eligible services.

net time

Use this command to synchronize a computer's clock with that of another computer or domain.

Syntax:

net time [*computername* | /domain[:*domainname*]] [/set]

Options:

computername	Specifies the name of the computer you want to check or synchronize with
/domain[:*domainname*]	Specifies the domain with which to synchronize time
/set	Synchronizes the computer's time with the time on the specified computer or domain

net use

This command connects a computer to a shared resource or disconnects a computer from a shared resource. Net Use without options lists the computer's connections.

Syntax:

net use [*devicename* | *] [*computername**sharename*[*volume*]] [*password* | *]]
[/user:[*domainname*\]*username*] [[/delete] | [/persistent:{yes | no}]]

or

net use *devicename* [/home[*password* | *]] [/delete:{yes | no}]
net use [/persistent:{yes | no}]

Options:

devicename	Specifies the name to assign to the connected resource or the name of the device to be disconnected. (Type an asterisk in place of the device name to assign the next available device name.)
computername	Specifies the name of the computer controlling the shared resource.
sharename	Indicates the name of the shared resource.
volume	Indicates the name of a volume on a NetWare server.
password	Indicates a password needed to access the shared resource.
*	Produces a prompt for the password. (The password is not echoed when typed.)
/user	Specifies a different user name need for the connection.
domainname	Indicates another domain.
username	Specifies the user name with which to log on.

/home	Connects to a user's home directory.
/delete	Cancels the connection.
/persistent {yes | no}	Saves or fails to save connections to devices (saved connections are restored at the next logon for this user).
/delete (yes | no)	Removes persistent connections.

net user

This command creates and modifies user accounts on computers. When used without switches, it lists the user accounts for the computer.

Syntax:

net user [*username* [*password* \| *] [*options*]] [/domain]

net user *username* {*password* \| *} /add [*options*] [/domain]

net user *username* [/delete] [/domain]

Options:

username	Specifies the name of the user account.
password	Assigns or changes a password for the user account.
*	Displays a prompt for the password, which is not echoed when typed.
/domain	The action is performed on the PDC of the current domain. This parameter is needed only with Windows NT Workstation (by default, Windows NT Server uses the PDC).
/add	Adds the user account to the database.
/delete	Removes the user account from the database.
options	The available options are shown in Table A-2.

net view

This command lists resources being shared on a computer. Used without options, it displays a list of computers in the current domain or network.

Option	Description
/active:{yes | no}	Activates or deactivates the account. The default is yes.
/comment:"*text*"	Adds a descriptive comment.
/countrycode.*nnn*	*nnn* is the numeric operating system country code for the language files that are used for a user's help and error messages. (0 means the default country code.)
/expires:{*date* | never}	Specifies a date when the account will expire in the form *mm,dd,yy,* or *dd,mm,yy,* as determined by the country code. The never option sets no time limit on the account.
/fullname:"*name*"	Specifies a user's full name (rather than a user name). Enclose the name in quotation marks.
/homedir:*pathname*	Specifies the path for the user's home directory. The path must have been previously created.
/homedirreq:{yes | no}	Specifies whether a home directory is required. If a home directory is required, use the /homedir option to specify the directory.
/passwordchg:{yes | no}	Specifies whether users can change their own password. The default is yes.
/passwordreq:{yes | no}	Specifies whether a user account must have a password. The default is yes.
/profilepath[:*path*]	Specifies a path for the user's logon profile.
/scriptpath:*pathname*	*Pathname* is the location of the user's logon script.
/times:{*times* | all}	Specifies the hours during which a user account may be logged on.
/usercomment:"*text*"	Specifies a comment for the account.
/workstations:	Lists the computers from which a user can log on to the network. (No list or * means any computer.)

Table A-2.   Options for the Net User Command

Syntax:

net view [*computername* | /domain[:*domainname*]]

net view /network:nw [*computername*]

Options:

computername	Specifies a computer with shared resources you want to view.
/domain:*domainname*	Specifies the domain with computers whose shared resources you want to view. If *domainname* is omitted, Net View displays all domains in the local area network.
/network:nw	Displays the available servers on a NetWare network. If a computer name is specified, its resources are displayed.

ntbooks

Launches the online manuals for Windows NT.

Syntax:

ntbooks [/s] [/w] [/n:*path*]

Options:

/s	Accesses documentation about Windows NT Server.
/w	Accesses documentation about Windows NT Workstation.
/n:*path*	Lets you specify the path where the online books are stored. By default, the last used location is automatically used.

ping

Available only if the TCP/IP protocol has been installed, this command verifies connections to remote computers.

Syntax:

ping [-t] [-a] [-n *count*] [-l *length*] [-f] [-i *ttl*] [-v *tos*] [-r *count*] [-s *count*] [[-j *computer-list*] | [-k *computer-list*]] [-w *timeout*] *destination-list*

Options:

-t	Pings until interrupted.
-a	Resolves the address to the computer name.
-n *count*	Specifies the number of ECHO packets (the default is 4).
-l *length*	Specifies the length, in bytes, of ECHO packets (the default is 64 bytes; maximum is 8192).
-f	Includes a Do Not Fragment flag in the packet (to avoid packet fragmentation by gateways).
-i *ttl*	Sets the Time to Live field to the value specified.
-v *tos*	Sets the Type of Service field to the value specified.
-r *count*	Keeps the route of outgoing and returning packets in the Record Route field. (The count may be a minimum of 1 and a maximum of 9 computers.)
-s *count*	Sets the time stamp for the number of hops specified by *count*.
-j *computer-list*	Routes the packets, using the list of computers specified by *computer-list,* when consecutive computers may be separated by intermediate gateways.
-k *computer-list*	Routes the packets, using the list of computers specified by *computer-list,* when consecutive computers may not be separated by intermediate gateways.
-w *timeout*	Specifies the timeout interval in milliseconds.
destination-list	Lists the remote computers you want to ping.

print

Prints a text file to a local computer in the background.

Syntax:

print [/d:*device*] [*drive:*][*path*] *filename*[...]

Options:

none	Displays the contents of the print queue
/d:*device*	Specifies the name of the print device, such as LPT1, COM2, and so forth
[*drive:*][*path*] *filename*	Indicates the file to be printed

rename (ren)

This command renames files.

Syntax:

rename [*drive:*][*path*] *filename1 filename2*

or

ren [*drive:*][*path*] *filename1 filename2*

Options:

[*drive:*][*path*] *filename1*	Specifies the source filenames
filename2	Specifies the destination filenames

restore

This command restores files backed up with the Backup command.

Syntax:

restore *drive1*: *drive2*:[*path*[*filename*]] [/s] [/p] [/b:*date*] [/a:*date*] [/e:*time*] [/l:*time*] [/m] [/n] [/d]

Options:

drive1:	Specifies the source drive.
drive2:	Specifies the destination drive.
path	Indicates the destination directory. This must be the same directory as the one from which the files were backed up.
filename	Indicates the filenames you want to restore from the backup set.
/s	Includes subdirectories.
/p	Prompts for confirmation when restoring over files that are read-only or that are newer than those stored in the backup set.
/b:*date*	Restores files modified on or before *date*.
/a:*date*	Restores files modified after *date*.
/e:*time*	Restores files modified at or earlier than *time*.
/l:*time*	Restores files modified at or later than *time*.
/m	Restores files modified since the last backup.

/n	Restores only files that do not exist in the destination directory.
/d	Displays files that would be restored, but does not actually restore any files. (Used to test which files will be restored given any other parameters you've specified.)

rmdir (rd)

This command removes directories.

Syntax:

rmdir [*drive:*]*path* [/s]

rd [*drive:*]*path* [/s]

Options:

[*drive:*]*path*	Specifies the name of the directory that you want to remove
/s	Removes an entire subdirectory tree, including files

start

Executes the given command in a new window. Used with options, it opens a command window.

Syntax:

start ["*title*"] [/*dpath*] [/i] [/min] [/max] [/separate] [/low] [/normal] [/high] [/realtime] [/wait] [/b] [*filename*] [*parameters*]

Options:

"*title*"	Indicates the new window's title (displayed in the title bar)
/*dpath*	Specifies the directory to which the new window defaults
/I	Automatically passes environment variables from Cmd.exe to the new window
/min	Starts the new window minimized
/max	Starts the new window maximized
/separate	Runs Win16 applications in a separate address space
/low	Runs the application at idle priority

/normal	Runs the application at normal priority
/high	Runs the application at high priority
/realtime	Runs the application at realtime priority
/wait	Begins the application, then waits for it to terminate
/b	Runs the application in the background, without a new window
filename	Specifies the program to run in the new window
/parameters	Any parameters you want to pass to the program

subst

This command creates a virtual drive letter from a specified path. Used without any options, it displays all virtual drives.

Syntax:

subst [*drive1*: [*drive2*:]*path*]

subst *drive1*: /d

Options:

drive1:	Specifies the virtual drive that will be created
drive2:	Indicates the actual drive that contains the path
path	Specifies the path to use for the virtual drive
/d	Deletes a virtual drive

title

This command sets the title bar for the current command prompt window.

Syntax:

title *title_name*

Options:

title_name	Indicates the title you want to appear in the window's title bar

tree

This command graphically displays the directory tree of a drive.

Syntax:

tree [*drive:*][*path*] [/f] [/a]

Options:

drive:	Specifies the drive for which you want to see a directory tree
path	Specifies the directory for which you want to see a directory tree
/f	Causes the files for each directory to be displayed
/a	Uses ASCII characters to represent the tree, instead of the extended characters used by default

xcopy

This command copies files and is used when you need more control than the Copy command provides.

Syntax:

xcopy *source* [*destination*] [/w] [/p] [/c] [/v] [/q] [[/f] [/l] [/d[:*date*]] [/u] [/i] [/s] [/e] [/t] [/k] [/r] [/h] [/a | /m] [/n] [/exclude:*filename*] [/z]

Options

source	Specifies the source files to be copied.
destination	Specifies the destination for the files to be copied.
other options	See Table A-3 for a listing of Xcopy options and their results.

Option	Result
/w	Waits for user input before copying files.
/p	Prompts for confirmation when creating destination files.
/c	Continues copying after errors are encountered.
/v	Verifies the integrity of each copied file.
/q	Runs Xcopy in quiet mode.
/f	Displays filenames during the copy.
/l	Lists files that would be copied, but does not copy any files.
/d[:*date*]	Copies files modified on or after *date*.
/u	Copies only files that already exist in the destination directory.
/i	Assumes that the destination specified is a directory and not a file.
/s	Copies subdirectories, except empty ones.
/e	Copies all subdirectories, including empty ones. Use this with the /s switch.
/t	Copies only the subdirectory tree and not any files.
/k	Retains the read-only attribute for destination files. By default, the read-only flag, if present in a source file, is not set for destination files.
/r	Forces read-only files to be overwritten if they exist.
/h	Includes files that have the hidden or system flags set.
/a	Copies files that have the archive flag set.
/m	Copies files that have the archive flag set, and removes the archive flag from the source file.
/n	Copies files using the NTFS short filenames.
/exclude:*filename*	Excludes files specified in *filename*.
/z	Copies in restartable mode, over a network.

Table A-3.   Options for the Xcopy Command

WINDOWS
NT
Professional
Library

APPENDIX B

Service Pack Fixes for Windows NT 4

As of the date of this writing, three Service Packs have been issued for Windows NT 4. This appendix lists the issues and problems these Service Packs have fixed. They are arranged by type of problem. The listing is inclusive through SP3 (and SP3 includes everything that was in the earlier Service Packs).

The language used to describe each problem is, in almost all cases, the way Microsoft described the problem when announcing the fix. Some language may differ from the "official" description, but the problem should be recognizable nonetheless. The difference stems from the fact that my own queries to Microsoft took a variety of forms and drew a variety of answers (although all of the answers I kept for this appendix indicated a fix in a Service Pack).

16-Bit Windows Version 3.x-Based Applications

16-bit application stops responding when run on Windows NT 4.0

16-bit applications cause access violation in Ntdll.dll

WOW applications stack fault when launched by a service

WM_DDE_EXECUTE API causes a memory leak in the WOW subsystem

16-bit named pipe file open leads to WOW access violation

SetTimer() API causes memory leak in the WOW subsystem

16-bit version of Visual Basic 4 may hang Windows NT 4.0

32-Bit Windows-Based Applications

Limit of the number of simultaneously open root storage files

Error: The MAPI spooler has shut down unexpectedly

Microsoft Excel 97 causes a Windows NT access violation

A service may not set hooks on 32-bit GUI applications

CLOCK hangs and consumes 90% CPU when set to digital display

DDE client experiences intermittent DDE disconnects

Cmd.exe does not support UNC names as the current directory

DDE destroy window code may stop 0x0000001e in Windows NT 4.0

Delphi 2.00 and 2.01 users encounter error 998

Stop 0x0000001E in Win32k.sys when exiting applications

Access violation in AddAtom inside Kernel32.dll

Missing Eastern Europe font substitutes in registry

Bad parameters sent to Win32k.sys may cause stop message

Possible access violation in Win32k.sys under high stress

Excel charts lose color when pasted into Word

Backup Using Ntbackup.exe

NT Backup does not properly eject tapes on DLT tape devices

Verify reports errors when restoring a tape backup

NT Backup fails to back up Microsoft Exchange Server Data

Truncation of backup log in Eastern Europe or Russian NT 4.0

Backup of local registry does not work with Ntbackup.exe /b

Stop 0x7A or system lockup in NT Backup with MINIQIC

Backup fails on certain directories due to lack of permissions

Backup always reports time as PM

Compression is not supported on Quantum 4000DLT

Blue Screen

Stop 0x1E or 0x50 error on multiprocessor DEC Alpha computer

Stop: 0x0000000A when selecting NDS map objects

Stop: 0x0x0000000A after call to GlobalAddAtom()

Stop 0x50 in Rdr.sys if pathname too long in SMB

RPC service stops responding on UDP port 135

Pressing CTRL+ALT+DEL when logging on can cause blue screen

NetBT (tag=Nbt8) corrupts pool with Windows NT 4.0 SP2 installed

Access violation installing IIS

Memory leak in NetQueryDisplayInformation API

Stop 0x0000000A in Netbt.sys after applying Service Pack 2

Memory corruption on a Windows NT Alpha platform

Stop screen 0x00000050 caused by Fs_rec.sys

Stop 0x0000000a IPX sends browser an incomplete datagram

Stop 0x0000000A in Ntoskrnl.exe at logon to Windows NT 4.0

Blue screen when closing kernel mode handles from user mode

Stop C0000021A using MoveFileEx MOVEFILE_DELAY_UNTIL_REBOOT

Stop 0x0000000A during create file SMB

Configuration

Policy Editor crashes when using large custom ADM files

Windows NT does not display some fonts

Accented Greek characters are not being created

Memory leak retrieving OLE property values with Service Pack 2

Device Drivers

Mouse cursor freezes or fails with Microsoft IntelliMouse

Incorrect MediaType parameter on IBM PCMCIA token ring card

Windows NT 4.0 may not recognize SCSI devices using nonzero LUNs

NEC IDE CD-ROM drive CDR-1400C cannot play audio CDs

Windows NT 4.0 SP2 Atapi claims IRQ for unused IDE channel

SCSI driver description truncated in Control Panel

4 mm DAT driver reports DEC TZ9L supports setmarks

Windisk crashes during initialization when Compaq ATAPI PD/CD

Direct draw programs may hang NT 4.0 with S3 968 video chipset

Stop 0x0000000A in Hal.dll on multiprocessor computers

Access violation occurs in Spoolss.exe

Applications using OpenGl cause access violation in Opengl.dll

Printing to a PostScript printer may cause a Stop 0x0000003b

Stop 0x0000000A using OpenNT commands and utilities

OpenGL access violation on Windows NT version 4.0

No crashdump on Compaq systems with Smart-2/P (PCI) controller

Fatal system error in Ndis.sys allocating map registers

Stop 0x00000050 in Srv.sys when shutting down computer

Windows NT 4.0 not able to read some compact discs

Bugcheck 0x1e caused by Isotp.sys driver

Matrox video driver may fail on Alpha-based computers

PPC 4.0 Cirrus driver fails to redraw &amp, fill objects correctly

Screen corruption on Dell laptops using Cirrus video

IoCompletionPort causes blue screen error

Adaptec Aic78xx does not issue multiple tagged commands

Madge EISA stops responding on Alpha in Windows NT 4.0

Domain Administration

Re-creating Admin shares causes exception error

Choosing default domain name for RAS client authentication

Group policies not applied if DC name is more than 13 characters

Logon allowed when access denied to mandatory user profile

Deferred reconnections to password shares may not work

Computer name truncated when name resolution attempted

Length of PDC name may affect performance on a domain

Logon validation fails using domain name server (DNS)

Personal groups not visible if %Systemroot% is read only

Sharing violation when accessing user profiles

Access violation in DNS Manager when deleting cached domain

DOS-Based Applications

Corruption problem when running DPMI application

Map.exe does not set environment variables correctly

Lost record locks from MS-DOS–based program to NetWare server

File Systems

Programs that lock 0 bytes at byte 0 lock entire file

Helpfile word lists may be rebuilt after Daylight Savings change

Stop 0xA in Ntfs.sys during reboot

Chkntfs does not exclude FAT partitions from Autochk on boot

Stop 0x0000000A in Ntoskrnl.exe

Stop: 0x0000001E when opening My Computer

Stop 0x00000024 in Ntfs.sys

Removable Medium does not eject if formatted in NTFS

NTFS stream limitation in Windows NT 4.0

A client crash may prevent an NTFS volume dismount

NTFS does not prevent a file deletion during rename

CDFS does not complete IRPs correctly

Moving files can corrupt NTFS partition

CDFS incorrectly creates short filenames for some files

SFM file type and creator properties invalid

Windows NT 4.0 may not return valid response for SMB search command

File size data does not remain consistent after Defrag on NTFS

Cannot read files greater than 4GB

NTFS fails assertion under high stress during transfer

File Manager performs a move instead of a copy

Intermittent file corruption problem

Hardware Compatibility

Autosynch-compatible COM applications may fail w/ FIFO enabled

Windows NT 4.0 Setup fails on ThinkPad 535

ATDISK finds the same disk twice on SunDisk PCMCIA ATA adapter

Czech keyboard layout has wrong mapping

Conner 4 mm DAT tape devices fail after about 30 seconds

NTVDM support for Compaq Financial Keyboard scan codes

Multiprocessor systems randomly restart or stop responding

Joystick in Windows NT 4.0 does not work properly

Windows NT may fail to boot on Toshiba portable computers

Device failure message with Microchannel network adapter

IBM Thinkpads 760ED and 760ELD may hang during shutdown

Mouse buttons not swapped on German Windows NT 4.0

SMP full-duplex adapter configuration may cause a blue screen

ExitWindowsEx does not work with NEC Power Switch service

Multiprocessor computer hangs under stress using Halsp.dll

Dongle may not function under Windows NT 4.0

Mouse and keyboard can disappear when replacing drivers

Systems with 4GB or more of RAM cannot boot windows NT 4.0

READ_REGISTER_ULONG doesn't preserve ULONG semantics on Alpha

FPSCR is not being saved across thread context switches

Stop 0x0000007F may occur on Compaq SystemPro

Interoperability

FPNW causes incomplete display when executed from Windows 95

Delay when saving Word 7.0 file to Windows NT 4.0 Server

Corel fonts unavailable outside of English locale

Not all objects are displayed when browsing NDS trees

CSNW sends packets greater than negotiated maximum packet size

SPX data stream type header may reset unexpectedly

AddGroupNameResponse frame from Windows NT may cause WFWG to hang

CSNW cannot see more than 32 volumes per server

Event 2006 errors in Xcopy from Windows NT 4.0 to OS/2 3.0 client

Cyberbit Unicode font does not return correct charset

Macintosh

Stop 0x0000000A Sfmsrv.sys when copying file to Mac volume

Macintosh clients may hang temporarily with multiple Mac volumes

Files in Macintosh volume disappear from Macintosh clients

Macintosh clients connected to Windows NT Server appear to hang

Miscellaneous

Command extensions cause access violation in Cmd.exe

Slow Exchange client logons due to deadlock in Lsass

Event logging frozen while doing heavy logging; services CPU peg

Convlog.exe may cause access violation

FPNW returns time stamp with 60 seconds to clients

Nwlnkspx retransmission problem over a slow link

Dumpchk.exe incorrectly reports some dump files as invalid

Access violation in Cmd.exe processing batch file script argument

Request from Perfmon counter can cause excessive page faults

Access violation with long NDS context in CSNW/GSNW

Replace command with space character in the path does not work

Memory leak using RegConnectRegistry API

Windows NT kernel crashes while processing WM_NCCREATE

Windows NT Muldiv() function returns incorrect value

Cannot open truncated filenames from compact discs

NTFS generates cross-linked files

Bugcheck in Windows NT while running POSIX applications

OpenGL access violation with invalid OpenGL context

Windows NT 4.0 with more than 4 processors may stall & reboot

Nested "for" loops Using the '~' operators does not work

Brief 3.0 in NTVDM consumes 100% processor

SNMP query to Windows NT returns same value for NTS and NTW

Stop message occurs calling GetThreadContext/SetThreadContext

Data corruption on Windows NT 4.0

Network Services and Protocols

Programs run at priority level 15 may cause computer to hang

Connections to share-level server may fail

BUG: Wrong error code on NetBIOS call when using Nwnblnk

FPNW blue screens accessing or creating folders with long paths

DHCP Manager error: "No more data is available"

Cannot view long file names on network in 16-bit programs

Error message: Error access is denied

Service Pack 2 may cause loss of connectivity in Remote Access

IPX doesn't function correctly over token ring source

Message from Unix using Smbclient with long user name crashes

SET: Drivers fail to load when I/O address is above 0xFFF

STOP: 0x0000001E with status C000009A

Delay while establishing SPX II connection

Failure to obtain IP address via DHCP on token ring with SP2

IIS access violation for polygon with more than 100 vertices

NDIS driver fails to check functional address

FPNW doesn't convert the long filenames correctly

Stop 0x00000050 in Tcpip.sys caused by Winsock applications

Stop: 0x0000000A in Rdr.sys when Mailslot message > 512 bytes

Remote procedure call (RPC) service access violation

Grace logon remaining is not decremented when logging to BDC

Invalid directory returned when attempting to access FPNW

NDS login script fails when checking "If member of"

DHCPAdmin incorrectly writes the BootFileTable in the registry

FPNW server returns error when user opens more than 256 files

Dlc.sys sends frame reject (FRMR) and drops connection

Access violation in Services.exe in Eventlog.dll

CSNW and GSNW won't display NetWare servers via a SAP seed server

Cannot reconnect to TN3270 server with close listen sockets

Cannot communicate with computer running NWLink IPX/SPX

Incorrect file listing on NetWare server with Dir /TC command

Windows NT 4.0 DNS server stops responding to queries

Multiple processes are able to open the same Winsock port

Windows NT Ndis.sys and Netflx3.sys performance improvement

Running SNA server 2.11 on the Windows NT 4.0

Nwrdr.sys fails reading file with execute-only attribute

Policy not updated on workstation

Windows NT 4.0 fails to replicate to backup domain controllers

RPC over NetBIOS programs can't call from server to RAS client

Applications testing for directory existence fail

Slow list of folders and files with CSNW

Internet Explorer 3.0 on RISC computer cannot connect to host

Shortcuts created under NT 4.0 resolve to UNC paths

Nwlnkrip data structures corruption when using a demand-dial NIC

Stop message when IBM warp client connects to Windows NT 4.0

Printing

CreateQueueJobAndFile fails with queues other than print queue

Extra form feed with passthrough functions to text-only driver

Access violation in Spoolss when printing to a serial printer

HP LaserJet Series II prints extra small stripes or points

CSNW clients cannot delete print jobs on NetWare print queue

Unable to change font cartridge selection

Cannot connect to AT&T Advanced Server VMS or OSF print share

First line of print job lost when printing using Lpdsvc

Print jobs are deleted when printer is resumed after restart

Serial service won't stop with serial printer installed

Reactivation of paused print queues deletes print jobs

Warning event ID 4010 generated on Windows NT LPD server

Incoming fax jobs do not appear in print queue

0x0000001e when printing certain documents from Windows NT 4.0

Remote Access Service

Problem with DHCP decline feature in Service Pack 2

RAS client fails to connect to Service Pack 2 using NetBEUI

Remote Access Autodial Manager may fail for second user logon

RAS script with Set IPADDR may fail with 3Com Defender add-on

RPC over NetBEUI fails from Windows NT 4.0 RAS to Windows NT 4.0 RAS

RasEnumEntries() API leaks memory

RasEnumEntries return incorrect number of Phonebook entries

RasSetEntryProperties() fails to set options in Service Pack 2

Nbtstat error when using >25 dialout devices with RAS

Rasdial error with English text on non-English version of Windows NT 4.0

NT 4.0 RAS client slows over time due to lack of resources

RAS client IP addresses not returned to static address

Setup of RAS with multiple modems gives slow performance

RAS server cannot use DHCP to assign addresses with.PPTP filtering

Windows NT 4.0 RAS not releasing static IP addresses

RasSetEntryProperties does not save a full path script name

Security

Changing password in User Manager does not permit logon

Retail SP3 clients cannot connect to SP3 Beta 1 servers

Run logon scripts synchronously not applied to new users

Cannot unlock workstation if password change cancelled

Logon rights are not audited

An account that still has system access may be deleted

No output from Dbmon using OutputDebugString while debugging

Access violation in security!SspQueryContextAttributesW

How to enable strong password functionality in Windows NT

Setup

Unattended setup stops and says "Press any key to shut down"

Activating /W switch to prevent rebooting in Windows NT

System restarts every 5 hours if Workstation to Server upgrade

Sysdiff changes dates on files it applies to Windows NT

Video memory not correctly detected on Dell Latitude laptops

Sysdiff cannot delete files

NT 4 error message: "The INF OEMNADDI is missing the referenced file"

Windows NT hangs on shutdown with certain PCMCIA devices

AlphaServer hangs on install of Windows NT version 4.0

Windows NT 4.0 may hang or crash in Win32k.sys during setup

German time zone results in incorrect log times

Intermittent file corruption when compiling on NTFS partition

Video memory not correctly detected on Dell Latitude laptops

Changing colors on Cirrus Logic cards to 65KB can cause stop

Startup

Delayed WinLogon when drive mapped to local share

TCP/IP

Name release notifications not sent to WINS on shutdown

Bad network packet may cause access violation (AV) on DNS server

Netstat slow to list large numbers of connections

XADM: Store stops responding with high CPU usage

DHCP server offers duplicate IP addresses for Windows NT

Winsock apps fail on first attempt at NetBIOS name resolution

WINS static entries overwritten by duplicate group names

WINS restore fails on Windows NT Server 4.0

Telnet to port 135 causes 100 percent CPU usage

WINS may report database corruption with more than 100 owners

RIP table sent while shutting down when silent RIP set

Telnetting to port 53 may crash DNS service

New Windows NT Ping.exe prevents hanging other TCP/IP stacks

WebSTONE benchmark of IIS may show poor results for MP systems

DEC Alpha Windows NT 4.0 Servers with SP2 fail to lease DHCP addresses

Winsock applications may time out or fail with an error

Event 552: DNS was unable to serve a client request

Windows NT client: Primary/secondary WINS servers switch

Any user can log on to FTP server with disabled anonymous logon

MGET to an IBM host FTP server returns garbage characters

Duplicate route not removed after second redirection

Scavenging WINS database removes static entries

DHCP server service may stop responding

Lack of secondary address may cause DNS service to hang

GetPeerName() returns WSAENOTCONN after Select() returns success

Connecting to Windows Network resources from multi-homed machine

OS/2 with TCP\IP may refuse socket connections from Windows NT

Description of DHCP server service has a misspelled word

RAS clients run Winsock and RPC applications slowly

Internet server unavailable because of malicious SYN attacks

Delegation requires a stop and restart of the DNS server service

Windows NT 4.0 DNS server loses the forwarders settings

Windows NT operating system SNMP OID incorrect

NT 4.0 breaks SNA server 2.x server communication over IP

Unattended install prompts for new IP if zero is in address

DNS server glue data is deleted

Second recursive query sent from DNS server is broken

DNS delegations may fail

DNS zone transfer fails after WINS record added

Cache file entries disappear

Unnecessary DNS zone transfers

Zone files in multiples of 4KB may cause access violation

DHCP client may fail with NT 4.0 SP2 multinetted DHCP server

Winsock memory access violation in Ws2help.dll or Msafd.dll

APPENDIX C

NT/Win95 System Icons

T he system icons for all objects in a Windows NT 4 or Windows 95 system are contained in .dll files that are found in \%SystemRoot\System32 for Windows NT 4 and \%SystemRoot\System for Windows 95.

All objects in both operating systems have a Class ID, which can be viewed in the registry in HKEY_CLASSES_ROOT\CLSID. For those objects that have system icons when they display in Explorer or My Computer, you can view the source of the icon in the registry subkey HKEY_CLASSES_ROOT\CLSID\Object_Subkey\DefaultIcon. The object subkey is hex.

For example, the Class ID for My Briefcase is 85BBD920-42A0-1069-A2E4-08002B30309D. The default icon subkey shows a value of \%SystemRoot\System32\ Syncui.dll,0.

That means that the icon for the briefcase is the first icon that is in the file Syncui.dll. Most of the Windows NT 4 system icons can be found in the following .dll files:

▼ Moricons.dll

■ Shell32.dll

▲ Syncui.dll

In addition, some program files contain icons for the objects connected with that program (.exe files can contain icons just as .dll files can).

Most of the Windows 95 system icons can be found in the following .dll files:

▼ Shell32.dll

■ Syncui.dll

▲ Cool.dll (if Plus! is installed).

The following pages identify the icon numbers for each specific .dll file, so you can change the icons for system files or add system icons to objects that are placed in your system as a result of programming.

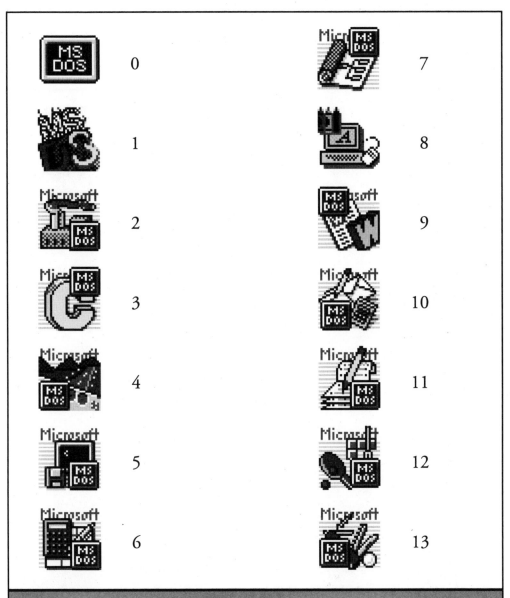

Table C-1.   Icons in the Moricons.dll File

	14		21
	15		22
	16		23
	17		24
	18		25
	19		26
	20		27

Table C-1.   Icons in the Moricons.dll File (*continued*)

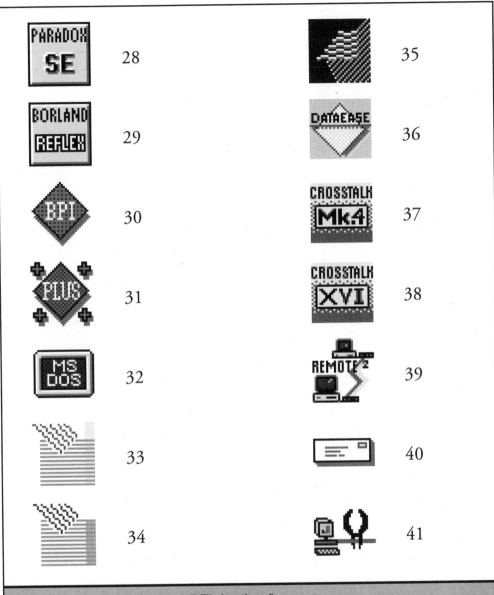

Table C-1. Icons in the Moricons.dll File (*continued*)

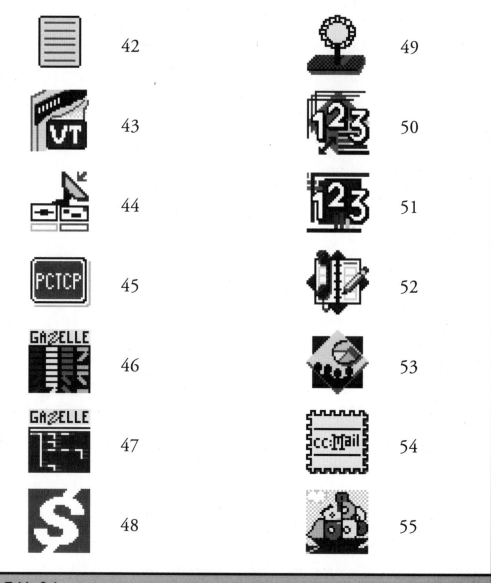

Table C-1. Icons in the Moricons.dll File (*continued*)

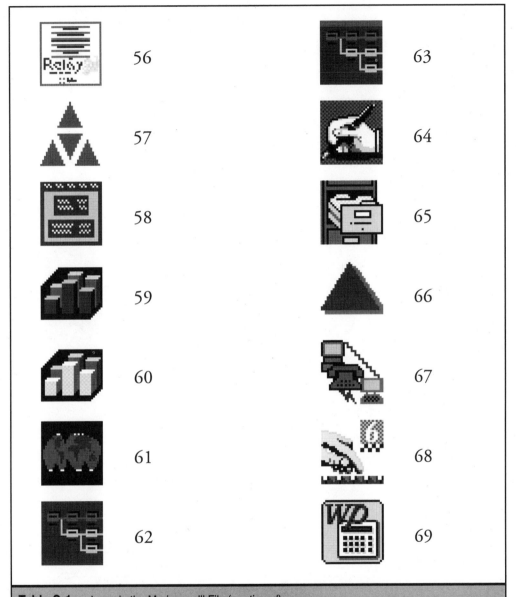

	56		63
	57		64
	58		65
	59		66
	60		67
	61		68
	62		69

Table C-1.   Icons in the Moricons.dll File (*continued*)

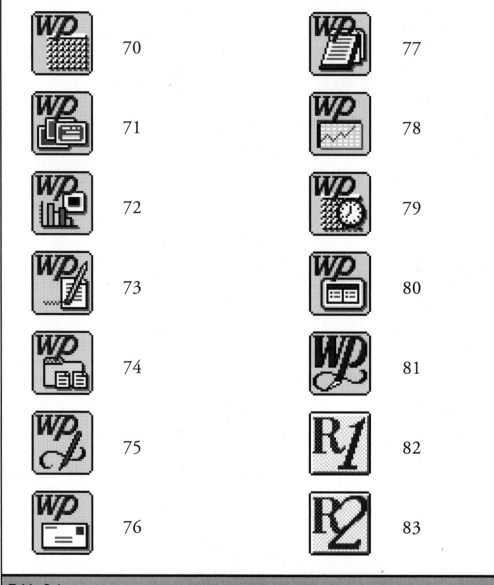

Table C-1. Icons in the Moricons.dll File (*continued*)

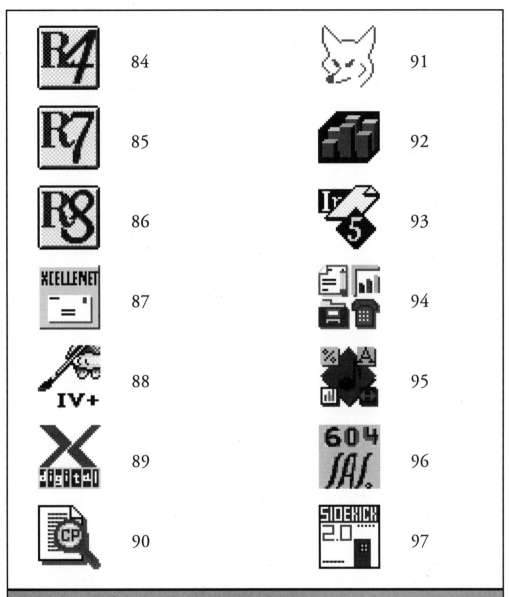

84	91
85	92
86	93
87	94
88	95
89	96
90	97

Table C-1.   Icons in the Moricons.dll File (*continued*)

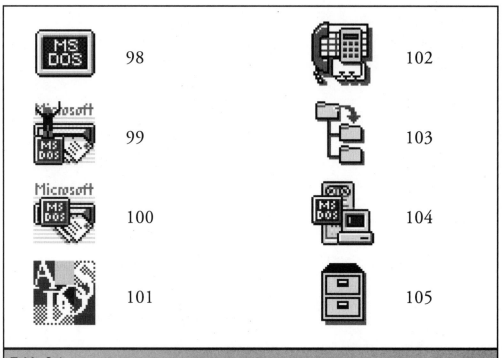

	98		102
	99		103
	100		104
	101		105

Table C-1. Icons in the Moricons.dll File (*continued*)

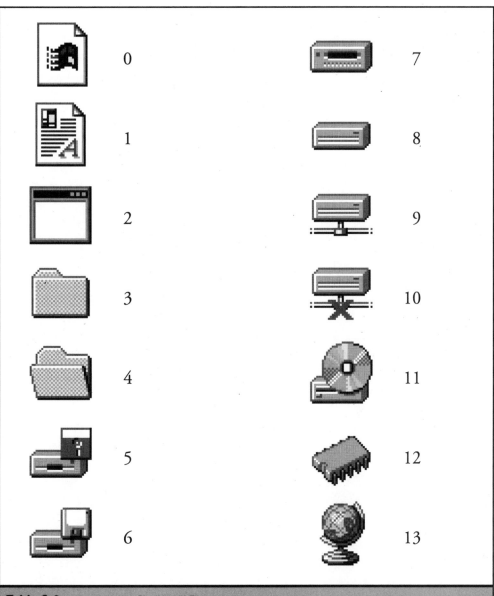

Table C-2.   Icons in the Shell32.dll File

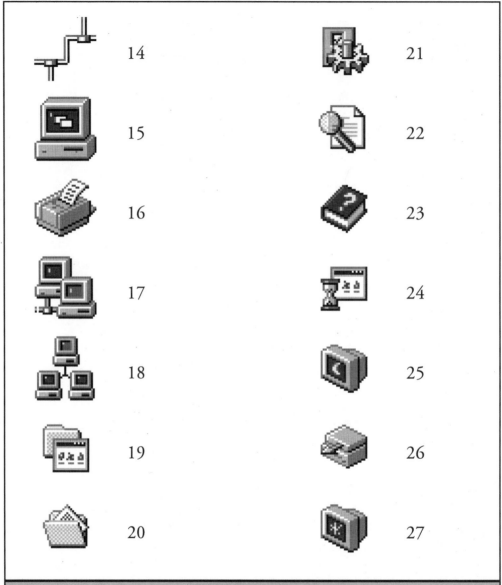

14	21
15	22
16	23
17	24
18	25
19	26
20	27

Table C-2. Icons in the Shell32.dll File (*continued*)

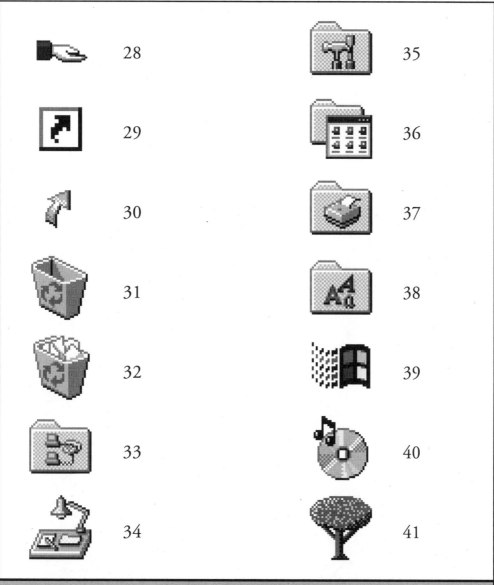

	28		35
	29		36
	30		37
	31		38
	32		39
	33		40
	34		41

Table C-2.   Icons in the Shell32.dll File (*continued*)

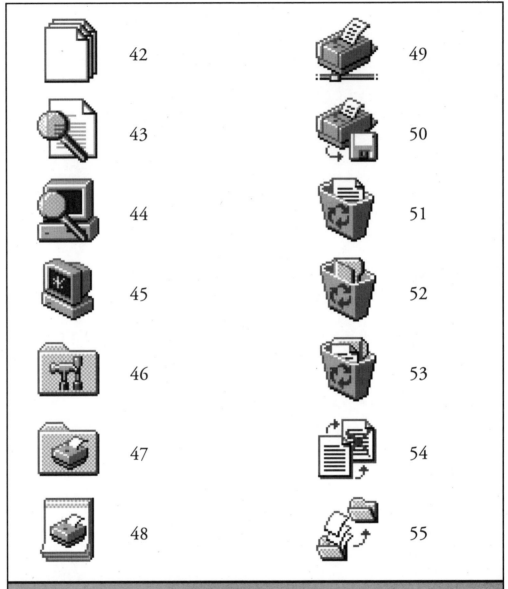

42	49
43	50
44	51
45	52
46	53
47	54
48	55

Table C-2. Icons in the Shell32.dll File (*continued*)

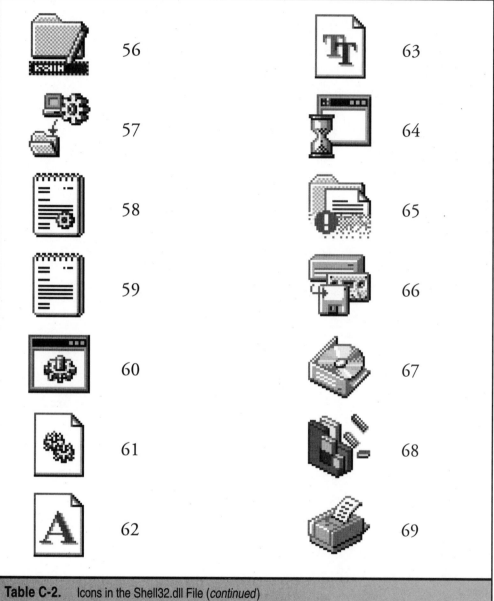

	56		63
	57		64
	58		65
	59		66
	60		67
	61		68
	62		69

Table C-2. Icons in the Shell32.dll File (*continued*)

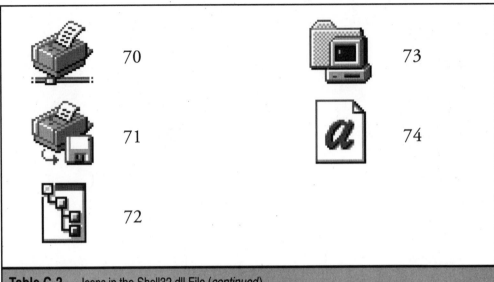

Table C-2.   Icons in the Shell32.dll File (*continued*)

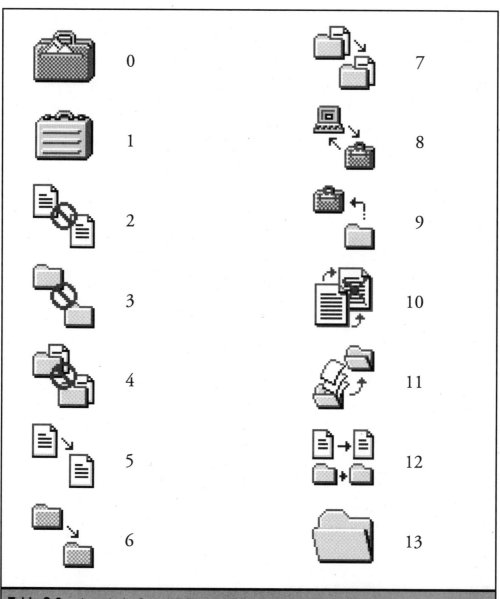

Table C-3.   Icons in the Syncui.dll File

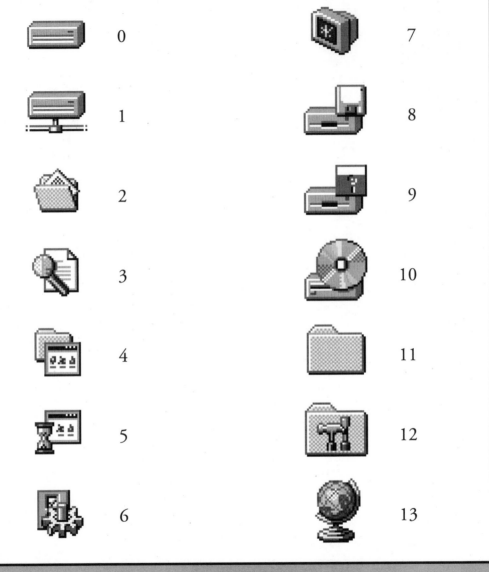

Table C-4. Icons in the Cool.dll File

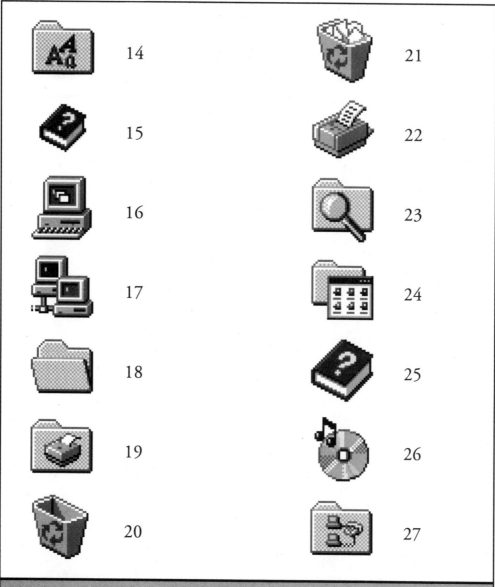

14	21
15	22
16	23
17	24
18	25
19	26
20	27

Table C-4. Icons in the Cool.dll File (*continued*)

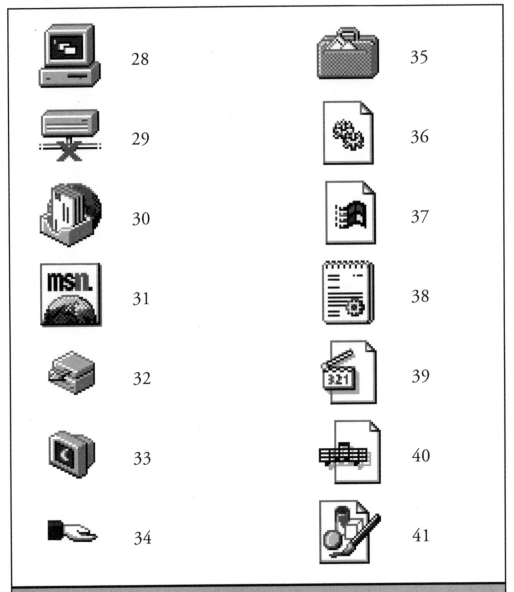

28

29

30

31

32

33

34

35

36

37

38

39

40

41

Table C-4. Icons in the Cool.dll File (*continued*)

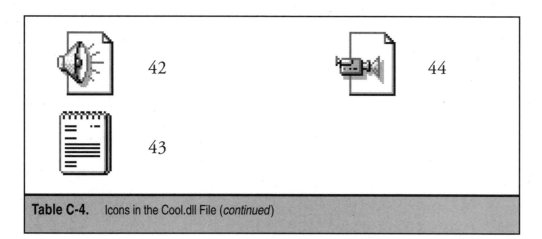

Table C-4.   Icons in the Cool.dll File (*continued*)

APPENDIX D

Shareware Guide

This appendix is a compilation of programs I've found, used, or heard about or otherwise have some reason to urge you to examine. The programs described here are freeware, shareware, or evaluation copies of inexpensive software.

The name of the program, the URL to reach it, and a brief description allow you to decide what to look at and then fetch it for yourself.

Remember the rules: Shareware is a honor distribution system, and if you're going to use shareware applications you must register and pay for them.

ApiMan

http://ourworld.compuserve.com/homepages/Germelmann/
ApiMan reads data from Windows API files. Useful for troubleshooting.

AssistBar

http://www.visualz.pair.com/index.htm
A customizable toolbar utility that lets you access programs, folders (including desktop icons), files, and shortcuts with a single click. You can add items to the toolbar by dragging them. And you can move the toolbar anywhere. This is a nice addition to the taskbar.

CardConv

http://ourworld.compuserve.com/homepages/Germelmann/
CardConv converts the files from those old Windows cardfiles into text files, Access databases, or Word.

ConfigSafe

http://www.imagine-lan.com/
For Windows NT and Windows 95, ConfigSafe monitors your system for any changes made to critical files, folders, the registry, and network settings. It can also restore your system to a previous configuration if the changes caused problems.

Directory Toolkit

http://home.sprynet.com/sprynet/funduc/
For Windows NT 4 and Windows 95, this utility compares files in two directories. If you have the need, it will synchronize the directories. This toolkit can rename, copy, move, and delete multiple files.

Diskeeper Lite

http://www.executive.com/
For Windows NT, this is a quick defragger.

Drag and File

http://www.canyonsw.com

For Windows NT 4 and Windows 95, this utility lets you drag to copy, move, or delete files across multiple directories and drives.

Drag and View

ftp://ftp.canyonsw.com

For Windows NT 4 and Windows 95, this utility uses easy mouse movements to view the contents of almost any file type.

DumpAcl

http://www.somarsoft.com/ftp/DMPACL.ZIP

Dumps the permissions (ACLs) for the file system, registry, shares, and printers in a concise, readable list box format. Great for finding holes in system security.

DumpEvt

http://www.somarsoft.com/ftp/DUMPEVT.ZIP

Dumps the event log in a format you can use in a database. Great for managing events and long-term tracking of security violations.

DumpReg

http://www.somarsoft.com/ftp/DUMPREG.ZIP

A Windows NT and Windows 95 program to dump the registry. For Windows NT, dumped entries can be sorted by modified time, making it easy to see recent changes.

FTP Explorer

http://www.ftpx.com

A file transfer protocol client for Windows NT 4 and Windows 95 that looks and acts like the Windows Explorer, making ftp a lot easier.

Internet Watch Dog

http://www.netwinsite.com

A Windows NT and Windows 95 utility that keeps an eye on your Internet services around the clock. It makes sure that all of your TCP/IP services are working and issues alerts when there's a problem.

ListDLLs

http://www.ntinternals.com/ntutil.htm

Lists loaded DLLs, including where they're loaded and the version numbers.

Listen

http://www.win-tech.com

For troubleshooting serial communications links, this utility uses standard Windows COM port drivers to tap into RS-232 transmit signals.

Magic Folders

www.pc-magic.com

Allows you to hide any folders and all the files contained in those folders.

Mail*Wiz

http://www.webgenie.com

Sends personalized e-mail to the members of any address lists you have.

Middle Mouse Button

http://www.digconsys.com/htm/homepage.shtml

Configure that middle button to do something useful, such as double-click.

Net Connector

http://www.baybuild.com/download.htm

For Windows 95, this simplifies Dial-Up Networking, eliminating many of the steps and waiting that waste time.

NTFSFlp

http://www.ntinternals.com/ntutil.htm

Creates NTFS floppy disks.

NTFSInfo

http://www.ntinternals.com/ntutil.htm

Displays more details about NTFS than your system does, including information about the Master File Table and the MFT-zone.

NTLocksmith

http://www.ntinternals.com/ntutil.htm

An add-on to NTRecover (see listing for NTRecover next) to overcome forgotten administrative passwords.

NTRecover

http://www.ntinternals.com/ntutil.htm

Access a dead drive from a good system over a serial connection. Then salvage the data using NT commands and utilities.

NTRegmon

http://www.ntinternals.com/ntutil.htm

A GUI device driver program that hooks kernel mode system calls to watch any activity in the registry.

NTUndelete

http://www.ntinternals.com/ntutil.htm

Lets you recover files deleted from the command line or legacy software.

Opalis Rendezvous

http://www.opalis.com

Data transfer and replication utilities for NT.

OpalisRobot

http://www.opalis.com

An evaluation kit for OpalisRobot, which automates administrative, maintenance, and communication tasks on Windows NT systems.

OuttaSight v2.0

http://rosa.simplenet.com/oos/

Allows you to hide applications.

Ping Thingy v2.53

http://indigo.ie/~zippy/download.htm

A quick and easy-to-use Ping generator. Ping Thingy dispatches ICMP Echo requests to a remote host and displays the results for each Echo reply.

RegEditX

http://www.dcsoft.com/prod01.htm

Registry Editor Extensions (freeware) that put a combo box on your screen to display a list of all the keys visited. Return to a key by opening the drop-down list and selecting it. The history list is retained for a record of your registry changes.

RegFind

http://www.intsoft.com

Searches the registry for keys, values, and data. You can display the keys that were modified before or after a specified date and time.

Remote Process and Shutdown Service

http://www.digconsys.com/htm/homepage.shtml

Starts processes remotely from another system, either attached to the network or dialed in. You can also log off or shut down a computer remotely.

SuperMonitor

http://ourworld.compuserve.com/homepages/NIFTY_TOOLS/

Tracks resource usage. Great to use if you're ready to find out which machines may need more RAM.

WindMail

http://www.geocel.com/windmail

A Windows version of the popular Unix Sendmail program. Send a message from a command line, CGI script, or batch file in Windows 95 or NT (evaluation copy).

WinZip v6.3

http://www.winzip.com/

The most popular file compression utility available for Windows. This new version has even more features!

WINDOWS
NT
Professional
Library

Index

NOTE: Page numbers in *italics* refer to illustrations or charts.

▼ NUMBERS

16-bit Windows 3.x-based applications, Service Pack updates, 436
32-bit Windows-based applications, Service Pack updates, 436-437

▼ A

access, auditing file and directory, 287
access restrictions, registry and, 196-198
Accessories menu, user profiles, *165*
Account Lockout, password policies, 116-117
Account Policy dialog box, passwords, *116*
accounts, corrupt built-in, 69-70

ACL (Access Control List), securing the registry, 211-213
Activation Follows Mouse option, Mouse tab (Tweak UI), 376-377
Adaptec FileArray, future of server safety, 288
Adapters tab, Setup Manager, 38-40
Add Sub-Directory dialog box, replicating directories, 81
Add to Log dialog box, Performance Monitor, 312
Add Users and Groups dialog box
    auditing, 329
    permissions, *213*
Add/Remove tab, Tweak UI, 384-386
addresses, static IP, 270-271
Admin$, special system shares, 158
administration, Disk Administrator, 336-337
Administrative Tools menu, System Policy Editor, 217-229

481

▼ B

F

G

M

▼ N

O

P

Q

 R

T

V

 W